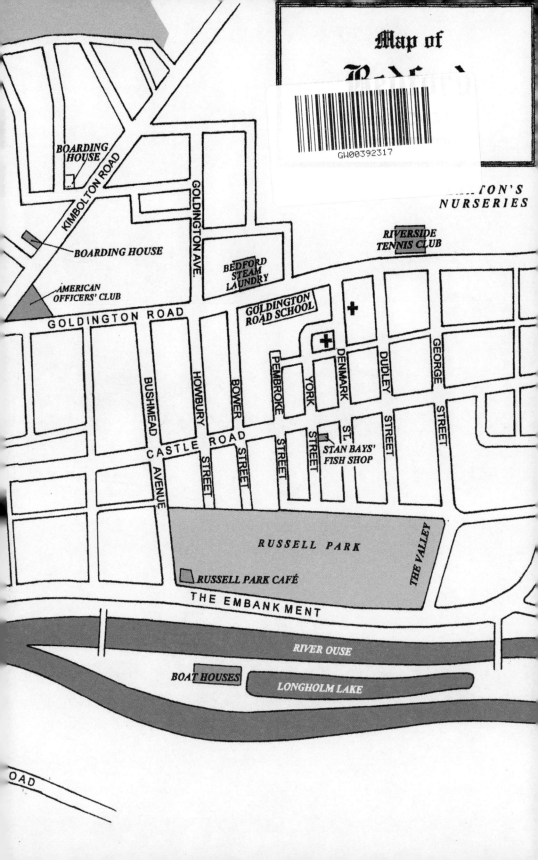

Map of ████████

...TON'S
NURSERIES

BOARDING
HOUSE

KIMBOLTON ROAD

BOARDING HOUSE

AMERICAN
OFFICERS' CLUB

GOLDINGTON AVE.

BEDFORD
STEAM
LAUNDRY

RIVERSIDE
TENNIS CLUB

GOLDINGTON
ROAD SCHOOL

GOLDINGTON ROAD

PEMBROKE

YORK

DENMARK

DUDLEY

GEORGE

BUSHMEAD

HOWBURY

BOWER

STAN BAYS'
FISH SHOP

ST.

STREET

STREET

CASTLE ROAD

AVENUE

STREET

STREET

STREET

STREET

THE VALLEY

RUSSELL PARK

RUSSELL PARK CAFÉ

THE EMBANKMENT

RIVER OUSE

BOAT HOUSES

LONGHOLM LAKE

OAD

Well Remembered Fields

David Bernstein (handwritten signature)

Well Remembered Fields

The Story of one school's evacuation 1939 – 1945

Editors: Martin Mitchell and David Bernstein

'On many a well remembered field
Have Owen's fought and won ...'

(Opening lines of the School Football Song)

First published in Great Britain 2003 by
Park Russell.

ISBN 0-9545687-0-2

A CIP catalogue for this book is available from the British Library.

Photo typesetting by David Stevenson.

Typesetting by Martin Mitchell.

Printed in Great Britain by Antony Rowe Ltd,
Chippenham, Wiltshire.

Dedicated to Owenians who fell in World War Two.

Acknowledgements

Our thanks to the contributors: 67 old boys (in both senses) of Owen's School, eight delightful wartime girl friends, one member of our host school, Bedford Modern; to Anita Amiel and Pamela Powell for permission to include poems written by their late husbands; Sheila Moses for editorial assistance; Vivian Moses for his research into the BBC in Bedford; to Alan Locke for his drawings plus his extra help with the chapters on education, radio and the cinema; 'WEO' Jones for his comprehensive review of religious observance in Chapter 8; Richard Wildman, Bedford Archivist; Pru MacGibbon, Archivist, The Worshipful Company of Brewers; David Stevenson for computer advice; Barry Hyman for proof reading; Ann Blackwell for secretarial help; and many others including Owen's School, the Bedford Modern School and their old boys' associations; the BBC archives; the British Museum Newspaper Library; the History of Advertising Trust; various advertisers; and the Imperial War Museum with whom the manuscript and unedited material are now housed.

A personal thank you to our wives, Lily and Sue, for their help, support and patience.

Finally, a special word in fond memory of those contributors who did not live to see the book in print: Frank Fenn, Ansel Harris, Dennis Jones, Geoffrey Rans, John Stockton, Ivor Walker and Bill Whitebread.

Martin Mitchell   David Bernstein

Foreword

This is the story of a school that was more than just a school. It is the story of a school remaking itself into a vibrant, closely knit, mutually supportive community as it grappled with evacuation and war. On 1 September 1939 – a sunny, warm day, not one meant for frenetic activity – 600,000 schoolchildren were uprooted from their London villages and summarily despatched by bus, train and even boat to the intended safety of the countryside.

Sixty-odd years later, some seventy old boys, now in their seventies, pooled their memories of those six momentous years of evacuation and war. This book is the result. Though we have grouped chapters thematically, this is only a rough and ready device to provide some order to our myriad recollections of a distant world, a lifetime away, which saw sacrifice and heroism on an unparalleled scale. It was a time of intense feeling where tragedy, despair, frustration, hilarity and exhilaration crowded our emotional space. How can we ever forget those years?

> Recalling the events of sixty years ago is not so much an exercise of memory but rather a series of acts of imagination. You remember an incident, a scene, a feeling, or an image, and in an instant the many details are filled in until the picture is as much a recreation of the scene as you can make it. But can you trust it? How much is wishful thinking? How much is invention? Maybe we romanticise it too much; or exaggerate the pain of a past injury. That period of wartime evacuation was a critical chapter in my life. It was a coming of age story. But how much is true and how much invented, I shall never know. Also, how much was due to the special circumstances of being moved to Bedford and all that went with it, and how much was normal growing up? I can never trust all those recollections, because they are now not real, merely parts of a story triggered by the past and shaped by the effort of remembering these times and by my life since then.   ME

> It's funny how songs, like people's names and obscure middle initials come back unbidden, but hide in the mind's recesses when you want them. You end up remembering the effort and earlier success of remembering, rather like remembering the photo taken instead of the scene itself.   DAMM

Foreword

The war leaves its mark consciously and unconsciously. I know I have
repressed memories of the evacuation. I know I was at times very unhappy and thankfully I shall never know why. More significant for my
state of my mind, having reached the age of seventy-five, is this feeling
of living in two separate eras that bear no relation to each other. The
earlier era carries for me the greater reality. Then there was self and collective identity expressed in vast national effort that touched everyone.
By comparison, the present era, with its obsession with markets and the
unrelenting pursuit of possessions that now engulfs even the youngest,
seems trivial and directionless. So there you are. I end up, because of
the wartime experience, still feeling that sense of displacement that I
felt as an evacuee.   MM*

---

* The initials are those of contributors whose full names appear on page 395.

Contents

List of Illustrations xiv

Preface xv

WAR

1 September the First 1

2 Countdown to Bedford 11

3 Early Memories 20

4 September the Third 32

BEDFORD

5 Home from Home 36

6 London it Ain't 45

7 Hosts 49

8 Small Town Life 57

SCHOOL

9 To Work 71

10 The Boarding House 78

11 'Most Difficult Circumstances' 87

12 'Training for Real' 93

13 Be Prepared 105

14 Fire Watching 112

Contents

15   'Do Not Rest Your Spades'   116

16   Unfamiliar Sports   123

17   'The Age of Bedfordian Football'   134

18   To be a Farmer's Boy   140

19   'A Most Enlightening Experience'   151

TEACHING

20   Teachers   160

21   The Headmaster   168

22   Past Masters   173

23   The Body of the Staff   178

AMUSEMENTS

24   Generous Auntie   189

25   Radio Times   199

26   'This Is Where I Came In'   210

27   Bikes   219

28   Boys and Girls   226

29   The Songs We Sang   235

30   Theatre of War   243

HOME FRONT

31   'Darkness Visible'   248

32   Life Was Full   254

Contents

33   We Never Went Hungry   263

34   The War Effort   276

35   Holidays – in the War   284

BATTLE FRONT

36   1940   293

37   War Once Removed   301

38   Closer Quarters   312

39   Yanks   322

40   On Active Service   331

THE END

41   Victory   352

42   Back with a Backward Glance   361

43   A Character Forming Experience   369

APPENDICES

A   Owen's School: A Brief History 1613 - 1945   381

B   Evacuation Activities of the London County Council   391

C   The Story of the Bedford Modern School – and another Dame Alice   393

Contributors   395

References   399

Index   407

List of Illustrations

1. Waiting to go
2. The card players
3. The danger of war
4. Air raid warning placard
5. Evacuation poster
6. Leaflet raid propaganda
7. River Ouse
8. Owenians outside 'school'
9. Study period
10. Boarding House
11. Modern School quadrangle
12. Army Cadet Force on parade
13. King's Scouts
14. Air Training Corps cadets
15. Fire Watching certificate
16. 'Dig For Victory' poster
17. The Gardening Club
18. Farming camp enthusiasts
19. Young farmers at work
20. The first eight
21. First to the tape
22. High jump
23. The Headmaster
24. The Prefects
25. Friday Evening Club: *Brains Trust*
26. Friday Evening Club: Revue
27. Owen's dramatics
28. Phyllis Dixey poster
29. Sir Adrian Boult
30. Squander Bug
31. Chad
32. 'Wings for Victory' savings certificate
33. *'Up Housewives and at 'em!'*
34. Advance notice of rationing
35. Fry's cocoa advertisement
36. Government blackout advertisement
37. BSA bicycle advertisement
38. Bikes at war

Preface

In 1939 my mother and I moved to a flat in a house in Green Lanes, Stoke Newington because I was about to start school at Dame Alice Owen's in Islington. Two weeks before my schooling commenced I saw the sea for the first time when we travelled from Holyhead to Cork in Southern Ireland, on board the SS Inisfallen. During those two weeks war broke out and it was not possible to return because it was considered too dangerous. Not long after, the Inisfallen was sunk by a U-boat.

For three months I went to the Cork Grammar School. In December we were able to return by train to Dublin and a quick zigzag trip by sea to Holyhead. During this time Owen's had been evacuated to Bedford, so after a brief visit to relatives in Birmingham we were just in time to have our windows blown out by one of the first air raids in England. My mother returned to our flat in London and I set off with my satchel and gas mask where I was billeted with a Mr and Mrs Rogers and their pet budgerigar. Owen's shared school with our hosts Bedford Modern School. We shared classes – one school in the mornings and the other in the afternoons – but my initiation was hardly a happy one because the Headmaster O.W. Mitchell stood me up in front of the whole school and, as I had come from Ireland, searched me for bombs. It was a joke, of course, but not a good one because from that moment on I became a bit of a loner. I always did prefer the company of the opposite sex – however, I did chum up with Vivian Moses and, later in the War, even though he was older than me, with Geoff Rowley, who was billeted with us when my mother moved from London to a flat in Bedford. This was fortunate because our house in Green Lanes received a direct hit. Nights were sometimes short because, if the air raid sirens sounded, we spent a great deal of time playing great deals of cards in an alcove under the staircase, and my evenings either going to the pictures or following Aileen Smith and other local beauties on my bicycle in Russell Park. Geoff and I have continued to keep in touch and, despite following different paths, both were given a CBE.

As matriculation approached, my Latin was so bad that I knew I would not pass so I told the Headmaster that I was leaving school. 'What do you plan to do?' he asked, 'Be an actor', I replied. 'But you haven't been in any of the school plays.' It was true – they would not even have me in the chorus of *Cyrano de Bergerac* – well there was a lot of dramatic talent at Owen's.

'I feel I should warn you', said the Head, 'Let me put it this way – the other week I went to my tailor for a new suit and he took more measurements than were absolutely necessary. Well, there are a lot of people like that in the theatre.' When I wrote my auto-biography I thought of calling it 'A Company of Tailors'.

However, after working backstage at Bedford's Royal County Theatre, I hitch-hiked to London and joined the Central School of Speech Training and Dramatic Art. I was sixteen and I only got there as they were desperate for men because the war was still on. There were two hundred and fifty girls and three other males - and two of them could have been tailors. Life was good.

Many years later when I was rehearsing *Evita* at Sadler's Wells I looked out of the window and saw 'Dame Alice Owen's School – founded 1613'. I pointed it out to my director Hal Prince. 'That's my old school', I said, 'but I've never been inside.' 'Why not go in the lunch hour?', he said. So I did. When I rang the bell a care-taker opened the door. 'May I come in? This is my old school.'

'Sorry guvnor, you can't. This is Council property. The School closed down the day before yesterday.' And it had been there since 1613.

A few years ago, my son was training to be a pilot at Cranfield near Bedford. So I suggested that he, my wife Rosemary and my-self should visit Bedford Modern School. On the wall outside was a plaque from Owen's thanking Bedford and the school. 'Come and see', I said excitedly and pushed open the huge door of the surrounding wall to the quadrangle. Inside were Woolworths, Boots, Marks & Spencer etc. Just shops – the school had gone. This is fate, I thought. I have no past.

One year I was invited – I assumed it was because I was an old Owenian – by Owen's, to attend a Lords Taverners meal to hon-our the England cricket team. And they were a great team – they would have refused to go to Zimbabwe!

I sat with Barry Norman, Peter Cook and Dudley Moore along-side the Headmaster.

After the meal the Head said 'will the old boys of the school rise and toast the guests.' I whispered to him, 'what do I do – half rise?'

He changed colour. He had no idea that I had ever been to the school!

Joss Ackland

1

September the First

Exodus and Genesis.

It was a warm bright Friday. It was the day the school leaving age was due to be raised to fifteen. One postponement of many that day. Other things happened. The ARP (Air Raid Precautions) was mobilised. The blackout began. So did conscription. Weather forecasts ended. Roads out of London were declared one-way. 'Scotland Yard obligingly issued a list of routes out of London for people leaving by car'.[1] The Government appealed to the people to be 'quietly confident'. Nevertheless, the decision to evacuate had already been issued (see page 15).

> *We come to school each morning complete with baggage and too much food. It is a queer life - unusual and exciting. The hardships of school life are gone. Everything is good fun; boys listening to records, some playing chess and draughts and lesser table games; others debating in the art room; an important fifth former assuring everyone that Hitler could not be so mad as to...* [*]
> *Arrow*, Owen's School Magazine, Michaelmas '39

Most boys, of course, knew each other. New boys had the task of settling in, in unique circumstances.

I got the Junior County Scholarship award in 1939 and my parents wanted me to go to Owen's. I was interviewed by the Headmaster, who left at that time. His name was Asman. So I was ready to go and was part of the evacuation scene there and I remember that, for a week before we left, we actually attended school every day already packed

---

[*] Authorship of *Arrow* extracts is given where known.

and we were entertained with epidiascope shows and things to keep us quiet. I was a newcomer, eleven years old and about to join the school at the very bottom.   VM

I knew nobody in the school other than my two friends from North Harringay School. The Boys' school was assembled in loose groups all wearing their school caps and some with school blazers and their haversacks, kit bags or attaché cases. With my father's help I searched for my two friends but was unable to find them.   AWL

A very special new boy was the Headmaster, O.W. Mitchell. This was his first sight of the school as Head. He had been head boy in 1916 before war service with the RAF in France. World War Two would make different though comparable demands on his talents.

We spent three or four days at the school waiting. We were excited. It was an adventure. The staff and senior pupils put on entertainment in the various classrooms. This was (apart from my interview) my first experience of the school building. We'd go home at the end of each day. One day we wouldn't.   DEB

The point was to bring us together every day, call registers, take instruction in how to prepare for evacuation – what clothes to pack, what food to take (I still have flashes back when I buy Ryvita; I'd never seen it before then).   GR

Reporting at school every day with multi-labelled younger brother in case he got lost in the strange and darkened corridors of the building. Fond farewells as we left home every morning ... fond greeting every evening once my mother had counted the number of cases and packages. My father had been called up six months earlier, being an RAF reservist.   DAP

> *Assembly in the Hall. We are going tomorrow. Terrifying warnings to those who come late. Some Owenians arriving at the eleventh hour with sand still in their pockets. Brown and bewildered they want to know where we are going. An important fifth former says Leicester or even further.*
>
> *Arrow*, Michaelmas '39

I said goodbye every morning as I left for school. I don't remember a special goodbye that morning although something had happened in

Poland and we knew about that. We most likely heard it on the break-fast time news.   VM

My brother (he was two years behind me) and I got there by ourselves with cheap suitcases and the incredibly annoying cardboard boxes that contained our gas masks that smelt awful and fogged up immediately. I remember lining up in the street in front of the school, horsing around, having a luggage tag tied onto us, and brimming with excitement. I had hoped for Kings' Cross and the LNER* since that at least held a prom-ise of Scotland.   DAMM

I didn't cry about going away. Boys of eleven don't cry. I don't recall any sense of insecurity or fear or concern, it was sort of fun that kids have, like going on an outing except we weren't coming back that evening. It was a secure environment. I was with the kids I knew and the teachers, in those days, were people who took care of you.   VM

There were certainly no tearful send-offs. My mother had young tod-dlers at home to look after, so we were sent off alone. We were men off to war. Twelve-year old boys do not cry (most having been educated by the *Boys' Own Paper* and Kipling).   DC

I have no recollection of saying 'Goodbye' to my parents!! I can clearly remember the night before watching my father very conscientiously packing all my belongings into a large brown backpack bought specially for the occasion.   DDW

> *Evacuation morn! Muster in front of the School. General jubila-tion. Staff and sixth form anxiously reading news-tapes at the paper stall. Only a matter of hours now.*
> *Arrow*, Michaelmas '39

The time passed very slowly. We were told we were waiting for news of the German invasion of Poland. This was to be the signal for our evacuation. In fact, we beat the invasion by one hour.

Just after ten o'clock the order came through and the evacuation was on. I found myself attached to one group of boys and we proceeded across City Road to the Angel tube station, then serviced by large lifts. I remember waving goodbye to my father through a window in the ticket hall.   AWL

---

* London and North-Eastern Railway

10.40am. efficient police and transport inspectors. A non-stop tube train to Edgware. Crowds on all the platforms. Efficient control again at Edgware. Evacuation noon! An endless stream of buses to take us to Mill Hill

Arrow, Michaelmas '39

Mill Hill station was on the London Midland and Scottish (LMS) line. There was a train waiting. The school embarked.

Not a flaw in the plan, yet. The sun is getting stronger. These pyjamas must be made of lead. One or two feeling the heat; medical aid right at hand. The train leaves at 11.45 and immediately packs are put up and sandwiches stuffed down. Most of them go in the litter baskets for there are more interesting things to do than eat. There is still no idea of our destination.

Arrow, Michaelmas '39

A full carriage. Excitement. Looking out of windows. One boy lost his cap. It seemed the train stopped a lot. Nobody, of course, knew where we were going.   DEB

Someone ran a book as to our eventual evacuation destination. Rumours and wagers were placed on everywhere from Toronto to Tewkesbury via Ballybunion so as to fool the Germans.   DAP

Some of the children had younger siblings to look after. Boys of twelve maybe looking after children of about eight years old so it wasn't just the children from our school, but most of the boys in our carriage were from Owen's.   HC

My brother, being the eldest in a closed compartment, was appealed to on the journey by a lad whose bowels were unequal to the excitement of the day. A paper bag was found and, the deed accomplished, thrown from the window.   MJC

At Luton station after one hour. It cannot be Luton. An important fifth former observes that this is the line to Scotland.

Arrow, Michaelmas '39

At Luton everyone got out. Three hundred boys milling about on the platform for five or so minutes. They reboarded and the train went on to Bedford.

There is a resilient myth that we were meant to go to Kettering and

Dame Alice Owen's Girls School was scheduled to go to Bedford. An official report written after the War referred to Plan 2 (see page 13) of which we were part: 'only problem with telescoping of transport arrangements leading to unexpected destinations'. For us it was a happy accident as one of our teachers, the Reverend R. H. Turner (having been a pastor of the Bunyan Meeting Free Church during the thirties) knew Bedford and the Headmaster of Bedford Modern School. The two Heads met that evening.

> *It is Bedford. Loudspeaker voices call us 'dear children'. What an insult! We are the first real Owenian pioneers in history. Scouts lead us out of the station at 1.15pm along the Midland Road by bus and foot to the cattle market. So that is what we are! The party is divided now and we begin to speculate on living accommodation. An important fifth former has heard of army huts and camp beds.*
>
> *Arrow*, Michaelmas '39

In the cattle market we were broken up into smaller groups of about twenty-four boys supervised by a member of Owen's staff and a local member of the WVS*, who were armed with clip boards containing addresses of people who had been canvassed in Bedford in the previous months and who had expressed their willingness to take an evacuee in the event of war breaking out.   AWL

We walked from the Midland Road station and my lot landed up in Goldington Road Infant School, which was actually a fair way, about a mile and a half, and when we got there we were issued with rations.
                                                                                                                            VM

... a brown carrier bag containing sufficient food for 48 hours... a tin of Donald Cook's corned beef, a tin of Libby's milk, two or three packets of biscuits and a half pound block of Cadbury's Dairy Milk chocolate bigger than any I had ever seen before.   AWL

At the village school we sat at desks while villagers trooped in to choose their favoured contribution to the war effort. Ian and I must have presented an unappealing prospect since the hall was nearly empty when at last a woman offered to take 'two who want to be together'. Thus we found ourselves billeted in the private lane running beside the school.
                                                                                                                            MJC

* Later The Women's Royal Voluntary Service

My main memory of evacuation day is one of waiting lined up in the school quad in forms. Waiting to get on the bus to Mill Hill station - waiting to get on the train and last of all waiting to be allotted a billet (being Webber I was at the end of the queue).   JW

We were divided into groups and a local lady or gentleman led us in crocodiles down nearby streets. The houses seemed large. We were presented to the homeowner in ones or twos and accepted - each time as I recall without discussion. I went to 72 Newnham Avenue. Mrs Ethel Smith, middle class, middle aged. Husband with dodgy lung (result of the Great War and gas). Younger sister Doreen. Very attractive. 'Any food I didn't eat?' I thought for a little while and said, 'Cold chicken.' 'Don't worry about that,' she replied.   DEB

The rest of us went along the street and when it came to my house there was a woman standing with, I think, a Scottish terrier. Someone said, 'do you like dogs?' and I said, 'yes', so they said, 'well come to us.'   VM

My own group under the control of Mr A.J. Hopkins, a mathematics master at school, and Mrs Edith Garlick, moved off up Goldington Avenue calling at various houses and dropping off brothers, pairs of friends and the occasional single boy. This started at about 1.30 p.m. and went on until about 5.30 p.m. by which time the group was down to four boys - none of them related or knowing each other.
It had been a long day and Mrs Garlick said that she herself had opted to take two girls but she was prepared to take these four boys. Thus it was at 6 p.m. that John Hudson, Howard Schama, Geoffrey Cook and Alan Locke arrived at 3 Glebe Road, Bedford.   AWL

In addition to gas mask and the recommended modest luggage, I took a football to help pass the time. Hence, many hours later, I found myself on Goldington Green in Bedford with a football that resulted in several hours of 25-a-side game. Eventually the numbers dwindled and I joined the tail end of a crocodile proceeding up Brookfield Road which proved to be a *cul-de-sac*. As we approached the last two houses there were just six of us to be billeted – two sixth formers and four very dishevelled fourteen year olds. The lady in the last house opted immediately for the respectable (?) sixth formers. That left Norman Tebbutt, Bert Seaborn, 'Mac' and me. The lady in number 88 had put her name down for a ten-year-old girl but she took pity on us and we became billeted.   WJW

Two of us were still being walked from door to door at six o'clock before accommodation could be found for us, albeit on a temporary basis.
                                KSK

Not all Owenians were able to muster with the school on 1 September.

> We went to the Angel on Saturday 2nd September and spoke to the Beadle, as the caretaker was called, to find that the school had all been evacuated and had finished up in Bedford.
>
> We must have found out that the Headmaster, O.W. Mitchell, was living in Harvey Road. We had had a series of generally unreliable motor cars but evidently the Morris 12, then in favour, was good enough for the journey.
>
> We set off early in the morning of Sunday 3rd September but I do not recall any fear or trepidation. RN

> I was on holiday at Clacton when the school was evacuated to Bedford. I returned the following day, 2nd September and somehow learned of the whereabouts of the school (we were not on the phone and my elder brother who subsequently took me to Bedford on the 4th September can't recall how we got the news). I can recall meeting the new Headmaster, O.W. Mitchell, who said there was a billet just round the corner from him. How could I refuse? So I spent the next four years with his namesake Mr and Mrs Mitchell and their twenty-six- year-old daughter at 19 Ouse Road, Goldington. KD

> The family was on holiday in Brighton. My father's business had been doing quite well and, unusually for that time, we had a small car. A few days after war broke out he used it to drive me from Brighton to Bedford. JL

> On the following Sunday I was dispatched in the company of my elder sister to Bedford. We travelled by Birch's bus. On arrival we first had lunch at the Railway Hotel, the only place we could find that was open. I remember that we had brown Windsor soup, a slice off the joint and two veg. I have a recollection that my sister thought the cost exorbitant. PP

In his autobiography, *I must be in there somewhere*[2], Joss Ackland, recalls the day:

> So with my clothes and toothbrush in a case, a satchel full of books, my gas mask hanging from my shoulder, and accompanied by my mother, I boarded a train and travelled the fifty miles to the little market town of Bedford. There I was deposited with my 'billet lady' Mrs Rogers and her husband, and, after a brief chin-up, tearless, smiling, lying farewell, my mother returned to London. For ten shillings and sixpence a week Mr

and Mrs Rogers sheltered me, fed me, put a warming pan in my bed, and we all played with their budgerigar who could talk and ring bells.

JA

Other eventual Owenians travelled to Bedford on 1 September.

Nobby and I kept company during the journey to Bedford. I've retained the impression of puzzling frequent changes of buses and trains. Later, I opined to Nobby that we must have been avoiding U-boats.   JS

As a ten-year-old, I was still at an elementary school, Duncombe Road in Upper Holloway, and trooped off with them to Bedford on 1 September. I think we walked from school to the Archway tube station to get to St.Pancras railway station. I recall, probably inaccurately, that the fifty-mile train journey took about four hours, for the most of which we were stationary, impatient but remarkably unconcerned. (A couple of years later, I did the same journey in more or less the same time on my new bicycle.)   DDW

Other eventual Owenians were initially evacuated elsewhere.

Early in the morning, duly labelled, we went to our school, Northwold Road Elementary School, with our boxed gas masks slung over our shoulders and suitcases in hand. I had won a Junior County Scholarship and should have been evacuated with The Grocers' School but for some reason it never happened. So here I was, accompanied by a tearful mother and a more restrained aunt, clutching the hand of my seven-year-old brother and promising faithfully that I would look after him. The children gathered in the playground, the weather was glorious. We were told by the Head, Mr Brimicombe, that we were to be evacuated to a place called Biggleswade.   MM

Our parents had taken us to school and followed us to the station. Some parents were weeping, others trying to encourage the children. After all, we were told, the War was only going to last two or three months, so make the most of it. No one knew where we were going, not even the mistresses or masters. Anyway, the train eventually stopped at Wisbech. My brother and I were put on a coach and we went to a little village called Leverington.   BS

On 1 September 1939 I was evacuated with the Jewish Free Secondary School to Soham, a three-mile-long village with 5,000 inhabitants. At three different billets the reception was similar, 'who wants a 'vac' from London?'   JNB

Mostly reception was warm and the lottery of selection produced more winners than losers.

> Billeting officer took Alan Smart and me to a Mrs Knight who said she couldn't take us. Just at that moment a lady came out from the house opposite. Could she take two boys? Just one. I was accepted as their son. They'd got three daughters - all younger than me. I was the son they'd never had. The youngest daughter had a lousy appetite so I got two dinners.   HG

> They gave me a reasonably warm greeting, introduced me to their son, who was about two years older than me, and I straight away settled down to country life in a good home. When I think back I had a great start to the War in my new surroundings.   GS

> My brother's and my own reception was very friendly but we always ate with 'cook', apart from the family - and did rather well as a result!   DP

John Stockton was greeted with an accurate prediction.

> Mrs Riches, our first billet lady, was the wife of the manager of the Maypole Dairy in Silver Street. He had been a dispatch rider in the Great War and took some pains to point out to N and me that food rationing would probably soon begin and could mean, for example, about two ounces of butter a week.
> Mr and Mrs Riches were a sweet couple who received us warmly and accommodated us comfortably. Nobby and I shared a bed and some weekend mornings we could hear either Mr or Mrs Riches read to the other extracts from their serviceman son's letter.   JS

> They also had a lodger in the house and I remember him particularly as he gave me a pair of ice skates.   VM

But it wasn't all sweetness and light. Adjustments had to be made by both parties.

> I was very unhappy in both billets. The first were serious churchgoers but with very unchristian traits. They had one son and I think most of our rations went to him. The second were from Wales - Salvation Army folks. I'm sure they were kind but this was my first experience of poverty.   GD

> We were well received but there was always a slight reserve rather than warmth.   GS

It has always puzzled Clive and me why we had so many billets. We weren't dirty or lousy, didn't wet the bed, weren't neglected by our parents, were moderately studious, but we were normal boys who could sometimes be noisy. We feel the explanation was that we were more or less forced on our billet ladies.   DHS

That evening the London paper *The Star* ran a headline 'LONDON'S CHILDREN WERE GRAND'. Half a million had been moved to new homes, from danger areas to reception areas.

The next morning *The Times* called evacuation, 'a triumph of preparation, organisation and discipline.'[3]

A correspondent in *Time and Tide* (6 September) wrote

> *The evacuation from London will be long remembered by the young evacuees as a star turn in adventure and by the rest of us as a star turn in organisation.*[4]

That organisation was a shared responsibility. Removing the children from London was the Government's. The responsibility thereafter was that of the reception area, Bedford and the staffs of the schools involved - the visitors and the hosts - and the boys themselves.

Meanwhile parents waited and wondered.

> The first thing we had to do was to send a postcard home to our parents to let them know where we were.   VM

2

Countdown to Bedford

Government - national and local - preparations for war.

'Deadly nightshade does not grow in Bethnal Green'

Over 600,000 children, half of London's total, were evacuated to safer areas of the country on 1 September 1939. The loss of population from Greater London was just short of 1.5 million. In the country as a whole, over 3,500,000 people moved from areas considered by civil defence planners to be vulnerable to mass bombing from the air. The evacuation of the Second World War was the greatest migration ever undertaken by the British people, greater even than the total of past migrations to the New World and the Colonies.

It was the culmination of a planning process based on highly pessimistic assumptions about the impact of mass bombing on civilian populations. What influenced the planners initially was the experience of bombing in the First World War.

The likelihood of a massive initial assault by bombers in the event of conflict was initially expressed in the first (1924) ARP report to the Imperial Defence Committee[1]. It was automatically assumed by some jittery committee members that those civilians most susceptible to panic would be the 'foreign, Jewish and poor elements'; and, more alarmingly, in the panic flight out of London the poor 'would flock into the wealthier areas where they would find prizes worth having'.

To prevent such socially destructive outcomes, the 1931 Evacuation Committee suggested cordoning the capital with police. The police pleaded shortage of manpower and asked for army back up. The army, whose business was fighting an enemy, was unwilling to divert resources to civil defence and the cordon idea was soon abandoned.

Such was the fear of a bombing attack, that Stanley Baldwin delivered a stark warning to the House of Commons in 1932, in terms frighteningly presaging the Cold War MAD (mutually assured destruction) doctrine:

> *I think it is well for the man in the street to realise that there is no power on earth that can protect him from being bombed. Whatever people may tell him, the bomber will always get through. The only defence is in offence which means that you have to kill more women and children more quickly than the enemy if you want to save yourself.*[2]

The ensuing years only too tragically confirmed Baldwin's fears. In 1935 the Germans rebuilt their air force. In 1936 the Italians dropped poison gas bombs on the defenceless Abyssinian population and the Nazi Condor Legion 'blitzed' Guernica. In 1937 Mussolini's air force dive-bombed Barcelona. Thousands of casualties resulted from these unprovoked attacks. With such evidence in front of them, the Government estimated that '... in this first terrible blow, [lasting 60 days] 600,000 people would be killed and twice that number injured', and London would suffer more casualties in proportion to its population than the rest of the country.[3]

(The actual numbers of casualties in Britain as a whole were 60,000 killed, 86,000 seriously injured and 149,000 slightly injured, in all a total number of casualties slightly under 300,000 or one-sixth of the expected number. Corresponding London casualties amounted to 168,000, of whom 29,000 were fatalities.)

This disturbing overestimate of casualties led to the grisly assumption by the Home Office of 'mass burials and burning of bodies in lime'[4] so avoiding the need to find 20,000,000 square feet of seasoned coffin timber each month. As a precautionary measure tens of thousands of shrouds, papier-mâché and cardboard coffins were stockpiled. The vast toll of death and injuries, the accompanying destruction of property, and the widespread distress and social breakdown that followed from the catastrophe would lead to

> *some 3-4 million cases of acute panic, hysteria and other neurotic outbursts during the first six months of air attack.*[5]

Such was the calculation of the Government agencies planning civil defence in the nineteen-thirties.

Strangely, the worst time for shaky nerves was not the 1940 Blitz on London, but the 1938 Munich crisis. People streamed out of London; eighty-three per cent of London children were registered for evacuation; the Government distributed 38,000,000 gas masks; 1,000,000 feet of trenches were dug and there was an emergency plan (Plan 1) for a mass evacuation of London in the event of war breaking out. In contrast to the *ad hoc* nature of Plan 1, was the detailed and long-range strategy for evacuation known as Plan 2, implemented on 1 September 1939.

Plan 2 came about as the result of political pressure. Initially, the concern of civil defence planners was how to provide protection from bombing. The planning of evacuation came second. Pressure from restive MPs on a somewhat dilatory Government forced a late amendment to the Air Raid Precautions Act of 1937. This required local authorities to assist the Government in the preparation of evacuation plans in addition to drawing up air raid protection measures. Further demands from MPs and from local authorities led to the setting up by the Government of the Anderson Committee on 24 May 1938 to 'review various aspects of the problem of transferring persons from areas which would be likely, in time of war, to be exposed to aerial bombardment'.[6]

Fifty-seven individuals gave evidence to the committee, among them the chief constable of Bedfordshire. The committee examined, with representatives of mainline railway companies and the London Passenger Transport Board, 'the facilities available for transporting persons from London to places of greater safety. As a rough basis refugees in the first instance would be taken on an average, fifty miles from the centre of London'.[7]

Fifty miles – the distance to Bedford – was arrived at after considering the need for evacuation trains to make return journeys on the day. A key factor was the capacity of railways to move evacuees to convenient railheads. This made advance pairing of schools from evacuation and reception areas an unnecessary complication. (Public schools, nevertheless, did get together, for example, Cheltenham with Shrewsbury, Dulwich with Tonbridge, St Paul's with Wellington, City of London with Marlborough — and Malvern went to Blenheim Palace.)[8]

The committee was prescient. Speaking of reception areas it noted '... in many places the risk will not be substantially greater than that bombs might be dropped in error, to relieve an aeroplane of its cargo when it had missed its objective'[9] (exactly what happened to Bedford).

The Anderson report, debated in Parliament on 26 July, was published shortly after Munich in October 1938.

With an impatient Parliament pressing the Government to plan for evacuation – there was a censure debate at the beginning of October – things began to move in line with the Anderson Committee's recommendations. Overall responsibility for evacuation was transferred from the Home Office to the Health Department and local authorities were made responsible for the reception and billeting of those evacuees designated as priority classes, namely schoolchildren, children under five accompanied by their mothers, expectant mothers and blind adults. An immediate requirement placed on local authorities was to carry out a survey of accommodation available to 'refugees'. (The term 'refugees' then was not used pejoratively and 'asylum seekers' had not yet been invented. The term 'evacuee' first appeared in an article in the *Times*, 24 November 1938.)

The country was divided into three areas – evacuation, neutral and reception, with populations respectively of thirteen, fourteen and eighteen million. A survey completed in January 1939 by 100,000 'visitors' (interviewers), covered five million houses and the eighteen million inhabitants of the reception areas. On the basis of one habitable room per person, some 6,000,000 rooms were counted. Not all were suitable and many had been privately earmarked, so at most there was room for 4,000,000 evacuees who had to be allocated to reception areas in such a way as to balance shortages of accommodation to surpluses with the need to minimise distances to travel; not an easy task given that much of the surplus lay below a line drawn from the Wash to the Bristol Channel. A further constraint on the planning was the allocation of entraining stations and the provision of buses at detraining stations for dispersal of evacuees to surrounding villages. (Even nowadays such a complex problem of optimal resource allocation within tough constraints would tax a top performing computer swimming with gigabytes.)

The greatest burden of organisation fell upon the shoulders of the

LCC's headquarters' staff at County Hall. An inner core of twelve dispersal officers for the metropolitan area, together with the education officers of Greater London, were responsible for managing an army of 41,000 workers comprising 1,000 official staff, 20,000 teachers and 20,000 volunteers. Each had to be primed with instructions for managing and directing station marshals at main line and exchange stations, party leaders, control point officers, nurses, and many others. Moreover, account had been taken of the needs of particular schools and routes. And when the time came to evacuate six hundred thousand from London, we can only marvel that, over the three days of the evacuation, there was not a single mishap or casualty, not just in London but across the whole country.

At 11.17am on Thursday 31 August the order to evacuate was issued to County Hall. Instructions were immediately conveyed to all parties and the evacuation commenced at 7am on the following day. Most travelled by rail, some by road. For rail alone it meant arranging 1589 assembly points for dispersal of parties to 168 entraining stations, followed by detraining at 271 stations in the reception area. Underlying this feat of organisation was the implementation of a multitude of individual operations across the country. The social historian, Professor Titmuss provides a list (see Appendix B) which is illustrative of the scope of activities to be co-ordinated.

The evacuation was meant to take four days and was completed in three; yet the saving of a day was fortuitous. Whereas 83% of London's children had been registered for evacuation at the time of Munich, now, after much cajoling, pleas and propaganda from the Government and local authorities, only 69% were registered. This was a strange irony, given that only a few months earlier, the Government had been rightly criticised for dilatoriness. Now it was the public that was dragging its heels and not listening too closely to appeals by itinerant Government emissaries who delivered a worrying speech to parents:

> *Suppose war were to come (please do not think for a minute that I think it is going to...), what would you do with your children? We have got to assume ... that bombers would come over ... and certainly they could carry and drop a far greater load of bombs than ... in the last war. Moreover, big and crowded cities ... offer a tremendous temptation to a ruthless enemy to try and deliver a knock-out blow in the first round - that is, in the first few weeks of war. The bombs may*

be aimed at military objectives ... but there is no knowing where some of them might land....

Would you not prefer to entrust your children to their teachers, to take them away to some safer place? ... One of the main objects of the Government in organising this dispersal of the children from our crowded cities is that they should not lose their education; we would make it our duty to try to carry on their school work ... The Government would pay their railway fares. The Government have accordingly planned ... the good old English rule of women and children first.[10]

Despite these urgent appeals by Government, the percentage of evacuees received compared with those expected in the whole of England was just 33%. Bedfordshire was among the top performers at 45%. The total accommodation available for evacuees in Bedfordshire was 111,000 and the number received by September 1939 was one third of the total and the second highest in the country, the highest being West Sussex. Fewer than 1,500,000 had travelled under the scheme tailored for 3,500,000.

We turn now to Bedford. It was the week after Munich. The country had breathed a collective sigh of relief. It could now attend to pressing matters that had been put on hold during the crisis. To quote a correspondent to the Bedfordshire Times concerned about evacuation,

... First of all it is important to get the digestive system back into proper working order. We cannot do this until we give some thought to constipation.[11]

As far as one can ascertain, the worthy burghers of Bedford needed no further reminders.

By the end of January 1939, Bedford's 'visitors' were well on the way to compiling a list of habitable rooms, but fears were being expressed as to whether Bedford was really a safe haven on account of its close proximity to Cardington, Henlow and Cranfield aerodromes; its large number of factories; and to cap it all

... there is already an unduly large (and dangerous) proportion of children living in the town for whom no safety provision has been made.[12]

The solution, suggested by this correspondent would be camps set up on rural ground to the north of Bedford, equipped with bomb-proof shelters. There had long been complaints in the local press of the lack of adequate bomb shelters. A correspondent sardonically asked whether the Borough Council was 'proposing to surround the schools with Sir John Anderson's bird cages...'[13] One correspondent enthusiastically suggested a colony to be built on the outskirts of Bedford for Spanish and German refugees, where they could live together in their own communities and so avoid friction with the local community.

The idea of camps to accommodate evacuees rather than private billets reflected a widespread objection to billeting in private homes: it would be 'worse than war', wrote one MP to Sir John Anderson, the evacuation supremo. Opposition came from MPs representing rural districts in the south of England; from teachers, housewives, local authorities, church bodies and Conservative and Labour associations. One council (not Bedford!) objected to accommodating 'the dregs of London',[14] an example of provincialism rubbing against racism. In retrospect, the less extreme attitudes are perhaps understandable. Evacuation was a journey into the unknown: never before had such a vast decanting of mostly working class city dwellers into rural districts been proposed. Prim country housewives, many begetters of today's Middle Englanders, worried about the lack of hygiene, morals and manners of indigent refugees. In the event, some of their worst fears were realised in a minority of cases: bed-wetting, scabies, urinating on carpets, verminous children dressed in rags – Angus Calder lists such complaints made to Women's Institute members. But it could happen in reverse as one Owenian recalls of his host's children:

> ... their smelly bodies, impetigo, head-lice and all the ailments which come from the lack of personal hygiene. With three in a bed I was lucky to escape with nothing worse than head-lice.   RSB

In May, with council blessing, a kibbutz style agricultural centre was established by an Anglo-Jewish committee at Tingrith, a small Bedfordshire village. Here it was intended that *Kindertransport* children would learn to be self-supporting, sell surplus produce to the market, and assist local farmers short of labour.[15]

In the same month, council billeting officers were doing their rounds, brusquely registering potential hosts and responding with bureaucratic joviality to refuseniks. The following excerpt from a letter to the *Bedfordshire Times* explains the process of registration:

> *...I was ordered to take in evacuees! No question of reason, circumstances or free will. People came to my house, counted the number of rooms, subtracted the number of inhabitants and then calculated the number of children to be put into my care. And that was that. I am not complaining of what we had to do but do object to the smug hypocrisy of it all. An acquaintance who raised a reasonable objection was addressed by a representative of the council thus 'Very well, I shall see that you get a half a dozen of the very worst that can be found. Good morning Mrs. Hitler!'* (Signed Materfamilias)[16].

By early May Bedford had agreed, somewhat under ministry compulsion, to receive up to 20,000 evacuees of whom 17,500 were to be evacuated under the Government scheme. It was estimated that 14,000 would be unaccompanied children. In the event the mayor, Mr. Braggins, was able to report in the first week of the War that, in the three days of evacuation, just over 13,000 of all classes had been received and, in the first day, all the school parties amounting to 4,921 in total had been billeted.

[A correction must be made to the memories of Owen's evacuees. They did not go to the cattle market on detraining, though that would have seemed to be appropriate; after all they were being herded. In fact, they marched to the fair ground, which was the central clearing point. Perhaps to townies, fair grounds and cattle markets look the same. Ed.]

Almost immediately on arrival, the Owen's Head, O.W. Mitchell, sent the following message of thanks to the *Bedfordshire Times*:

> *Sir, - Would you allow me a few lines to express on behalf of the masters and boys of Owen's school, London, E.C.1. our most grateful thanks to the people of Bedford for the way in which they have received us. It has been an immense comfort to us all to have such a cordial welcome and for the billeting arrangements and reception generally to have worked with such remarkable smoothness. We shall not forget and do our very best to be loyal, if temporary, citizens of your town.*
> O.W. MITCHELL
> Head Teacher[17]

In turn, Bedfordians expressed concern for the evacuees in their midst. There was a public plea for prams

> *... as the town is overfull of mothers who have no means of airing their children except by carrying them.*[18]

As for unaccompanied evacuee children, a letter to the *Bedfordshire Times* warned:

> *We country folk should put them on their guard... Deadly nightshade does not grow in Bethnal Green.*[19]

Other things were to prove deadly. 183 people were crushed to death while seeking shelter in Bethnal Green tube station on 8 March 1943.

3

Early Memories

Growing up in thirties London.

War Chronicle of the thirties

1931	September	Japanese invasion of Manchuria
1932		Japan occupies China north of Great Wall
1933	January	Hitler becomes Chancellor
	October	Germany leaves the League of Nations
1934	June	'Night of the Long Knives'- consolidation of Nazi power
1934	July	Civil war in Austria, semi-Nazi regime established
1935	October	Italians invade Abyssinia
1936	March	Germans reoccupy Rhineland
	May	Abyssinia annexed by Italy as war ends
	July	Outbreak of Spanish Civil War
1937	April	Guernica bombed to destruction
	July	Outbreak of Sino-Japanese War
1938	March	Annexation of Austria – *Der Anschluss*
	September	Munich Conference
	November	*Kristallnacht*
1939	March	Annexation of Bohemia and Moravia
	March	Madrid falls to Franco - end of Civil War
	March	British Government guarantees Poland
	August	Soviet-German Non-Aggression Pact

*Y*ears of Wrath is the title of cartoonist David Low's scathing record of the '30s and '40s. One can see why from the above list of calamities. The earliest memory we record below, by a somewhat precocious child, concerns one of the darkest days of the thirties, 30 January 1933.

> I have a clear memory of going with my father one Sunday morning and there on a newsagent's placard board I read 'Navis in power in Germany'. I suppose I had not heard of Nazis and that was the nearest that I could get. I was less than five. Whether I knew what it meant I actually don't remember. VM

By April 1933 pogroms against Jews were a regular occurrence.

> My first political consciousness was at the age of seven in my last term of the elementary infant school. In 1933 bits were published in the *Jewish Chronicle* of Jews being pushed around in barrows. That was a moment of sensitising me which was sustained and I was fiercely aware of the rise of Hitler and that affected my commitment ever since. I remember October '33 when Hitler took Germany out of the League of Nations. A cousin had just been born and there was a gathering of friends and that bit of news spread around that gathering. AH

The second half of the decade regressed, war after war - Abyssinia, Spain, China. The vicious and unprovoked Italian assault on Abyssinia, its use of gas bombs brought protests from the more politically minded members of the public and from members of Parliament. Despite the personal appeal by Haile Selassie to delegates at the League of Nations to take action against Italy, the League was powerless, without the support of Britain and France, who were opposed to any direct action such as sanctions or closure of the Suez Canal. America could only express outrage, not being a member of the League. British and French policy was to avoid any action, which could alienate Mussolini and drive him into the arms of Hitler. The *Magnet* comic published anti-Mussolini propaganda.

> We regarded Mussolini's attack on Abyssinia as a mad dog act, and felt particular sympathy for a primitive people assaulted with modern weapons. The schoolboy magazine I read, called The *Magnet* ran a series entitled *Muccolini's Circus* with the villainous circus owner Muccolini as a thinly disguised Mussolini. The stories included several digs at Italian barbarities. We spent fairly frequent holidays at Ventnor, where we had friends and it was at Ventnor that the Emperor Haile

Selassie initially stayed after his expulsion from Ethiopia in May 1936. Once or twice we saw him on the veranda outside his hotel.   WEOJ

The British fascists, of course, supported Mussolini.

White painted signs on walls in Dalston: **NO SANCTIONS**   DEB

The Left rallied to the defence of the Abyssinians.

My father took me along to demonstrations in support of the emperor Haile Selassie, also known as the Lion of Judah. I saw him as some kind of Biblical warrior. We hailed his courage and condemned the League of Nations and the British Government for failing to support sanctions against Mussolini. But the greatest condemnation was directed at the Italians for their relentless air bombardments and the use of poison gas against civilians.   MM

And for Ian Appleby...

I remember feeling sorry for Haile Selassie and his lions.   IA

Not only comics but toys also played their part in involving kids in the war.

His troops all seemed to be barefooted. The local newsagent introduced lead soldiers of Abyssinians and Italian blackshirts, at one penny each.
AD

Two months after Mussolini annexed Abyssinia in May 1936, Franco invaded the Spanish Republic and the Spanish Civil War began, crystallising political alignments in the country between left and right, with many on the left volunteering for the International Brigade. In 1936 Victor Gollancz founded the Left Book Club, which became the intellectual centre of the campaign against Franco. In May 1937 Guernica was razed to the ground by the Nazi Condor Legion. Picasso recorded the horror of the event in an unforgettable and shocking set of images. The awesome fate of Guernica and later Barcelona made a deep impression on the planners of civil defence.

Our horizons were not drawn so wide - Abyssinia was far away and appeared to be of little political concern: the Spanish war initially was for the Spanish until the bombing of Guernica.   RC

The thirties I remember very vividly as I was politically aware of the Civil War and the agitation of left wing groups. I lived in North London but I belonged to a club in East London in Mare Street. I met many people who came back from Spain. I had a friend, who lived near Sevenoaks. He ran a left wing holiday camp. My brother and sister and I would be sent there for weekends and weeks at a time. There we met many people who were communists and others who were left wing. There were always lots of political discussions, particularly with people who had come back from the Civil War.   HC

I became involved politically in the Spanish Civil War, being taken to demonstrations by my father and to committee rooms above the local co-op to help in the preparation of leaflets supporting the Republicans. It wasn't long before the committees came to us. My father had established a Left Book Club discussion group at home. People came for talks about Spain, socialism, the rise of Fascism and Nazism, and the growing threat from the Fascist powers. On one never-to-be-forgotten occasion at home a group of refugee Spanish dancers gave a sparkling demonstration of flamenco dancing in support of fund raising for the Republicans.   MM

I took my line from my family that Franco was a dangerous ally of Hitler and Mussolini and his victory was a triumph for the Axis placing us in greater danger. We were disappointed that Russia was unable to give the Spanish Government more support. My parents and grandparents were very anti-Catholic and regarded the Roman Catholic Church in Spain as particularly reactionary and oppressive.   WEOJ

I passed by a street vendor selling bagels from a large stick and I noticed a youth of around 18 munching bagels. He was wearing a black heavy leather windbreaker, a garment unknown in Bethnal Green and a boy explained that he had just returned from service in the International Brigade.   AD

(The British Battalion – one of many International Brigades that fought with the Spanish Republican Government against the Fascist invaders led by Franco – was formed between December 1936 and January 1937. Consisting of some 2,000 plus volunteers, it fought in many of the major battles, among which the fiercest were the defence of Madrid and the last desperate assault across the River Ebro in July 1938. Casualties were high with a quarter killed and a half wounded. The last brigaders were withdrawn at the end of 1938. The Spanish Civil War which began in July 1936 ended in victory for Franco and fascism in March 1939.)

At home the British Union of Fascists was active in the streets of East London stirring up hatred against the Jewish population.

Fascism was all around us in Gunton Road, Upper Clapton. Chalked on walls, hoardings and lampposts were the Mosley versions of the swastika, a lightning flash within a circle, bearing the initials PJ for 'Perish Judah'. Fear of the nascent British fascism swept through the comfortable homes of Gunton Road. Many neighbours joined the thousands of anti-fascists in the historic battle of Cable Street in 1936, when the Mosleyites were routed in their attempt to march through the East End.   MM

In 1938, I clearly remember seeing evidence of Oswald Mosley's British Union of Fascists in Wood Green High Road on Saturday afternoons, not the marching and fighting that went on in Clapton and Hackney, but the selling of *Action*, their news sheet, and street corner meetings ending with the speaker giving the Nazi salute to a shout of 'Heil Mosley!'.   AWL

The seeds of Fascism grew out of the Great Depression of the twenties and thirties...

I recall two episodes during my boyhood (say 10-12, 1938-39). On one of my weekly Sunday visits to my Jewish grandmother in Hackney, I had reached Ridley Road on foot (it was thought safe then for a child to walk freely in the city - as I did all the time); there was a row of drummers dressed in black, their snare-drums draped in black velvet embroidered in gold with the fascist flash; as they tattooed, hundreds of men in black and youths in grey shirts came from all directions, formed a broad column, hoisted flags and banners, and marched east through the Jewish area where my grandmother lived with my uncle. I walked alongside, quite excited. My grandmother and my father, when I told them, were appalled, frightened, and warned me to be aware in future. I learned later that the Fascists were met later in the day by militant unionists in a pitched battle. My father also told me that defence patrols led by Jewish athletes and boxers (Kid Berg was a legend!) existed in the East End for the protection of women and children (is this true?). The police were not trusted (this is certainly true).
The other 'incident': I was going one autumn evening to meet my father at his workplace (Ogus and Moscovitch who had a furniture-making shop behind East Road); to get there I crossed Nile Street, where there was a permanent street market, where that night there was a smart black-shirted man in jack boots (Mosley?), lit by a naphtha lamp haranguing a crowd of working people from the back of a flat-bed lorry. I

met my father, told him, and we took a different route home, along East Road. It was unsettling, even though our Labour MP Dr. Jager defeated a fascist candidate (Joyce?), and despite the Trade Union and left resistance to the BUF. The police were not helpful.

But the over-riding thing for me was the Depression, the dole, unemployment and poverty, and, in my immediate life then, the real misery for my father, a generous, bright, highly skilled craftsman, who had to leave the Jews' Free School in Brick Lane, where he was doing very well, at the age of thirteen to help, with his wretched apprentice's pittance, support his brother and widowed mother.   GR

Frank Fenn's experience of Fascism and anti-Semitism was both different and familial.

My mother's family was not as systematically anti-Semitic as some of the Fenns. My grandfather cleaned the windows of Jewish shops on Stratford Broadway, my uncles collected bets for at least one Jewish bookmaker, and the family boasted (I have never verified this) of a distant family connection, through my grandmother, with a West End chorus girl called, I believe, Bunty Payne who married one of their heroes, the Aldgate Tiger, Jack (Kid) Berg. But, like the Fenns, they had moved from the old East End 'because the area was changing, going down', and much of their conversation about Jews was disparaging and based upon the crudest stereotypes.

My first actual encounter with British Fascism took place some time in the mid 1930s. I passed a BUF meeting near the old Midland Railway Station in Leyton High Road one Saturday evening and saw, to my great surprise, my Uncle Len addressing the crowd. I stopped and listened; I remember only a few words from his speech. 'What did we fight the Great War for?' he demanded. 'To make a land fit for Hebrews to live in?' The crowd applauded enthusiastically. When I got home I told my father. He shook his head with some distaste and took the first steps in my political education. The process took a giant step forward about two years later when I went to Owen's and, for the first time, knowingly met Jewish boys of my own age. And that was a defining moment in my life.   WFF

The third war of the thirties, the continuing Sino-Japanese War, impressed not only young minds but also a future 'rivers of blood' politician.

The Sino-Japanese War, with its many strange sounding place names registered with me a good deal. In our circle of acquaintances there was great indignation and demonstrations over Japanese atrocities generally and in particular their ill treatment of British nationals in the Far East. Our regular newspapers, the *News Chronicle* and *Daily Herald* highlighted these. Somehow a poem written by Enoch Powell in 1939 in a magazine reached our household. I found it very stirring.   WEOJ

> *Murdered, deny who can,*
> *Here lies an Englishman.*
> *The steel that through him ran*
> *Was tempered in Japan*
> *And while his native land forgets,*
> *And bows the knee to threats*
> *His vengeful spirit whets*
> *The German bayonets.* [1]

1938 was heavy with fearful expectation. The annexation of Austria by Hitler; his threats to annex territory in Czechoslovakia (conceded to him on a plate at Munich) convinced many that the war was likely sooner or later, despite Chamberlain's promise of 'peace in our time' on signing the Munich agreement.

I knew that Neville Chamberlain had flown to see Hitler and had come back waving his famous paper promising 'Peace in our time'. We all heaved a sigh of relief and the Germans marched into Czechoslovakia.
AWL

The 1938 crisis was in term time and I went to school with a knapsack containing various items as specified by the authorities, including food for 24 hours. No evacuation took place, Chamberlain returned from Munich with the fatuous piece of paper 'peace in our time'. Being at that time a precocious student of politics, I did not believe it. Press reports revealed that the evacuation would have been a shambles.   PP

A few days later I was in a cinema with my dad. Newsreel. Chamberlain waving his piece of paper (signed by Herr Hitler). My dad shouts out, 'it'll be torn up next week'. I feel embarrassed. He'd never done anything like that before. But then people cheer him and clap. And I feel proud.
DEB

In Gunton Road, you would hear the neighbours gathered on their doorsteps and people in the local shops talk fearfully of war within a year - this despite the euphoric headlines in the press assuring us of peace. Signs of war preparation were in the air, literally. I remember seeing my first barrage balloon, over Hackney Marshes, looking like a floating elephant minus limbs and with a stunted trunk. Even more alien looking was the sight of my family donning the gas masks supplied by the Government later in the year. We became humanoid insects. I was only ten. I had no idea of war. Wearing a gas mask was fun, a good way of frightening girls in the dark and frightening yourself.   MM

Ironically, for some children the days before Munich were full of lively anticipation.

In the lead-up to the Munich, stacked in the corner of each classroom were knapsacks stuffed with emergency clothing etc., which each of us had brought to school to be grabbed, presumably, in the event of an immediate departure. Instead, Mr. C. came back to Heston waving his 'silly piece of paper' and the *Daily Express* carried the bold headline 'PEACE IN OUR TIME'. Joyce and I trudged back home, disappointedly, with our no longer needed knapsacks on our backs.   JS

When evacuation plans were rumoured at the time of the Munich crisis I was excited at the prospect of going away from home on what I regarded as a great 'adventure' and was bitterly disappointed when told that it was 'all off'. The enormity of the political tension of that time passed me by - my nine-year old mind held no concept of the dangers of war.   SB

Not every child in September 1938 was so euphoric about the possibility of war. A prophetic and frightening image of the devastation to come played in the cinemas and terrified Joss Ackland.

In 1938 the newspapers, the wireless and the neighbours all talked of the possibilities of war with Germany, and men who had been so long on the dole now found work digging air-raid shelters. One day I had to go to a large grey building where I was fitted for a gas mask. Then, with the grotesque black rubber Martian face with its huge perspex eyes and metal Schnozzle Durante nose tucked inside a cardboard box hanging by a string from my shoulder, I went home to imagine the worst. That evening Mother took me to see the Alexander Korda movie of H. G. Wells's *Things to Come*. Open-mouthed and round-eyed I watched the dreadful results of the holocaust, with the little boy, with his tin drum hanging by a string from his shoulder, lying dead in the rubble. Later that night I knelt by my bed and prayed long and hard. 'Please don't let there be war.'   JA

The Trinity 1938 *Arrow* reports on discussions in the Debating Society on political issues. H. A. Moore, the school captain, spoke on Extremism. Edmund Dell, who later became a Treasury minister, opposed the pacifist line of the Peace Pledge Union. Other topics discussed were the dangers of fascism and support for the League of Nations. Sixth formers, most of whom would shortly be called up, were only too receptive to political analysis.

> ... the vagaries of the school timetable had left our history tuition in the hands of a young man fresh from college who gave us a brilliant exposition of the politics of the day, including an analysis of the economic and foreign policy of Nazi Germany. It might have been above our heads, but like all good teachers he treated us as thoughtful, capable young adults and left us in no doubt that the ultimate outcome of Nazi policy was the attempt to dominate Europe through conquest and conflict. So, as the events of that school year unfolded, through the Munich crisis, the annexation of Austria and Czechoslovakia and the pact with Russia, like most of my friends I could see that war was an inevitable outcome of the dramatic events that filled the newspapers and the radio bulletins. DB

Dennis Jones was made aware of impending war by the arrival of refugees from the Nazis.

> My grandmother facilitated the arrival of the Ullmann family minus father. Mother and two sons came from Germany with only suitcases, settling in a nearby flat. Departing later for the USA, they left behind for us a magnificent clockwork model locomotive and some blue and white china they'd escaped with. Another refugee from the Nazis we helped was Rudi Lichtenstein, a diminutive and exceedingly livewire chemist, anxious to develop and market his newly formulated 'lemonade', before likewise moving Stateside; he presented my brother and myself each with a smart necktie. DMJ

The long, tragic shadow of the First World War also played a role in preparing young minds for war.

> My father had served in Gallipoli and then had his arm shattered on the first day of the Somme, so I grew up in a house that mistrusted the Germans and supported Churchill's 'stop them now' pleas of 1933 onwards, so I was well aware that war was likely. GRo

> Mansfield, the Headmaster at my elementary school, was exemplary in the manner in which, from 1938, he made clear to us the extent to which we should take the threat of war seriously, justifying, therefore, the necessity of possible removal from our homes, without at the same time putting the fear of God into us. Later, in the War, when children

had become seriously home-sick, and no bombs had yet fallen on London, he went out of his way to stress that the Germans, as he well knew from his own WW1 experience, were certainly aggressive and skilled enough to pose a great threat to London, in spite of the air defence systems (balloons, AA guns, etc) which we might believe would keep them at bay.   JS

Near us in Ryde Vale Road lived the Madman. Reputedly shell-shocked in the '14-'18 war, he daily walked out, smart in suit and trilby, epitome of repressed violence, stick waving, gesticulating and yelling the forbidden four-letter words. We children cowered uncomprehendingly from a reflection of horrors past and to come.   DMJ

I must have had a pretty good image of what the First World War was like, at least from a kid's perspective. I must have expected something similar. In 1934 coming home from school, I passed a placard on a wall which showed a picture of Big Ben toppling over, presumably having been hit by a bomb and it said 'War in 1938?' and I found that very frightening.   VM

One of the reasons we did not fully understand the horror of war is that the survivors of the generation that endured World War 1 engaged in a conspiracy of silence about what they had endured and felt and seen – too awful to be willingly remembered and spoken of to their wives and children. World War 2 was very different in that regard – the horrors were far more widely known and shared for many reasons. Anyway, how could a Jewish father say, even if he knew, to his 12-year-old son, 'if the Germans come here, you can look forward to Dachau'? Our teachers were silent. I really wonder what was going on in senior classes in 1938.   GR

In 1938, I was nine years old and a pupil at Newington Green Primary School. One day I was looking out of the window during prayers and saw they were digging trenches in the Green. Knowing about the Great War, I thought they were going to be the front line - it turned out to be preparatory work for air-raid shelters.   DHS

Shortly after Munich, Ernst vom Rath, the Third Secretary of the German Embassy in Paris was assassinated by seventeen-year-old Herschel Grynszpan in revenge for Nazi persecution of his family. The Nazis, led by Goebbels, Hitler's Chief of Propaganda, used the assassination as the excuse to launch a pogrom against German Jews. On the nights of November 9 and 10, gangs of Nazi youth roamed through Jewish neighbourhoods breaking windows of Jewish businesses and homes, burning synagogues and looting - hence the name *Kristallnacht* or night of the 'broken glass'. In all 101 synagogues and almost 7,500 Jewish businesses were destroyed. 26,000 Jews were arrested and sent to concentration camps.

In November 1938, an appeal was made to world leaders to at least save young children from annihilation by the Nazis. The appeal was largely ignored. The US Congress rejected the appeal. One country alone gave refuge to 10,000 young children. That country was Great Britain.

The Nazis insisted on three conditions: the sum of £50 per child (approximately $250) had to be paid; the children had to be between the ages of 3 and 17 years old; and they had to leave without parents or families.

The children travelled in sealed and guarded trains to Holland, and then on to England where they were received with open arms. The funds were donated by the public. The children were placed in foster homes, schools, farms (see page 17) and orphanages. Over 80% of these children never saw their parents again; they perished in the Holocaust. Of the fortunate 20%, two came to Owen's.

> My two late brothers, Felix and Erwin and I were among the fortunate 10,000 Jewish children from Germany, Czechoslovakia and Austria who - unaccompanied by their parents - were admitted to Britain late in 1938 and in 1939, on the eve of the outbreak of war, in what were called *Kindertransports* and who would otherwise have been exterminated by the Nazis during the war. Of these 10,000, some 25-30 or so were evacuated to Bedford when the war broke out. WT

At the end of March, after Germany annexed Bohemia and Moravia in flagrant breach of the Munich Pact, the Government issued its guarantee to Poland. Collective security discussions held in August between Britain, France and the Soviet Union failed and on 23 August 1939 the Soviet Union and Germany signed a non-aggression pact.

> After Munich came the event that split the family: the Nazi-Soviet pact signed in late August 1939. Progressives everywhere were dismayed. My father tried to defend Stalin. My grandfather, like my father, an escapee from Czarist oppression, considered the Soviet regime to be no better than the Czarist regime it replaced. As for Stalin, he was no

more than an evil bloodthirsty murderer. There was a furious argument between my father and grandfather, which was only put into cold storage when the Nazis invaded Russia in June 1941.   MM

4

September the Third

The day war broke out.

Friday they arrived. Saturday they explored: parks, the river, shop windows. They tried to find old friends and make new ones. The weather kept fine.

War was imminent. Adults were never far away from a wireless set. On this last day of peace the boys were more preoccupied with their new life.

Nobody forgets where they were the next day when they heard the news. Some heard it first hand.

The declaration of war was a very sombre occasion sitting around the dining table listening to the wireless.   JW

I remember us sitting around the wireless and listening to Neville Chamberlain saying we were at war with Germany. Even at 10 years old I could feel the drama of the situation.   DHS

It was Sunday morning and everyone in the billet was in the sitting room listening to Neville Chamberlain's broadcast. His sombre tone impressed an 11 year old.   AD

I recall the radio message by Chamberlain and subsequently adjourning to Goldington Green where a number of school colleagues had gathered.   RC

Declaration by Chamberlain sent us rushing into the garden to see any German bombers. Immediately ordered back into billet in case we got hurt.   DAP

I distinctly remember sitting with the family in the house in Bedford listening to Chamberlain's broadcast that morning. I didn't know how long we thought the war was going to last.   VM

Remember hearing the news but did not think the war would last.   IA

I was in the local meadow playing with some boys who managed to steal my pocket money.   BF

I quite clearly remember hearing Chamberlain's broadcast on the BBC National Programme while standing in the dining room of 3 Glebe Road, and realising that this was it. I don't remember whether I was alone but I certainly felt alone. There were those who said that the war would be over by Christmas including Foulsham's Old Moore's Almanac. I don't think any of us believed it.   AWL

It was a fine sunny day and I was in the garden, where my foster parent, who was a keen vegetable gardener, was explaining to me how to grow onions, when Chamberlain came on the radio through the open kitchen door. My host reassured me that it would be all over by Christmas.
                                                                                                    DDW

Most boys got the news soon after eleven.

I do remember that we found Harvey Road outside the town in Goldington and as we stopped outside number 2 a woman ran out of a house opposite saying that war had been declared. It was just after 11 a.m.   RN

I had gone fishing in the Ouse with a net. I came back after 11 a.m. I was at the side door of the house cleaning my muddy shoes. Mrs Smith came out and said, 'War has been declared'. 'It was expected,' I replied.
                                                                                                    DEB

I had been out playing in the woods and on returning I could see that Mrs Clark was very upset and had been crying. She then told me that the declaration of war had just been announced on the radio, and the whole household was very subdued for some time.   GS

Pauline Fowler, who was evacuated to Bedford with her younger brother, soon to be an Owenian, had been told by her mother that she would soon be joining her.

The Doctor took us to church in her little car on Sunday September 3rd, where we were told from the pulpit that England was at war with Germany. On our way back from church, to our delight, we saw our Mum, sister and baby brother Patrick, walking towards Landsdowne Road. She had kept her word to us and brought her other two children out of London. PF

There are those who heard, and those who heard about, Chamberlain's broadcast. More intriguingly, there are those who recall the first siren that morning and those who are adamant no siren sounded in Bedford.

I do not believe that the air-raid sirens sounded in Bedford on the first day of war, as they did in London. I'm sure the good Mr and Mrs Riches would have sheltered us under the stairs if a warning had been sounded. JS

The siren blew. We stood around. Sister Doreen was a telephonist at the Bedford exchange. Rumours abounded. Bedford, hearing that Coventry had been blitzed, rang the Coventry exchange who in turn had heard the same about Bedford. DEB

In the garden of our billet was a mostly complete Anderson shelter. Very shortly after the declaration of war on the radio, the sirens sounded. We all went into the shelter followed by the two sixth formers from next door and then the lady of their house wearing her best hat, gas mask, fur coat and carrying a briefcase which we understood to contain her house deeds, insurance policies, etc. It was a false alarm. WJW

In London, of course, the siren did sound.

In September 1939, outside term time, my parents kept me at home. The 3rd of September. Once again, Chamberlain was on the wireless 'no such undertaking has been received' and we were at war with Germany - then immediately the air raid sirens – but it was a false alarm. PP

'The day war broke out' found me in Homerton Hospital East London with diphtheria (they called it the fever hospital in those days). CCo

Other incidents impinged that Sunday, one heavy with tragic irony given that a war against fascism had just been declared.

I remember the announcement on the radio. I was in the garden. I came into the house. Mrs Wright was tearful and I felt shaky. But before that happened about 9 o'clock she said to us 'Come on children, it's time to go to church'. I remember that so well. Standing in the room with my brother and feeling very nervous, I said, 'We don't go to church'. 'You don't! Why not?' She was clearly affronted by my heathen response. I mumbled, 'we are Jewish'. Her reaction could not have humiliated me more.

'Oh! You wicked children!' I will never forget that. But, to be fair to her, she treated us well and never referred to Jews again – at least in our hearing.   MM

Mick Horkins, for the same reason, didn't go to church that day (or any other).

Heard announcement on the radio. Ran down the road to tell the people who had gone to church.   MHor

That night the RAF dropped six million leaflets on Germany.

5

Home from Home

Culture clashes.

It was random. What choice existed belonged to the hosts. The guests – welcome or unwanted – had no option. A minority of reception officers attempted to meet requests such as number, age, gender. But the real task was to fit supply to an unexpressed demand.

Had there been world enough and time, the differences might have been ironed out. Might. Consider the potential incompatibilities: class, background, age, religion, beliefs, habits, culture. It was far more complex than the cliché of deprivation meeting affluence or city confronting countryside. Though such encounters did take place.

> For the first time in my life I saw beautiful countryside and met wonderful country folk.   RD

> The neighbours were interesting. Some were expecting the worst from evacuees. Others were sympathetic and friendly from the start.   GCk

Owen's boys were predominantly middle class, but many of those had been born into working (hard working) class homes. Most had gained school entrance through scholarships. Most lived in easy reach of the Angel. Dickens described the Angel as the place 'where London begins in earnest'.

Life was earnest. There was little mollycoddling either at home or school. Evacuation was a fact of life for most, a job to be done and, by and large, a great adventure. And what is an adventure without the gamble of the unknown?

Given the incompatibilities, it remains a wonder that so many of the *ad hoc* arrangements made in early September lasted years, some the entire duration. Indeed, today, a few contacts are maintained.

Did the young, the eleven-year-old new boys, find the wrench harder to take? Possibly: after all, for them it was the start of two new lives. Or was it tougher on those two or three years older who found the pattern of their school life disrupted? Or were the preoccupations of the senior boys the most pressing: soldiers-in-waiting who first must need to clear the hurdles of general and higher school certificate? Who can say? There is no stereotypical evacuee experience. All lives were changed. War does that. Those who lived through it are, arguably, less fazed by change than others.

The *Cambridge Economic Survey*, written in January 1941, described evacuation as a 'powerful, social ferment … for strangers and for those who took them in.'[1] For many reception areas, evacuees were evidence of an underclass they had never seen before. For many Owenians it was the reverse. But, class apart, each coupling of host and guest meant that both parties had to accommodate, become familiar with alien speech, different dress, strange eating habits.

It was a period of adjustment often followed by abrupt re-adjustment if, like Alan Locke, you changed billets.

> The Garlicks were certainly much more prosperous than my parents were and the house was larger and more fully furnished and equipped. The differences were not intimidating, however.
>
> By the fourth week, it became obvious that Mrs G could not cope with four raucous boys, despite having a living-in housekeeper and so John and Howard were found other billets. I stayed on for a further three months with Geoff Cook until I too proved too much of a burden and was handed on to friends of the Gs, Charlie and Florrie Fowler of 51 Denmark Street.
>
> Denmark Street was a bit of a culture shock after Glebe Road. Mr and Mrs F, too, had no children of their own; the house was an end-of-terrace two-up, two-down with a kitchen. The downstairs 'front room', well equipped with a three-piece suite, carpets and a standard lamp, was never used, but always set aside for the visitors that never came.

This went hand in hand with the culture of never using the front door. In fact, if anyone knocked at the front door all activity in the house stopped in anticipation of dreadful news. No, the back door was used always by everybody who came to the house.   AWL

Malcolm Campbell, similarly:

I was packed off to a household in Brereton Road. I only once set foot on the doorstep; my first mistake was to arrive at the front of the house. I was quickly informed by Mrs C that nobody (except, I later discovered, a visiting cleric) crossed the frequently scrubbed doorstep. Also, after morning descent, access to the upstairs of the house was not permitted again until bedtime and I was never allowed to be in the house alone.   MJC

There were other culture shocks higher on the Richter scale.

The Vs were very religious. I was expected to go to Sunday school at 10 a.m. followed by Morning Service at 11 a.m., Sunday school again in the afternoon and Evensong later!

They had no children of their own and, although kind, really didn't know how to look after an eleven-year-old like me. I wasn't very happy and consequently moved to 147 Bower Street off the Goldington Road, the home of Mr and Mrs M and son Derek (14) and daughter Gwen, a little younger. The family attitude was liberal to say the least. I was allowed out until past 9 p.m. and offered cigarettes (!) I was twelve years old! Me being me, I loved it.   RCa

I learned to appreciate a new culinary culture, which excluded kosher food. Of course I missed lokshen soup and chopped liver, but started a lifetime seduction to the joys of sizzling bacon, the aroma of pork sausages wafting out of the kitchen and the burnt crispiness of Yorkshire pudding.   MM

There were four of us in my first billet. I suspected Mrs S accommodated us in order to avoid soldiers being billeted with her. She was unsuccessful and subsequently two soldiers, one a sergeant, joined us. We lived downstairs in the basement and slept in the attic.   MC

I had a bed with no mattress and I had to sleep on wads of newspaper instead.   BC

Second billet with manager of local fleapit, long way out of town… saw lots of horror films from the back row of the cinema.   IA

Our billet was in 150 Shortmead Street, with Mr and Mrs R who were in their 70s and a brother, Bill, who was about 60. I think we were a bit of a problem for them for they had never had any children, but they were very kind and she was a good cook, especially with the restrictions of rationing. We used to have a lot of bread and cheese and raw onions, which I really enjoyed. The house was a typical cottage with gas lighting, a kitchen range for heating and cooking, an outside water tap, shared by the other cottages and an earth lavatory at the end of the garden.
This was nothing like home, but at ten years and five years, it was a bit of an adventure to us. Our room was an attic that was reached by opening a door in the living room and going up a tiny winding staircase with a rope banister. It was always freezing cold – the winter of 1939-40 was one of the coldest on record.   DHS

But culture shock wasn't all one way.

I spent my evacuation years (1939-44) with the same family in a semi-detached house in Irwin Road. From the first day I entered a world completely different from my home in Shoreditch for I had never experienced having my own bedroom or using a toilet and bathroom inside the house. I am sure my experience was not unique and I, like many others, gained immeasurably by the introduction to middle class life style of order and concern for others.   RCo

The whole family gave me their seal of approval. It was a nice middle class home in a nice middle class town. I can always remember being impressed by the absence of brick walls between houses and thought it was great to see people in adjoining gardens. .   KD

They lived in considerable comfort. They had a gardener and a maid and they took in, I think, three of us. There might have been a fourth at one time. The wife was very English, tallish and angular with a marked sharp diction, not unkind but not overtly sentimental. We lived in the servants' quarters and had our lunch and the evening meal with the servant. Once or twice a year as a special treat we were invited in to the drawing room and had a few minutes' polite discussion with the man and his wife. So we were left very much to our own devices. I suppose the servants looked after us although I think we looked after ourselves. We hardly saw them at all. I am pretty sure we had our own entrance.
                    HCu

The foster parents weren't so called. The deputy mum was called 'billet lady' though there was no general term for deputy dad. You would expect that experience of child rearing would have been an advantage if not a pre-requisite. In fact, many of the most successful relationships involved childless couples. In retrospect, it is not so surprising. Evacuees filled a gap.

> I was billeted with two spinsters and their elderly father and they spoilt me.
>
> AD

> I moved billets – from middle class detached to working class two-up-two-down and back-to-back. An outside lavatory. Near Russell Park. And the window cleaner's wife was a plump friendly lady. Almost her first words were, 'We're having rabbit for dinner. Do you like rabbit?' I said yes though I'd never had rabbit. Her name, strange to relate, was the same as my previous billet lady, Ethel Smith. She too was childless.
>
> DEB

> Both the Garlicks were pillars of the local Baptist Church in Mill Street and they had no children. Mr G was a director of a firm of monumental masons in the town and also owned a confectionery wholesalers.

> Mrs G had her own choral group and she opened bazaars, so we considered ourselves very comfortably off.
>
> AWL

> I was lucky. My hosts, Mr and Mrs H, took me into their circle of friends and I lived with them until I left the school in December 1944. They had no children of their own and it must have been quite an upset for them and for the old mother who also lived in the house and with whom I got on very well. Some years later my parents told me that in the event of their death in the blitz the Hs would have adopted me. RN

It didn't always work out.

> They were well intentioned but also middle aged and childless. Our relationship can best be described as perfunctory. The lack of parental support and encouragement that I had enjoyed before the war gradually began to affect my schoolwork.
>
> WFF

> I lived with a childless couple. They already had an evacuee two or three years older than me. The husband worked in the railway sheds. He was a big gentle kind man. His wife could not have been more different. She was dirty; rarely washed her hands. I am sure I never got my share of the rations despite the extra money she received from my

parents. Breakfast was bread (with dirty finger marks on it) and never with butter.

The worst was the fact there was something going on between the wife and the other evacuee. She tried to involve me in these activities. I was shocked and horrified and wrote and told my parents. My mother came, with a friend, to collect me very soon after. The joy when the 'lady' of the house answered the door and I heard my mother's voice cannot be described. I ran to the door and this woman put her arm around me and told my mother what a good boy I was and how happy I was. Without going into detail my mother said she'd come to take me home.   J Wes

Of course, if a parent actually accompanied you then things were very different. Or, rather, the same.

Our home life there was a continuation of pre-war home life, except for the absence of my father in India.   DMJ

Life for some became grand.

The Gs' house was much larger than my terraced house in North London; they had four bedrooms, a large kitchen and a wash-house where the laundry was done. They had a live-in housekeeper, they were on the telephone and they had a car (a Rover 12 I seem to think) although it was garaged separately, a short way from the house. The house had a cellar via a grating in the side entrance. The Gs never actually did any shopping. They placed orders for groceries over the telephone and Mr Lindford delivered them by a carrier bike. The same happened with the bread from Mr Northwood.   AWL

One of the rear bedrooms was used by the owners as a dressing room and the other one was occupied by the live-in maid, a strapping southern Ireland lass named Mary. So I was allocated the prestigious second bedroom with the front-facing bay window over the lounge below. I do not think that Mary was particularly pleased that I had joined the household either, since it meant an appreciable amount of extra work and cooking for her to embrace. Whilst not being actually unkind to me, I can recall a number of occasions when I was given a shove or two and subjected to her sharp tongue, when the master and mistress were out of earshot.   KRC

Those boys who were fortunate enough to be billeted in the very best houses enjoyed the best of possible times, one group even lived in their own private wing with their own leisure room, and existed virtually independent of their host family, being fed and attended by the various live-in servants. Another of my friends was able to invite me to enjoy tennis on an excellent grass court in the garden of his new billet. KSK

I remember being billeted on a family owning land, buildings and timber yards, etc. They were very good at the start... There were all kinds of things that were right for them but wrong for me or the other way round... My life in Bedford was so different from my life in London. My surroundings were very pleasant but the people I was staying with had a completely different lifestyle. It was a large detached house surrounded by trees and a large garden with allotments. They had servants, a permanent cook and considerable help in the house.   BS

Basil Leverton had the unique experience of living with a family he had already met in a previous life.

I was very fortunate indeed, to be in a family home with people I knew. They had a double fronted house and I had my Boosey and Hawkes drum kit there in one front room, plus wind-up gramophone and Mrs R endured it, on reflection, nobly. The other front room had a removable billiard table and Mr R taught me Russian billiards.   BL

Geoff Cook, who shared a billet with Alan Locke, also found a link with his new acquaintances.

Early in my stay, I had been given the Gs' holiday photograph album to look at. One of the entries showed a group of about two dozen people on an outing seated in an open charabanc. The legend was 'Ventnor 1924'. (It was, I'm told, usual for such an organised outing to include a group photograph.) Yes, there were the Gs but to my great amazement my mother (still single at the time) and her younger sister were with the group. (On telling my mother, she unearthed a similar photograph.) This little incident did much for my standing; it was told by the Gs to their friends for many weeks afterwards.   GCk

Behaviour changed.

In my real home there was the major difficulty of having to be very quiet during the day including weekends, while my father, who worked nights on the printing presses in Fleet Street, was sleeping. It was good to be released from that.   DDW

I remember Mr A used to get very upset as I would go up and down the stairs a lot to the bedroom or toilet and he thought I was wearing out the carpet.   HC

Mr and Mrs A were extremely house proud and every part of the house was shining and largely unused. On the arms of the armchairs in the rarely used lounge were two ashtrays on each of which reposed a cigar. These were just for show and never smoked. We were quite happy there but had to be careful not to leave finger marks anywhere. We were in bed by 7.30 every evening but could hear the wireless from downstairs. CL

Mrs G had not ventured out of the house for a number of years (she was very deaf and terribly snobbish), unless Arthur the chauffeur was summoned in his Daimler for a Sunday outing. The hairdresser and the dressmaker or doctor always called on us when required – a bit of a different lifestyle now for me also. KRC

Few, if any, had to adjust as Mervyn Crossick.

There were six of us, four adults – husband, wife and two sons and two evacuees. We shared three bedrooms and one outside loo. There was no bathroom.

We never ran out of toilet paper. Mr C worked on the railways as a freight guard and brought home railway timetables and my job was to cut and trim. I used to 'sit' and study these and became quite expert on how to travel, where to change and what time you might arrive. During the winter months my expertise lessened. The draught under the door truncated the time spent studying.

In the toilet was stored a galvanised zinc bath. Bath nights were infrequent. There was a ritual to be observed. The bath was first taken from the toilet and fitted in the kitchen. Baths could only be taken with soft water. It was, therefore, necessary to fill buckets from the rainwater butt at the side of the house. The water was carried through to the kitchen and poured into a gas copper. When the water was hot enough it was transferred by bucket to the bath. Doors to the garden and living room were locked. Bath night had arrived. My father must have realised the occasional nature of my ablutions and I was given extra money to take advantage of the public baths. I was constantly faced with the dilemma of whether to pay for a bath or buy an extra doughnut from the Co-Op. More often the Co-Op won.

The living room, measuring probably about twelve feet square, was the centre of the family's activities. There we came and went, did our homework, ate our meals, listened to the wireless and talked. Mr C's father was our landlord and he came round once a week to collect the five-shilling rent. The front parlour was used only for matters of importance; Mr C's father was always entertained in there. I was shown into it once when an uncle arrived from London to break the news to me that my mother had died.   MC

6

London it Ain't

Building a community in the country.

Owenians were proud of their city. Displaced, they became professional Londoners.

> Being a Londoner made us feel a little different from Bedfordians. They seemed parochial. I know I made little personal contact with them. And I wonder whether in turn they found our streetwise, London ways perhaps a little too exotic for a quiet nonconformist, country town.
>
> MM

Bedford was small-time.

> 'Home' meant relatives, friends and familiarity and initially Bedford seemed small. RC

> Bedford was a small town, a very different environment. In London I had a fair amount of freedom to travel around on buses and trams *ad lib*. There was no problem in going long distances in London. VM

> Whilst in later years I realised that Bedford was a good town, compared with London, we all considered it a dump. GS

There was an instinctive desire to convey a metropolitan superiority. However, Bedford promised adventure and to some might even compare favourably to life around the Angel.

> Amongst us thirteen-year-olds, there was an air of excitement at the prospect of war and, since Islington was not a particularly attractive place, evacuation in the event of war was almost to be welcomed. KD

London may have been bigger but Bedford was roomier. Some boys who had grown up in flats now lived in houses for the first time. Some discovered freedom.

> I seemed to be semi-detached. Generally, I could come and go as I liked with few questions asked. How different from home where my mother liked me to stay within reach in the street (our playground) after I returned from school. MM

Some discovered the joy of gardens – and the proximity of green fields.

> There was a football field close by. Better than chalking cricket stumps on a brick wall in Fairbridge Road, or inadvertently breaking a window with an out-of-control spinning top. DDW

They may not have admitted it but Owenians succumbed to the charm of Bedford. Though first impressions weren't reassuring for one late arrival.

> For an inner city kid Bedford was an eye opener. True, my first acquaintance with Bedford on a damp, overcast day, pounding the streets, seeking accommodation, stomaching rebuffs, was anything but charming. MM

Sixty years later, for some at least, there is no contest.

> Bedford, compared with SW London, was an easy winner. Open-air experience, Ouse-centred activities and contact with, and integration into, the rich life of an historic market town. DMJ

> I still recall the smells of Bedford... hops, barley and yeast from Chas Wells' brewery; chocolate from the Meltis factory; something appetite-banishing from the British Restaurant; something sweet and pastoral on Goldington Green; and something uniquely horrible in Green's Store, a kind of downmarket Marks and Sparks next door to Woolworth's. MJC

Bedford was a country town. Country to the average pre-war Owenian was an occasional, annual at best, experience; not something accessible, let alone visited on impulse and a bike.

> Bedford is a pleasant country town with easy access by bike to the countryside. For London boys, hemmed in by miles of unbroken

streets, Bedford plus bike provided a ready mobility, which London
lacked.   MM

My memories of the early days of evacuation, still as an elementary schoolboy, are just snapshots of that life. I did things that London
would not have afforded. I climbed trees, tended my own garden, fished
in Cardington Mill and I got there on a bicycle that I bought for 2s.6d.
                                                                         DBa

Bedford as a town was clearly a much better environment for me to
grow up in than the streets of Islington regardless of the war. In the first
year, living in Acacia and London roads, we were on the southern edge
of the town. We spent a lot of time exploring the countryside which was
just down the road.   DDW

The Ouse! A stone's throw from Castle Road was this magnificent river
unhurriedly flowing through richly blossomed embankments, spanned
by a picturesque 'Chinese' suspension bridge. This was, indeed, a river
for leisure, unlike my own local river, the Lea, which for centuries had
been mainly a working river. I could not imagine the elegant Ouse at
Bedford lowering its dignity by ferrying overloaded barges, drawn by
sweaty, snorting carthorses, a common sight on the Lea of my childhood.   MM

After living in London, being so close to the country left indelible
impressions on me. The differences in the seasons became dramatic;
hiking to school after heavy snow, skating on the open pond after
freeze-up, picking wild flowers and berries, cycling or hitching rides to
nearby villages, all of these were new experiences for a youngster who
was raised in London.   ME

**For some evacuees living in villages before joining the school or
'commuting' (a word not known then) to lessons from a rural billet, the countryside experience was more intense.**

Village diet including beestings (colostrum – first milk of cow after
calving) made into thick custard. A single blue egg would be taken
from a moggy's (moorhen's) nest, and returned to the clutch next
day to placate mother bird, another being filched for the table. Farm
labourers enjoyed the Bedfordshire clanger, an elongated sliced bread
roll, one end meaty, the other jammy, washed down with cold tea from
a bottle kept in the hedgerow. Pond and ditch yielded wild watercress.
Scrumping, we targeted Cox's orange pippins.   DMJ

Bedford was manageable. There was a definite centre from which radiated river and parks and significant streets. It didn't take long to orientate, to know the location of the four cinemas, the theatre, bus station, train station, town hall, library, department store, Woolworth's, cafés, amusement arcade and the soon-to-be Mecca, the billiard hall.

London was a collection of streets. You could get a handle on Bedford. That was difficult to do even in Islington. Besides, Owenians didn't all live their lives in Islington. In the evening they scattered by bus, tram, tube. Whereas in Bedford...

> No travelling time – less than five minutes' walk to the Modern School. PP

> A critical social factor was the ease in which there could be a life after school because everyone lived pretty well within walking or cycling distance of each other. What a difference from the hassle of London buses going to and from the Angel and our sports ground. DDW

> I spent the evenings (until it got too dark) calling on friends, hanging around Bays fish and chip shop with other Owenians, or searching out schoolmates in Russell Park. I never felt lonely outside the billet. In Bedford the school was my community. We all shared a sense of displacement, which made it so much easier to strike up friendships. In London the friendships were looser; school was a place you went to for instruction and put behind you when you came home. You didn't belong to it in the way you did in Bedford. MM

Bedford was both welcoming and alien. Or, looked at another way, we were the aliens. We lived in other people's homes, studied in a strange school. But a school is not just a building.

> We had a very strong community, because we had the school and that was of immense importance in the way we developed. VM

And the history master hailed the rebirth of the school.

> *We were indeed fortunate in being sent to Bedford, for it really was possible for the School to start its life anew there. The river in its varying moods, was a constant source of pleasure, and there was much to discover in a town so rich in historical associations; perhaps most famous of all, its prison, which we fortunately only saw from the outside.* H.K. Olphin (Diary)

7

Hosts

Strangers taking in strangers.

'... the least unexpected war in history'. [1]

Neither hosts nor guests quite expected what they would encounter, or whom. Owenians were billeted across the town and different social classes and occupations, be they salesman, shop-owner, teacher, window cleaner, prison officer, ex-mayor, or assistant postmaster – in all, a rich source of characters.

> For entertainment the lodger would plunge a carving knife between the fingers of his moving hand at high speed.   AJ

> The method of my billeting selection was interesting in that two brothers and two other boys were lined up in the Shire Hall to be inspected by a bespectacled gentleman in ginger plus-fours with a matching cap and walking stick. He walked up and down two or three times before pointing at me with a stick, announcing his selection. (He told me much later that he chose me because as I was the smallest one, he thought my appetite would be the least demanding.) Outside, on the pavement was his old Raleigh bicycle with a basket at the front and I was instructed to put my case in the basket and push the bike whilst he led the way to meet the lady of the house. One stop at a pub in the High Street and an even longer one outside the Conservative Club in St. Peter's Street resulted in us taking at least two hours to arrive at 12 Bushmead Avenue, near the rugby ground on Goldington Road.   KRC

Martin Mitchell was taken round Bedford streets by a senior prefect named Jonas.

Our worst moment was when a gnarled and dishevelled old man with leering expression and a nose decorated with a lattice of purple veins and a tip that hosted a snotty globule, appeared at the door. 'I'll 'ave 'em,' he grunted. Seeing our fear and repulsion, Jonas winked, as if to say, 'Don't worry.'

'Of course, you'll have to take their parents,' he said. That did it for the aspiring foster father. He muttered some imprecation and slammed the door.

At last, Jonas found us an engaging hostess, Mrs Knight, at 150 Castle Road. It couldn't have been more conveniently placed; a stone's throw from York Street fish and chip shop – ah! those apple fritters - and at the end of York Street the meadow lands of Russell Park.

Mrs Knight was a white-haired, gently spoken widow, clearly a lady of breeding. The house inside had the appearance of a shrine. She showed us proudly around. The hall, stair well, living room and bedrooms were cluttered with photographs, emblems, cups and trophies, honouring a man with a handlebar moustache. Sepia photographs told us that we were in the hallowed presence of an athlete, cyclist, swimmer, mountaineer, billiards player and master of many other sports that I no longer remember. It seemed almost sacrilege to admit two louche London schoolboys into such reverence, let alone provide them with lodgings. But Jonas's sales patter overwhelmed the poor dear. To be fair, we got on very well with Mrs Knight and did try very hard (though not too successfully) to behave ourselves. MM

Mr C worked on the railway as a freight guard. He worked shifts and a 'knocker up' would bang on his bedroom window with a long pole in the middle of the night to wake him. MC

Mr J was a retired plumber, a bit of a martinet, who had been a member of the volunteers (Territorials), for many years and had served throughout 1914-1918 as a sergeant major in the Royal Engineers. He did not take to me, a stroppy self-opinionated teenager. Mrs J was a remarkable lady, eldest daughter of a remarkable man – Bill N, said to be the man 'who brought trade unionism to Bedford'. After being sacked and blacklisted for his activities, Bill N had a number of situations and eventually became a senior official of the Prudential.

The daughter, Ethel, was the eldest of five children and married a Bert B, also a member of the volunteers, who also served right through the 1914-18 war. Bert B had a large shed at the bottom of the garden, where he conducted a business as a self-employed coach trimmer. PP

Mr H suffered a chest problem and coughed rather enthusiastically and produced a lot of phlegm, which meant from the armchair he could make the fire grate. You knew it was a direct hit from the sizzling. GC

Extended families were common (and in the days before the welfare state, very often necessary) – in both London and Bedford. Owenians often swapped one for another.

Auntie Blanche came down from Cheshire to help with the house. Auntie Blanche had the reputation of being a bit of a dragon. Certainly a strong personality, fortunately for us she took to us boys. Auntie Blanche organised the household duties and Johnnie and I were put in charge of the 'washing machine'. This was a metal container activated by turning a handle connected to a paddle outside the machine. We competed to be the fastest operator.   PP

Mrs L was a well-built Irish lady who had married a soldier. He had achieved the rank of sergeant and was already in France. His parents lived opposite in one of the older cottage type dwellings; the L family had originated in the village of Harrold. There were two children: Doreen, who obviously resented the invasion of the premises by a Londoner, was employed in the town and George, about my age, was still at school.   RC

Mrs S's cousin and her husband were bombed out and came for a prolonged stay. Mr and Mrs P were different, maybe a social class apart. Mr P read books. His face was ruddy, especially at lunchtime. I would pass him the plate and he would breathe alcohol over the mashed potatoes.
DEB

Sometimes both parts of a couple made lasting impressions.

Mr and Mrs T were always at each other's throats and on one occasion Mrs T attempted to stab Mr T with a carving knife.   BC

She was of reputedly German extraction and was in a constant dither over the blackout effectiveness at the rear windows, which looked over the vacant spaces of the village green. He joined the Home Guard and his night patrols often meant a shot rabbit to enhance our rations. RC

After three happy years I was very disappointed when Mr. Crees told me he was being transferred to a bigger branch in Oxford and that, when I returned after the summer holidays, it would be to a new billet. They presented me with a large Cassels' German/English dictionary as

a going away present. The nature of the gift, to a boy who was study-ing German, was indicative of what a kind and thoughtful couple they were.
NC

Mr H was a well-known character in the district. A small, wiry man, he was always filthy dirty – wore the same suit every day, with braces and a thick leather belt, shirt with a stud but no collar or tie and a heavy watch-chain across the well-worn grimy waistcoat, and hobnailed boots. He did his own 'snubbing'. He would never use the bathroom but always washed himself in the kitchen. His nose was perpetually dripping.

He rode a large, very old, 'sit-up-and-beg' bicycle; on one side of the handlebars hung a bag with his tools (he was a carpenter) and on the other side a bag for collecting horse manure. He also collected discard-ed cigarette ends and spent every evening unravelling the tobacco from them, which he then used to roll his own. He smoked this non-stop and once a fag was lit it never left his mouth. He would keep it stuck to the tip of his tongue, which he kept moving from side to side to prevent his lips from getting burnt.

Mrs H was a very large lady constantly embarrassed by her husband, Will. She worked part-time at the Bridge Hotel and would bring home any leavings from the plates in the restaurant – chicken and chop bones and various scraps, ostensibly for the cat, but she and Mr H would sit in the kitchen and make a meal of them!
CL

A less bizarre but no less impactful couple is remembered by John Webber.

Tom A was a Bedfordian, ex-army, over six feet tall, who worked as a storekeeper at the council yard at the bottom end of Newnham Avenue. Edith A was a housewife – not strong and had no children. Having two London children 'forced' upon them must have been a bit unnerving for them as was having a father figure forced on me as my dad had died when I was two years old.
JW

Some took in evacuees for the wrong reasons.

First billet was with former police sergeant and wife who took on four evacuees in order to increase income. Felt our hosts' authority when on the Sunday we were prevented from playing cards because it was the Sabbath.
DAP

Some hosts were ill equipped to take in evacuees. Martin Mitchell realised this. Despite trying to behave themselves at Mrs Knight's,

he and his fellow evacuee

... did exasperate her on occasions, especially when we stayed out later than promised and she would remonstrate with us. Now I see that it was unfair to have inflicted us on her. One of the penalties of evacuation was the awkward intrusion it made on people's daily lives. The mixing of different cultures and backgrounds did not always work out. So Mrs Knight, generous of spirit as she was, tired of us, or let me put it the other way round: our mischief was too much for such a genteel soul. The clincher was the injury our football inflicted on the rose bed in her lovingly tended garden. So after six months she asked for us to be found a new billet.   MM

The penalties and intrusion were expressed in a letter to the editor of the school magazine dated 30 October 1939.

Sir,

'Quot homines non solum tot sententiae sed mores.*
I think what has struck the Bedford hosts of evacuees more than anything else is the difference in customs and ideas between themselves and their guests. We belong to the same race and we speak each our own version of the King's English. But the structure and pattern of our lives is so different that many of us are finding it difficult to adjust the family **modus vivendi** *to include the newcomers.*
Living at high pressure in a confined space is difficult even for well-assorted groups of human beings. We know that there must be a measure of compromise. But we do expect that the young should recognise that it is easier for them to adapt themselves than it is for us who have already worked out our own way of life, and that they should make their contribution to the national effort, increased self-control and thoughtfulness. We appreciate that many of you are making a great effort to come up to our expectations.
Life is enormously more complicated than it has ever been before but to counterbalance the extra work there is amusement and satisfaction to be derived from getting the last ounce of efficiency from the household machine. We must juggle daily with pots and pans to produce on a stove intended for two, meals for six or seven. We are learning to order and deal with food in quantities which six weeks

---

*As many men, so many minds or opinions.
Terence, Phormio II iv 14

ago would have made us gasp. Boys are acquiring the household arts perforce for it is only by the cooperative effort that it is possible to get everything done. It is certain that by the time the war is over we shall all be more adaptable than heretofore.
Yours sincerely,

Mrs. M. K. M. Anderson.
Arrow, Michaelmas 1939

A woman wrote to *The Times*

The evacuation has caused us to lift up the stone and see what is crawling underneath. Let's make a promise that at the end of the war we won't just put the stone back. [2]

Some hosts were only too prepared to take in evacuees – for dubious reasons.

My mother found out that the extra rations and various goodies that she had been sending for my sister and me had never reached us and had been kept by the As. CL

My mother on occasion sent Mrs H some cash to help my home comforts but that wasn't to be because it was a visit to the Goldington Arms that enjoyed the comforts. GCo

Kingsley Martin in his *Critic's Diary* in the *New Statesman* (23 September 1939) sympathised with some billet parents. 'There is the difficulty which working class households find in keeping middle class lads on 8/6 a week.'*[3]

I fancy that the billeting allowance was not unwelcome, but they seemed to welcome the chance to be surrogate parents and they fulfilled their responsibilities admirably. He was an amusing, inveterate hobbyist: an angler who tied his own flies and split bamboo to make his own wonderful, hexagonal, flexible fishing rods – he used to take me fishing, and I still recall the texture and sweetness of fresh caught roach; I was initiated by him into gardening; he also raised budgerigars, and rabbits and pigeons. He took us for Sunday walks (did we want to go?), played family board games with us, and took us to visit their family.
GR

---

*The rate was soon increased – 10/6 (52½ p.) for those aged 10-14; 12/6 (62½ p.) for 14-16; 15/- (75p.) for 16 plus. But at Bletchley, where Enigma was solved, the rate for adults was one guinea.

Doug Wade was taken into five different houses in the first year. He recalls particularly the third billet...

> A strange family with one son a couple of years older than me I think, who was odd. I was obliged to bath in the water which the mother had already used. Then I got pneumonia. DDW

... and the fifth:

> The fifth one was with a master at Bedford School and his wife, in Warwick Avenue. Russell Turner was with me. We were well looked after but the atmosphere was austere and it got to me. The four of us were together only at meal times. Otherwise they withdrew to their sitting room which was off limits to us. DDW

Some hosts, unused to sharing their home, chose not to trust their guests.

> If, during the day, Mrs A wanted to go out, we had to leave the house even if we were doing homework. Bearing in mind the vicious cold of the 39-40 winter, this was not pleasant. After the Easter holiday we were told that new billets were required for George and me. We asked what we had done wrong but were told there was no complaint but the As felt that they had done their bit for the war effort! GRo

In the face of unfair treatment Owenians were nothing if not resourceful.

> Dennis Elston and Norman Blythe lived at the bottom of my street with a spinster lady. She had a little dog that she idolised. The best chair in the living room was reserved for the dog. One weekend the lady went away. The boys didn't allow the dog in the house, let alone on the chair. HG

Sometimes the lucky roll of the dice compensated. When the police sergeant and his wife felt they couldn't cope with four evacuees, Dave Pratt and his brother were moved to another billet.

> ...a Canadian family who were about the kindest and most considerate people anyone could meet. We soon realised how lucky we were to have to move and were very happy indeed with our wonderfully hospitable new hosts.

It was here that we were introduced to peanut butter sent over in food parcels from Canada. I have never been a marmalade man and have eaten peanut butter just about every day during the last 60 years. DAP

There were delights other than peanut butter. For Andrew Jones the memory is so vibrant he recalls it in the present tense.

A boy in the fourth form (I have not forgotten his name) is billeted where the husband works nights and the wife, it must be told, takes hospitality to the extreme. He has many friends. AJ

Others resisted the temptation.

Alan Beecham lived with my billet lady's sister-in-law. She was lonely. Husband away in the army. Alan – being a big lad – had to lock his door on occasions in the night. HG

The people of Beds took us to their hearts and a few with hearts took us to their beds.

8

Small Town Life

Adjusting to a new environment.

The stirring events of the outside world seemed to impact little on our Bedford lives. So much was apparently unaffectedly permanent.   MJC

A 21st century observer in *The Guardian* reflects on this permanence.

> *Bedford is the very vision of an ordinary provincial, market town that keeps its pavements spick and its morals span ... the kind of proper place that shuts up shop at 5.30 pm ... not only has a handsome centre, with all the right civic equipment in appropriately pompous red sandstone facades, but continues to look after it.*[1]

Bedford's heritage was manifest in its buildings, statues (Bunyan and John Howard) and its rituals.

> One thing that did impress me in Bedford was the ancient ceremonies. When I went to school one day I saw the Assize judge bedecked with wig and ceremonial clothes going to the court which was the main court for Bedfordshire... Bedford was a small town compared to London with some very interesting shops.   BS

Of course, London had interesting shops but we viewed them from trams and buses, whereas in Bedford we walked or cycled to school or to other pursuits and had time to investigate and to compare notes.

Most notorious of all was Rigby's in Mill Street, a junk shop with a wondrous, grubby, untidy and incoherent display in the window and beyond. Here were sold 'preservatives', rubber sheaths allegedly recycled. They were branded, Rigo, after the shop owner.

Rigby's shop in Mill Street held a morbid fascination for us. As memory serves, his window displayed assorted oddments of the type then known as 'surgical goods' – in this including both new, and salvaged and re-packed, preventatives. Entering those musty premises, sounding the plangent doorbell, was a spooky experience. He once told me he kept a lion upstairs – which had scary overtones. Becapped, in a dark, crumpled suit, an inexplicably sinister red ribbon tacked around an upper arm, he patrolled the riverbanks, reputedly reclaiming discarded condoms for recycling. It was surprising to learn at our last reunion that Bedford's colourful character, and his disgusting shop, are fondly remembered.   DMJ

By the school, were the outfitters, OVR BOYS, with their pretentious spelling   AJ

(... and up-market, scholastic and blazered clientele.)

There was one arcade off the High Street with select but small shops and a restaurant, the Cadena, where relatives not posh enough for the 'Dujon' (in the Dudeney and Johnston's department store) took boys for a lunchtime treat. The arcade also boasted a forbidden penny-in-the-slot machine.

You pushed your penny and a crane hovered over a variety of tacky china objects. You turned a wheel to control the direction and the opening and shutting of its claws ... nine times out of ten you would win nothing except maybe a few sugar coated caraway seeds which covered the base of the cabinet. But one day with my first and only penny I caught not one but two prizes, an ashtray and a figure of a kilted jock. I hurried back to my billet to show off but nobody believed me. How much time and money had I wasted?   DEB

Time could be better spent elsewhere.

The museum was another source of fascination. The shrunken head of an Aborigine with black hair and eyes remains in my memory.   RN

Museums, churches, the town hall, the Corn Exchange, statues, all less than a hundred yards from the Modern school. Plus, twice a week, in St Paul's Square, the Bedford Market. It had been mentioned in the Domesday Book and became the subject of the third of a series in the *Arrow* called *Looking Around*, a familiarisation programme for us strangers.

Bedford might well have been called the town with the wandering market. For centuries parts of it had been scattered all over the town; and it is probable that the districts were built around the various sections of it, just as they are now built around the Schools...Sheep were sold near the Modern School and men had to tramp along muddy lanes to buy poultry in St Peter's... Eventually Town officials began to clear up and collect the oddments. They decided to erect a market in St Paul's Square by pulling down the old buildings...and a great step was taken when the old Moot hall was removed from its place in the Square. Civic buildings retired discreetly from the main thoroughfare after this, and in their wake went the private houses and the coaching inns. The result was the present Market Square.

C. Propper, *Arrow*, Trinity'40

Bedford had been important, a centre of trade, the townsfolk influential enough to persuade the monarch to grant them the privilege of holding a market. According to the *Arrow*, the king was anxious to keep on friendly terms with Bedford's duke who 'might easily cut off communications with the North'. At one time Bedford market was so powerful that neighbouring markets were suppressed. But decline set in during the fifteenth century. The author philosophises on the purpose of markets and their future. They will survive because they undercut the chain store and, in the case of Bedford, 'because of its sentimental associations and... attractive appearance'.

Market day on Saturday is one to avoid. It means heat, dust, crowds and a white-coated policeman fighting a losing battle against an avalanche of traffic rolling down Market Hill. But Market Day on Wednesday presents a far different sight. Then there is space and shade. There is time to take a broad view of the scene. The white stalls sheltering by St. Paul's Church resemble a typically French provincial town. The parish church, the idea of a market, the weather-beaten faces of the traders, give one the impression that within that quiet square is Bedford's link with the past, a historical connection in a town which has taken very little trouble to preserve its old associations.

The Market Square harbours a wealth of reflections and images of antiquity. Whilst men are disturbed by their present environment, this memorial of the past will long survive its proper function.

Arrow, Trinity '40

But for a group of Owenians one constituent of a market was

missing.

> Walking around the Saturday market in St. Paul's Square they were struck by the lack of vendors' cries. They spotted an empty stall, went behind it and began the cries of Petticoat Lane – 'Yorkshire blues two pounds for freeha'pence [⅝ p.]. Do you suffer from colds, catarrh or stomach pains? I've got the very thing – Spanish Cemiana – but for Gawd sake don't give it to the children' and many more. They won a large audience before being moved on. Bert Seaborn was one of the criers, I recall.
>
> GRo

Not that Bedford needed to import 'snake oil' merchants, as Dennis Jones recalls

> ... there was the old man who trudged in weekly all the way from Cambridge, sockless in boots. Preaching socklessness, that this item was neither good nor necessary, barefoot he demonstrated the application of foot-toughening oil sold in glass bottles.
>
> DMJ

Around the corner from St. Paul's Square stood the library.

> The town library, opposite the school in Harpur Street, was cosily wood-panelled. Books such as *All Quiet on the Western Front*, *Lars Porsena* and the Gorbals saga *No Mean City* were checked out with a knowing wink.
>
> DMJ

The town library's proximity to the school, plus an appetite for reading matter of all sorts, guaranteed steady patronage.

> I used the public library regularly and rapidly exhausted the supply of Edgar Wallace and P.G.Wodehouse - and a great author of adventure stories, Percy F. Westerman. Also, a first glimpse of *Gray's Anatomy*.
>
> KD

> Very much used and very much appreciated for offering works, among others, of John Buchan, Baroness Orczy and various crime writers. JS

> I spent, like many others, a lot of time in the library; at one time I was reading a book a day, mainly *Just William* and *Biggles*.
>
> DHS

> My hosts thought I was strange and told their friends that 'the boy laughs at books'. I had to be in bed when Big Ben struck nine p.m. and they did not seem to know that pocket money went on batteries for reading under the blankets in winter.
>
> RN

The public library was handy. It was magic. It had collected editions of *Punch*, which I devoured.   DEB

It also had more topical fare.

As my billet did not have any daily papers, only the weekly *Bedfordshire Times*, I was an avid reader of the library papers.   AD

It was difficult to get at the daily papers because the seats in front of them were regularly filled with dossers, including one who always wore his hat and tried to sell you his gold watch. He never did receive a sufficiently high offer.   AWL

Alan Locke was not alone in meeting interesting characters.

A fellow habitué of the reading room was an elderly man with an Alf Garnett moustache who carried with him a faintly disturbing smell. He was making copious notes for a work he planned, entitled *The Call of the Omnipotent*. When I was summoned to my medical for the Navy I found that he was employed to empty the urine buckets.   WFF

But there was ample compensation for Frank Fenn in the reading room.

It is one of my life's richer ironies that I owe much of my love of the cinema and of American literature to my truancies from 'Flash' Hardwick's English language and literature classes. I am greatly indebted to him. I spent the time at the cinema, usually the Empire, and in the reading room of the public library. Strangely enough, I never met a member of staff there. It was there that I first encountered, in a rather haphazard way, the novels and short stories of John O'Hara, Steinbeck, dos Passos, Hemingway, Sherwood Anderson and William Faulkner. I also discovered other American writers whose names I had first read on the credit titles of films I had enjoyed – Sid Perelman, Nathanael West, Daniel Fuchs, and Horace McCoy. And all this when I should have been studying *The Tempest*; *Victorian Narrative Poems* (Browning and Christina Rossetti had, similarly, to wait their turn), and Conrad's *The Rover*. In the 1960s I taught the last named for nearly a year before I remembered it had been one of 'Flash's examination texts. It was in the library, too, that I nurtured my interest in History, which 'Dicky' Dare re-awakened in the Sixth form; I discovered Robert Graves and the left-wing novels of Jack Lindsay. And of course, I read and re-read the six or so books the library possessed on the Cinema (I still own copies of three of them) and one book on Jazz – Wilder Hobson's *American Jazz Music*.   WFF

Bedford's rather magnificent public library in Harpur Street was also a haven for those boys who could not easily do their homework in their billets.
                                                                              AWL

An identical metaphor is employed for a somewhat different location.

What would we have done without the Billiard Hall? This was our second home and regardless of how good our billets were, on a Sunday afternoon we had to go out of the house and the Billiard Hall was a haven.
                                                                              GS

As I got older I became addicted to the Billiard Hall. All my pocket money went on the game. It was a very calm atmosphere.   DHS

This calm haven, located above Burtons the tailors, held other attractions for Andrew Jones.

The tea came from gleaming silver urns, and was served through the steam by a young woman with eyes of china blue and a halo of golden hair. Rather like Lynn Bari, the B picture favourite.   AJ

Oasis to some, den to others, focal point, magnet, the Billiard Hall rarely led Owenians into temptation.

One December, a friend and I apologised to our Latin mistress, Miss Sherwen, that we would have to miss the next morning's class as we were going to be working at the post office helping with the Christmas mail. It was a lie and, even as I sloped off, I felt bad about it.   DEB

But the school recognised the contribution the hall made to our welfare.

For a while, so popular was the Billiard Hall, that there was an unofficial school rule that non-sixth formers should occupy no more than two tables. There was also a school snooker competition in which members of staff including 'Dicky' Dare and, I believe, 'Boo-Boo' Davison took part.
                                                                              WFF

Snooker became a non-official school sport. I believe there was a knock out competition – and I am still playing regularly.   KD

Always a lot of Owen's boys in the afternoon, sometimes free tables. One boy in the upper school could have become professional.   IA

Mick Morris had his own cue. That's how good he was.　　　　HG

The Hall also provided some of us with an occasional source of additional income. We grubstaked Mick Morris in matches against Eastern Counties bus drivers and conductors and such local notables as the boxers Chris Lovell and Tony Arpino. The latter, son of the local ice cream king, was a courageous but largely unsuccessful fighter with something of a glass jaw. He was of somewhat menacing Mediterranean appearance and, in spite of a rather high-pitched voice, was occasionally seen as a minor heavy in British movies and on the West End stage.　　WFF

Frank Fenn, Mr Memory, brings our recollections of small town life into the recent past.

My favourite memory of the Billiard Hall is that, one afternoon, for the one and only time in my life, I actually won a frame of snooker. It was against Reg Perrin, the future producer of 'Pot Black'. Reg considered that my glasses handicapped me as a player; and sometimes wore a pair of empty spectacle frames to even things up.　　　　WFF

But there was another, less profane, side to small town life...

When Terry Waite (special representative of the Archbishop of Canterbury) was held in captivity as a hostage he received a picture postcard from Bedford. It was addressed simply 'via Hisbollah, Lebanon'.

It showed a stained window from the Bunyan Meeting Free Church. John Bunyan is seated in his cell penning Pilgrim's Progress. The window was installed in 1978 to commemorate the third centenary of the book's publication.

Another card lists all the pastors and ministers of the church beginning, of course, with John Bunyan and including, pre-war, the Reverend Ralph Turner who subsequently became a master at Owen's, and forged links between it and Bedford.

Evacuation widened horizons. For many it meant change, often enforced; for some a dark side to belief (the 'wickedness of the Jews' confronting, among others, Martin Mitchell); for most a realisation that there were other choices on offer.

In an area of small terraces between Midland Road and Bromham Road were many little chapels. Cheek by jowl in Mill Street in the centre of town were a Baptist Church; the Howard Chapel, established by John Howard, the leading anti-slavery campaigner; and the Bunyan Meeting House, built on the site of an earlier church where John Bunyan had been minister.

> John Bunyan's great legacy of benign non-conformism prevailed (I felt it in the air) surviving pranksters' attention to the St. Peter's Green statue and demolition of his birth cottage at Elstow by an out-of-control US Army lorry. DMJ

> Bedford, with its non-conformist tradition, had organised religion at its heart. No wonder one member of the American Eighth Air Force described it as 'a cemetery with traffic lights'. AWL

Bedford was dotted with many Anglican churches including St. Paul's and St. Peter's, a Moravian Church (frequented, utilised and popularised by Owen's master 'Gus' Cumming), Seventh Day Adventists, the Society of Friends, and the Panacea Society.

Behaviour was dictated by pre-war upbringing and, if there was no clash of beliefs with one's hosts, then faith could be pursued. Devout hosts would prefer that their new charges joined them in the congregation. For most Owenians the shift was not too difficult. But for Alan Locke who called himself a lapsed Methodist – his father a regular attendee at the local church and his mother an agnostic – Bedford was a shock.

> Mr and Mrs Garlick were Baptists but Mrs G could not stand the minister at the Mill Street church. His pulpit manner was mainly bluster, his sermons poorly constructed and he introduced a hymn, during which the collection was taken, with a direct statement that 'we want some money'! Mrs G and a small group of soloists would perform religious songs and readings in various churches and meeting halls around the town, many of which I dutifully attended in those early months of the war. AWL

Fellow billetee Geoffrey Cook was equally discomfited since he had been an Anglican chorister in his Church of England church in Holloway.

Changing billet mostly meant changing one's form of worship. Not in Alan Locke's case however.

At Denmark Street Baptist church I witnessed my first full immersion adult baptism. The altar table had been removed and a trap door beneath lifted up to reveal a seven foot by four foot three inch white tiled sump filled with warm water (where from?) and several supplicants were dunked in this one after another, in black robes made of blackout cloth (what else?) their splutterings being drowned (!) by the lusty singing of suitable verses of a hymn by the congregation. Full immersion was guaranteed by Reverend Ferguson standing in the well in a pair of waders. The saturated souls on emerging groped their way into the vestry to dry off and avoid pneumonia.   AWL

Ron Nash obediently joined his billet parents in their regular high church attendance but ...

After a year I became bored with the incense and went round the town to see what else was on offer. Somehow I found my way into the Bromham Road Methodist Church which was much less formal and morning and evening services and the Youth Club were always well attended and I even signed the Pledge.   RN

Seeing what else was on offer was a temptation many boys found hard to resist. But few tackled Bedford's menu of offerings as religiously as W.E.O. Jones. His comprehensive review of religions merits inclusion in full.

What was the impact of the arrival of a large school, with a high proportion of Jewish pupils [see below, Ed.] but with a strong Christian tradition, on the religious community in Bedford?
Obviously there was some infusion of enthusiasm, dedication and talent into local churches. The Headmaster, O.W. Mitchell became an Anglican lay reader. The Rev. Ralph ('Tub') Turner who had been Minister at the Bunyan Meeting in Bedford before the war was appointed to the staff in 1939, (there is a story to the effect that he personally persuaded O.W.M. to remain in Bedford rather than pressing on further north). H. 'Gus' Cumming became a pillar of the Moravian Church, a protestant group which had spread to the town from Germany in the 18th century. I recall that on one occasion when the Moravians did the School a good turn 'Gus' bribed a large number of boys to attend one of their services; I think he used Horlicks tablets which were a substitute for sweets and he even provided money for the collection! A good many boys must have taken up with the denominations their families had supported. For example, David and John Price were regulars at St. Cuthberts (Anglican) and sang in the choir there. At all events, when the boarding houses were established it became their

custom to turf boys out on Sunday morning – destination Church! So the local ecclesiasts must have benefited, if only numerically.

So far as I was concerned, the 1942/45 period, during which I was in Bedford, was an interesting one because, my religious belief being at a formative stage, I was able to explore and experiment almost endlessly in this field. Bedford, with its strong non-conformist tradition, was a town of many churches, and I treated them like a sort of religious cafeteria. The C of E I avoided because my family sent me there at home, although I regret that I never attended a Church service conducted by O.W.M.

I went fairly often to the Moravian church partly because it was near the Boarding House and partly because my friend B.L. (Barry) Skeggs went there. Although I liked some aspects of the services, the minister was a poor preacher who read his sermons and I became fed up with the Moravians after a while. Better preaching was to be had at the Bunyan meeting (Congregational). Those old Owenians who went to the 1999 reunion will remember visiting there. When Ralph Turner, made return visits I found his sermons affective and thoughtful. The Methodists also provided food for thought.

The most hospitable reception I had was at the Society of Friends (Quakers) who met in a house near Midland Road station. I was pleased to be able to get up and say something whenever I felt like it during the services. Although I admired the Quakers and made several friendships, (appreciating, for example, their support for conscientious objectors confined in Bedford prison) I couldn't go along with their view of the war. In turn, they respected my opinions.

On a less worthy level were my visits to the Christian Spiritual church which met in the Co-Op Hall on Sunday evenings. Like several other boys in the Boarding House, I went there to enjoy a spectacle. G.W 'Butch' Baker was rather reluctant to let us go. There was a visit from the celebrated medium, Mrs Helen Duncan who was later accused of being a fraud and was the last person ever to be prosecuted under the Witchcraft Act of 1735. I can remember nothing very remarkable about her performance.

I had a fundamental angle from the Crusaders' Bible Class which was held at changing venues on Sunday afternoons. This consisted almost entirely of Bedford School and BMS boys who were pleasant and friendly enough. The only other Owenian I can remember attending was called Colin Cuff; he was a year or two older than me. The Crusaders did much good work among the more affluent schoolboys and some of their moral lessons went home so far as I was concerned. However, I thought them rather narrow and the fact that membership was confined to boys attending what were then called secondary schools imparted an element of snobbery which seemed inconsistent with their teaching.

At this time, Bedford appeared to be a headquarters for the Panacea Society, adherents of Joanna Southcott, a strange early 19th century prophetess. They lived in a few houses grouped round a small clock tower situated (if I remember rightly) near the Goldington Road. Joanna had left a box which was supposed to be opened at a time of great national crisis by 24 diocesan Bishops, who would find therein instructions on how to proceed. The Bedford lot kept on putting advertisements in the papers saying, 'Why don't the Bishops open Joanna Southcott's box?' Fascinated, Barry Skeggs and I bluffed our way into the citadel but were unable to communicate effectively with the Southcottians who, although courteous and agreeable, seemed to inhabit a totally different world. (Incidentally, Ralph Turner maintained that the box had in fact already been opened and found to contain only rubbish, apart from a pistol tied to the lid which was designed to go off on opening: it didn't!)

The main school assembly was, I felt, pedestrian and uninspiring, and reflected everyone's tiredness at the end of the day. Nevertheless, I enjoyed singing what might today be regarded as chauvinist and sexist hymns such as *Men of England, who inherit, rights that cost their sires their blood.* Some of the hymns were essentially solos sung by 'Gus' Cumming, although I helped a bit.

A lot of boys, however, found this assembly very boring. Any mistake, defect or eccentricity on the part of those conducting the service was the subject of selected *sotto voce* comment. For instance, one master, Captain Cole, was often selected to read the lesson, and indeed he read rather well, but he had rather an excess of saliva and a regular jibe was 'here's old Cole come to give the Bible a bath again'. A favourite trick during prayers was to select a boy standing with his hands behind him and place some object therein. On one occasion this was an inkbottle, which the victim failed to grasp, and created quite a row when it descended on the floor. The offender was spotted and duly bent over for a couple of juicy ones on the traditional spot.

One way or another I found out a fair amount about the religious views of the staff. O.W.M. of course, had a strong faith and was worried by the presence of atheistic views in the upper part of the school. He said, 'I shall consider myself as Headmaster to have failed if boys go out into the world from this school mocking at the idea of God'. Personally, I thought that some of the boys who adopted an atheist viewpoint were trying to be clever but one had to recognise that others, scientists in particular, were sincere enough. It is interesting to note that the scientific staff (Armitage, Baker, Clarke, etc) were all Christian believers.

P.H. 'Flash' Hardwick was a devout Christian, who belonged to a very exclusive sect of brethren, so exclusive that all the others who called themselves brethren were all wrong. Other members of the staff who were religiously inclined found it difficult to discuss spiritual matters with him and concluded that his religion was not one that made him feel nearer to the other people, although they respected his deep piety. Ralph Turner was my form master (IVB). I had a soft spot for him because he always found time to talk to me and answer my many questions. He was also capable of giving most interesting 'RI' lessons. Another master who helped me a lot was D.H. 'Laddie' James. He had a very good mind and really got down to a study of the Bible. 'Laddie' was himself on a religious quest and went the rounds of many churches. My form master when I first came to Owen's (2A) was J.M 'Nobby' Knowles who was a member of the Society of Friends and a skilled scripture teacher. Another master with strong Quaker sympathies was J. 'Fishy' Salmond.

The pre-war Headmaster, the Rev. H.W. Asman, continued to contribute to the spiritual life of the school. It was his joy to conduct the annual carol service but in 1944 he was (if I remember rightly) very ill indeed and his place was taken by the Rev. H.D. Bagot of Holy Trinity, a good friend of Owen's. But Mr. Asman was back in full health and voice by 30 November 1945 when he gave the address at the Thanksgiving Service on the occasion of the school's return to Islington at St.James' Clerkenwell. This was so great an occasion that the *Arrow* reproduced the Order of Service in full. The vigorous Asman sermon drew from the history of the 1930s the lesson that those who want peace must be prepared for war. Rather reluctantly, and regrettably, I accepted this view at the time and my opinion has not changed. I believe another half a century or so of history has again vindicated it.

It is to my discredit that I made little attempt to speak to the many intelligent Jewish boys about their beliefs and I had no real idea of what went on upstairs in the Jewish assembly. I cannot understand why, given that I was so curious and probing in some areas, I almost entirely neglected this one.

WEO

W.E.O. Jones's excursions into Bedford's non-conformism has a historical resonance for Jews.

Bedford was first settled by Jews in the wake of the Norman conquest. The historian Martin Gilbert in *An Atlas of Jewish History*[2] lists Bedford as a town with documented evidence of a Jewish presence up to the expulsion of the Jews from England in 1290 by Edward I.

Jews returned to England at the invitation of Oliver Cromwell in 1656. In the religious census of 1803, Offa Street, Bedford was noted as having a small community of six Jews who met in a private house. It is possible that a small community lived in Bedford continuously until the outbreak of World War Two, when the numbers expanded as a result of evacuation from London.

One of the factors that may well have encouraged the post-Cromwellian resettlement was the town's non-conformist tradition, inspired by John Bunyan, a tradition that tolerated dissenting religious practices.

Ansel Harris felt very comfortable with non-conformism.

> ... I had a marvellous billet, a Methodist family; he was a director of a leather company and our friendship sustained for years and years...
> I went to chapel with them on Sunday evening. I had no problem with the Jewish/Methodist mix. I never had any problem because my roots were so secure. My Jewish commitment was so positive. Because I was kosher she fed me on tomato soup and kippers. AH

The resident Jewish population of Bedford ws never large enough to support a synagogue. A substitute place of worship was provided by Ansel Harris's father. The Jewish Centre, as it became known to many visiting Owenians – both Jews and Gentiles – was a haven for so many and much more than a place of worship.

> ... for years afterwards he talked about the four years in Bedford as the pinnacle of his life's work. He helped with the education at the Centre. Over time he liaised with the authorities, liaised with Mitchell, with the Mayor, he became a sort of non-elected community leader.
> ... My parents took this house – and without a blueprint and not knowing where it would lead to – but did so in order to provide for these homeless, refugee children. Bear in mind that it was within five weeks of the outbreak of war that they took that decision. It so happened that things developed: they were able to utilise the space. They had Hebrew classes there, Jewish adults came in and it was an open house for visiting troops, American troops and so on. So it grew organically rather than from a preconceived conception.
> My father felt that he was the ambassador of Jewry. He knew there were Jewish boys at Owen's. He developed a certain affinity with Mitchell. Mitchell, I know, as they got to know each other, expressed concern about the left wing influence among the Jewish boys He explained to Mitchell where the boys came from and why they were influenced by

the left wing. Of course, there were Jewish boys who were not left wing and were very much establishment boys.   AH

The Jewish Centre responded to the needs of the times. Whether you were a soldier about to be posted, a US airman fresh from operations over Germany, a hard pressed townsperson, an Owenian scholar, you would be greeted by the Harrises with a smile, a warm handshake and a hot meal, kosher, of course. But their first commitment was always to settle the homeless, refugee children.

> ... He got Willie Tomaschoff into Owen's. He got two boys into the Bedford Modern School.   AH

Panacea Society (see p.67) postscript.
According to a Channel 4 television documentary in August 2003, the box is still unopened. From the same source we learn that 'only those who make it to Bedford will survive the Apocalypse'.

9

To Work

One school building - two schools working.

The most important task in September 1939 was, physically, to arrange schooling. This, however, could not be properly attended to until billeting was completed. One of the masters, G .W. Baker, was appointed school billeting officer. Later, he would, with his wife, inspire, set up and manage a school Boarding House (see next chapter). Initially, his job was to get difficult Owenians resettled and to deal with those latecomers, who, according to Dare's official history of the school, 'trickled in when the school was found to be located in Bedford'. Within a few days most of the school had found itself a new home.

> *At first concentrated in the central and eastern parts of the town, the boys so frequently changed their billets that the Owenian net eventually spread over the whole town, north, south, east and west. Moreover, the new set up gave to the school many of the characteristics of a boarding school and Mr. Mitchell wisely treated it as such from the start. To deal with the inevitable domestic problems which would arise he 'zoned' the boys into residential areas, each with a Housemaster and a House Matron, who could relieve him of many of the personal relationships, billeting difficulties, health problems and the like, leaving him free to handle the heavy administrative business.*[1]

Owen's was lucky. Bedford had fine educational facilities. Oliver Mitchell met his opposite number, H.W.Liddle, the Headmaster of Bedford Modem School. BMS was a Direct Grant grammar school not unlike Owen's. While Owenians enjoyed a glorious late summer finding their feet, discovering each other and what their new location had to offer, the two Heads and the staff were in intensive consultation. 'Things', as Dare says, 'were fixed up harmoniously'.

On 13 September, we assembled at the Modern School to hear rules, explanations and the date of the start of the new term.

> *A 'double-shift' system was devised by which the Bedford boys occupied their premises in the mornings from 9am to 1pm while Owen's took them over from 1.30pm to 6pm. This at first cut down the teaching time because boys had to be home before 'blackout'.* [2]

Looking back, at a school evacuation reunion in September 1999, Jack Levy OBE, praised BMS's generosity and the friendly relationship.

> Two progressive schools working together in double harness ... success was achieved without a major disagreement or serious misunderstanding during the six-year stay. In consequence, the standards of our academic work remained astonishingly high. I have to say that, as an academic myself, I have wondered ever since why children have to go to school all day!
>
> JL

Philip Fawkes compares pre-war with war-time school routine, to the advantage of the latter.

> Before the war school term routine involved rising at 6.30-7am, walking to the station to catch the 8 o'clock train to arrive at Islington for 9am prayers, seven classes of 40 minutes, breaks of 15 minutes morning and afternoon (school milk in the morning ⅓ pint) and an hour for lunch in the refectory. Finish school 4.30pm. Return home just before 6pm. supper and 2 or more hours homework. At weekends you had 3 hours homework, which often took me more!
> On being evacuated, we had only half the schooling and consequently half the homework. A half-hour travelling time (15 minutes, each way) and don't forget we had summertime all year round. And double summer time in the summer. Oh the freedom!
>
> PFa

No morning school was a strange experience that autumn; not only for Owenians.

> You would see clusters of Owenians drifting aimlessly on the streets of Bedford. I don't think we were very popular with its worthy citizens. We crowded their pavements, invaded their stores and those of us with bikes, cluttered their roads.
>
> MM

There were other more worthwhile and lasting benefits.

> I found the academic routine in Bedford quite congenial. There was time available, not only for visits to the local milk bar but for browsing and study in the local library adjacent to the school and I would spend time there several days a week. JL

BMS enjoyed a complementary freedom.

> The biggest impact of Owen's School on me in my earlier years at BMS was the absence of afternoon school. We used to start at 8.50 (I think) and end at one o'clock with three periods before break and two afterwards. Sport was in the afternoons and as far as I can recall this was on most days of the week. Saturday was special in that we ended after only four periods (which were only 35 minutes instead of the normal 40 minutes) — a great treat. But often there was a three-line whip to support the first XV or first XI on the sports field during the afternoon.
> GW

But for Owenians the pleasures of a week of five fully free mornings were short lived. It was soon realised that half days were not academically sufficient and, more importantly, as winter encroached, so did the hours of blackout. Owen's solution was in line with that of other schools.

> *An evacuated school would commonly take it in turns with its hosts to use existing buildings, and whatever halls, rooms or warehouses could be found nearby so that all children had full time education*[3]

The school rented various other premises around the town and afternoon sessions became shorter.

> The school hired venues for morning lessons: the Co-op, the Liberal Club, the Oddfellows Hall - I've met many odd fellows but never an Oddfellow - church halls, the Riverside sports pavilion, and even a pub (The Angel, nostalgic that). No longer aimless, droves of boys tore from one venue to another, by foot or on bikes, whilst the older masters cycled sedately, and the younger ones, with gowns flying, usually led the race. MM

> *These scattered premises involved a good deal of travelling about; it did enable the School to run a complete timetable and was, in fact, rather fun.*[4]

Staff and pupils adapted. Though the furnishings and fittings, decorations and portraits, might initially intrigue, the rooms became ordinary classrooms. Occasionally, however, there were incidents which might not have taken place in more conventional surroundings.

> There was a very large room on the first floor of the Co-op Hall over-looking Midland Road. It was used for examinations. There were about sixty of us at desks in rows. One master was invigilating. Halfway through the morning a man entered and walked out of the window. It was difficult to concentrate. After about ten minutes he re-appeared. One senior boy (Ray Schwalb) spoke out: 'He was on an elastic band all the time'. It takes a lot to make you laugh in an exam room.   DEB

> Riverside tennis club pavilion. It had a gas fire. I had a brilliant idea one day. I'd take a potato and roast it for lunch. We started lessons. There was gradually a smell. Miss Cast said, 'What's that smell?' I explained. She said, 'don't pay any attention to that, pay attention to me'. So I did - and let out a wolf whistle. She went red but that was all.   HG

No such irreverence in the afternoon.

> In the afternoon we became a proper functioning school with quadrangle, headmaster's study, draughty classrooms and an Assembly Hall.
>   MM

It took considerable effort to realise that the school was being shared, that the desk you filled had that morning contained another boy's belongings. There was little evidence around the walls of BMS ownership.

If, given the separate schedules, there was no contact between the two sets of schoolboys, there was hardly much more in the town itself. Only a handful of BMS parents played host to Owenians. BMS boys did not frequent Owen's favourite locations. Neither did those from the more up market Bedford School. On the other hand, fraternising with other 'alien' schools such as Rye Grammar and especially King's Warren Girls from Plumstead was frequent and, as we shall see, in the latter case, of some consequence.

> I know of no Owenians who forged a friendship or any kind of association with a BMS boy. Is this to be a matter of regret or even surprise?
>   JS

Owen's boys with some exceptions (see later) found most of what they needed in each other.

> The school had such an overwhelming presence in our lives. Our contemporaries, the people we talked to all the time, were all there. There were a few people that I knew from other schools but mostly it was the kids in our school. So it is very difficult to divorce my intellectual life from the school. There was the music and the debates but again they were with my contemporaries at school. VM

> I think the closest contact with BMS was on the cricket field when, for example, our First XI played their Third. That showed us where we stood alright! — except that I now know that we were probably cleverer and certainly more streetwise. JL

A similar assurance of superiority is expressed by a noted sporting Owenian.

> Friendly but suspicious rivalry with BMS boys, as Bedford girls were very attracted by Owen's new faces and accents, as were British girls on the arrival of American forces in the UK later. DAP

BMS boys were perhaps given less opportunity to be streetwise. In common with those from Bedford School, they were not allowed to go into shops. They seemed more regimented.

> BMS boys wore caps as we did. Some sported a white pearl button on the middle of the top of the cap which indicated that the owner couldn't swim. Whether this was a safety or a shaming device we couldn't say. DEB

> When they could swim they used to go to the town bridge and ceremoniously throw their buttons into the Ouse. IA

> The Bedford School and BMS caps were apologies for caps that were worn on the back of the head. We began to ape this despite instructions that each boy's cap should be of the correct size (mine was seven and three eighths) and be worn correctly. I can only think of a few boys who obeyed. AWL

Caps were the only item of Owen's school uniform that were mandatory.

The school outfitters, T.R. Roberts of Upper Street, Islington, suffered bomb damage and could not be expected to supply uniforms at a distance of 50 miles, so as the pre-war uniform of black blazer, white shirt and grey trousers (with grey socks and black shoes) was outgrown, it was not replaced. AWL

Streetwise Owenians looked and felt different from their local equivalents.

The freedom to dress as one wishes, save for the school cap, led to some notable departures from the norm and the Headmaster was moved to warn two boys (Simon Bronkhorst and Paul Simpson) that bold check sports jackets worn with yellow shirts and ginger-coloured corduroy trousers was a step too far, and must be reined in. AWL

The cap, however, was sacrosanct. There was one bizarre exception.

The only satisfaction I derived from my stay in hospital was that my entire wardrobe had to be fumigated and some of it destroyed. While I awaited replacements I was reduced to wearing a pair of pre-war plus-fours. They did not go well with a school cap. Even my form master agreed. 'It would make the school look ridiculous,' was his verdict. And so, for some weeks, I received a much envied dispensation. WFF

Though wearing school caps *à la* BMS was frowned upon, one millinery refinement was officially adopted: the straw hat or boater, but not yet in our story. Not in the winter of 1939 when the country was putting itself on a new footing and Owen's was becoming, *force majeure*, a different school.

The war and evacuation altered the situation considerably. Some of the senior staff stayed on longer than they might have done, some of the existing staff took on responsibilities and exercised an authority they might not otherwise have achieved, some of the younger and more interesting members of staff went off to war, and some of their wartime replacements might not have been employed at Owen's in peacetime.
The school itself could not function as it had done in London. Owen's before the war was, I suppose, a pretty typical city grammar school. Even with after-school activities (not always available easily to boys like myself who lived at a distance) the working day was short, the pupils on the whole were reasonably bright and motivated; disciplinary problems were, I suspect, rare - a playground fight was about as bad as it got - and delinquencies were minor; parental support was taken for granted (and

given), and families were generally stable. But, although the grammar school ethos was based largely on the nineteenth century public school, the grammar school was not *in loco parentis* for the bulk of its pupils twenty-four hours a day, seven days a week. It could, in fact, get by with a fairly rudimentary system of pastoral care.

In order to cope with the situation in Bedford Owen's had to change. Oliver Mitchell was now responsible all the time for a few hundred boys nearly all of whom, by the very nature of evacuation, came, quite literally, from broken homes. But first, of course, he had to get the show on the road; the schoolwork and sport, the provision of workable time-tables. That the school came into operation so quickly is greatly to the credit of the Headmaster and his staff. WFF

To judge from contemporary accounts, the Owen's experience was unusual. In 1940 *Mass Observation*'s Tom Harrison and Charles Madge summed up the achievement of evacuation in the first four months of the war. 'It has made a chaos of the education system.' [5]

There was disruption in Bedford but no chaos. Though Frank Fenn adds a note of caution.

Even a year is a very short time in education and I suspect, when I look back, that it was well over a year before the school really began to function successfully in its new environment and to pay more than a routine attention to the general welfare of its pupils. WFF

10

The Boarding House

Our surrogate public school.

The provision of hostels for children difficult to billet and for second-ary schoolchildren was... a prominent feature of the evacuation scheme. ... to give more active encouragement to the establishment of hostels.[1]

And so it was, after an unsettled year as a member of the awkward squad, wandering like a refugee from one indifferent billet to another, I became a resident of the Boarding House. I discovered that I wasn't the only billet gypsy. A number of London schools had been parked in Bedford. The population had grown and suitable accommodation had become scarcer and so at the end of 1940 the school opened a hostel sponsored by the LCC and, presumably, requisitioned by the council or the Government.

'Butch' Baker, the senior chemistry master and his wife managed the establishment. Some thirty or more of us, flotsam of the evacuation, were packed into seven or eight dormitories at 48 Kimbolton Road, a large, late Victorian/early Edwardian house. It only just managed to be detached, squashed between two other large houses. The front of the house was covered in a thick growth of ivy that cascaded down the walls, just leaving enough room for the windows to let in light.   MM

It must have been difficult to heat such a large house, especially in wartime given the restrictions on the use of fuel. We have the testimony of W.E.O. Jones.

Conditions were very spartan by today's standards. At No.48 there were generally fires on the ground floor on winter evenings and in the dormitories there was a good supply of blankets. Otherwise, I can remember little in the way of comfort. It was bare boards in the dor-mitories and, of course, no heating of any description there. Shortage of toilet paper was a perennial problem. (I had no experience of living at No.5 [the annexe] in the winter but conditions there seemed to be equally austere.) When we broke up for the Christmas holiday in 1944 I stayed behind for an extra day for some reason. The weather was bitterly cold, and as I wandered to the empty No.48 it struck me as one of the bleakest dwellings I had ever seen. WEOJ

From the beginning it was called 'The Boarding House'. The word 'hostel' was eschewed: it was too common for a grammar school with public school aspirations. 'Boarding House' was more in keeping with the school's status. Possessing a Boarding House was the nearest the school got to being a fully-fledged public school.

According to Martin Mitchell, a long-term resident, the social order was on the whole benignly hierarchic.

At the top of the hierarchy were the two Bakers. Mr and Mrs 'Butch' maintained a strict but not too oppressive discipline, but he was a stickler for homework. He would wander round the dining room tables that served as our collective homework stations on weekday evenings, commenting sarcastically at sloppy work or unsolved simultaneous equations. This public exposure of inadequacy unnerved some, whilst others learned to acquire protective thick skins and, in the manner of derisive schoolboys, would mock 'Butch' behind his back. This was sensible since 'Butch' notoriously had a short fuse. MM

He also had a loud habit.

Life was condensed into formulaic statements. Snappy phrases meant everything and became shorthand for recollection of key events. Jim 'Greaser' Meurice shouting at George 'Nosy' Parker. Mr Baker entering our Common Room and saying, 'Meurice, moderate your language.' Then returning to his own room across the hall as a loud belch reverberated in our room. So, 'Meurice, moderate your belches' was born. Hardly a fragment of song floating before you, and I can't remember who said it, but a phrase that somehow condensed the essence of Boarding House life. DAMM

But 'Butch' was more than just an occasional belcher.

He was an 'old hand' at the School even at this stage, having taught there since 1926. He had been a postmaster (major scholar) of Merton College, Oxford, an achievement which his son Colin was to repeat 30 years later. If a trifle self-opinionated, he certainly combined consider-

79

able academic prowess and personal astuteness with practical ability. For example, on one occasion I broke two windows in the Boarding House on the same day, one as a result of a friendly wrestle in the morning and the other through a quite serious fight with a boy called Colin ('Schlew') Welch in the evening. I was impressed, firstly by the efficiency with which 'Butch' traced all concerned with the evening row and made them pay for the damage, and secondly by the deft way in which he personally fitted new window panes. On the other hand 'Butch' had a quick temper which sometimes led him to chastise boys too severely. This defect was probably exacerbated by the strain he was under, being school billeting officer apart from his teaching and Boarding House duties.   WEOJ

When a boy was too senior to be chastised in the usual way, reprimand of last resort was a visit to the Headmaster.

Oliver Mitchell was a great Headmaster. One time Baker sent me to him to be disciplined for climbing in late into No. 48 when he had locked me out. Tom Dash let me in from the side alley by opening the third floor bathroom window, which I reached via strong drainpipes. OWM let me off, but poor Tom got a hard time from the Bakers (their bathroom was on the second floor below). He didn't so much let me off as get me to understand Mr Baker's problems of running No. 48. Please don't do it again – so I didn't. It was a kind of turning point to be asked to act responsibly instead of being ordered to.   DAMM

Mrs Baker had the invidious task of managing the domestic side of the House.

She always seemed to be busy and, indeed, carried a heavy burden. Besides having to contend with all the wartime shortages, she was on a limited budget. One aspect of her regime was that she had a good intelligence system. e.g. we never knew how she discovered it was a group from our dormitory at No.5 – the overflow annexe – that climbed into the greenhouse there and removed substantial quantities of grapes. Most of the time 'Kitty"s attitude to her charges combined exasperation with affection. But I think the latter was a big element because I recall how she wept when the Boarding House finally closed its doors. WEOJ

One can only admire Mrs Baker's efforts to overcome wartime rationing.

We were often ravenously hungry or thought we were, though I hasten to add that Mrs Baker did a brilliant job with the ration books. Spam,

80

which in those days had nothing to do with unwanted Web detritus, was a staple diet, with tomatoes and veg. You couldn't get anything yuckier than Spam. Then, there were her exotic concoctions: fake chicken and bogus duck, made from rice, disguised cheese, potatoes, lard and God wot, the sort of culinary extravagance that nowadays sends vegetarians into transports of lip smacking delight, after they had properly substituted margarine for lard.

Her skilful juggling with ration books meant that on Sundays there were extra microscopic helpings of fried bacon on fried bread with fried powdered egg and even on occasions, real fried egg. The trouble was that there was a stampede of desperate Oliver Twists for seconds. At this point the hierarchy asserted itself and the post-puberty boys with greater hormonal needs were favoured with the extra helpings.

On Sunday morning, non-churchgoers had their own priorities and would go foraging at Joe Lyons for their highly desirable apple pies, which in later years I would take with a Bisodol tablet. They were packaged in little, easily opened, cardboard boxes, unlike today's impenetrable shrink-wrapping.

Whenever we got the chance we would raid the kitchen, fortifying ourselves with inedible slices of so-called Woolton loaf, made more palatable with sneaky smears of lard.   MM

Many complaints were made about the Boarding House food, but given the circumstances we didn't fare too badly, our diet being adequate if very monotonous. We were heavily dependent on the rather tasteless wartime bread and on potatoes to fill us up. Dinner at mid-day was the one really good meal of the day - a meat and two veg. arrangement usually. Breakfasts were pretty microscopic apart from the bread - a very small helping of cereal or a piece of bacon one felt might easily blow out of the window or an occasional egg. There was bread and jam and tea after school and a cup of cocoa and a small snack before going to bed. A lot of us supplemented this fare at Joe Lyons, particularly on free mornings, or went out for fish and chips (much queuing) at night.

Attention tended to be concentrated on the mid-day dessert because of the 'Boarding House song', which I think originated at the Friday Evening Club. The part of it I can remember went:

> *Listen all you people, I've got a tale to tell.*
> *Its all about the Boarding House; some people think it's hell.*
> *All we get is rice and prunes,*
> *We get it every day*
> *And now again just for a change they give us prunes and rice,*

And rice and prunes, and prunes and rice, and rice and
    prunes
And rice and rice and rice and rice and prunes and rice
And prunes and rice...

And so it goes on interminably. Later, when Japanese conquests in South East Asia cut off rice supplies the following lines were added:

Listen all you people I've a sorrowful tale to tell
There's no more rice in the Boarding House but perhaps it's
    just as well.
A bowl of semolina has come up in its stead
And together with prunes and custard, it's part of our daily
    bread.

There was a *sub-rosa* alternative version of the last two lines:

A bowl of semolina has come up in its place
So what did we do? We turned around and chucked it in
    'Butch''s face.

WEOJ

It appears feelings towards the Bakers were somewhat ambivalent.

The Bakers' efforts were not, I am afraid, much appreciated. Probably they acted as a focus for our discontents with evacuation and with the hardships of wartime living.   WEOJ

But no one could have been more appreciative than Ron Coyte.

1943-1944 was a difficult year for me, my health was not good - being constantly ill with asthma, and I was in hospital for long periods of time, which meant not a great deal of time being spent at school. Each time I came out of hospital I would return to the Boarding House, and Mrs Baker would look after me like a second mother. I only have good memories of the way she nursed me in what can be a distressing illness.   RCo

Supporting the Bakers were a number of masters. W.E.O. Jones, the Pepys of the Boarding House, recalls each member of the supporting team.

The master in charge of No.5 Pemberton Avenue (the annexe) was Mr J.M. ('Nobby') Knowles who was at Owen's for a relatively short time (1941-44). However, he was a suitable choice, having had previous experience of Boarding education, including a spell at Stowe. He was a kindly and considerate man with a good sense of humour who, I think, really enjoyed the company of boys, although he could be strict. Like the Bakers, he was very hard working, and had many problems, including the lack of domestic help and complaints from the neighbours about the amount of noise emanating from the premises. For some reason there was a feud between boys in both Boarding Houses and a most unpleasant (although slightly mentally handicapped) man who did odd jobs in the town. One day when this man was cutting a hedge in Pemberton Avenue some of our number squirted him with water from a garden hose and knocked him off the steps on which he was standing. Poor 'Nobby' had then to deal with a drenched and infuriated man whose language turned the air a deep shade of blue. Fortunately he was a fairly small man and Nobby managed to get him off the premises, after which he caned those concerned severely.

In addition, there were various masters who 'lived in' from time to time and assisted in the running of No.48, provided relief at No.5 and so on. Among these was H.A. ('Gobbo') Bradding, an old boy who had recently left and taught temporarily at the School - I believe he was waiting to go up to Cambridge after the War. But he was too familiar a figure to be treated with much respect. One visiting master at No.5 who made a particular impression on me was Captain W.P. Cole, a former Army Educational Corps officer and a ferocious disciplinarian. I remember he explained once that he thrashed delinquent boys in the same way as he had thrashed lazy servants in India. At one stage a mistress named Miss M.M. Lowe was put in charge at No.5. She was a very pleasant and efficient lady but the wretched 'fags' gave her a terrible roasting. The Headmaster threatened to send them Captain Cole on a permanent basis and perhaps it is a pity he didn't. Eventually J.M. ('Fishy') Salmond took over and stayed until the end of the War. I don't know much about his rule but I am sure it was both kind and firm.   WEOJ

We learn that the hierarchy beneath the Bakers was pleasantly benevolent.

At the top was Harold (Annah) Caplan, later to become school captain. He kept mainly to himself and was treated with ingratiating respect by the lower orders. Occasionally, he and his dormitory mate, Donald Alexander Morgan Mackay – you could hear the skirl of bagpipes on the mere utterance of his name – supervised our homework. The latter achieved everlasting fame in later life as an Oxford rowing blue.

Leading the lower ranks, the Fourth Form and Remove, was the power-fully clever Geoff Rans, King of the Gramophone, in the front room, and jazz auto-didact. Among the near bottom of the heap was myself, a Third Former, and at the very bottom were the tiny tots of the Second Form, one of whom was Barry Skeggs, I remember; and the youngest of all, the Bakers' own son, Colin. I made many friends: Bert Caplan, who suddenly left to join the merchant navy, and who, sadly, died recently; Peter Jones, a regular prize winner, and the brilliant, icy-cool Alistair Mackay, all room mates on the top floor, overlooking the copious garden.   MM

Some insight into life in the dormitories is provided by two long-term denizens, Jock Mackay and, as ever, W.E.O. Jones.

Setford, Ellis, Taylor and I shared a room on the third floor facing Kimbolton Road. Frank Taylor had an air rifle. Setford—a future geographer—had a map of Europe pinned to the bedroom wall. Our war aggression was taken up in shooting at Berlin once we tired of shooting at a mouse, or rather a mousehole since the mouse could rarely be induced to appear. Once we took down the map and were horrified to find a large area of wall missing behind the target area. So the map went back up in a hurry. I've often wondered whether our mouse eventually died of lead poisoning.   DAMM

My clearest memories are of the boys in my dormitory at No.48 in the last year of evacuation. There were five of us, which was about the usual number. G.T. (Geoff) Dimmock was an intelligent and athletic boy with a strong personality who took the lead in most matters. K.C. (Kevin) Seeger was a pleasant character with the nerve of the devil. A regular exploit of his was to get up early before the Bakers were about, go down to the kitchen where the cook was preparing breakfast, and brew up a pot of tea, which he served to us in bed. B.L. (Barry) Skeggs was a good and loyal friend to me the whole time I was at Owen's. He was a prominent sportsman and had considerable musical talents, but what I liked most about him was his zest for life, and I think this feeling extended to the others in the dormitory. L.I.S. ('Liz') Smith was a slightly eccentric studious boy who did not fit in and got rather a raw deal. 'Liz' was a tremendous sleeper. One morning when he had fallen asleep as usual after being called, the four of us got up, replaced the 'blackout', collected our clothes, crept out of the dormitory and in due course went down to breakfast. The meal was best part through before authority noticed 'Liz' was missing. You can guess the joy with which 'Butch' discovered him still in the land of nod – a pretty rotten trick, really.

Of course, the boarders had the faults of boys everywhere. Dormitory raids and feuds were common and could take a nasty turn. So could fights even though these might start playfully. There was plenty of bullying of all kinds and those who savaged the Lower School at No.5 tended to get a dose of their own medicine when transferred to the senior House. I can remember one occasion when my face was so much slapped that it ached for days. Anybody who was a bit eccentric was likely to be persecuted e.g. Colin Welch, mentioned above, who was a very sensitive boy received so much ragging he ran away at least once. Alan and Colin Baker had a separate room and were generally considered to lead a privileged existence, which was (rather illogically) resented. WEOJ

All sorts of things went on. For instance the, students used to race newts that they had given chloroform to, silly little things really. BS

The Boarding House stay was very brief. It was memorable because of an incident in the middle of the night when I found myself suddenly awake in an empty dormitory. If my recollection is correct the Boarding House boys had quite a cache of ammunition and arms which they disposed of that night; dumped in the Ouse. There was to be a dormitory inspection the next day. I know that some of the boys had bullets. I recall at least one incident when a bullet was thrown into a fire in Bedford Modern School with very noisy and dangerous consequences, which could have been fatal. This was during a lesson in German with Miss Lowe who was incapable of controlling the pupils. JWes

The teeming life of the Boarding House flourished in spite of the wintry rigours of the accommodation as described above by W.E.O. Jones.

Kevin Seeger remembers his spell there as

... an enjoyable time and a good experience. I can remember being coached by the sixth form boys prior to taking school certificate. KCS

The school was the larger community and within that community was an even tighter, closer community. Of course, there were animosities, spite and bullying. MM

There was a bully by the name of D and we eventually got rid of him. We learned later in life that there were reasons why he was a bully. But two of us didn't like it and enough was enough and so when he attacked anyone they would yell and we would take over. That's how we got rid of him.

BS

After homework, quite a few of us would gather in the front room for jazz edification. Geoff Rans was a born discographer, an expert on jazz byways and obscure labels. He held us in thrall to his presentations on New Orleans, blues and boogie and in his destructive, illustrated dissertations on the spurious claims of swing to represent any part of jazz.

MM

The only experiment in public school life ever undertaken by Owen's, worked. Emergency hostels were set up in 1940 by the Government for those 'unsuitable for billeting'. There was no reason at that time to think that 'unsuitable' billetees would fit into the stricter regime of the Boarding House. That they did with minimum friction is partly due to the Bakers' management skills; partly to the ability of these 'unsuitables' to construct a vibrant collective life; and partly to their easy accessibility to the wider social life of the school. And in any case what alternative was there? It was wartime, after all. In 1947 there was a proposal to move Owen's out of London and accept boarders. No doubt, the successful example of the Boarding House was in mind. Would it have worked? We shall never know. The decision was to continue as a State school.

11

'Most Difficult Circumstances'

Tough times settling down.

YOUR COURAGE, YOUR CHEERFULNESS, YOUR RESOLUTION WILL BRING US VICTORY   **Official War Poster**

For Owenians, and Britons generally, autumn 1939 was strange and unsettling. Re-billeting frequently followed billeting. Early excitement faded into grim realisation that evacuation, if not the war itself, was real and maybe lasting. A phrase forced itself upon the national consciousness — 'the duration'. As in the Great War, there were blithe assurances that the war would be over in months if not weeks (even in 1940 Chamberlain tried to assure the nation that Hitler had 'missed the bus'). But we began to doubt this and 'the duration' took hold.

It took less time for participants in evacuation to realise that they had made a mistake. Just as a pet 'isn't just for Christmas' so evacuation wasn't temporary. Both hosts and guests realised this but it was easier for the former to do something about it, to fix up new accommodation, directly or via the billeting authorities or, as we saw previously, through the Owen's billeting officer. Unsettled boys told other boys, their teachers and their parents.

Change of location was a fact of life in Britain. From 1939 to 1945 there were 60 million changes of address in a population of 38 million. By the beginning of 1940 four out of every ten children evacuated in the UK had returned home. We can find no Owenian in this statistic.

Owen's was more fortunate than many evacuated schools.

> *Two London secondary schools were billeted so far from the nearest*
> *secondary school that after four weeks it had still not proved possible*
> *for them to start work ... In Norfolk one London school was spread*
> *over no fewer than 23 villages ...*[1]

There was unhappiness: incompatibility of boy and billet parents; bullying and other forms of intimidation by a fellow schoolboy; loneliness; deprivation of the comforts of home.

Homesickness prompted the odd Owenian to catch a bus or train home. John Stockton, who joined the school a year later, was in Bedford with his primary school.

> More and more kids became homesick. It was not uncommon for 10 and 11-year olds to set off to walk from Bedford to London — indeed one of the Oare Brothers, billeted next door, set out and had walked as far as Cardington before being picked up and brought back to Bedford.   JS

Going home, legally or illegally, was difficult. The first required a permit from the Headmaster. The second was made virtually impossible by the imposition of weekend roll calls.

Overall, the problems faced by resourceful grammar schoolboys, in a middle-class environment, were as nothing compared to those researched by Peter Hennessy.

> *Many evacuee stories are heart-rending, ranging from homesickness,*
> *protracted coldness or indifference towards vulnerable little children*
> *by those who reluctantly took them in, to downright physical or men-*
> *tal cruelty and even child abuse.*[2]

But those difficulties were not a direct result of the war itself. For the majority of Britons in 1939 there were few effects of actual war. This was the 'Phoney War' though we don't any of us remember calling it that at the time. It was also known jokingly by ally and enemy respectively as *drôle de guerre* and *sitzkrieg*. We may have called it the Bore War. Indeed, as Angus Calder asserts, 'Many people remember the war chiefly for its boredom'.[3]

Whatever we (or the nation) called it, the war that autumn was not what we were expecting. Where were the devastating air raids the Government had warned us of, that the newsreels of the Spanish Civil War had prepared us for, that *Things to Come* had fixed in our imaginations? And what our billet parents had told us of the previous World War (though many tactfully preferred not to) bore little resemblance to what we read in the papers, let alone what we saw in Bedford.

The weather added to the unreality. Whereas the summer had been one of the wettest in recent history, there began in the last week of August a long spell of sunshine. We spent the early days of September in the open air rather than in billets. Our holiday was extended by the negotiations between the two schools. It was not until mid-September that we were informed of the start of term time.

One of the oddest features of the phoney war was the continuation of leaflet raids by the RAF. By the end of 1939 they had dropped eighteen million of them. Ostensibly the purpose was to sow dissent but subsequently apologists suggested others: to accustom flight crews to the dangers of night flying and, at that early stage of hostilities, to discourage reprisals.

> I remember a cartoon very early in the war, in a newspaper. The scene is an RAF debriefing. The pilot is apologising for releasing a pile of leaflets without first untying the string. 'Good Lord!' exclaims the officer, 'you might have killed somebody.'   DEB

Of course, the war was far from phoney for merchant seamen from day one, for the souls aboard the Glasgow liner *Athenia* torpedoed on 4 September, for the 500 victims on the aircraft carrier *Courageous* sunk on 18 September in the Bristol Channel and the battleship *Royal Oak* sunk on 18 October in the Scapa Flow with the loss of 833 men. Soon after, the *City of Benares* was torpedoed on her way to Canada. Among the dead were child evacuees.

The war was real also for William Tomaschoff, the *Kindertransport* refugee (see Chapter 3).

Tomaschoff two years later won a scholarship to Owen's but was not yet a British subject and could not avail himself of it till May 1942. Meanwhile he stayed in Bedford where he found warmth and friendship. At the newly formed Jewish club he met not only fellow refugees but also Owenians. Tomaschoff found a tolerance of religion and dissident opinion (see Chapter 8).

The Jewish boys had their own assembly; if I remember a rather ramshackle affair in a room off the gallery over the Assembly Hall. Prayers led, I think, by a local Rabbi, in Hebrew, were mechanical. The main (Christian) assembly held in the hall below was controlled by the fearsome scrutiny of the Head, who could spot the slightest display of irreverence in the massed ranks of worshippers.

There was also a third assembly in the gallery itself, officiated by Andrew Rothstein, who was the only member of his congregation. The Head, under pressure from Andrew's father, a well known Communist, had granted Andrew a formal dispensation to practise atheism, so he would religiously conduct daily readings from *Das Kapital* and occasionally vary it with the more apocalyptic excerpts from the *Communist Manifesto*.   MM

Other dissidents took a leaf from the RAF's book. Several leaves in fact.

As a central London school we had no idea of the out-of-school restrictions placed on pupils at schools in provincial towns. After a while the Headmaster began to introduce such rules for Owen's.   GRo

The revolution came and went within 24 hours and sprang from the Headmaster's refusal to let boys travel to London at the weekends during the term, because of night bombing. This was enforced by roll calls.

Some half dozen 5th and lower 6th formers objected, not so much to the principles but to the methods, and placed the blame on the new Headmaster and they plotted insurrection, by entering the BMS premises overnight, slashing the curtains in the Great Hall, destroying sets of books, etc and then leafleting the boys in the quadrangle. AWL

At break time, from the top window of the Modern School a shower of leaflets wafted down onto the quadrangle bearing a rude message about the Headmaster's rules. There was much hilarity and copies were picked up by the masters and of course, shown to Mitchell. 'Oh well! A one-off.' But no! The same thing happened the next day with a different but equally censorious message. This was wonderful - Scarlet Pimpernel stuff, and it was taken seriously. The next day several masters were in the quad looking up and around to see from where they were being launched.

They soon found out as leaflet number three floated down. Top floor window. Halloo! The hunt was on but by the time they had climbed several floors our hero was not to be found. I should here remind you that the top floor ran along only one side of the school and there was only one staircase giving access so a trap was easy to set. On the next day, Friday, several of the fitter teachers stood at the foot of the stairs to apprehend our hero should he dare to try again.

The ringing cheers that greeted leaflet four stung the teachers into action. Up they went but there was an empty corridor with a breeze coming through an open window. They were thorough. They posted a sentry at the foot of the stairs and searched the classrooms one by one. Empty. They looked up but no loft entrance. Somehow he had escaped but how? They never found out but the flow of new restrictions dried up. 'How was it done?', you ask. Apart from the classrooms there was one other door on that floor bearing the legend, 'Modern School Photographic Dark Room — Keep Locked'. It was locked so he could not be in there. But the lock had a scored mark on it and the culprit had a penknife with a strong blade that could spring the lock. He opened the door, then launched his leaflets and in seconds was in the darkroom behind a locked door. The most successful leaflet raid of the war! Who was it?   GRo

Mr Mitchell had all the school in assembly and asked for those responsible, or anyone who had any knowledge to come forward. A group of boys, eventually found to be the malefactors, sat close to me. They were all in the same year as me. 'Well Anti' one said to me, 'are you going to Mitchell or will you wait for him to come to you?' 'Wait for him to come to me!' was the obvious answer. I was suspicious, since this group had not been close buddies in London. I believe one of them confessed first. The ringleader, on being expelled, reputedly thanked Mr Mitchell for starting him on his life of crime!   PP(nickname 'Anti')

There was no real incitement to revolt, and it was all too novel for most of us to take seriously. Nevertheless, it must have rocked our relations with BMS.   AWL

There was another leaflet raid: different location, different cause though equally revolutionary. It occurred at the end of religious assembly.

Somebody threw over the balcony onto the body of the hall, leaflets demanding the Government lift the ban on the Communist Party. In 1939 the British Communist Party declared the war was an Imperialist war because the Russians had signed a pact with the Germans and the British had taken some action against the Communist Party, I don't know what. It was against this ban that the pamphlets were thrown over.   VM

The war would change of course. In 1941 the Soviet Union would become our allies. And long before that the RAF would be dropping messages of another sort.

The Headmaster summed up the school's first wartime months in the Michaelmas term issue of the school magazine. He referred to the

> *... quite remarkable spirit of courage and cheerfulness shown by the School as a whole in most difficult and trying circumstances.*

Were the virtues he commended an unconscious echo of the ubiquitous official poster quoted at the head of this chapter? If so, he was in good company. Young Princess Elizabeth used the same nouns in her first ever broadcast praising the country's children.

> *Every member of our party in Bedford can feel proud of a School that is going ahead with numbers but little diminished, school work of no mean intensity, and games and outside activities by no means less energetic than in normal times.*

> *We get a bit homesick at times, we do not always like the process of adapting ourselves to new conditions, and we find ourselves a little more tired at the end of the day than we have been as a rule. But the courage and the cheerfulness are still there, in abundance, and we're going to make a success of it – we're going to see the thing through!*
>
> O.W. Mitchell, *Arrow*, Michaelmas '39

12

'Training for Real'

Recruits – raw but ready to serve.

'Don't you know there's a war on?'

It was more than a catchphrase. It was the ready response – by a shopkeeper or a foster parent – to any request.

The war was all around us.

> A game we played walking to school was counting the signs of the war. White paint on the kerbs. Masked traffic lights. Notices in shops about shortages. Re-inforced windows. Uniforms.   DEB

We were part of the war. The Government and the Ministry of Information endeavoured to make us believe we were serving in a front line. Everyone had to contribute to the 'war effort'. We were told we were doing our bit by being evacuated – and staying evacuated. As the war dragged on, there were more active contributions – collecting scrap metal, digging for victory, buying savings stamps and participating in savings drives (see Chapter 34). But most of us sought a more tangible form of expressing our patriotism. Sooner or later, of course, each of us would be in uniform. How could we shorten the delay?

We were keen. As Paul Fussell notes in his book *Wartime*, 'war must rely on the young, only they have two things fighting requires: physical stamina and innocence about their own mortality'.[1]

Occasionally, recruiting officers would visit the school. Geoff Rans remembers a brigadier addressing the sixth form and an exchange with Nat Solomon.

> Brig: ' … 20% of the natives (sic) are troublemakers'.
> N.S. (innocently): 'What percentage of the natives are educated?'
> Brig: 'Oh, about 20%'. GR

Many boys joined local units of pre-service training – the ARP, the Air Defence Cadets or the Local Defence Volunteers (formed in 1940 and later rebranded by Churchill, who would have made a brilliant marketing man, the Home Guard).

It was not till early 1941 that the school itself organised its own corps activities with the Air Training Corps and, in the following year, the Army Cadet Force.

> I joined the ACF where I became a first class shot – not otherwise very military. But we knew we were training for real. DP

> I did a number of camps with the ACF and the training seemed relevant as we all felt we may one day have to join the Forces as everyone of our age seemed to do. DHS

In the spring term of 1941 the editor of the *Arrow* admitted that interest in the school magazine had been 'overshadowed by … other, more momentous interests'.

> *These, it is true, have been mainly for the older boys. The first is the announcement, at the first assembly of the term, that a contingent of the Air Training Corps would be formed in the school. Since that announcement a considerable number of boys have given in their names, and we eagerly anticipate a school contingent, officered by members of the staff.*

> *An Air Training Corps will evoke that corporate spirit drawn from military discipline and the wearing of a uniform...it will show that those taking part are not 'merely schoolboys' in this war...*
> R.E. Davenport, *Arrow*, Lent '41.

That the ATC, launched January 1941, should be the first corps formed reflected a mystique. As Anthony James comments, in the HMSO publication, *Informing the People*, this mystique was 'reinforced during the early months of the war when [the RAF] seemed – wrongly – to be the only arm of the services actually in contact with the enemy and later, by its visible and clearly vital

struggle with the *Luftwaffe* in the Battle of Britain.'[2] It was also reinforced for Owenians by news of recent colleagues taking part.

The ATC's commanding officer was a senior master, G.A
Hutchings. After four months he reviewed progress.

> *Before the Lent term opened, the idea of an Owen's Flight had
> been born. Early in February the Flight came into being, some
> sixty Owenians welcoming among them a contingent of twenty-
> five of their comrades in evacuation from Rye Grammar School.
> Training then began, and a strange period of improvisation, O.S.
> sheets, Aircraft Recognition from magazine cuttings, and drill
> founded on rather hazy memories and some helpful hints from
> Home Guard members. Some of our experiences were amusing,
> as when our four officer-candidates, up for interview before a
> Selection Board, spent a wintry morning at a local air station
> being marched about in the slush and narrowly escaping being
> mistakenly enlisted for the duration of the war as ground staff
> R.A.F. Some have been just trying, as when a new order from H.Q.
> checked our hopeful plans for a visit to the R.A.F. station to which
> we are quite regularly affiliated, leaving us to envy those who were
> not so restricted. During this period, routine training was relieved
> by visits from Pilot Officer Walker, who gave us an interesting
> account of life in the Initial Training Wing, and from Squadron-
> Leader Hudson, who visited us from Cranfield, gave a lecture to
> the whole school, and was most cordial in his assurances of future
> help and interest.*
>
> *Now most of the essential Training Manuals have arrived, equip-
> ment and uniforms are promised for the near future, we have been
> visited and addressed by the Commandant, A.T.C. himself, and we
> begin to feel that we are, after all, the real thing. It is hoped that a
> number of cadets will have a chance of spending a week in camp dur-
> ing the summer holidays.*
>
> *Arrow*, Trinity '41.

There was real enthusiasm. To qualify, boys had to be sixteen on
31 July of the current school year. The corps, anxious not to quell
the enthusiasm of younger boys, formed a B flight, which trained
with their seniors in preparation for subsequent full membership.

The limited strength of the flight entitled it to only two officers
(the second being Mr Olphin) but other teachers from Owen's

and Rye Grammar School provided part-time instruction.

Mr Hutchings concluded his *Arrow* piece with a call to arms.

> *Lastly, a few words to all Owenians who are already sixteen or will reach that age during the next school year. There is already an Owen's School Flight. As Owenians, do you not think that an Owen's School Squadron would be more worthy of a school of our numbers? As Londoners, have we not a special interest in the war, which the R.A.F. is waging, and something of a personal quarrel to settle with the Luftwaffe? And as citizens, who owe to the community in which we live educational opportunities which will give us an advantageous start in life, surely we have a duty to help to defend that community in a way for which that education has specially fitted us. Aeroplane production has speeded up: the urgent need now is for trained aircrew.*
>
> *Arrow*, Trinity '41

Initially, the Army Cadet Force unit collaborated with Bedford Modern School. Together they formed No. 33 Platoon Home Guard Company, attached to the 3rd Beds Battalion. A teacher, W.J. Pearce assumed the duties of C.O. with the rank of Lieutenant.

> *It is not so very long ago now that Mr. Pearce, like Falstaff before him, felt himself to be the not-too-proud possessor of a 'ragged regiment'. For we were a ragged lot, rookies on parade, trying so hard to appear nonchalant when we turned left instead of right. We felt the resentment of all apprentices at the fact that there must be a beginning somewhere, and that we should have to undergo the agonies of the effort. Grins there were in plenty, many of them sheepish. But we had a godfather in Sgt. Maj. Harvey, who was a veritable Penelope in his patience and in his hope that we should make the grade. His gentle encouraging did much to create the necessary atmosphere of harmony and co-operation. To cut a story short, we finally mastered the drill, forming up in ranks, achieving and maintaining our dressings, and everything else that goes to make an orderly squad.*
>
> *Uniforms, of course, were eagerly awaited, for are we not all romantics? Cadets had already been enrolled in the platoon, still more and younger recruits were at the door, and yet the long expected khaki had not reached our A.H.Q. It was not until after we had returned from the Easter Holidays that dawn came to dispel our gloom...we stampeded through determined drizzle on a Tuesday afternoon, ne-*

gotiated the side entrance of the house of refreshment, and there were introduced to the peculiarities of Army fitting.

Now we were soldiers – at least that's what we thought we were. We still felt rookies, but not hopeless rookies and we looked forward to drill with our Platoon. The first Sunday we were graded into sections, and made valiant efforts to impress our hardened critical audience. We were not altogether unsuccessful, for drill comes easily with concentration and fitness.

We have taken part in ceremonial parades, and have learned much of great profit to ourselves. We are steadily becoming more proficient, smoother in our action, quicker off the mark. Rifle drill has been started and even rifle shooting for some. We still, of course, do silly but forgivable things like presenting arms smartly when we ought to be to attention at the "order", we still find ourselves gazing into the steel-blue eyes of our left-hand neighbour when we ought to be staring at the ears of the man on the right. Things like that are silly, but understandable, and are soon eradicated – we hope. The Regiment loses, bit by bit, its tatters and looks a lot less ragged than of yore. We are jumping to the occasion. We are becoming soldiers.

L.W. Madden, *Arrow*, Trinity '42

Later, under two other Owen's teachers, Captain Tingay and Captain Lloyd Williams, the force became an independent company known officially as F Company, 2nd Bedfordshire and Hertfordshire Regiment.

Its full strength reached the grand total of eighty-four cadets, N.C.O.s and officers. Two of their number went on later to win distinction at Sandhurst - S.Bronkhorst (who won the Belt of Honour in 1945) and F.R. Taylor (who gained a commission in the Scots Guards). The Force also was presented with a painting of the Bedfordshire Regiment for gaining the highest percentage of certificate 'A' successes in the country. After the war 'F' Company was transferred to the H.A.C. in London, becoming 'B' Company of the H.A.C. Cadet Battalion.[3]

Corps life added a new dimension to our evacuation. Boys discovered new skills, skills they might use in later life.

The ATC was probably the most popular corps to join in preparation for eventual call up. We all became dab hands at Morse and aircraft recognition, even beating an RAF team on one occasion.

Did it prepare me for the RAF? Well, I was given some examples of parachute training and learned, successfully, how to jump off a chair, ladder, and then after being harnessed to some sort of winch, the side of a hangar. This early training served me well, since one of my jobs in the RAF – I cleaned latrines as well – was to nudge first time Army parachutists out of gliders. MM

I joined the ATC early on and ultimately became Flight Sergeant – in charge under the officer. In fact aircraft had become something of a hobby and I was a whiz at identification from the printed silhouettes published for the Observer Corps, which in the ATC we had to study. I also made 'Airfix' kits in those days! Maybe it was no coincidence that my first job after graduating from London University was in aircraft design. JL

Penguin published a book on Aircraft Recognition. It ran to three million copies.

We were red hot at Aircraft Recognition. Many of us bought a publication called the *Aeroplane Spotter* (3d every Thursday) which gave three-dimensional silhouettes of British and foreign aircraft that were far superior to any produced by the HMSO. We had regular practice in aircraft recognition with the considerable number of planes flying over Bedford and our interest was increased with the arrival in 1942 of the Americans at Thurleigh, a newly opened USAAF airfield, and five miles from Bedford. Our skill was recognised in inter-squadron competitions, where we not only wiped the floor with other town ATC squadrons but also the local Observer Corps. AWL

The Corps was also red hot at drill, seemingly by accident.

We met on Friday mornings at the Riverside Club which had grass tennis courts and all our marching and drill was done on grass. As a consequence, when we met other ATC squadrons, as we did in summer camps, we out-drilled them so thoroughly that we made ourselves rather unpopular. AWL

Philip Fawkes noted in his diary:

As a member of the A.T.C. I have made several trips to Cranfield and am due to visit the American Air Force Station at Thurleigh where there are many Fortresses. I have passed my proficiency. We have two periods of two hours each week on Tuesday afternoons after break & Saturday mornings. D.Pratt used to be our flight sergeant but now

Foulger has taken his place. We have 'marches past' during visitation & Church Parade. We have navigation, (Astro & Dead Reckoning), Morse (Aldis & Buzzer) drill, P.T., Met., and principles of flight, anti-gas and armament. PFa

Years later he recalls

… a week at a RAF camp Wisbech, with flights in an Avro Anson. We had what the pilot described as 'a ropey landing, what!' bouncing from one wheel to another, fortunately the Anson had a very strong undercart. PFa

I remember my first flight, as a passenger in a small monoplane. I returned to 12 York Street and told Mrs S that I had seen the house from the air. She didn't believe me. I said something like 'who was flying – you or me?' which was probably the only time I was rude to her.

DEB

Peter Senn, editor of the *Arrow* and subsequent writer of the William Hickey column on the *Daily Express*, had a more adventurous first flight in a more important plane.

We walked, the four of us: the pilot, the observer, Davis and myself. The wind, blowing across the great airfield, was ruffling our hair and I could feel my parachute harness cutting into my thighs. The two airmen were joking. The pilot, with his clear grey eyes and small black moustache, was typical of many I had seen that day on the aerodrome. The observer was older, more sober. I looked at them both and then at the planes in the distance. For a brief while I was part of all this.

We neared the planes – huge black Blenheims – and, reaching ours and having had our parachutes tested by the observer, we clambered in, myself on to the navigator's seat – a small and uncomfortable piece of leather in the very nose of the machine– and Davis into the seat next to that of the pilot. Adjusting his helmet, the latter followed. I looked at Davis; he seemed a trifle apprehensive, experiencing the same feeling, as I was, doubtless, that queer, jumpy emotion one gets before a race.

Suddenly there was a roar like ten thousand devils as the pilot opened out first one engine and then the other and the fuselage seemed stricken with ague as it vibrated against my back. Then we began to move, slowly at first as we taxied along the runway behind two other planes and then faster and faster until we were roaring across the ground at a speed which sent the blood bubbling through my veins like rich, red wine. A slight jerk and we were up and I watched, almost casually, as the earth slowly receded.

We climbed steadily, then straightened out. I had asked the pilot to fly over Oxford, but revealing a lamentable false sense of values, he had elected to go to Cambridge. With a wave of his hand he now yelled, "Here we go" and yanked the joystick over. The next minute the world seemed to have gone crazy, for the earth, hitherto flat and even beneath us, was now standing on end in a vertical plane. My stomach lifted slightly but righted as we came out of the bank and I settled down to enjoy a calm and pleasant trip.

I glanced out of the window where I could see the port engine thumping away and tried to imagine myself flying the plane; but I shivered as I thought of this terrifying monster getting out of control. Away to the left I could see some silver specks – I realised they were barrage balloons. Beneath us the world had an appearance of unreality. The fields were too even, too exact; the houses like toys. I saw a winding, trickling stream, which, I idly supposed, was the Ouse, though I could see little evidence of a large town around it. I suddenly began to feel philosophical. Up here, I thought, one could view affairs in their true perspective; one could realise how small was man, and how petty his worries. The next minute I was feeling anything but philosophical, for we were dropping like a stone, and I could do nothing but clench my teeth, close my eyes and grip my fists. It was the old nightmare of falling off a bus come to life. At five hundred feet (as I later learnt) we pulled out of the dive and five minutes later my stomach caught up with the rest of my body. I opened my eyes to see Davis grinning all over his face at my discomfort. The sky was black now, and rain was beating on the fuselage and trickling down the windows and a small spray was playing on the back of my neck. The pilot pulled off his intercom mask and yelled, 'weather too bad, going back' and once more the earth spun round as we banked. Life now seemed to be one perpetual round of adjustment, for no sooner had we pulled out of the turn than we were dropping again, and just as my stomach had recovered from the first experience it went on its travels again. But I lived, and the descent to earth, which I had been expecting to be the worst stage of the journey, proved, instead, to be a gentle downward glide. Down, down, down till, with a few slight bumps, we were once more taxiing across the ground.

Arrow, Trinity '42

In the last year of the war a Peter Senn landing of a Wellington bomber would not be so gentle (see Chapter 40).

The Corps was part of 691 Squadron and flew from various aerodromes.

> I flew in an Oxford from Twinwoods and looped the loop in a Tiger
> Moth at Bircham Newton. RN

> We did get some practical flying experience with 691 Squadron at
> Twinwoods aerodrome very near Thurleigh in Dominie biplanes and
> Oxford monoplanes. I distinctly remember on one occasion flying in an
> Oxford with four of us cadets aboard and the pilot was wrestling with
> the trim wheel, unable to stop the aircraft from alternately pitching up
> and down, until he saw Ron Nash walking about in the back of the air-
> craft, whereupon he instructed him to 'sit on that bloody mainspar and
> stay still'. Better flying experience was had, of course, on the summer
> camps and I remember flying in formation with two other aircraft, all
> Martinet target towing planes, and peeling off from 5,000 feet in a dive
> to 2,000 feet. Terrifying. AWL

**Both Alan Locke and Ron Nash were to remember another day
at Twinwoods when the Americans used it (see Chapter 39). An
unofficial visit, as was an earlier one by Dave Pratt.**

> One Saturday morning three of us cycled out to RAF station at
> Twinwoods. At 6.30 am we were taken on a 3 hour air-experience
> practice bombing flight to Berwick and returned to cycle back to the
> Meltis ground to play in a 1st XI match against Bedford Athletic in the
> afternoon.

> Shortly afterwards, four of us went to experience service life at RAF
> Cranfield where we had to share our modest house on the base with
> four members of the WAAF, each of whom, I assure you, was much
> more worldly than the combined experiences of four Owenians. DAP

**Longer visits to military airfields took place during one- or two
- week camps in the holidays.**

> We were fortunate enough to go to Burton Wood, an American base,
> which wasn't very far away and we would cycle there wearing our
> uniforms. We weren't allowed to go into the large aircraft, the Flying
> Fortresses. We used to watch them practising strange circles and
> bumps and after a couple of weeks asked them what was going on. They
> told us that they were flying blind and things could often not go very

well. We were also very privileged to hear about a very secret device on the Halifax crafts called H2S which gave a picture of the ground when flying at night. Most interesting was the course in navigation: what to do when you were lost: how to deal with weather: what to do in emergencies: how to behave in a plane: how to deal with visiting airfields and climbing over aircraft and how not to stand in places that you shouldn't or touch anything that would cause any mishap. We would be examined on all aspects of this training. The greatest thrill was to visit aerodromes where we were allowed to take part in flights.   BS

A rather exciting - now, but then terrifying - experience occurred at RAF Witchford. Don Hall, Martin Peters and I were selected to fly in a Lancaster on a formation flying exercise. On gaining our position in the formation, a small stream of liquid appeared outside the aircraft and a smell of petrol within. Breaking formation, we were instructed to don our parachutes. It is impossible to explain the expressions on our faces but a 'whiter shade of pale' is inadequate.
Needless to say, the parachutes remained unopened – we made an emergency landing at the US Air Force base at Glatton where we stayed for the rest of the day enjoying US Air Force hospitality.   IW

ATC camp was always exciting with quite a lot of flying. Whilst at RAF Bircham Newton, Norfolk in July 44 my brother flew in on a training flight, commandeered a wagon and the two of us called on my uncle at an adjacent aerodrome, Docking.   KD

Being in uniform made us believe, if not that we were the real thing, then very close and that we could fool the less attentive into accepting us as part of the genuine 'war effort'.

During the war, the Derby was run at Newmarket. Dave Barnett and I reckoned we could hitch-hike from Bedford in a couple of hours. So we put on our ATC uniforms and had no trouble getting there. We backed Midas each way. It came second but the bookie did a runner. It was a great day – and we had no trouble getting back.   DEB

The flight's hopes of becoming a squadron were dashed. The formation of the ACF drew off much of its potential strength. Mr Hutchings' review in the Lent 1944 issue of the *Arrow* told of other disappointments.

Again, we are still without a real home of our own, a headquarters where we can equip a permanent Aircraft Recognition Room, wire a Signals Instruction Room and leave all our gear set out for instant

*use instead of having to pack up and lock away after every parade.
Opportunities to fly have not recently been as frequent as they once
promised to be and the much-advertised alternative, gliding, has not
so far come our way.*

Arrow, Lent '44

(The war would end before ATC cadets would gain gliding certificates at Southend civil airfield.) Nevertheless, the CO is not too
discouraged.

*We are now equipped on a generous scale for instruction in all aircrew
subjects...our weekly Flight Parade has developed a definite 'Service'
atmosphere...and we are fortunate in having no lack of Instructors.
And we have achieved definite success in these three years. Twenty
Cadets have joined the R.A.F. or the Fleet Air Arm and one the Army,
either direct from this Unit or after further service in a University Air
Squadron. Of these, eight have been specially selected to take Service
Short Courses at the Universities for training for Commissions. We
have gained 31 Proficiency Certificates. All the above figures include
Owen's School Cadets only and take no account of the successes
gained by our comrades of Rye Grammar School, whose contribu-
tion to the growth of the Unit has been invaluable. Last December a
hastily mustered team under Corporal Fawkes, came first in a local
Aircraft Recognition Competition in which the other A.T.C. units of
Bedford and the Spotters Club were represented.*

Arrow, Lent '44

The Army Cadet Force was to score a similar success.

Army Cadet Force Commanding Officer Lloyd Williams led us proudly
on parade and we wore the black and yellow flash of the now defunct
Beds and Herts Regiment on battledress sleeves. Target practice was
with Lee Enfields adapted for .22 ammo.
Brigadier Foss VC was a great character and whenever his '14-'18
military achievements received mention, as on speech days and other
formal occasions, this was to his acute embarrassment. Inspiring us
on field days, he maintained a fatherly interest in all our soldierly ex-
ertions. Although his war had been the previous one, his enthusiasm
never waned.   DMJ

I joined the Army Cadet Force and got promoted to Lance Corporal!
The Area Commander was a Brigadier General who had won a VC in
World War 1, but we considered him a bit of a Colonel Blimp. However,
at an ACF Camp we all went up in an Army glider where all the boys

were semi-conscious and terribly sick – but he just sat there enjoying the experience. We had a lot more respect for him after this.   GS

The Brigadier was less than pleased with one cadet.

I remember training with wooden rifles. Then with real Lee Enfields. They were heavy. My uniform smelt of chemicals and fitted me in places. My most poignant memory was of girls I knew laughing when they first saw the uniformed me in Castle Road. My most embarrassing memory (possibly of the war) was wheeling 180 degrees not 90 degrees at a parade of honour when I was right marker.   DEB

Instruction, however, improved. The ACF had ten instructors under a Regimental Sergeant Major of the Royal Fusiliers. Captain Tingay took bayonet drill. The cadets took other subjects themselves after attending training courses.

The School Company met 'A' Company (Bedford Town) in a map-reading and general knowledge match in the BMS Hall on November 24th.The School won by a narrow margin, Cadet Davis showing outstanding ability to recognise the badges, ranks and flashes of the various regiments.

Arrow, Lent '44

Corps training stood the cadets in good stead when they graduated into the real world – initially civilian or university but eventually and inevitably military. For some it was active service, for many more national service post-war but for all of us, in either of the two corps, the transition from school life to service life was eased by the lessons we learned 'training for real'.

13

Be Prepared

Was there ever a more successful scout troop?

There was another school corps with its uniform and tradition and open to Owenians of all ages. It lacked the glamour of an association with the regular services. It lacked obvious topicality. The war it was connected with was that in South Africa. Baden-Powell had been a hero at Mafeking. The Scout motto shares his initials.

> *'Would you like a cup of tea, sir?' This question sounded like a voice from Utopia to the ears of a tired member of the school staff, as he rested in a Bedford schoolroom, after the somewhat tiring journey from Islington on the day of our evacuation. The answer was 'yes', in a tone of surprise, surprise because of the unexpected offer, which came from a boy in his party, who had been travelling without any apparent means of producing such a beverage. The boy, like a number of others, was a Scout belonging to a London Troop. He had lived up to his Scouting motto and was prepared.*
>
> J.A. Davison, *Arrow*, Michaelmas '39

The author of that piece from the school magazine's first wartime issue then referred to another example of preparedness by another Owenian who 'saved a life from drowning in the Bedford river shortly after our arrival here'.

The author was Mr Davison, the art teacher. He was known affectionately as 'Boo Boo', the name of a chimpanzee at London Zoo. Mr Davison is credited with the idea of inaugurating an Owen's troop. Evacuation had severed scouts in the school from their London troops. With the Headmaster's approval, a meeting was arranged at the end of the first month of the war. Held on the entrance steps of the Town Library (opposite the school) it was attended by eighteen boys who formed themselves into a troop.

> *The Modern School very kindly gave us the use of their room in the Tower. Here we held our first indoor parades when we could do so without interrupting any class that might be in the room underneath.*
>
> J.A. Davison, *Arrow*, Michaelmas '44

That Christmas Mr Davison appealed for new members.

> *Although we are already large in number, there is still room for others who have been members of troops at their own homes. Later it is hoped to be able to welcome boys of the school who are not scouts already. The times of parades are: Tuesdays, 10.30am, Court of Honour; Fridays, 10.30am, Troop Parade; Sundays, 10am, Religious Service.*
>
> *Arrow*, Michaelmas '39

The troop numbers grew.

> The scout troop at Owen's really took off and eventually had over 100 members formed into eleven patrols, with Eric Vincent and me as Troop Leaders. We had so many King's Scouts that we formed a club.
> I remember the day when I was summoned to the Headmaster's study, where O.W. Mitchell requested that I should not call a meeting on a day when the school had an important event as he liked to have more than two-thirds of the school present.   WJW

> *The troop was so large that it was necessary for some part of it to meet each day after school. The whole troop met on Saturday afternoons. The formation of Air Scouts enlarged our numbers so much that the troop became a group of three divisions with a membership of 140. Unfortunately, there was but one Scouter (the ideal proportion is one Scouter to 15 Scouts). Nevertheless, we continued for about four years with this disproportion, always hoping that other Scouters would come to our assistance. As no further help came, the number of meetings and members had to be decreased.*
>
> *Arrow*, Michaelmas '44.

Apart from its regular Scouting in the open air around Bedford – knot tying, Morse and semaphore signalling and games – the troop did much useful work. It liaised with the local ARP in message running and First Aid.

As a Scout I became involved in the ARP as a messenger – I can't remember taking any messages but when there was an air raid I would make my way by bicycle to the ARP post and sit around. As a result of these efforts and for my fire watching I received a certificate at the end of the war from the County of Bedford Civil Defence thanking me for the 'unstinted and valuable service' I had rendered to the organisation.

BF

Another of our activities has been the sorting and packing of waste paper and delivering it to the district dump. This is work of national importance, but for several reasons we have not been able to carry this out on as large a scale as we should like. Amongst the reasons are the lack of trek cart, the breaks in attendance because of holidays and weekend leave and in having no room in which to do the sorting. Perhaps we may be able to find some way of overcoming these difficulties. In the meantime we confine our efforts to dealing with the waste paper produced by the school. This in itself is an item of no small dimensions!

J.A. Davison, *Arrow*, Lent '40

An Air Troop was inaugurated. It occupied its time signalling, aircraft spotting, model making and visiting local aerodromes. Many air scouts eventually joined the ATC, and, according to Mr Davison in a review of the troop's first five years, 'gave a good account of themselves'.

The activities of the Land Scouts include help in Wolf Cub Packs, entertainments in Nursing Homes, concerts in aid of various good causes, assistance to the running of weekend and holiday camps for evacuees. They have excelled in both Morse and semaphore signalling; a challenge offered to the Bedford Troops was not accepted. Hundreds of proficiency badges have been gained and a record number of King's Scout Badges awarded, and there has always been a good proportion of 1st Class Scouts.

A special word about King's Scouts may be opportune. The training for the badges includes subjects which will help the Scout in his social work. Outside examiners take most of the tests and the award is made on their recommendation. We hear from time to time how some of these Scouts who have left the school are progressing.

Arrow, Michaelmas '44

The progress of an Owen scout who left the school as war was declared was noted in the *Arrow*.

From all the scouts in blitzed areas who had been recommended for bravery were chosen four King's Scouts. The party, led by a Londoner, have gone for a tour of Canada, their duty being to show the Canadians what British scouts are doing in National Service, to relate experiences in air raids and to advise in Civil Defence. The leader of this party is an Old Owenian, Stanley Newton, winner of the Art Prize in 1939, and a Holborn Troop Leader.

Before leaving this country the party were engaged with interviews, press conferences, photographs and newsreel pictures. They also broadcast on 'In Town Tonight'*. They were honoured by a 'send off' from high Government officials and by leaders of the Boy Scout Organisation.

W.J. Whitebread, *Arrow*, Trinity '42

The Owen's troop was an undoubted success.

The 95th Beds and Herts Scout Troop was at one time the largest in the country. Patrol meetings were held in the room at the top of tower at Bedford Modern School and the fearsome charges of British Bulldog took place in Bedford Park. We camped in Pavenham Woods and I learned the art of preparing a vast boiler of rice custard for my Cook's badge. Scout's pace – run a minute, walk a minute – seemed to get me home quicker. We collected waste paper for the National Service badge.

RN

The scouts were very popular at school and we had some great times. Friday nights were the best when we went to Bedford Park and played such games as British Bulldog which was fairly rough to say the least. I do recall four of us taking a 'Journey Badge' where we had to <u>walk</u> several miles and camp for the weekend. Coming home we were exhausted and thumbed a lift in a car complete with our staves and rucksacks and kept quiet about the whole of this episode.

GS

Not everyone found the appeal of the scouting movement to his liking. Was this description in the summer 1940 *Arrow*, written by a keen Troop Leader, T.A.Simmons, a turn-on even then?

Scouting is an attempt to reach, chiefly through outdoor games, camping and woodcraft, some of the subjects not contained in the school curriculum, subjects which promote character, health, and

---

* A topical live broadcast from London every Saturday evening, featuring interesting people who were 'in town tonight'.

citizenship. It helps a boy to live a life of fuller enjoyment. His keen desire for romance and adventure is put in the right direction. He is encouraged to think less and less of himself and more and more of others. Or as the Chief Scout puts it, to replace Self with Service, to make the lads individually efficient, morally and physically, with the object of using that efficiency for the service of the community.

T.A. Simmons, *Arrow*, Trinity '40

Some recruits left after only two or three weeks. Martin Mitchell fought his dislike of the ethos and lasted longer.

I don't know why I joined the scouts. It just wasn't me. I couldn't really buy the King and Country routine, although I liked the idea of tying knots. My shaky allegiance petered out after a few weeks. The scoutmaster, 'Boo Boo' Davison, must have breathed a sigh of relief; especially after the embarrassment I caused him. But it was his own fault. He shouldn't have given me the scout's handbook to read when we were camping. Browsing through it I came across the helpful advice that, should you experience a nocturnal emission and it worries you, then speak to your Scoutmaster about it. Normally, one wouldn't dream of telling anybody; it was a sodden, unmentionable experience. But in the tent that night as we mulled over the solemn advice with great hilarity, the five of us thought, what a jolly good idea to seek enlightenment from 'Boo Boo'. And so the following morning at breakfast, we said in a single voice in front of our fellow scouts, 'Please, sir, we wish to make a submission.' 'What about?' 'Emission, sir, nocturnal emission. What is it, sir? It's mentioned in the handbook.'

A gust of chortles swept through the troop. Poor 'Boo Boo' turned crimson. 'We'll talk about it some other time, now let's sing. All together now!' He had recovered quickly but the laughter outlasted the song.

MM

Mervyn Crossick was an enthusiastic member of the Scout Troop.

I particularly enjoyed dressing up in the uniform: the shirt and shorts, the scarf held in place by a woggle, the sheath knife tucked into the belt and the Canadian Mountie style hat. The hat could be used as camouflage and we only had to lie down, prop the hat up in front of us and we would become invisible. Sadly, I was never able to test this theory. But my real problem was the staff. This essential part of the scout image was a thick pole approximately five feet long and about an inch in diameter.

Its uses were manifold; bush fires could be beaten out, crowds kept back, bridges built and shelters constructed.

I had been told that its overriding purpose was subduing mad dogs. We would immediately recognise these animals by the foam pouring from their jaws. The pole had to be held horizontally with two hands, arms outstretched, at about slavering jaw height. I was assured that when this posture was taken it would provide irresistible bait. The dog would snap its teeth shut on the centre. Then a quick kick on the underside of the jaw would result in the collapse of mad mongrel and general acclaim of heroic activity.

When wearing the scout's uniform you immediately felt this heavy responsibility to society. I ignored blind people hoping to cross roads and pregnant women carrying large shopping bags whilst I peered hopefully at every animal I passed looking for the telltale signs of insanity.

MC

This metamorphosis was part of the movement's pitch. As Troop Leader Simmons maintains:

> *It caters not only for the bright boy but also for the so-called dull boy who often does so well that he gets a feeling of greater self-respect.*
> *Arrow*, Trinity '40

The lessons to be learned included discipline, pluck, chivalry and resourcefulness. Owenians rarely lacked the last.

> There was a collector's passion in our troop and an obsessive desire to acquire badges we could sew on our shirt. We all started with the Missionary badge because the examiner, an elderly lady, was known to be a soft touch and served home made lemonade and biscuits during the examination. We had to explain how we made and served beef tea to an invalid and if we got that right a certificate was signed, the badge obtained and proudly displayed. Nobody ever failed. MC

This incident may not be exactly what scoutmaster Davison had in mind when he taught each scout, 'to use his initiative not only in his own interests but also in those of others'. This virtue would be reinforced at camp.

> *Here the theory, which he has been learning in the winter months, is put into practice from the correct way to use an axe to the preparation of a meal, from how to be cheerful, to doing his part in a Troop*

concert and many other things, including the importance of sanitation.

J.A. Davison, Arrow, Michaelmas '44

Mens sana in corpore sano. Baden-Powell's tenets, inspired by one war, were appropriate for another.

14

Fire Watching

Not quite a protection racket.

The other school preoccupation more important than reading the school magazine (see page 94) was fire watching. In
spring 1941 the editor wrote:

> *Co-operating with the Bedford Modern School, parties consisting of
> two masters and six boys each, spend a night in the school building
> in case of an incendiary attack. The boys have been through a brief
> training. There are seven parties and working on alternate nights
> with an equal number from the B.M.S., one duty is required of each
> person every fortnight. The first duty was taken by the Headmasters
> of our two schools, Mr H. W. Liddle and Mr O. W. Mitchell. Thus we
> find the spirit of the school assumes a concrete form.*
>
> R.E. Davenport, *Arrow*, Lent '41

Angus Calder notes in *The People's War* that though the danger
from incendiary bombs had been appreciated well before the
War, 'the authorities' approach to the problem of fire prevention
had been slow and halting'. Individual citizens could purchase a
stirrup pump for one pound but they were in short supply.

> *Wardens, police and Home Guards, acting with the supplementary
> fire parties organised from local residents in some areas cornered
> most of what was going.*[1]

Ad hoc parties were commendable but concentrated on residential property. What of the commercial, industrial and unoccupied
buildings? Prompted by the blitz on London, Coventry and other
cities, Herbert Morrison decreed on 31 December 1940 the beginning of compulsory fire watching. Regulations were enforced
which could 'compel all men between sixteen and sixty to register

for that purpose'.[2]

> The school was no exception. Boys over the age of sixteen were encouraged to form fire watching teams, which kept watch, on a two hours on, two hours off basis, in the school premises. The additional attraction of this was that we were paid for our labour at the rate of half-a-crown [12½p.] an evening. We received instructions on the use of a stirrup pump for extinguishing fires caused by magnesium incendiary bombs. I believe the nights, alternated with Bedford Modern School, included weekends.   AWL

It's doubtful, however, if any Owenians regarded fire watching as a real job of work.

> Fire watching at the school could not have been too serious. I was in the gymnasium the night that a naked climber was called down from the top of a rope. Not a pretty sight. Could we really have chloroformed a mouse and nailed it to the underside of the table in the prefects' room?   RN

> Fire watching at BMS building had great appeal apart from the payment made. Great fun with wonderful nightlong games of tag (I remember bringing down a very active member of the staff with a vigorous rugby tackle in the darkened corridor). Cooking baked beans on the gym gas ring. Being rightly accused of being involved in one squad's less than conventional way of putting out a fire in the watcher's room.   DAP

Though Geoff Rowley didn't enjoy the experience.

> Fire watching at the Modern School in a room in the Tower was a terrible bore but one never knew whether Allen's Works might have attracted a raid on Bedford.   GRo

If some found compensation in the sense of duty fulfilled, others found companionship – and not only with fellow students.

> Once the Battle of Britain was on we fire watched. There was a good group unity – and that included masters. I got to know 'Flash' Hardwick more easily on a more friendly level.   BL

Bedford Modern School was not the only building Owenians kept an eye on, as Ken Deadman reminds us.

My wartime diaries record frequent fire watching at Bedford Modern School, BMS Boat House and the Moravian Church! Presumably there was a stipend apart from refreshments. KD

The Moravian Church led some into temptation.

I fire watched at the Moravian Church. Who was it that played boogie-woogie on the church organ? ME

When we went fire watching we used to spend half the time playing on the organ. VM

But fire watching was not just fun and games.

Fire watching – always a joyful occasion to get away from supervision for the night – almost made heroes of those of us who were on duty one night. We were ready as usual with buckets of water and sand, and prepared with stirrup pumps and the methods to handle incendiary bombs to keep them from burning through the roof. There was plenty of smoke that night but not from the roof or a bomb. It came from under the Assembly Hall. There was a crawl space maybe four feet high with two feet of dense smoke at the ceiling but enough clear air underneath to let us get under the stage without dying in our ignorance of carbon monoxide poisoning. It turned out to be an electrical fire, a smouldering fire that might have burned down the school as easily as any thermite bomb but even after the firemen arrived the adrenalin levels burned fiercely in our veins. DAMM

Fire watching started at the boathouse after there had been an incendiary raid in which the boathouse was hit with the loss of a couple of boats. There was no heating, and lighting was by oil lamps. We sat on the top of a large table wrapped in blankets. We rarely went to sleep. I can't remember whether we got paid for this but we were certainly paid whilst fire watching in the Church near to the bus station. BF

My first watch was in the Moravian church and it was the night Bedford was bombed. I remember going to the ambulance station and getting one or two people off the stretchers. About 6am I thought I had better go home and tell my parents where I had been, as they hadn't realised that anything had happened that night. AH

By 1944 all men who worked less than sixty hours a week and women who worked less than fifty-five were obliged to fire watch for roughly one whole night a week 'unless they were already civil defenders or Home Guard'.[3]

Yet in the same year a whimsical not to say frivolous piece appeared in the *Arrow*.

> *What is 'fire watching'? It may mean –*
>
> *(1) Watching a fire or fires (2) Watching for a fire or fires.*
> *If they are fires they may be real or imaginary. It depends.*
> *Then there are different sorts of fires e.g. grate-fires (excluding the celebrated one of London) and grateless fires, just as there are fireless grates. Don't we know it?*
>
> *(1) Watching a fire – We can either watch a fire in our house – a pleasant occupation – or our house on fire which is not so pleasant. We can also watch a house on fire, the psychological reaction depending on our relations with the occupier.*
>
> *(2) Watching for a fire – This means that as soon as we have observed a fire, our part of the job is finished and we can go home.*
> *It was this interpretation of 'fire watching' that led to the introduction of the term 'fire fighting', but if we are paid for fire fighting, ought we to be paid when there is no fire to fight? Ask the 5th and & 6th forms. As for myself I prefer the term 'fire watching' to 'fire fighting' because you can (sotto voce) go to sleep while you are fire watching, but to do so while you are fire fighting could have disastrous results. You might put out the wrong fire!*
>
> B.L. Vulliamy, *Arrow*, Lent '44

Bedford had been relatively free of incendiary bombs. Fire watching was largely a sinecure and a good opportunity to chat, indulge in hobbies or horseplay or write a diversionary piece for the *Arrow*. This one was signed 'Bon Bon!'

You may be surprised to know, given the year and the real fires and the 'real job of work' being done by Londoners and other citizens, that the pseudonym was that of a member of staff, who, of course, taught French.

C'est la guerre.

15

'*Do Not Rest Your Spades*'

Digging (sowing, weeding, growing) for Victory.

Two days after the war began, farmers were urged to increase food production. A month later, the Minister of Agriculture broadcast to the nation. Half a million more allotments would provide potatoes and vegetables to feed another million adults and one and a half million children for eight months out of twelve.

> So let's get going. Let 'Dig for Victory' be the motto of everyone with a garden and of every able-bodied man and woman capable of digging an allotment in their spare time.[1]

Over 800,000 allotments were being worked in 1939 and by 1943 close to one and a half million. Millions of instructional leaflets were distributed. Owen's boys needed little urging. They were anxious to disturb the lawns of their billet parents. This enthusiasm was marshalled by the school itself.

> Still another very popular new activity was found in the school gardens – seventy allotments on the eastern boundary of Bedford where optimistic gardeners laboured arduously under Mr. Olphin's direction to increase the nation's food supplies and (in a few cases) make a profit for themselves.[2]

A less sanguine version of events is provided by Alan Locke.

> The school secured the lease of about half an acre of ground at the top of Barkers Lane in Goldington, which was split out into various segments for any boys and staff interested. Very little guidance was given and the activity fizzled out after about three years.   AWL

But those who participated did so with enthusiasm and, eventually, some skill.

> I was a keen allotment holder – I even played a major, not to say perilous part in the digging of a most useful well in the middle of the school's allotments. I especially recall the incredible task G.T. Dimmock and I undertook in conveying – by swaying wheelbarrow – a staggering load of pig-manure some distance to the Owen's acreage. H.K. Olphin was officially in charge but George Armitage was in fact much more in charge (and 'hands-on'); he even interrupted a chemistry lesson to upbraid me for the state of my cabbage bed...   JS

The spirit of Owen's gardeners was expressed by J.Groom of form Remove A in a verse.

> REMEMBER THE GARDENER
> *Let's dig up the land and pull up the weeds*
> *To win the food which England needs,*
> *With a rake, a fork, a spade and a hoe*
> *We'll go to grow, to dig and to sow.*
> *For the turnips, the peas, the 'tatters' and beans,*
> *The onions, the sprouts, the carrots and greens,*
> *Never mind blisters, the mud, dirt and toil,*
> *Just roll up your sleeves, and dig up the soil.*
> *Owenians, dig, and just dig with a will,*
> *For King and for Empire to have a 'rill mill.'*
>   *Arrow* Michaelmas '40

'Rill mill' (or real meal) was a popular catchphrase from the radio programme *Happidrome*. Many boys took pride in contributing to the welfare of their billets.

> 'Impey' the gardener and I got on well and he taught me how to grow potatoes, asparagus and tomatoes and more or less everything we needed to be self-supporting with fruit and vegetables. When Impey was called up I was expected to take over his mantle.   KRC

> I was an enthusiastic supporter of Bert Olphin's 'Dig for Victory' squad. The field we used wasn't far from the billet. Despite our sampling the produce, some did arrive back at the billet.   JW

But, lack of enemy activity permitting, the billet wasn't the only recipient of the vegetables of their labours.

It was always an impressive sight, on the first day of the holiday to see the allotment holders among the boys heading home – these 'Dig for Victory' zealots would be seen lugging onto the Birch bus bulging sacks and indeed suitcases, heavily packed with, largely, green and root vegetables of an amazing variety.   JS

The first year's efforts were duly reviewed in the *Arrow* by the master in charge.

> *During recent months we have been harvesting the produce; and even though the drought affected some of the crops, we are satisfied with the first year's results. Some among us with business instincts proudly display balance sheets showing "a hundred per cent profit" – if they ignore all labour costs!*
>
> *It is certainly true that although there are some sixty plots, practically all of them yielded well. In some cases results were outstanding. Several boys had onion beds of extraordinary value and carrots – where they had been properly thinned. Beans, peas, potatoes were generally satisfactory...*
>
> *The competition at the end of July was the climax of the year. For several weeks everyone had been busy hoeing, weeding, making edges straight and neat and generally trying to make the garden the best ever. The judging was done by three members of the Bedford Council's allotment committee ... There have been times during the year when nothing but grumbling, threatening and driving have kept the garden scheme going. But for the efforts of that day I have nothing but praise. Not one of the seventy-five gardeners failed to give a good account of himself. The judges expressed their pleasure at what they had seen, and a hope that we could carry on with our work. Let us hope it was no coincidence that the first two prize winners also took first and second position respectively in their form!*
>
> *But I must again end with a warning against any feeling of complacency. Gardeners like politicians are 'learners all their lives'...I am sure that if the people who discover old Chinese proverbs searched long enough, they would find one running something like this: 'He who sets the least seeds gathers the biggest harvest.'*
>
> H.K. Olphin, *Arrow*, Michaelmas 1940

The second place in the best garden in the competition section was a fourth former called Norman Tebbutt. A contemporary, Bill Whitebread, comments:

Tebbutt was one of the keenest allotment holders in Bedford, leaving school to go on a farm in 1942 and is a farmer to this day, responsible for probably the largest crop of organically grown potatoes in southern England. WJW

A less successful competitor nevertheless learned something about life.

The allotment was shared with 'Bollop' Robinson who unfortunately died a number of years ago. (Curiously I made a pact with him that at midnight on 31 December 1999 we would meet under Marble Arch and I just don't know, if he had lived, whether I would have kept that appointment. It just goes to show the odd things we sometimes talked about as schoolboys.) On the allotment, Bollop and I did manage to clear the ground and raise some vegetables for our billet ladies but our efforts were puny compared with the prize-winning plots. Nevertheless, I can still remember feeling resentful when we had worked very hard and then on competition day the judges swept past our allotment with hardly a glance and on to the more magnificent ones. Surely they could have stopped to give us a word of encouragement or advice. This accidentally taught me a lesson for later life when I too became an event judge – never ignore any entrant, however apparently hopeless. JL

Digging went on outside the school gardens in co-operation with billet families.

Mr Ralphs had about one quarter of an allotment near his home which I worked with him from early on, alone once he rejoined Beds & Herts. BL

There was my involvement with Mr Bale's allotment. I learned all about digging which I loved and at which I became very proficient and I spent many hours in Mr Bale's company on the allotment. We grew potatoes, celery, onions, carrots, rhubarb, beetroot, marrows all of which were used in the home. BF

I went with Mr Carter to help him on his allotment and, although I knew nothing about vegetable gardening, I offered my help to clear his cabbages and Brussel sprouts of the plague of Cabbage White caterpillars which infested them. I must have filled two or three buckets with the wriggling creatures and my reward was to see his green stuff flourishing whilst his neighbours' plants were eaten to shreds. DB

And Owenian digging went on outside Bedford.

Some had allotments but we also bussed out to work on Bedfordshire farms. Together with loosely guarded Italian prisoners of war and closely guarded German ones, all in brown garb with identifying coloured back patches, and recruited Land Girls in wide-brimmed hats, green jumpers and khaki jodhpurs, we picked peas and potatoes, scythed thistles and stooked sheaves. The Italians especially seemed content with their lot. We received fourpence halfpenny an hour.

I recall one hot summer's day harvesting and a hot and bothered Land Girl peeling off her regulation green jumper to cool off. Right beside her, engulfed in that welter of sweat and pheromones, I experienced those youthful stirrings H.E. Bates describes so well.

On one occasion we had to clear a rick of rat and mouse infestation. Whacking its sides released scampering showers of the unfortunate creatures; we clubbed them mercilessly, later jocularly dumping a sackful of corpses in the High Street. DMJ

Most Owenian endeavour on farms happened in school trips to farming camps (see Chapter 18).

The rise in proficiency and recognition of gardening's place in school life can be plotted in the *Arrow*. Departing scholar-gardeners had their wellies filled by others.

> *There will be a short meeting for all gardeners ... We seem to have heard that announcement very often during the past weeks – I am writing on the last morning of the term – but it is with considerable satisfaction that I now record that the school gardens, or rather the school gardeners, are in splendid form.*
>
> *When I wrote these notes last, I appealed to the Middle School to fill the ranks. The response has been almost embarrassing in its enthusiasm. I will confess now that when the veterans left – several of them are already farming – I wondered where the recruits would come from. There was no need for fear. The Removes saw there was a job of work to be done, and one after another besieged me with demands for land, until now I am gradually being driven off my own plots.*
>
> H.K. Olphin, *Arrow*, Lent '43

Gardening became a school 'sport', i.e. a competitive activity among the four school houses★. Mr Olphin continues:

★ Cloudesley, Colebrooke, Hermitage, Myddelton. The origins of the house names are given in Appendix A.

I like, too, the thoroughness with which the work is being done. Digging was excellent, seeds were set carefully, another well has been sunk. In fact – and I say this with no disrespect to the fine work of previous gardeners – we now have that mixture of enthusiasm and experience which should give us our most successful year. Awarding House points is a headache. It is rather hard to penalise the good plot because there is a slight kink in the path but at the moment there are only such minor faults to be found! More power to your elbow, every one of you.

Arrow, Lent '43

Seasons come and go – as do Owenians. Writing later in the year, one *aficionado* was encouraged by the maintained standards.

The Fates indeed have looked with compassion upon our garden-ing efforts in the Lent Term. In this most active season of the year the weather managed to hold good and enable the many budding enthusiasts to commence – in many cases their first year – with a flying start. Needless to say, the gardening programme for 1943 was embarked upon with some doubt, not to say trepidation, since the po-tential stalwarts consisted almost entirely of new gardeners, largely from the Remove Forms who, called upon to fill a very formidable gap, have not only satisfied all expectations but have guaranteed a steady supply of competent workers for 1944.

Testifying to this new spirit is the wonderful change in the appear-ance of the originally small plots, for even the younger among the ranks can boast of a three or four-rood holding.* Meanwhile, enthu-siasm is aroused and maintained by means of a system of judging the gardens approximately every fourteen days, and under the guidance of Mr. Olphin the spirit bodes well for the future.

D.O. Jones, *Arrow*, Trinity '43

Later still that year the same contributor strikes a suitably wintry note.

Often the rewards of our labours have seemed pitifully few in return for the time spent, and yet somehow, those of us who derive more from gardening than mere profit, find a satisfaction and exhilaration peculiar only to ourselves in the pursuit of an interest all too long as-sociated with secluded bachelors and the like.

---

* Although the value of a rood varied locally, it generally represented a quarter of an acre (just over a tenth of a hectare).

The long, dreary winter months lie ahead now, and whilst there can be but little comfort in the prospects of cutting a few wet, shivering kales on a cold January morning, the time has already come for the preparation of a programme for 1944. The exigency of a situation, aggravated still further by the recent rearrangements in the school routine, has necessitated the resignation of many of those members of the Remove forms who displayed such talent last year and has thus rendered the task doubly difficult.

Climatic conditions too, not always come up to our expectations, a deficiency which we feel sure to have proved dispiriting to the uninitiated: one, indeed is expected to possess a remarkable philosophy of life.

D.O. Jones, *Arrow*, Michaelmas '43

He is encouraged, however, by the success of the annual competition and the fact that the judging was taken away from the Bedford Allotments Committee and entrusted to 'the versatile Mr. Dare... proof of just how self-supporting the gardening community has become'.

Progress was marked also by the words of the Minister of Agriculture quoted in the same article:

We can all justly congratulate ourselves on what we have achieved... carry on, then, with the good work. Do not rest your spades, except for those brief periods which are every gardener's privilege.

16

Unfamiliar Sports

Enthusiastic beginners triumph over new challenges.

If war brought problems there were compensating opportunities, for example in the field of sport. More especially as the fields in question were more numerous and closer at hand than those at the end of a tedious bus journey through North London, and the sports were often new and challenging.

> We were very sports minded and lucky to have the opportunity to take on new sports, such as rowing, fives, river swim, etc. Who ever heard of rowing at the Angel Islington? GS

Bedford Modern School rowed, played fives, tennis and rugby. Owen's was — and is — a soccer school. To one senior boy evacuation was an opportunity to switch codes. S.J. Waldman wrote a letter in the first school magazine of the war. He supported his appeal with emotional rather than rational arguments. Rugger was 'a better game' and those who disagreed had not tried both.

> *Everyone will agree that very few people who have played both games prefer soccer — and this is a striking proof that Rugby is a better game. Association football is probably popular in the school because of the healthy and enjoyable exercise that can be derived from it. With Rugby, that healthy and enjoyable exercise can be obtained, with a little bit extra. That little bit extra is indefinable, but it is that which makes people loath to revert to Association football after having changed to Rugby. Even the keenest of footballers will be an even keener Rugby player.*
>
> *Arrow*, Michaelmas '39

In later life Stanley Waldman, a noted judge, would no doubt demand better proof. But in 1939 none could accuse him of prejudice. He was in fact the goalkeeper of the soccer first eleven. The *Arrow* wrote of him, 'His positioning, his daring and his dodging are real assets to the team'. His letter continues:

> *There are three more reasons in favour of the change. First, few matches have been arranged so far. If this inactivity continues, football will be ruined in the school. Then again, one game of Rugby can keep a larger number of boys occupied than a game of Association football. Lastly, we have a great chance of success in making arrangements for Rugby matches when we share the very same building as a prominent Rugby school.*
>
> *Now is the time to change to Rugby; we have a wonderful opportunity to learn a new game. Many of the staff, it appears, would assist in this changeover. Knowledge of Rugby would be invaluable if we were to find ourselves in a Rugby district when we leave school.*
>
> *There could be no better opportunity for making a change for the better than this and I sincerely hope that the movement will receive whole-hearted and active support throughout the school.*
> Arrow, Michaelmas '39.

A fellow member of the soccer team, L.W. ('Nobby') Madden, answered the goalkeeper's 'aggressively stated opinions' in the following term's *Arrow*. He chose to discuss, not the two games' merits, but organisation and time.

> *In order to derive any satisfaction from the change, the sport obviously must be attempted on a thoroughly organised basis, and I maintain that it will take two or three years for the Rugby tradition to seep into the school and much longer before the standard of play will be anything approaching that of the two schools here, whose boys are coached in its tradition from birth...*

(You can see these genetically streamlined rugby babies ready to take the field as they exit the womb.)

> *... by the time that we shall have a proficient first fifteen, we shall be back in London - or is that too pious a hope? Here is an instance of such a state of affairs. Luton Modern School took up Rugby four years ago – their first team now plays Bedford Modern's third fifteen. If we intend to challenge Rugby schools in London – and it is extremely doubtful our being accepted, as the Rugby schools are in an entirely*

different league – the experience will be rather embarrassing and the result unsatisfactory.

Some supporters of the change, more sincere than sensible, advocate that we could switch back to football in London, but they will find that the time devoted to Rugby will have considerably weakened our standard of football, so much so that we should be in the unenviable position of 'Jack- of-all-trades' – and novice at both. Rugby can never become our major sport, and its acceptance now must inevitably be detrimental to our football.

Arrow, Lent '40

But was this in fact a battle about the game's merits or organisation? Wasn't Waldman really saying, 'why can't we be more like Bedford Modern School and Bedford School?' Couldn't Owen's, in other words, take on some of the characteristics of a real public school?

The sharp sighted reader will discern between the lines, the smoky outlines of a class battle, with the common people (association football) pitched against the privileged minority (rugby). The burning issue was subsequently debated. The principal speaker, Norman Tebutt, secured the defeat of the rugby faction by seven votes to six but failed to prevent a seduction of the masses, twelve voting to give rugby a chance. The chance, however, was not taken up.

The river, on the other hand, and the proximity of pools provided sufficient opportunity for new sports.

Swimming regularly in the BMS baths, I reached a fair standard of crawl and back crawl. Miss G. Wills coached us. We swam against Aldenham, BMS, Carlton School and Stowe. The Commercial Road and Newnham baths were on the river, but cold and less popular. DMJ

A number of us used to swim in the Newnham River baths. One year it was announced that the baths would open for the season at 8am on 1st May. Challenges were issued as to who would be first into the water off the top board. Cometh the day and at 7.50am, seven or eight of us, half undressed, were waiting. We rushed in and Ken Deadman led the charge. He let out a shout of triumph as he leapt into space and the plate with his two front teeth shot out. They fell with him and he made three or four vain grabs in mid air. Needless to say, with the remaining bodies landing with huge splashes in the next few seconds, his teeth were washed away to settle somewhere in the oozing mud.   GRo

Meanwhile, in the muddy Ouse, hardy souls tackled the River Swim. There were 'lifeboats' at various stages along the half -mile stretch, between the Plaza cinema and the suspension bridge. But probably the real danger lay in the river itself.

This event (open to all who could and wished to) would surely be disallowed now on both health and safety grounds but we all survived.
                                                                        DMJ

Now, as a doctor, I wonder about the many types and quality of bacteria and other organisms the dark brown water harboured at that time.
                                                                        JNB

Ron Nash took part in the first river swim. It was a handicap race. The sports master was Taffy Lloyd.

Taffy had made a mistake in handicapping as I won. I still have the cup, a poor thing, not engraved. He gave it to me outside the common room and admitted that he had not expected me to finish.   RN

Subsequent prizes were won almost exclusively by Dennis Rosen. Coming second was an achievement.

Coming second to Dennis Rosen, in 13 minutes 13 seconds, was my highest aquatic achievement, 'Gus' Cumming hauling me out by the boathouse. Crawlers won, the bulk of the floundering Owenian armada drifting downstream at dog paddle, sidestroke, trudgen, a skiff accompanying stragglers. I recall our varied crawl styles. Dennis Rosen's streamlined surge, Conrad Lynn's all elbows and head rolling but getting there damn fast; and Denis Bayly's bilateralism. None of us, however, was fit to touch the hem of BMS's local hero Trevor Aughton, Olympic freestyle choice, human torpedo, whose 100 yards in 54 seconds wasn't far behind Johnny (Tarzan) Weissmuller's then world record of 51 seconds.   DMJ

Nobody could beat Dennis Rosen who was able to swim rapidly using the crawl. I could only do the breaststroke and was very careful not to put my face into the dirty water; if I remember correctly, I came about 30th. However, Bernard Fox seemed to derive the greatest pleasure of all by coming last.   JNB

Bernard Fox was honouring a tradition of not taking the event too seriously. It began with the initial river swim.

> Some wags started the swim wearing school caps and playing cards on
> the water.   RN

In the event the contest was both serious and fun. Rather like the London Marathon with its elite competitors and fun runners.

> I recall the manner in which the 'serious' competitors somehow greased
> themselves overall and the day Geoffrey ('Flooge') Rans completed the
> swim doing backstroke from start to finish. Since he swam diagonally,
> from side to side at fairly sharp angles I reckon he must have swum
> nearer five miles than the actual straight half -mile.   JS

What a shame in those days there were no sponsored swimmers. What you earned was the satisfaction of finishing and a point for your house.

> ... regardless of whether you finished 11th or last in the field. Being
> Owenians, we decided it would be more fun to come in last in a field
> of over 100 so that was the challenge. As a result there was much tack-
> ing backwards and forwards across the flow being pelted by the non-
> swimmers with sticks, stones and goodness knows what as we passed
> under the suspension bridge.   DAP

> It was as prestigious to come last as first. So while Rosen and all the
> other good swimmers set off for the suspension bridge I turned round
> and set off for the town bridge. Even then I had to threaten the small
> people at the back to let me 'win'.   HG

The really serious river sport was rowing, though not all Owenians were as dedicated as those in the fours and eights.

> One thing I did learn, how to row. Certainly enough to show off, taking
> out girls in a hired boat. But I never mastered poling a punt; most punts
> in Bedford were paddled, not poled.   PP

Lack of mastery could be dangerous.

> I vividly recall watching a boy taking out a skiff by himself. He was
> markedly overweight; his posterior overlapped the side of the seat, so
> he looked as if he was sitting in the water. He was very scared because
> any imbalance of the oars tilted him sideways. We, standing on the riv-

erbank, were equally frightened and amused simultaneously.

JNB

Though nobody could row at the Angel, there were, prior to evacuation, odd enthusiasts such as Douglas Wade and Martin Mitchell.

Before the war, when I was less than ten I used to sneak away with a pal to catch a steam train for two stops to Alexandra Palace to spend half an hour on a pond in a little paddle boat which looked more like an orange box. So when in the third form, I think, we were asked if anyone would like to learn how to row I thought that I was on my way to Heaven.

DDW

There were rowers on the river Lea. I used to look at them with envy as they easily shot past the barges. And here in Bedford I became one; alas, not an outstanding one, although I was accepted in a reserve four.

MM

When eventually I took the bow seat in the first eight I knew that I had arrived.

DDW

Life for the oarsmen revolved around the boathouse and its guardian spirit.

The school boathouse was maintained and boats constructed, by Jack Bowers. Crafting magnificent shells and clinkers, he welcomed us into his workshop at the back, with its piled shavings and reek of glue and varnish. I still have the wooden Owen's crossed oars calendar Jack made for me for 3/6d.

DMJ

He was a craftsman *par excellence*, a creator of the sleekest craft ever to skim the waters of the Ouse. His cherished creations lined the walls of his boat shed, which reeked of glue and polish. Where are the Jack Bowers now when fabricated fibreglass has replaced the precious feel of those lovingly crafted hulls?

MM

Jack Bowers was a father figure to many an evacuee (though neither party would have then suggested it).

He had the advantage of not being a parent or a teacher. He also had the gift of not talking down to schoolboys so he was good to talk to. DDW

Though his talk was gruff.

I was often on the receiving end of Coach Jack Bowers' lashing tongue. He would cycle on the towpath, one hand holding a megaphone, bellowing, as I vaguely remember, various imprecations of the sort, 'Mitchell, lift your oar out, pull, stop tickling the water! Are you a joker? Turn your blade round, you're going the wrong way, don't you know your brass from your oboe?' Why did he keep harping on about musical instruments?   MM

Rowing had its attractions for non-oarsmen.

Being small, rowing was not my forte but I was allowed to cox Myddelton House second four - once! I became so excited that I allowed our crew's blades to touch those of the other house, thus ending my rowing career, except as a spectator.   JNB

John Stockton was both cox and oarsman.

I coxed the First Eight, later rowed in Lightweight VIII, which won medals on the Tideway Lightweight Race, rowed in House Fours. Highlights were two appearances as First VIII cox at Henley Royal Regatta.   JS

It took time for Owen's to be truly competitive. Initially, the eight rowed against other schools' lesser crews. But, not long before the school left Bedford, came the historic victory against the BMS first eight.

When we eventually beat BMS it was like winning the war!   GS

It was said that Jack Bowers had known before the race we and the BMS crew had clocked the same time in the last rows over the course just before the race itself, which was above the Town Bridge to the suspension bridge. On the day, we won by over a length — and I was ceremonially tossed into the river in front of the boathouse. At the last Bedford reunion, members of that winning crew were present, Duggie Wade (bow), Dennis Mack (5) and self (cox).   JS

For Doug Wade this was the 'climax of the whole evacuation period'.

Owen's had learnt a completely new major sport producing later one Oxford Blue (Donald Mackay) and, in my day, some four oarsmen in the first eights of various Oxford colleges. Even now, over 50 years on, I still recall frequently the powerful sensation of being in the bow of an eight which is running well.   DDW

Running less well, no doubt, were the also-rans in the school regatta.

> Owen's, much influenced by the BMS, started its own regatta and I had
> the dubious honour of stroking the football crew against the cricket
> crew. We found the effort totally exhausting and at half way had a pre-
> prepared picnic before going on to win by what they call a canvas.
>
> DAP

> I had a modest flirtation with most sports including unfamiliar ones
> - rowing (rejected through not pulling my weight) and fives (brutal self-
> inflicted injuries). KD

BMS, the most generous of hosts, made their fives courts available. The version was that played at Rugby school in contradistinc-
tion to those played at Winchester and at Eton where the basic
game allegedly originated. It necessitated the use of the hand (i.e.
five fingers) within a leather glove. It was played in a court. The
bruises were indeed self-inflicted.

> I remember one afternoon when Joss Ackland and I, equipped with
> some fives gloves from I know not where, undertook an attempt at the
> game in the BMS fives court but ended up indulging in a sort of crude
> fisticuffs. That was the launch and the conclusion of my fives career. JS

Others persevered – with much success. The captain of fives was
allowed a boast in the summer of 1942.

> *Many and varied have been the new activities undertaken by Owen's*
> *during its wartime career, but surely it has never been so successful*
> *in such a short time as it has been at rowing and fives. This is no idle*
> *statement, for there are not many schools who, within a very short*
> *time of taking up these sports, can compete – and compete success-*
> *fully – with schools who have been playing them all their lives. This is*
> *especially true of fives for it was only after a term's hard practice that*
> *we played and beat The Bedford Modern School. That is the secret of*
> *fives more than of any other game. The fundamental pre-requisite*
> *of a fives player is not so much the ability to hit the ball hard as the*
> *knowledge when to hit it and this knowledge can only be obtained by*
> *practice.*
>
> R. B. Chatterji, *Arrow*, Trinity '42

Alas, success, or rather playing the game, was short-lived.

The conclusion of the school's two year affair with the sport was marked in the *Arrow* in Spring 1944 with a piece written by an all round sportsman, R.B. Chatterji (who was also editor). Referring back to the introduction of fives he writes:

> *In those days material and enthusiasm necessary for our success were available; now the former is non-existent and the latter is the privilege of the energetic few. It is almost certain that after this term fives will die out, we hope with a bang and not a whimper.*
>
> *Arrow*, Lent '44

Wartime shortages had restricted the game's growth and instilled a sense of fatalism.

> *... Many, realising the potency and inevitability of fate, had more wisdom than Oedipus and did not struggle to escape the Nemesis of the veto of the Ministry of Supply. The remainder all played regularly, automata to the spirit of fives - for what else will explain their attendance at the courts on mornings when the temperature was something unbelievable? ...They played with feverish energy, for they liked playing fives and that is a good enough memorial for any man.*
>
> *Arrow*, Lent '44

The following term, a similar refrain was heard concerning tennis. We had taken up the sport in 1941 and managed to lose to the Girls Modern School. But in 1944...

> *The Tennis Club is experiencing many of the unfortunate but presumably unavoidable vicissitudes which, however, are only to be expected in time of war. Tennis balls, for instance, are exceptionally scarce and the school is sadly reduced to having only fourteen reconditioned balls; on this account, and also to save wear on our only two courts, club membership has necessarily been limited to Sixth Formers. Also, our groundsman, Mr Fishlock, has only a very meagre petrol ration with which to run the mowing-machine, although bad players have the advantage of being able to claim the result of a backhand spin to the sudden dropping of a ball deadened in a patch of daisies. On top of everything, bad weather has impeded our tennis playing as well as the landing in Normandy.*
>
> Denis Rosen, *Arrow*, Trinity '44

The report ends with a plea.

*More players, however, will be needed next year and perhaps some-
one with foresight may be able to obtain a few dozen tennis balls?*

Arrow, Trinity '44

One new sport required less equipment – cross-country running.
In Bedford, of course, it was easy to come across country. Barry
Skeggs was exceptional in bringing metropolitan experience.

Back home in London our next-door neighbour used to train runners.
I used to run (as it happens to my girlfriend's house) under his supervision. He taught me a lot about energy conservation, such as not leap-
ing over a stile but going over carefully. Not jumping a ditch but going
down and then up out of it. Much less energy is used up. I entered the
school cross-country race and managed to come sixth, much to my
father's amazement. He was quite thrilled and I got some extra pocket
money for that. BS

The sport began for Owen's in 1940.

*One new sport that Bedford has given us is cross-country running.
It was very successful though yet in its infancy. It made excellent
groundwork for training for the athletic sports, and it is to be noted
that the regular enthusiasts did very well in their events. We owe our
thanks to Mr. Lloyd for his work in finding us a course, and next year
we hope to get permission to use the B.M.S. course and give this most
enjoyable sport the popularity it deserves.*

Arrow, Trinity '40

*It ought to be clearly understood that there is the world of difference
between cross-country running and racing. There's no unhealthy
strain in running; and it constitutes excellent training for the sports.*

J.L. Lloyd, *Arrow,* Trinity '40

Cross-country running was re-christened 'the Steeplechase'. The
1944 event was won by Keely from Lauffer who 'had only just
returned from a scholarship examination'. Morris was third and
Skeggs fourth ahead of Deadman.

*Others worthy of mention include Solomon, who nonchalantly took
the lead from the start and as nonchalantly surrendered it less than
a hundred yards later ... And so the second Steeplechase finished.
Long may such races continue in days to come as the yearly trial of
strength, but in those days, remember it was born in Bedford.*

R.B. Chatterji, *Arrow,* Trinity '44

It died there too the following year. In Spring 1945 the report begins:

> *Occurring as it did at a time when events of worldwide scope were happening every day, the Steeplechase of April 27 1945 will perhaps have been forgotten, if not already, at least by the time this* Arrow *appears.*
>
> J. Stockton, *Arrow*, Trinity '45

That day allied forces were converging on Venice, Milan and Trieste and the Soviets captured Berlin's Templehof airfield. In San Francisco delegates were drawing up the constitution of the United Nations. In Bedford the last cross-country race was won by Alf Nunn.

> *Now it 'belongs to the ages' to the closing chapter of Owen's stay in Bedford. In years to come, when we are plodding over our own course along the lanes of Totteridge we shall look back with affection and delight to these our initial efforts up Cemetery Hill, over the ploughed field and round by Clapham Oak.*
>
> *Arrow*, Trinity '45

Finally, baseball, or more frequently, softball. The Yanks arrived, made friends and supplied equipment. At the Friday Evening Club the 'school's expert' D.W.Cowling gave an epidiascope lecture on the game and its history in America and Britain. We formed teams in the park and gave them names.

> Played baseball with the Bedford City Giants. We had a senior boy who was in the Hornsey Red Sox. I forget his name but remember that the Red Sox beat the American All Stars team when they came to the UK.
>
> IA

Whether we would have played softball, fives, tennis, rowed, run cross-country or swum with such frequency had there been no war it is impossible to say but it seems unlikely. One of the attractions of the unfamiliar sports was their democracy. They were unfamiliar to virtually everybody. We learned from scratch together. A level playing field, though by no means literally.

17

'The Age of Bedfordian Football'

Out of our league–but who would have believed it?

Bedford had one advantage over London: the school playing field was a short bike ride or a decent walk from the school itself. Located to the south east of town, its presence could be detected by the smell. For the field belonged to the adjacent factory. The factory belonged to Meltis and the smell belonged to chocolate. Chocolate was soon put 'on ration' but the smell was there for the duration, suggesting to some of us that it was a ruse to fool German spies into believing that the factory was still on a pre-1939 footing and not engaged upon some vital war work.

Bernard Fox's landlord

> ... worked in the Meltis sweet factory in a reserved occupation. I never learned what in fact he did. BF

In 1940 bands of wire were stretched across the field, between the football pitches, to entrap invading Nazi gliders.

The *Arrow* for Michaelmas 1939 contains no reports of soccer. Games were played but among ourselves, between houses and in the lower school between forms. But outside, the school played no competitive soccer. The local schools played rugby. The soccer captain voiced his frustration in the spring of 1940.

> *The war has had a doubly disastrous effect on the Football Club, this season. First, because the fixture list has necessarily been altered and cut beyond recognition, and, secondly, because this has happened when the school team is, in my opinion, the best for some years.*
> R.E. Davenport, *Arrow*, Lent '40

134

Four matches were arranged and played in that second term of the war: one against the masters, one against a local village side and two against Saint Cuthbert's Reserves, a thriving club connected to a church in a working class area. For the first of the games against the more mature Saints the team was reinforced with three masters. Owen's lost 1-2. In the second game, without the benefit of staff, Owen's fought back from 0-2 to draw 2-2.

So began a wartime history of competing mostly against youngish adults rather than schoolboys. This did the school's prowess no harm at all. The opposition was varied: first it was works teams, village teams, athletic clubs; then Forces' elevens; eventually a few schools. One, Rye Grammar, was evacuated to Bedford. Matches with the others took place mostly away from Bedford, mostly in the holidays or half term, sometimes in London, bombing permitting. Aldenham, an up-market public school shares its governing body with Owen's, the Worshipful Company of Brewers. John Webber remembers the contrasting adversaries.

> ...The 'Shiners' a window cleaning XI (a rough lot) and a posh lot Aldenham Public School, Radlett. JW

> My best memory of the Meltis Ground was of a 2nd eleven game against a team from a firm of window cleaners who called themselves 'The Shiners'. Their goalkeeper turned out in his firm's cap with a glossy peak and a very heavy padded cloth. The goals, except for the 1st XI, had no nets and the crossbar rested in slots at the top of the posts. From a corner one of our boys nodded the ball just inside the post and the keeper thrust out both hands, hit the post which leaned outwards and the crossbar fell onto his head. He recovered after a time but his cap saved him. It was one of those incidents that could have been serious but which had us rolling on the grass in mirth. GRo

The Shiners all worked for the same company, Doves. To have called themselves that would hardly have fitted their self-image. They were not above borrowing a player or two from the seemingly less macho London school. Ken Deadman made a couple of guest appearances.

The company had a slogan, 'Somewhere Dove is shining'. There is a cherished, though apocryphal, story that their competitors Church asked a group of Owenians to invent a rival slogan. The result: 'In our Church there are no stained windows'.

There was no second eleven in the first year but in the following Owen's fielded four elevens, including under sixteen and under fourteen. The juniors joined in, playing against the evacuated elementary school teams and had a very promising league going until many of these schools returned to London. As the captain wrote in the *Arrow*, 'Soccer has been revived with added keenness and interest this term'.

Honours were more or less even for the first eleven though the first game went badly.

> *This game was enjoyed by our attack, who somehow found time to watch it; our defence though, found it more like hard work.*
>
> L.W. Madden, *Arrow*, Michaelmas '40

The standard slowly improved. A victory was squeezed out against a works team.

> *The inside forwards dribbled and fiddled in familiar style, and our finish in the centre was up to our usual standard, which is not saying much. But we were a team at last. We had found our footing.*
>
> *Arrow*, Michaelmas '40

One team provided regular and tough opposition - a reform school five miles out of town. Goalkeeper Barry Skeggs recalls

> ... the inmates crowded round my goal and said if I didn't let one in they would burn me with their cigarette ends. Of course I took no notice.
>
> BS

It was not until 1941 that the school first team played against 'normal' pre-war opposition. It served as a benchmark.

> *Our matches against Tollington School were refreshing after playing a whole season against teams heavier and faster than most London school teams. We found ourselves outplaying them.*
>
> R. E. Davenport, *Arrow*, Lent '41

By late autumn 1942 the team captain was able positively to take stock. His comments have an almost Churchillian tone.

> *No one need have any fears for football at Owen's. Three changing and absorbing years have taught us many a profitable lesson and by far the most important is, that if there are setbacks, confidence in our*

> *ability will save things in the end. Never yet has an Owenian team
> disgraced itself or the school on the field and we feel proud to be told
> that we play as good football as any under-eighteen side. So trot out
> gallantly, Football Club, secure in the knowledge that you can show
> them a thing or two. If on the field 'we fill the unforgiving minute'
> with its 'sixty seconds worth of distance run' we shall not fall far short
> of Kipling's idea of a man. Something stronger than a tough body in
> football is a rough will; and with a stout heart, a bold plan and a
> song on our lips we shall yet dictate to Fortune.*
>
> L. W. Madden, Arrow, Michaelmas '42

In late October 1943, during the half-term weekend, the school
played in London against the Belgian Institute. 'Rather in the nature of an international' remarked second master, Mr Dixon. In
the same season during the Christmas holidays two more games
were played in London. The first was against Highgate School.
In September 1939 they had been evacuated to Westward Ho in
Devonshire. They had returned to Highgate, however, in January
1943. Highgate had a formidable reputation.

> *This was a great day for Owen's football. The cynics said, 'Why,
> they've even beaten Aldenham. What can we expect?' However,
> nothing daunted, the team accompanied by a motley crew of sup-
> porters, climbed the dizzy heights of Highgate Hill to give Highgate
> their first beating by a school team on their own ground for ten years.
> The ground was rather muddy, and our opponents much heavier; but
> we came out on top. The team was not quite as fast as usual, but we
> may well blame the after-effects of Christmas over-indulgence.*
>
> H. Seaborn, Arrow, Lent '44

The following day – the after-effects presumably well and truly
over – the team met and defeated Hornsey Police.

There was optimism in early 1944. The war could soon be over.
A 'veteran' footballer contributed his thoughts: nostalgia for the
old school ground in Whetstone and anticipation of the coming
season.

> *Now we remember that we are among the last of those evacuated to
> Bedford to have ever played at Oakleigh Park. Indeed, some even of
> the present 1st XI have never seen the old ground. And we realised
> that the age of Whetstone footballers will, when this present eleven
> leaves, have finished.*

Next year will see the age of Bedfordian football come into its own. We have had our struggles, our hopes, and our disappointments: you have yours to come. We had a high standard to maintain; you must surpass it. Your task, if the school remains in Bedford, will be difficult – Owen's has a reputation for good football. Your task if Owen's returns from exile will be more difficult still. For, among all our former rivals, except Tollington, whom we have played down here, the school's soccer ability will be comparatively unknown. You must ensure that it becomes known, feared and respected.

We, then, the Oakleigh Park footballers, realising that 'the old order changeth, yielding place to new' wish you good luck and successful seasons!

H. Seaborn, *Arrow*, Lent '44

If the adversities of wartime honed the skills of Owenian footballers and made the good better, there were individuals who could have shone in any context. One was Dave Pratt. He built a close friendship with Gordon Brice, a boy from BMS (a rare event) whose interests he managed to divert from rugger to soccer. So successfully that Brice eventually played as a professional for Luton Town and other clubs.

When I was fifteen he arranged for me to get a trial with Luton Town with whom I signed amateur forms and played in a number of games in the wartime leagues. I was asked to go to Wolves by the renowned Major Buckley but declined the opportunity due to travel difficulties and a later college commitment. DAP

George Cowan was another star. He and Pratt were selected to play for 'London Schoolboys in Bedford' against Hertfordshire Schoolboys on the Hitchin Town ground.

George was a splendid goalkeeper and if my goal proved to be the winner, it was only because George made a magnificent penalty save. DAP

Professional soccer, after an initial shutdown for reasons of safety (i.e. the danger of bombs on crowds), was permitted, indeed encouraged, as a relaxing spectator sport. Leagues were regional and teams often unrecognisable from one week to the next. Players would be in the services, occasionally on leave, often transferred (in a military sense that is). Guest players were common and absences on the day quite frequent. One Saturday afternoon,

Owenian soccer ace Ray Schwalb was standing on the terraces to watch Reading when a man circumnavigated the pitch carrying a board with a scrawled message asking if a spectator would like to play. Ray volunteered and, in borrowed gear and wrong size boots, acquitted himself well.

Another spectator: another match. Future rowing blue, Donald Mackay was at the Meltis field. There was no second eleven game for him so with three or four mates he was a sideline supporter with the railway line to Luton at his back.

> Bert Seaborn ... had the ball stripped from him just in front of us. 'Oh Bert!', I said in desperate disconsolation. 'Why don't you come out here and do better?' he snapped. Frank Fenn came to my rescue, though I think he was always equipped with a quip waiting for the right occasion. 'You don't have to be a horse to judge a horseshow'. How true.
>
> DAMM

In spring 1945, when reasons for optimism about the war's successful end were better founded, the captain's notes remained cautious about the future – but not the future of Owen's soccer.

> *One last word. Perhaps – we fervently hope so – next season we shall be back in our own homes. If so, it will mean that Owen's will once again step into the arena of school football. May we therefore, without idle boasting but with justifiable pride, issue a warning to our coming rivals? Watch out, you Londoners! Owen's is preparing for battle again.*
>
> *Arrow*, Lent '45

18

To be a Farmer's Boy

Down to earth farming camps - agriculture shock.

Owen's wanted to help on the land. In the first year of the war 'Gus' Cumming, a master who had done so as a schoolboy in the summers of 1915-18, wrote to local agricultural experts.

> *The Eastern Counties seemed, however, to have all the extra hands they wanted. What with Bedford School and Norwegian refugees, we didn't stand much chance. Well, now if the East were replete, what about the West?*
>
> H. Cumming, *Arrow*, Michaelmas '40

He contacted Bristol University who sounded interested and promised an early reply. Fifty enthusiasts attended a meeting one day after school. All wanted to go. All told their parents. One turned up a couple of days later to enquire what the school was about 'trying to make her son leave school and take up miserably paid farm work?' As for transport, the boys would go west by bike. But then came the 'early reply', three weeks later, 'We were wanted by neither East nor West'.

The Headmaster accordingly wrote a letter to the *Daily Telegraph*. And then things happened.

> *Letters arrived in shoals. Some gave us good advice. Some gave us bad advice. Some thought us foolhardy. Some sent their condolences. Some actually offered us jobs. These were seized upon – except the very best one in the Western Highlands. I thought of my forbears in Nivoulish 'na Briachan, and dropped a bitter tear. Picture Post wanted to come and take our photographs. One lady wrote in red ink and enclosed her photo. Unfortunately, she was under some misap-*

prehension, as she wanted 'a few of your undergraduates with a bit of cash to spare' to come and dig her garden and meet some of General de Gaulle's adherents. I sent her a charming reply, written in my best French, regretting she was living in a scheduled area.

H. Cumming, *Arrow*, Michaelmas '40

Eventually some two dozen Owenians were fixed up in different parts of the country...and different sorts of work. Basil Leverton remembers being allocated to Camoys Court near Stadhampton, Oxfordshire. He returned there to harvest after he left school in 1941 and kept in touch with the widow of the owner until her death. He recorded a contemporary account in the *Arrow*.

In a bout of enthusiasm I volunteered for harvesting – not without trepidation, for I feared my ignorance would prove too much for the most patient of farmers. My first four days of work taught me more about farming than I had learnt in sixteen years. I remember the cowman's disgust on learning that I was still at school: 'Be you staying till you're twenty?' expressed his thoughts. I found that not too much was expected of me, and numerous mistakes were overlooked. Working all day in the open in the perfect weather made me feel very fit, and I returned to London a better man. One unfortunate event marked my visit; the farmer celebrated 'Harvest Home' by falling twenty feet from a rick, with disastrous consequences.

B. Leverton, *Arrow*, Michaelmas '40

This experience sat incongruously with that of Peter Senn.

Squash, golf, swimming, shooting and riding (duly clad in borrowed jodhpurs), with an occasional spot of work, would aptly describe my holiday 'farming' activities.

My employer, owner of a grocer's, haberdasher's and post-office in the village of Queen Camel, Somerset, required me to clear a patch of land in his garden, but my excavating labours were varied either by trips to collect or deliver groceries, and when the postman was absent we took over. The expression on the housemaid's face when, handing her a parcel, I proudly proclaimed 'I'm the postman!' will forever be a delicious memory.

Picnicking in the Mendips and thence to Cheddar, visiting Sherbourne, Wells, Bath and Tewkesbury (where my most poignant memories are evensong at the Abbey and dry Martinis at the 'Bell'),

meeting Somerset characters – one who forecast earthquakes by his lumbago, especially – time passed very pleasantly.
P.D. Senn, *Arrow*, Michaelmas '40

Another intrepid Owenian, R. E. Davenport, wrote of evening tennis parties and playing for the village cricket team against Forces' opposition who included 'a West Indian test player who had recently bagged the wickets of Hutton and Compton'.

As the years passed, so the organisation improved and the work became serious. Individual employment (with a few exceptions) gave way to school farming camps. In the *Arrow* 'Gus' laid down some sound advice for farming aspirants.

> *1. This is a work scheme, not a holiday scheme. The farm labourer's week is sixty hours: that is your minimum. Harvest-time always calls for more. Any boy or parent asking what 'leisure' arrangements are being made should be shot. So, too, should all parents and boys who assure me that the wages paid do not interest them: they merely want to have something to do in the holidays.*
>
> *2. The usual cash payments for juveniles living in are ten to twelve shillings per week. Don't expect any more; you will be disappointed. If you do happen to get any more, treasure it as a windfall.*
>
> *3. Boys should be over sixteen and be prepared to stay throughout the harvest – anything under a month is useless from the farmer's point of view in the present labour shortage.*
> H. Cumming, *Arrow*, Michaelmas '42

And stay they did. It is doubtful whether many of them, after the first day's labours, thought they would last the course.

> We started out under canvas but before not very long the persistent rain drove us into the great barn to keep company with an owl together with one or two rodents. JS
>
> *Arrive with rain, fagged, push bikes uphill, down hill, over stones, into an imposing Elizabethan farmhouse: supper, attic, evacuee beds, thank the Lord, drop off.*
>
> *Awake, arise, feel forever fallen. Introduced to work; weeding by hand of wurzel field; see wurzels when weeds pulled; takes days – night-*

mare; back no longer straight, arms lost sense of touch. Noisy supper with comment, reach attic, thank the Lord, drop off.

Next day, ditto, only easier; repeat again until flax carried; I'm pitching – spear nobody, sweat a lot, laugh a lot. Rain again while waiting for harvest, so brush – hooking – fed up. Dip sheep on Sunday, messy but enjoyable. Outbreak of 'fly', a nuisance; ewe under shed, pretty bad, drag her out, dies in night, dig grave in morning; what a life! Fending [sic] all day, bullocks get on nerves, always in barley, not farmers – cowboys.

L.W. Madden, Arrow, Michaelmas '42

Have you ever weeded a beet field? This one had had the blight, and after about ten minutes my hands were fitfully black. Hoeing turnips is an easy job – if you do it in shifts of five minutes with half-hour breaks. I was hoeing turnips for four days without respite. At last, the unmistakable sound of the cutter could be heard and I was ordered to follow it to 'stook' the corn. First oats, then wheat, then barley!

R.E. Davenport, Arrow, Michaelmas '40

But, as 'Gus' advised, once the painful first week is over there is nothing to beat farm work – and farm food.

Get your hands hard and your back supple and it's good fun. Otherwise, why should four of the groups have reserved their bunks already for next year – even to the extent of leaving their clothes to maintain a sort of squatter's rights?

H. Cumming, Arrow, Michaelmas '42

As regards the unbeatable farm food, there are conflicting opinions.

The conditions at these camps were very basic and the food awful. GS

School agricultural camp at Kirton Lindsey. Lifting potatoes on a lunch of lettuce leaves between plain bread.   AJ

We had lunch supplied by the farmer on the job. It usually consisted of a large piece of bread with a chunk of cheddar cheese. It was great. BF

Chas Baker, on the other hand, remembers not the food but eating by the light of an oil lamp.

By 1943 there were over a thousand harvest camps in Britain.

63,000 children worked on them in their summer holidays.

Owen's ran a farming camp at Upton in Somerset. A rival school from North London, Highbury County, also had a presence there.

A contemporary account penned by the anonymous Tityrus appeared at the end of 1942. It covered an eight week period during which Rostov fell, the Americans landed on Guadalcanal, Churchill went to Moscow, six thousand men (mostly Canadian) raided Dieppe, Rommel was pushed back in North Africa and there was street fighting in Stalingrad.

> Between July 27th and September 25th we had at least 124 meals and the orderlies, on an average, must each have peeled no less than 1,000 potatoes. Together with some 18 Highbury boys we did over 3,000 hours farm work. From this the ardent statistician will gather that one hour's farm work can be produced by 1.2 potatoes, since there were six orderlies...we were fortunate in possessing two very capable cooks in D.M. Jones and J.Price, both of whom could turn out a very pretty Home Guard pudding, thereby winning the respect (temporarily, at any rate) of Highbury.
>
> D.M. Jones, *Arrow*, Michaelmas '42

The same D.M. Jones recalls the scene a little differently a half-century later.

> J. Price and I were camp cooks and porridge burnt in the billy can.
>
> DMJ

Kevin Seeger would appear to have been more efficient. Having attended one farming camp, he opted to go again as one of the cooks believing the work to be preferable to weeding.

> We had to be up in the morning about an hour earlier than the working party to prepare breakfast. The porridge was always made the night before and put into a hay box overnight where it continued to cook and was piping hot in the morning.   KCS

> I got up early to make scrambled eggs for thirty. Using dried egg powder, of course, with water and milk. I managed to burn it. Most of it got eaten though.   DEB

Life was hard and life was fun.

Talking in tents after lights out resulted in an impromptu mass beating in the marquee. We queued, bending low, each to receive a resounding whack from 'Nobby' Knowles. For a treat we were taken to see the movie *French Without Tears*.   DMJ

We had a particularly unpleasant person in our party, I can't remember exactly what he did but it warranted the old fashioned, well tried and very effective Owenian punishment, namely, the blacking of the posterior with shoe polish. Not taking his punishment 'like a man', he told the master in charge 'Boo Boo' Davison, who, for some reason thought I knew all about it. I was duly summoned and told that 'you could rest assured that whoever was responsible would be sent home immediately'. I had to find out who was involved and report back. I did...with every single member of the camp's signature...needless to say nothing more was heard of the incident.   RCa

The work was varied.

... Potato picking, pea picking, weeding huge fields, onion shaking, getting drunk on rough cider, feeling ill on trying Turkish cigarettes (I've never smoked since).   DHS

I was meant to be carting sheaves from a field some distance away. I tethered the horse too tightly. It went round and round in the middle of the field.   IW

We pulled sugar beet in a field that seemed to go on forever. I got the unlucky job of going down a row wearing a sack banging the beet together to clear the mud and leaving them for the next chap to pick up, chop off the heads and throw into the cart which always seemed to be coming round too quickly!   RN

Very often the work was weeding and the use of any tools rather limited. On one occasion it was a field of young onions and the distinction between leeks and onions is not very great. We worked on our hands and knees down the rows. You can imagine our disgust when the following day we discovered that the field had been ploughed up because the crop was not a good one.   KCS

I helped to get in the harvest learning how to make stooks with the sheaves of wheat, how to use a pitchfork and how to make wheat stacks to store the wheat until the threshing machine arrived. Then I was given the job to clear away the chaff. At first it was easy but as the day wore on it became very difficult as there was so much of it and it was hard to clear it away from the machine. One got covered in dust. I was promoted to unloading the sheaves of wheat from the stacks on to the trucks to go to the threshing machine. The skill in taking down the stack was to make sure that it did not collapse. Eventually, I was allowed to unload the wheat from the truck and toss it up with a pitchfork to one of the men who fed it into the thresher. There were many other jobs around the farm, most of them of a back breaking variety: potato and pea picking, weeding, hoeing, etc. We were paid for the work, which was great, and when the four weeks were over we were very fit.   BF

In the summers of 1941 and 1942, Derek Davis, Rob Weston, Tom Dimmock and I went to help gather the harvest at a farm near the village of Terling in Essex. The farm was owned by a former Colonel of the Gurkha Regiment, who had a badly bowed leg from a wound. Our quarters was a room over the stable with four mattresses on the floor which suited us well once we had grown used to the smell. It was hard work and long hours and the Colonel was the hardest worker of all. We were well fed and we were invited into the sitting room each evening to hear the 9pm news on the radio. With four horses to work with we each adopted one and enjoyed grooming them at the end of each day.   GRo

Gerry Shaw, of course, was less pleased with food and conditions.

I even recall us having to go on strike due to the bad conditions, but it gave us a chance to fraternise with the land girls during our working day, even though we had great opposition from the Italian prisoners of war who worked with us. Another boy, Derek Briggs and I went to a village dance on a Saturday night at a camp in Lincolnshire and struck lucky, meeting two local girls who invited us for tea the following day. Instead of 'hanky panky' at their house we got stuck into the food because we were starving – and they must have thought London boys were very different from the norm!   GS

London boys, for their part, were often surprised by the locals.

I remember one of the old farm workers telling me that he had never been to Doncaster which could not have been much more than ten miles away and did not believe our story of trolley buses and how they worked.   RN

Owenians, by and large, enjoyed the life.

We stayed in an old Rectory. During the day we had the backbreaking job of potato picking. Being 'orrible boys we found that if the tractor was going too fast we would, when we stopped for a break, put a potato over the exhaust which meant the tractor wouldn't start!　　RCa

Farming camps were the thing during the longer summer holidays when we were unable to go home to London. Great fun! Ten shillings a week with perhaps an extra pound as a bonus at the end of a 4-5 week stint.　　DAP

Sometime later…

On another farm the farmer had a Jaguar. In his absence, an Owenian tried to drive it in the driveway and succeeded in reversing it into a rockery and so puncturing the petrol tank. No bonus that year!　DAP

Many of the most deeply etched memories concern the staff.

First thing we did at Haxey farming camp was digging the latrines. I remember 'Pop' Dixon coming round and trying to get me to drink Senna tea to keep me regular. I said I would if he would. Then I thought I hope nobody else says that to him.　　HG

At camp sleeping on straw-filled palliasses on dormitory floors. One large chamberpot per room, each emptying it in turn and facing the twin challenge of a utensil filled to the brim and a gauntlet of jostling boys. In flagrant defiance of the regulations, out of the window it goes. Nobody knew that 'Boo Boo' passed beneath returning from the local. *Après moi*, it could have accounted for the reduced rations.　　AJ

Little did I know that the very first experience of life in the raw was to happen in the serenity of this camp. The adult ladies and gentlemen camp leaders always went swimming in the nearby river early in the morning. Upon their return they would dry themselves in their tents. However, one of the female members decided not to close her tent flap, turned stark naked towards where us little boys were and smilingly, full frontally, talked to us. I say no more other than I liked what I saw and still do!　　RCa

A more rural encounter involved Martin Mitchell.

The farm was near Boston, a small market town in Lincolnshire, not all that far from King's Lynn. Our task was 'stooking', placing sheaves of bound grain stalks in upright orderly rows. It is tiresome work and, for the less conscientious, skiving off was routine. So it was that one afternoon I joined Tom, the farmer's son.

'Come and see our bull.' His face was full of mischief. When we got to the field I could see why he was so gleeful. The bull was in the act of mounting a cow. 'Come on, let's get closer. What a whopper!' He spoke with a proprietorial pride. And, indeed, it was most impressive. Just as it was about to enter, the bull saw us, gave a frightening bellow, slid off the cow, spattered her rear and sides and came charging at us. It was terrifying. We got out of the field as fast as we could run and just managed to pull the gate shut. But our ordeal was anything but over. I felt a powerful blow to the head and Tom was sent spinning. His father had witnessed the fiasco and was beside himself with rage. 'You fools, you idiots. You've cost me at least one calf. That bloody bull's expensive. You'll pay for this,' he yelled at his son, 'and as for you, you can eff off'. He reported me to 'Gus' who was in charge of us. 'It's back to Bedford, my boy,' said 'Gus' with a heavy sigh. I never went farming again.   MM

John Stockton and his colleagues weeded cabbages in the company of a veritable caricature of a Somerset yokel, who all day, every day, sang a succession of lewd ballads.

All in our tent were anon singing word-for-word (I shall here go so far as to repeat the opening lines of one of these genuine folk-songs).

> *I took my maid for a ramble*
> *Along a country lane.*
> *I gave her a shilling, she weren't willing,*
> *So I gave 'er 'alf a crown...*

The next – and final – verse had the same quality of brevity, but packed in a quite unacceptable level of bucolic obscenity. But this folk ballad became, for all but one of the occupants of our tent (something of a man of faith), the unfailing lullaby at 'lights out' played on a bugle...It is, perhaps, somewhat sad to think that this rather disgusting example of West Country Work Songs is one of the very few surviving mementos of this particular Owenian agricultural undertaking.   JS

In addition to the scheduled camps there were occasional *ad hoc* farming jobs in the environs of Bedford. This sample of the real thing had limited attraction for some...

Away from Bedford I did a limited amount of farm work one harvest time, chiefly stooking corn. Quite enjoyable actually on a nice day but not something I ever wanted to do much of. I suppose I was, and am, irredeemably 'townie'   JL

... but in no way dissuaded others.

We did some agricultural work going pea picking locally, I believe outside Elstow.   RN

Most years I went farming organised by the school, usually in Lincolnshire. On one occasion my brother was at RAF Cranwell and I met up with him in the Grapes, Sleaford on a few nights. I also did a stint of freelance farming in August 1944 at a farm just outside Kempston. Working 9am to 7pm, 5 days earned me two pounds, three shillings and fourpence.   KD

Henry George, however, managed a little better, if a little fortuitously.

We'd go farming from Bedford on odd days. Went by lorry with ladies. One day one of the ladies said, ' Don't do any work, we're on strike, we want a shilling a bag.' Got 14 shillings for a day. Good money.   HG

Lorries were organised by the War Agricultural Executive.

In the spring and summer months there were one or two lorries and anyone who wanted to could get on about nine in the morning and spend the day in the fields planting onions, picking peas, raking potatoes or whatever. It was quite enjoyable and adventurous and gave you a holiday from school and it had a financial benefit at the end of it. Occasionally, when in Bedford, instead of going to school, you could leave your bike in the square (no problem with it getting pinched then) and hop onto the lorry. There were a few native farm workers there and some Italian prisoners of war and the Land Girls who were more interesting than the natives!   HCu

But what did the school think about Harry Cuming's non-appearance?

Can't remember ever having some ingenious excuse. The whole existence encouraged initiative and independence...we were given enormous amounts of responsibility.   HCu

Memories are idyllic and exciting.

The River Barle was crystal clear and an icy swim. We sampled scrumpy. This was Lorna Doone country.   DMJ

In May 1943 we were on a farm very near to RAF Cranwell and each day a dozen or so Lancaster bombers flew over at treetop level to our great excitement. Shortly after, we heard that these planes had carried out the Dam Busters' raid. What we had seen were the practice flights—beneath the radar.   DAP

Yes, there was a war on – and, as Chapter 36 relates, many Owenian young farmers experienced it first hand.

19

'A Most Enlightening Experience'

We make our own entertainment - and surprise ourselves.

In 1938 the Senior Chief Inspector of the Board of Education predicted that an evacuated school would probably operate a double shift system with a local equivalent. Therefore 'some thought should be given to ways of occupying the spare time that children would have at their disposal.'[1]

He recommended that both native and evacuated children should be as fully occupied as possible during that part of the day that school buildings were not available. At all costs the children should be provided with means of ignoring 'those opportunities for mischief, boredom or unhappiness which a superabundant leisure may produce.'[2]

In the early days of the war, under the guidance of hard-working teaching staff, various activities were enjoyed – sports, walks, visits, after hours talk etc. The 'opportunities for mischief' were less frequent as soon as supplementary buildings were organised for morning lessons. Here again, the education authorities were prescient. A Board of Education circular issued a few days before the war recommended that those schools operating a double shift system should secure other buildings

> 'to eke out the accommodation' and to provide some shelter for the school which was not in session. So far as possible the visiting school was to retain its own individuality as a separate unit with which its pupils would be familiar although there would naturally be scope for close collaboration with the local school.[3]

Owen's retained its own individuality all right – with team activi-

151

ties both inside and outside the school building. Choice was the problem, not boredom.

Every generation is told by its predecessors: 'in my day we made our own entertainment'. Wartime Owen's did. Of course, some boys were used to the experience. Bill Whitebread for instance.

> Before the war I was in a Scout troop which, being founded from a church choir, had musical talents which were often displayed at concerts and Gang Shows – including the famous London Gang Show by Ralph Reader and his 'Boy Scout' pageant at the Albert Hall. When a Scout Troop was formed in Bedford, this pre-war experience proved invaluable at camp-fire sing songs.   WJW

In a sense, Owen's was a twenty-four hour school. The boys' welfare was the school's responsibility. Teachers would, when required, act *in loco parentis* and supervise out-of-school activities. These would continue, despite the blackout, after the final bell, in locations around the town. And the school's concern extended to the weekend. There was a Saturday morning chess club and another in the afternoon called simply the Saturday Afternoon Club. Mr Olphin recalled its early days in Spring 1941.

> *Winter weekends sometimes drag a little. It's all right when there's snow or skating about. But a wet Saturday afternoon is a different proposition, and it was to fill this gap that the 'Saturday Afternoon Club' was started. The idea was to provide some sort of show every Saturday during the winter months for boys in the school and their friends. The backbone of the programme has been the picture shows, and for these our thanks are due to Mr Davies of the Richard Cobden School (evacuated from Camden Town) who has so gladly given his time and advice for our entertainment. During the Lent term we have tried to put on a more varied programme. We are prepared to try anything – once.*
>
> H.K. Olphin, *Arrow*, Lent '41

> At the Saturday Afternoon Club a magician entertained us. He picked up a top hat and asked the audience of eleven to twelve-year-olds what they would like to have from the magic hat. We all shouted out the obvious requests (money, sweets etc). 'Did I hear petrol coupons?' asked the magician pulling out a petrol coupon. No he didn't.   DEB

The club met opposite the school, above Braggins the drapers, in the Victory Hall which, according to Bedford archivist, Richard

Wildman, began life as the Victory Tea Rooms, set up by two ladies after the armistice in 1918. This also housed the more serious, *quasi* adult, congregation known as the Friday Evening Club. Its original location was the church hall on Goldington Green.

It was a good place for beetle drives – and meeting the local girls.   JL

Neither facility, however, was on offer at the Friday Evening Club.

Geoff Rowley was one of the club's progenitors.

I always looked on the Friday Evening Club as my baby. The format of a moderately serious first half and a lighter second half, led to the second half becoming a variety show which I compèred and helped to organise.

GRo

Strange to relate, it was not till Spring 1942 that the club merited a mention in the *Arrow*.

It is to the ideas, persistent efforts and guidance of Mr Olphin that the club owes its existence and to him and his production council of form representatives it owes the quality of its shows. Nurtured by them the baby has reached the lusty youngster stage, full of verve and vitality. It is now a favourite in the school. Almost an institution, in fact. But it wouldn't have been but for Mr Olphin.

To see Owen's at play is a most enlightening experience. At first, it is true, there were comedians and mimics in abundance – but a few good ones. Musicians had ambitions – but not the ability to realise them. Ideas, too, were not inexhaustive, and the means of implementing these limited. Yet out of such confused elements has come a succession of hot turns – the Music Hall Boys, the Ranch hands, the Gay White Coons* – turns with originality and some neat touches.*

Anon, *Arrow*, Lent '42

As noted above, there was always a serious element cheek-by-jowl with the fun. Sometimes the prefects held forth on matters of the moment, such as co-education.

---

* Gay White Coons – in those non-PC days – was a regular BBC minstrel show, i.e. white singers and musicians (mostly banjo players) who put on 'black face'.

> *We heard at first hand scathing invective clothed in the veil of innuendo.*
>
> Anon, *Arrow*, Lent '42

The popular BBC programme, the *Brains Trust* (see Chapter 25) sired an Owenian version formed by the teaching staff with the Headmaster the question master.

> *We learned that boys should not swell wartime queues, that work is actually done in co-ed schools, that history is a means of stating the obvious, that revolution is part of evolution, and bluff means success.*
>
> Anon, *Arrow*, Lent '42

The variety programme was accompanied by an orchestra ('one piano, one fiddle, and a ukulele out of pitch'). Frank Fenn could do a mean Max Miller.

> *Fenn and Perrin did their lifelike impersonations. The former can almost make us believe that the Holborn favourite is there; the latter's characters talk amazingly like Perrin, but Napoleon's farewell to his troops was a novel touch.*
>
> Anon, *Arrow*, Lent '42

The idiosyncratic character of the club was never better caught than in this conclusion.

> *We know that the prefects can prevaricate, and the masters educate. The boys supply the humour. Of fun, fiddling, fooling, we have them all, not to mention enlightening instruction. Maybe not the slickest of shows, but we would back it against many. And anyway what do we care? We are at play.*
>
> Anon, *Arrow*, Lent '42

The format was retained throughout the club's history. The *Brains Trust* returned the following term. Alas, Frank Fenn was unable to appear in the variety show but 'Lily' Groom led a chorus including 'Flooge' Rans, Nat Solomon, and Mick Hooley in the ever-popular *Captain Ginger*. Other stalwarts over the years included Joss Ackland, 'Nobby' Madden, 'Dippy' Draper, Geoff Rowley, George Cope and, of course, Frank Fenn.

> *Resident pianist Marius Parker, played sweet and sentimental arrangements of two evergreens of jazz, while, in direct contrast to*

Bill Bailey, our Bill gave a faultless arrangement of Lady be Good *followed by boogie bashed out in his own inimitable technique. Huggins tried a creditable best with an arrangement of two concertos – Tchaikowski in B mi. and Grieg. Although the piano is unsuited for such a task, the effect was very sound. Then came an entirely new venture. 'Six claws on a Jo.' William Bailey with his Basie swing, Parker smacking melodious chords in the middle regions, and Hooley beating an effective eight beat bass. The three combined to play a* 'Dark Town Strutters' *that has never been equalled.*

Undoubtedly Ovis was the high spot of the show, a performance even more creditable in view of the fact that he took the job on a moment's notice. His perfect imitation of Tommy Trinder (complete with straw hat), and of that low aristocrat, Vic Oliver (for which he played a squeaky violin), were his masterpieces, while his pièce de resistance *was Disney's* Donald Duck.

Anon, Arrow, Lent '42

The following term marked the passing on of old stagers (Bailey, Perrin and Parker). But a new pianist was discovered in the shape of Mr 'Jigger' Cohen. And the ever-resourceful Mr Olphin opened the first show of the term with an illustrated lecture on the historical cartoon. 'Nobby' Madden followed that with one on Jazz.

The next subject was 'Is History Beneficial?' As usual Mr Bronkhorst dragged in what is for him the ever-fascinating subject of the opposite sex on the excuse that we learn by our mistakes.

Once more the show has gone on with the serious and the light, the topical and tomfoolery. Musical solos, duets, mimicry and Solomon have been our menu. The lectures have been of a high standard and the acts have at least been vigorous.

P. J. Saunders. *Arrow*, Michaelmas '42

The next term's report again regretted the end of an era and the fact that the search for new talent had not been entirely successful. Though it did result in a song recital by the Headmaster.

The comedy items were interspersed with musical interludes, the best of which was F.V.Hooley's arrangement of the theme from the Warsaw Concerto.

W.F. Fenn, *Arrow*, Lent '43

Other items that term included a debate between the masters and the boys, a school *ITMA*, a photographic quiz, a debate on 'there's no such thing as progress' and a one man show by the chemistry master, Mr G.H.Armitage...

> *who gave us in true Norman Long tradition, 'a song, a smile and a piano.' The songs were of 1890 vintage, the smile was Mr. Armitage's own, and the piano was played by permission of the Modern School.*
> W.F. Fenn, *Arrow*, Lent '43

The report ends, once more, with a passage in the minor key.

> *At the moment there is the possibility of one more show in the present series. After which the Friday Evening Club will go into retirement until next Autumn. Many of the present performers will have left by the time that the club starts again. They feel that they have contributed something to school life by helping to entertain their schoolfellows and hope that those who follow will carry on the good work to the best of their abilities, until the School's exile is over (-and after? Editor.)*
> W.F. Fenn, *Arrow*, Lent '43

The club's best days were past and no report of its activities ever again appeared in the *Arrow*. But memories remain fresh. Frank Fenn, who wrote the last report, recalls being persuaded by Reg Perrin and Geoff Rowley to become involved.

I greatly enjoyed the challenge of putting on some sort of show once a fortnight. Bert Olphin pretty much allowed us to do our own thing and seemed to be quite happy to ignore the many *double-entendres* scattered through our scripts. My own favourite memories include Bert Caplan's sketch smoking a small saxophone, Simon Bronkhorst's singing Kipling's *The Ladies* to ukulele accompaniment; Reg Perrin's impression of a cinema organist; Mick Hooley's muted trumpet solo on 'Jim'; 'Marius B' Parker leading *'Six Claws on a Jo'*; and, of course, 'Lily' Groom with the occasional violin solo and *Captain Ginger*.

As to my own appearances, I always enjoyed doing the Max Miller and Billy Bennett routines and was quite proud of a sketch called 'If Hollywood made a movie of Owen's'. It included, of course, Lionel Barrymore as the headmaster ('Gentlemen of the Brewery') and a Katherine Hepburn impression ('I'm Miss Cast. I'm terribly Miss Cast'),
WFF

Not all acts achieved that standard. David Bernstein partnered Alan Locke in a comedy crosstalk act.

We called ourselves 'Lockjaw and Heartburn, the two ailments'. We were probably right. At least, to judge by the laughter, we weren't contagious.   DEB

'Moggy' Mitchell, on the other hand, won plaudits for a unique act. John Stockton called it

An unforgettable turn as a refugee from, can you believe it, a concentration camp, reminiscing both movingly and hilariously about 'ze little vogel' that he found as a pet, I believe, in the camp – the sheer sophistication of such a piece of 'entertainment', at that particular time, is really quite breath-taking!   JS

The artiste, however, wonders …

I still have a queasy feeling about a sketch I did of a concentration camp inmate lovingly caring for a lame bird. I wonder if it was in the best of taste.   MM

John Stockton believes that the major reward for acquiring fifth form status

… was the immediate access it gave one to the Friday Evening Club, surely an institution that was one of the most precious adornments of the School's Bedford achievements! How marvellously exciting it was, each Friday evening to crowd into the gallery in that hall by the library and to be treated to such an uproarious display of all kinds of talent! *Captain Ginger*, of course, and the night the 'management' got the Headmaster onto the stage to warble, in a baritone fashion, about Grimsby Fishing Trawlers. 'Come back Viking. Come back Daphne etc. etc.' are lyrics, which stay in my mind.   JS

Bill Whitebread has a special memory of Oliver Mitchell on stage.

It was at one of these concerts in my last year that, dressed in 'drag', I sang 'You made me love you' sitting on the Headmaster's knee. Perhaps it was as well that I left a few weeks later!   WJW

Frank Fenn remembers a one-man sketch concerning a light-house keeper – in which Dennis Robinson ran alternately clockwise and anti-clockwise round a chair. Another sketch sticks in his memory.

Soviet version of *Workers Playtime* featuring a Russian Murray and Mooney cross talk act.

Straight Man: Ladies and Gentlemen, by way of a change, a little manifesto entitled 'The Communist Party Manifesto'. A spectre is haunting Europe, the spectre of …

Funny Man: 'Ere I say, I say, I say. What is it that the bourgeoisie and the proletariat inherit?

Straight Man: I don't know. What is it that the bourgeoisie and the proletariat inherit?

Funny Man: Death. It comes to us all.

Straight Man: I've no wish to know that. Kindly leave the Central Committee.   WFF

There were other sources of merriment. The Riverside Tennis Club was an evening haunt.

There were impromptu shows at the Riverside in the evenings. I set up a bar where I served lemonade and tea and bits to eat. I called it Dave's Dive.   DEB

Uniformed Owen's did their entertaining bit at training camps.

We were welcomed to the RAF Smoking Concerts where talented cadets scored great hits.

Arrow, Michaelmas '43

Individual forms put on shows.

I do have a memory of getting together on one or two Saturday mornings when I was in Olphin's IIA, and staging a sort of 'comedy' show which featured Hitler & Co, in which Geoff Dimmock played Goering, his chest covered entirely with medals (the lids of polish tins). I have an idea that it was then we saw the first signs of Joss Ackland's histrionic gifts. Later, in Ben Knowles' IIIA and RA, we also staged Mock Trials and the occasional sketch – one such involved a 'serious' operation, and from the abdomen of the prostrate and anaesthetised Colin Welch, rendered senseless by the apparent injection of pints of brown ale, there was drawn a positive string of alien objects including a chamber pot, a mouse-trap, toilet roll, etc.   JS

And towards the end of the war House Parties were initiated. At the end of Michaelmas 1944 the four houses put on three shows. Cloudesley and Colebrooke merged into Cloudesbrooke. Their show was called 'MY GAG' (the initials of the two house captains,

Malcolm Young and George A. Goold). Two minutes in and a beam was dislodged. Ray (Reading FC) Schwalb held up both it and the show instead of making his entrance.

> *The* pièce de resistance, *however, was the Sinatra Cup. Weintraub informed all and sundry that he couldn't sleep a wink last night, and undaunted by cries of 'Shame' and 'No wonder', pocketed coins benevolently thrown on to the stage by a vociferous audience. The final judgement went to Swinnerton, a close head from Cakebread. Mr Swinatra sang an encore.*
>
> "Amber", Arrow, Lent '45

In the following term's magazine, though there was a report of a show put on by form IVA, a bigger stage assumed precedence. This Arrow is subtitled VICTORY NUMBER and countless Owenian performers did their number in the streets and parks of Bedford and, to all intents and purposes, brought down the curtain on evacuation.

And, sad to relate, on the Friday Evening Club. The editor's parenthetical question in the Arrow of Lent 1942 ('and after?') was answered in the negative. The club was a response to the war situation. As leading light Mick Hooley comments over half a century later:

> Extra mural activities were probably our greatest success. The Friday Evening Club went from strength to strength. Could we have done this in London? FVH

20

Teachers

The unsung 24/7 heroes of the evacuation.

'The teacher has proved himself an able, adaptable and willing horse,' commented *The Times* in late 1941 but warned of 'a danger of overloading him with too many onerous duties.'[1]

> As a teacher I realise how much I owe to those teachers in Bedford – they gave so much time and energy to our education and welfare.
>
> DHS

Retired teacher Doug Sutton speaks for most of us. Time, energy, education, welfare – these chapters are about all four. Demands on the teaching profession arguably were never fiercer. Adjusting to new surroundings at school and whatever passed for home, possibly commuting to London to spend time with family, awaiting call-up if you weren't recognised as being in a reserved occupation, or, if at the other end of the age scale, putting in extra years of longer days.

Teachers were on duty most of their waking hours in a variety of extra-curricular duties. Apart from the sports, hobbies, Scouts, cadet forces mentioned elsewhere, there were the frequent spells of being *in loco parentis*, offering advice, providing treats, tendering sympathy. (Mind you, in those days a shoulder could be offered without raising eyebrows.) Then there were the duties unconnected to schooling – as an air-raid warden, in the Home Guard or fire watching.

(On 5 February 1942 the Headmaster reported to the governing body 'that there had been a satisfactory response by the boys and their parents to the formation of a Home Guard section, that it would be commanded by Mr Pearce and be attached to the

Bedford HQ Company.')[2]

Life changed for individual teachers. As Frank Fenn has reminded us…

> Some of the senior staff stayed on longer than they might have done; some of the existing staff took on responsibilities and exercised an authority they might not otherwise have achieved. Some of the younger and more interesting members of staff went off to war; some of their wartime replacements might not have been employed at Owen's in peacetime.   WFF

> The staffing at Owen's School during the war was very interesting. Maths and science staff found themselves in reserved occupations, the arts subjects were not so lucky and we found ourselves losing younger members of staff to the services. Oliver Mitchell had taken the precaution of persuading several members of staff, who were about to retire in the early years of the war, to stay on. These included George Armitage, Chemistry; W.H. Clarke, Physics; H.G. Dixon, Maths; and also Second Master; and Mr. Jesse Smith, Geography. In place of the younger staff came the first female members of staff including Miss Baker, French; Miss Sherwen, Latin; and Miss Cast, Classics.   AWL

It will be seen that academic standards did not suffer. Jack Levy believes Bedford had an unseen contribution to make.

> It has, of course, to be remembered that Bedford itself was a town with a fine academic tradition. So the infrastructure and psychological atmosphere were there.   JL

To teachers and Bedford Vivian Moses adds bikes.

> Having talked to people in the years since I left, I think we had a remarkably fortunate experience for our secondary education partly because of the calibre of some of the teachers and also because of a sense of community. Here were a group of kids away from home in a congenial environment. Bedford was a small town and we soon became mobile with bicycles so we were able to get around the town very quickly. VM

Whatever the causes, the result was, to Moses, a rounded, educated, well-balanced, and for the most part 'intellectually savvy' group.

The style of teaching was traditional, formal, disciplined – all characteristics we would have recognised at the time – and old-fashioned, which we probably would not.

Doug Sutton recalls his first impression of the school.

> It was well run with a distinct emphasis on the right attitude to work. Homework was a must and you were punished if you failed to do it.
>
> DHS

Alan Locke recalls a school artefact which was part of the discipline.

> I remember that we kept 'journals'. These were in effect school diaries of each individual boy and our examination and our homework results were recorded in them each day of each week. This not only enabled staff to check on how we were doing but also added an incentive to us to try to outstrip our peers. I'm sure it was responsible for the sense of competition among us and when we returned home for holidays, we discovered how much better we were doing than any of our friends who had stayed behind in London and whose education was patchy to say the least. (I mentioned holidays because during the period of the phoney war we went home for Christmas 1939, Easter 1940 and summer 1940.)
>
> AWL

Competition we accepted – not that we could refuse – in sport (it was enshrined in the School song), examinations, social intercourse, as a fact of later life.

Discipline, by and large, we accepted also. It was an unavoidable aspect of total war. We knew from the press, radio and encounters with authority that following rules would improve our chances, whether of survival or a fair share of off-ration goodies.

Whether we had the same respect for authority is another matter. In the classroom authority ostensibly went with the job but in reality had to be earned and teachers who abused their privileged position earned the contempt of their critical pupils. Authority, we knew, was not dictatorship. Dictatorship was what we were fighting. The highest epithet we could give a teacher was 'fair'. We wanted to be treated justly and consistently and if the punishment or harsh word were deserved, so be it.

Authority would be challenged after the war when the side effects could be less threatening. Meanwhile there was a job to be done by us and the nation as a whole. For the duration, authority would be largely unquestioned. Come victory authority's top man would be overthrown – in his own words, 'immediately dismissed... by the British electorate from all further conduct of their affairs'.[3]

Though not as well provided for as Churchill, teachers had various means with which to reinforce authority. They still have, though not all that we students encountered are permissible today. The Headmaster's cane was for the really major offence; one master's small wooden 4 by 2 equivalent for frequent knuckle-rapping; a book thrown across the class to impart hurt rather than learning; the offender made the butt of the class; the imposition of detention after hours; or a verbal rejoinder ranging from the witty one-liner to the sarcastic, even offensive, put down. Most successful – and covertly most admired – was the silent non-reaction, calm in the face of the enemy.

Had we been asked the role of the teacher, most of us would have replied 'to get us through the exams' i.e. General School Certificate (preferably with Matriculation exemption) and, two years later, Higher School Certificate, the forerunners of O and A Levels.

A significant part of traditional teaching was by rote – feeding the memory rather than the mind. Nevertheless, since examiners were testing one's grasp of information rather than one's wisdom, and incidentally checking that the syllabus had been adequately covered, rote worked. Up to a point, says Harold Caplan.

> In the early stage the boys who got the scholarships were ten or eleven and had learned by rote and had an ability to learn quickly. When you got further up the school and had to manipulate knowledge then different brainpower is needed. I can remember people who were top of the class in the second form became rather moderate by the time they got to sixth form.   HC

> The work was very conscientious but not very inspiring. My personal intellectual broadening came when I went into the Forces. School didn't excite me, didn't spark lines of thought, lines of development even though I got prizes and got a place at Cambridge. It was a class based form of teaching and it succeeded.   AH

Dennis Jones, who otherwise regards Owen's wartime educational standards as excellent, believes

Mathematics taught by rote would have benefited from a more philosophical approach. DMJ

One history master had rigorous but different techniques to help pupils prepare for the certificates.

Our teacher was noted for spending the whole lesson dictating notes on the subject. He probably kept the same syllabus notes forever. AD

Certainly subsequent forms found the previous year's notes virtually identical. Each member of the class would copy a complete set of notes if possible during the vacation.

His staff colleague's technique was analytical and, applied elsewhere, might have earned him a living as a tipster.

Dare had an almost mystic ability to forecast questions in both the General School Certificate and Higher School Certificate history papers. By analysing subjects which had gone before, he would regularly come up with ten forecasts of questions in the next examination paper. Since there were only likely to be six questions, he would almost invariably score with at least five. This allowed you to concentrate on those likely subjects to the exclusion of all others with consequent astonishingly high marks. AWL

The teaching was geared to getting you through the School Certificate and, although there was an all round education, it helped people with lesser abilities. BS

All round education? Probably, by the standards of the day. A mixture of arts and sciences and though there was an early separation into C.P. Snow's two cultures, the barriers came down in the Literary and Debating Society. Religious instruction was strictly Anglican. There was no teaching of comparative religion although a sizeable Jewish minority attended a parallel service in the 'gods' during morning assembly. Current affairs did not have to be taught. We were alive to world events and felt close to them. Many of us were also politically active.

Certainly by the sixth form people became serious and there was a learning atmosphere. We used to study together, maybe have discussions but not interchange information. There would be four or five people sitting at the table working away, often in the [school] library.

> The [school] library was an important place for all the boys. It was also a social place.   HC

The classroom, too, was, of course, an important place.

> Our education was firmly class based: no pupil centred teaching for us. A combination of efficient discipline, conscientious teaching, meticulous monitoring of homework and a full teaching timetable with double shifts in the afternoons in the first year, and then morning lessons at various locations in the subsequent years, ensured good exam performances for most of us. Other factors drove educational standards: competition between us to overtake each other in form position; I like to think maybe somewhat romantically, the collective spirit of attachment to the school, and an implicit understanding that we had to perform.
>   MM

The ambience of war and our displacement bred resolution and self-discipline. Another key factor is the route by which some of us got to Owen's School.

> We were scholarship boys coming from inner London with LCC Junior County Scholarships or, if outside the area, with Owen's Foundation Scholarships, and so we were already primed to perform.   MM

Martin Mitchell's mum rewarded him with sixpence for getting the scholarship. Doug Sutton's dad gave him a pound.

> I bought a football shirt, socks and shin pads and football boots and had one and sixpence change, enough to buy at least a dozen Sam Hester's cream buns.   DHS

For boys 'already primed to perform' there were other rewards.

> I went steadily through the fifth form and VIB and VIA without undue effort and having a pretty good time all the way. The form teacher in both sixth form years was H.G. Dixon, a brilliant mathematics teacher who shared the Upper Sixth maths work with Mr. Hopkins, also an excellent teacher. In fact, I found that when I left in the summer of 1943 to attend Imperial College, having successfully gained the Higher School Certificate in Pure Maths, Applied Maths, Physics and Chemistry, almost all the first year university mathematics had been covered with 'Pop' Dixon!.   JL

In the sixth form Doug Pearce took Zoology, Botany, Physics and

Chemistry.

> The debt one owes to these excellent teachers. There were four of us doing the same subjects – Philip Cashmore, Brian Ellis, Conrad Lynn and myself – and we were all able to get into Medical Schools on our results.   DPe

Geoff Cook is another who recalls sixth form science with affection.

> They were mostly happy years and I remember with much gratitude the influence of George Armitage in Chemistry, C.E. Le Min in Physics and, especially, A.J. Hopkins in mathematics. They were very good teachers and were easily approached.   GCk

Of course, approach was easier in Bedford. Physical and psychological distances were less. Harold Caplan however, expresses a somewhat contradictory view.

> It was an unstimulating sort of education. The books we had were old. Notes were dictated to us which we would learn. We would do a little lab work, chemistry and physics. It was the same in the sixth form. I wasn't much of a student and just did as I was told. I think by the fifth form I started to use my own initiative and teach myself, by reading around the subject. I'm a naturally curious chap so I don't feel it was the quality of the teaching that got me to teach myself. I don't know if it was inspired by the masters but by the time of the School Certificate others seemed to start working and taking things more seriously.   HC

Geoff Rans is also critical.

> We learned 'subjects' from teachers, but not how to think and come to know and embrace new things: for the most part we gave that to one another.   GR

All in all though, judged by academic achievement, subsequent careers and over half a century of contemplation, the record is good.

> We were wonderfully well served by the teachers of our day.   JS

Perhaps sufficient recognition has not been paid.

I think that teachers during evacuation have been a neglected group. For example in the evacuation programmes on Radio 4 in 1999 teachers hardly got a mention.   JL

We shall attempt to compensate a little in the next three chapters.

21

The Headmaster

A meticulous manager in extreme circumstances.

The Headmaster was one of the most remarkable men at his job that I have ever met. He ran the school on the lightest of tight reins and he could afford to do so because all the boys and all the masters knew all the time who was boss. His appearance was very strange with huge bat ears and cheeks so sunken that you thought he would starve to death next month. But the eyes were so alive and alert and the man was so full of energy that you forgot the way he looked. PK

Tall, gaunt, eyes piercing, he could have been a stand-in for Raymond Massey. DEB

Oliver Worden Mitchell's presence was awesome. To be in it, of course, generally meant you had done something wrong. Not always…

I remember my first interview along with my mother when he accepted me for the school. He replied to a question 'Yes, he will certainly go on to university, he is the academic type' so I naturally liked him from that moment. PK

Frank Fenn took longer to appreciate the qualities of the new Headmaster.

Like most of the younger boys in the school, I viewed the arrival of Oliver Mitchell with a certain amount of trepidation. He bore an unfortunate resemblance to Josef Goebbels and had none of Asman's surface amiability. From then on he remained a remote authoritarian figure and I don't remember having any contact with him until late in the fifth form. WFF

168

Things then began to improve.

> Throughout my sixth form life he took a friendly interest in my progress, was always kind and encouraging, and he certainly kept me on a pretty long lead. For a while he tried to counsel me into going to RADA until he realised that my eyesight was deteriorating (perhaps affected by the bombing). He was pleasantly surprised when Dare said that I should try for a History Scholarship in Oxford and, when I applied for my first teaching post, he wrote a positively glowing reference. We were miles apart politically and philosophically, but I cannot do anything but think well of him. WFF

> I have nothing but the greatest admiration and affection for the man even if this is by no means fully shared by all Old Owenians. Apart from what OWM obviously and unarguably achieved in more than simply holding the school together throughout its evacuated life, I have nothing but good memories of his presence and the manner with which he addressed himself to us, collectively and as individuals. JS

Nat Blau remembers the Head's silences.

> From Mr Mitchell I learned to sit and not talk when he was indulging in long pauses, later of great value when I was registrar to Sir Russell Brain, the great neurologist who, though highly and widely knowledgeable, was a poor conversationalist. JNB

There were few pauses, however, in the now legendary confrontation between the two Mitchells, the Headmaster and young Martin.

> It happened in 'Gus''s class. There was I in the front row sitting innocently and inconspicuously, when he suddenly confronted me.
> 'Your badge, in your lapel, what is it?' I knew, instinctively, that whatever answer I gave, would lead to a perilous outcome. 'Just a badge, sir.'
> There was absolute silence in the class. 'Gus' stood next to OWM, a barely suppressed smile lurking on his lips. I took that smile as an expression of alliance with me. The rumour was he didn't get on well with the Head.
> I removed the badge. He looked at it closely. It bore a hammer and sickle and a red star.
> 'Are you a Bolshevik?' he demanded. 'Well, not exactly, Sir.'
> 'Not exactly? What does that mean?'

I really wanted to say that I supported the Bolsheviks against the Mensheviks, having just read about the historic schism between the two factions in 1904. Instead, I said, 'It's just a badge, Sir.'

'Then why do you hide it behind your lapel? Are you ashamed?'

At last, I found some courage, 'No, Sir, but I thought if you saw what it was you would confiscate it.'

'Exactly. It's confiscated, and I want you to report to me after school.' He swept out of the class wrapping his shroud around him.

Later, in his office, he lectured me on the evils of Communism. 'Look, you are an intelligent boy, you get good results – how can you support such an evil system?'

'Well, Sir, the Russians are our allies.'

'And they won't be after the War, mark my words. You won't wear such a badge again in the school, do you understand? Now go.'

'Yes, Sir.' I desperately wanted to ask him what he would do if I wore the Scouts' badge.   MM

Martin Mitchell respected his namesake.

He was a strong, if not very popular, Head who showed considerable leadership in pulling the school together after the disruption of the evacuation and in maintaining the highest academic standards.   MM

He was also a disciplinarian.

I was pleased to find I had been made a school prefect, but less pleased when the new Headmaster, O.W. Mitchell, introduced gowns for prefects. We wore the short black 'bum freezers' with pride at first, but this was soon dispelled by the mockery and jeering we endured from the younger boys. I have often wondered if those gowns stayed the course, but perhaps clothes rationing put an end to them. [No – they stayed. Ed.] I did not enjoy the discipline that fell to the prefects in those difficult times for the school and although I had always been fairly enthusiastic about school, I was rapidly becoming disillusioned with it.   DB

Although I remember OWM as a kind and forgiving man (given the provocation of my 'attitude' from time to time), I must have infuriated him. I found myself at the time quite without sympathy for him. Why? I hated his puritanical attitude towards sex. Did he not know, had he forgotten how interested in sex, pornography, and obscenity adolescent boys are? I – and some others – had passed around some old indecent rhyme, and it came to his attention. Obviously, though, he had to 'do something' (Why?).

OWM: 'Would you want your mother to see this?'

Me: 'Surely, you don't think I was intending to show it to her?'
Responses like this do not endear you. More serious, however, was G.W. Baker's interception of my YCL* mail, which he opened and took to OWM. I was summoned to Mitchell's office. I was extremely angry and asked by what right GWB opened and they both read my mail. He said that he was *in loco parentis*. I told him that my parents did not open my mail and that my membership was legal, the USSR was our ally, and an old boy was head of the Tass agency, my father approved, etc. I find behaviour of this sort incomprehensible, un-forgivable. I was indirectly punished for this, even though he did his duty by me for the most part, and I am grateful for that. The benefit of this to me was to show me how not to treat my schoolboy charges when my turn came.   GR

Oliver Mitchell engendered deep respect, loyalty rather than af-fection. He was the man for the times.

He was a good Headmaster in difficult times and had to lead a very disparate and probably difficult bunch of staff.   AJ

He was pitchforked into a new school in a new, very different environ-ment than he must have envisaged, and made a success of it.   FVH

That success would be recognised by the admission of Owen's into the Headmasters' Conference, the fraternity of public schools.

The cohesion of the school staff, right through the war, was what brought it through the conflict and returned it to what was left of London in 1945. A great deal was due to the remote and autocratic role of the Headmaster, who was younger than many members of his staff, but blessed with a vision of what he wanted the school to be.
(He wanted Owen's to be acknowledged as a Public School and part of the Headmasters' Conference. It was, briefly in 1946-7, but when the post-war Labour Government began to meddle in its status, he thought that this would not continue and he resigned in 1948 to take up the Headmastership of the Royal Grammar School, Newcastle – a Public School.)
His staff had remained loyal, not because they felt isolated in Bedford, but because the tradition was to earn your place in the school and be-come part of it. They enjoyed seeing a continuous stream of boys grow, develop and prosper in their care. They were comparatively well-paid,

* Young Communist League

had job satisfaction and did not want the changed demands that advancement into administration would have meant.

For the boys, though few realised at the time, Bedford offered a safe haven, with few distractions, leaving an opportunity to concentrate on academic excellence that could never have happened in London. AWL

What Mitchell and his staff accomplished during 1939-44 is absolutely admirable. They brought us through a very difficult situation with no great harm done, and the school in good shape for the years to come.

GR

We had a fine Headmaster. OWM was an Owenian and he believed in his school. Doubtless well supported by his senior staff, he took it to Bedford, made it flourish there and brought it back to London in good heart. Quite an achievement! GCk

22

Past Masters

Senior staff's great staying power.

The war meant a longer working life for senior staff. This benefited the school by reinforcing continuity and the senior staff by encouraging the four of them to develop new skills or, indeed, reawaken old ones.

H.G. Dixon

The Second Master (i.e. Deputy Head), sixty at war's outbreak, H.G. Dixon, was heavily involved in planning the school's evacuation from the time of the Munich crisis in 1938. He was a loyal ally of Mitchell whom he had taught in the Head's previous life as an Owen's schoolboy.

> *I had known that upright figure for thirty-six years... a keen imperturbable, handsome master, speeding along the school corridors... bounding up to the wicket to deliver some of his fast ones with all the verve of a schoolboy.*
>
> O.W. Mitchell, *Arrow*, Lent '48

Dixon himself had also been a schoolboy at Owen's arriving at age eight and leaving for Cambridge as Head of School in 1898.

His added workload in the early days of the war had a downside, particularly for those who appreciated his teaching qualities.

> Dixon was also the Deputy Headmaster and spent a lot of his time doing other jobs so missed a lot of his lessons. HC

Jack Levy calls him 'a brilliant mathematics teacher' – and Mitchell, in his tribute on Dixon's death in February 1948, 'the supreme example of an English schoolmaster.'

One advantage of a life lived at the one school is that you can empathise more easily with your audience. Part of him remained a schoolboy.

> He always put questions in the form of an anecdote which started with 'I was walking down the Balls Pond Road when a lady dropped a pease pudding on my head from a third floor window; if the pudding weighed 1½ pounds and the height of the window was 50 feet what was the force or speed with which it contacted my head?' etc. CL

> For School Cert and below he was one of the two best maths teachers I have ever come across. It was my great fortune to be demoted to the maths 'chuck outs'. WFF

This meant for Frank Fenn, coming under the influence of Dixon. Later in his teaching life he used 'Pop''s routines.

> When you were taught maths by 'Pop' you stayed taught. WFF

Hamlet Gell Dixon was Second Master for the greater part of the war. Too avuncular and close to the boys ever to have made Headmaster, he was the bridge between boys and staff. His calming and modifying demeanour had a great steadying influence on the school. He was responsible not only for the evacuation of Owen's but also for its early reassembly in Islington.

He came back to the London school premises in 1944 after the V1 doodle-bugs and during the V2 rockets to re-establish a second form of London-based boys in order to have the school running when the bulk of school returned in 1945, as was expected. He finally retired in 1945 after 44 years.

G.H. Armitage

George Armitage was due to retire in December 1941. He carried on for another three years. He had joined Owen's as second Chemistry Master in 1905 and in World War 1 joined the Royal Naval Air Service (Chemical Section) and worked on the Brock explosive bullet which helped overcome the menace of the Zeppelin.

In the 6th form I took Zoology, Botany, Physics and Chemistry. Mr. George Armitage, the chemistry master, was incredibly good and even gave me private coaching in the school holidays at his home in Barnet.

DPe

In the BMS building during the Chemistry School Certificate paper one boy didn't understand a word in the question. 'Miscible', he pondered out loud and looked enquiringly at the invigilator, Mr. Armitage, who was walking up the aisle. Armitage, without looking at him, uttered the following as a mantra 'Misco, miscere, mixi, mictum.' DEB

I think the teacher I felt closest to later on, when I was in the sixth form, was Armitage. I was very interested in Chemistry at that time and I don't know if he was a good chemist but I liked his lessons. He had a good sense of humour. VM

George Armitage behaved on occasions like a slightly demented conjurer and I still treasure a reported exchange from a chemistry demonstration. Armitage (starting back from the apparatus): And now what have we here? Tebbut: Flags of all the nations and the King? WFF

On his retirement, fellow oldie H.G. Dixon wrote of his 'powers and thoroughness as a teacher and as a disciplinarian' and the resulting contribution to the success and subsequent careers of Owen's scientists.

In the same issue of the *Arrow* the Headmaster praised his immeasurable services to the school

> *No one has done more to help the school during the last five years...*
> *my warmest and sincerest gratitude to him and Mrs. Armitage for*
> *standing by the ship during the worst storms, at no small sacrifice to*
> *themselves, long after they were quite honourably free to go.*
>
> O.W. Mitchell, *Arrow*, Michaelmas '44

J. Smith

Another who honourably stayed on was Jesse Smith who is remembered, it must be said, less for the geography he taught, than for other subjects and anecdotes, not all of them apocryphal.

He was rather deaf so a boy would go to the front of the class holding a pencil and penknife and ask *sotto voce* whether he could go to the toilet.

'Yes, do it in the wastepaper basket', Jesse would reply. Uproar in class. We really were bastards.   CL

A gentle man tormented by boys. They nailed his gown to the door. They swayed in unison and denied they were moving. He was much liked.   AJ

Sometimes, before he returned to the classroom, after a liquid lunch, we would tilt all the pictures on the walls, put all the desks skew-wiff and turn his desk around. On seeing this on one occasion he put his hand to his head and retired very rapidly.   CL

Dare wrote of him at the time of his retirement:

> *He was a man of many parts and seemed able to handle a variety of subjects – English, Maths, Latin, French – with equal facility and thoroughness... Geography he made a living reality.*
>
> *Arrow*, Michaelmas '46

To many, such as Barry Skeggs, Jesse Smith was a marvellous teacher. He remembers a great day.

> 'There is not going to be a geography lesson today, instead we are all going to listen to something which will be yours for keeps. Many of you won't be going to university and I am going to teach you about the Stock Exchange so listen very carefully.'   At the end of the lesson each of us was given a share in the Stock Market and we had to follow it up in the weekends. He said if you watch your yield and study it carefully, you won't go wrong and you will always have an income. I was given Triplex. Triplex was a glass that every car had to use. The shares cost 33 pence at the time. When I left three years later it was worth just 35 pence and I asked how this could happen and was told that the directors had expensive lunches!   BS

W.H. Clarke

The last of the quartet of senior citizens was W.H. Clarke, who retired in July 1942 having served the school almost forty years. A Fellow of the Physical Society, he was respected for his clarity of intellect, an attribute much in evidence during the Czech Crisis of 1938 and the real thing the following year.

Not for the first time does a tribute in the school magazine refer to the power of discipline.

He was there to do a certain job and the boys under him were there to do another, and he saw to it that these jobs were done... As discipline is the one thing education and the world today needs perhaps more than any other, we are most thankful for his sound, virile and realistic powers of control.

H.N. Asman/H.G. Dixon, *Arrow*, Trinity '43

He was known as 'Point' allegedly because he used the word many times in class. Those of us with little enthusiasm or little application for physics would count the usage and bets would be wagered. The philistines would also listen out for something else.

Mr Clarke was a physics master who had a slight lisp, so that when he announced in electrostatics an experiment with a 'pith-ball' it gave rise to giggles and smirks behind hands, to which his response was 'there is a certain amount of lewdity in this class!'   CL

None of the science staff impinged much upon my consciousness unless they possessed qualities suitable for imitation or parody – 'Point' Clarke's curious way of saying 'pith-balls' and 'porous pots' and so on.

WFF

But he was respected by all who sat is his class – if not at the time then certainly in later years.

The boys have learned from him that nothing shoddy, nothing second-rate and nothing superficial will do.

H.N. Asman/H.G. Dixon, *Arrow*, Trinity '43

Dixon, Armitage, Smith and Clarke provided continuity, maintained traditions, reinforced discipline and each in his idiosyncratic way gladly gave the school his Indian summer.

23

The Body of the Staff

Pen pictures of pedagogues and pals.

Nobody knew, and few could have imagined, the effect that the upheaval of transporting 380 boys and their teachers could have had on the continuity of the boys' education or on morale – or on the demands, initially mostly extra-curricular, which that upheaval imposed.

> There can be no disputing the fact that Owen's Boys School came through the war as a functioning and successful unit was due to the quality of the staff of the school and to their wives and families.   AWL

Alan Locke also cites two contributing factors:

> The expected immediate bombing of major towns never took place while both warring sides weighed up the situation – and we were fortunate to find ourselves in a large cohesive settled county town blessed with an abundance of good schools.   AWL

The atmosphere in Bedford in the war's early months encouraged many of the staff with wives and children to settle in the town.

> With a few exceptions, the staff's private lives remained private, few boys knowing where they lived, nor seeing any of their children, most of whom went to Bedford schools. Staff simply materialised, as did the boys, at the appointed places and times, for lessons, by bicycle. A very simple, smooth running regime where staff were acknowledged for their seniority, abilities and qualifications and boys were acknowledged in their turn for their eagerness to learn, their wit (very much in evidence) and their *esprit de corps*.   AWL

The body of the staff was made up of career men. They were nobly reinforced by the senior members coming up to retirement age who opted to stay on (see previous chapter) and a third group who would today be referred to as supply teachers. In this group were female staff members.

The career men specialised in English grammar and literature, history, geography and the arts. Teachers of maths and science had special 'reserved status', which gave them near immunity from call-up but the younger members began to disappear as the increasing call of the services took away the youngest then the not-so-young.

The following incomplete roll call of impressions some sixty years later must begin with the one teacher killed in action.

> During the North African campaign, I remember the shock I felt when Mr Mitchell announced during assembly that Mr H.C. Swift had been killed in action. He had been my form master during my first year at Owen's in Islington, in 1938-9. DPe

> The death of Swift in action caused great sorrow. DP

(His obituary appears in Chapter 40.)

Another second form master soon to go off to war was Michael Duane.

> The very first form master we had I remember, I liked him, and I think he taught Latin. He was a nice chap. VM

> I remember Michael Duane (by then in the army) turning up at the Moravian church in command of a tank, which he parked outside while he took 'Gus' and one or two of us for a drink. WFF

> One handsome young member of staff, Mr. Michael Duane returned from the war as a Major in the Tank Regiment and was later to achieve notoriety as Headmaster of Risinghill comprehensive school in North London, or 'Raising Hell' to the education establishment, where his progressive ideas were frowned on by both parents and the local education authority, resulting in his removal from active teaching to a role at the London University Institute of Education. AWL

I met him again in 1960 when I went into teaching. He was my first Headmaster at Risinghill School, not more than three-quarters of a mile from Owen's.   DHS

Many years later, when he had been removed from his headship at Risinghill and had become something of a celebrity in educational circles, I was asked to introduce him as a speaker at a conference in Oxford. He arrived at the last moment and I had no time to identify myself to him. He was a little disconcerted when I began with the words, 'I have great pleasure in introducing Michael Duane. One of his minor claims to fame is that he rendered me valuable assistance in failing School Cert. Latin...'   WFF

J.M. Knowles was remembered differently.

An effective teacher of both Chaucer and Marlowe. He had a talent for getting us to write pastiche and parody.   WFF

The particular master for whom I had – and have – the strongest respect and real affection was J.M Knowles. He had a knowledge and love of English literature in its many forms from the sublime heights to Jerome K. Jerome's *Three Men In A Boat*, which he imparted to a priceless degree...

In the wider role of form master, he administered, guided, and encouraged all the quite disparate individuals in his forms with an effectiveness and lack of partiality that drew from everyone of us the deepest affection and respect. 'Ben' Knowles was a Quaker, most unobtrusively, and I believe a conscientious objector. I have to insist that he could have rendered no greater service to his country than teaching some of its sons!   JS

J.M. Knowles had transferred to Owen's from Highbury County School in January 1941 and returned there in the spring of 1944. In between he successfully took over the newly formed boat club.

But, in addition, we owe him a debt for his keen and personal interest in Farming and Camping. The combined Highbury County and Owen's Camp which he ran each summer in Somerset has been a model of efficiency and good comradeship, and many happy memories will remain with those who were fortunate enough to take part. His versatility has also been admirably demonstrated in his running of the second school Boarding House at 5 Pemberley Avenue. The heavy duties attached in this position – comprising as they did, being father, mother, nurse, guide, philosopher and friend in a large crowd of small orphans of evacuation – might have daunted any other man, but Mr Knowles has shouldered them with his characteristic diligence and conscientiousness, and has thus filled an important place an the organisation of the School in Bedford.

Arrow, Trinity '44

'Gus' Cumming was another who played many parts: drama director, pillar of the Moravians, farming superintendent.

To have seen him urging on the slackers, haranguing the farmers, patching up the halt and lame, or chasing the truant and the delinquent was a delight and an inspiration beyond words.

Arrow, Trinity '44

I was very fond of Cumming. He was my form master in the second form. Although he used to shout a lot you could feel he was a good-natured, caring sort of person. HC

And yet this caring person brandished a weapon.

He could not have existed in today's climate, as his deterrent was a 4 by 2-inch piece of wood which he concealed in his gown and hit out whenever he considered it necessary. This was 'Willy' who was remembered by all who suffered from it and no doubt many scars are visible today! But for all this 'Gus' was loved by all his students and was a great person. GS

His eccentricities (notably 'Guillaume', his 'peace maker') were never overdone. JS

'Gus', clever and odd, with his little 'Willy' tried to convert all to Communism. IA

He was, I think, rather a shy man whose lower school persona (and the whole 'Willy' routine) was an elaborate survival strategy designed to overcome disciplinary problems with small boys in his early days as a teacher. WFF

Frank Fenn was in touch with 'Gus' for a longer period than many of his contemporaries largely because in the later 1950s and early 1960s...

We occupied similar positions in the Further Education sector. We both ran large and successful departments at Walthamstow and Oxford and were often invited as guest speakers and 'stirrers-up' at educational conferences.   WFF

Another member occupied with complementary activities was H.K. ('Bert') Olphin.

He gave me some excellent tutorials in nineteenth century history when I was preparing for the Oxford scholarship.   WFF

George Cowan too benefited from 'Bert''s out-of-class attention.

I was never an enthusiastic scholar until H.K. Olphin told me to cut out sporting activities and do the homework at his house in Goldington. It worked for him and me – scraped through School Certificate. I think I was the first Olphin babysitter. Olphin was a great man and had a great influence on my future life.   GCo

Olphin was one of those members of staff who showed their mettle in rising to the occasion of keeping boys interested and involved.

Bert initiated not only the school allotments for the growing of vegetables but also the Saturday Afternoon Club which involved film shows and light entertainment and also later the Friday Evening Club where the boys entertained themselves with songs, sketches and sniping at the staff.   AWL

Mr Olphin ran the school allotments and the Air Training Corps. He arranged our first flight, in a De Havilland Rapide.   AJ

R.A. Dare, like Olphin, taught history. He had a way of making it stick.

He used for example mnemonics 'But George's Rotten Crazy Gang Never Really Secured Complete Power.' A clue to the initial letters of George III's Prime Ministers.   AJ

So, gentlemen, how can I ever forget you: Messrs Bute, Greville, Rockingham, Chatham, Greville, North, Rockingham, Shelburne, Chatham, Pitt. The mnemonic is now a personal mantra for ancient meditating Owenians.   MM

Once upon a time I knew what the initials stood for. So we were taught history like that… the reasons for this one, two, three, four, there's a mnemonic. I can't say that was the best way of learning but some of it stuck. VM

Dare was addicted to dreadful puns and loved the groans that greeted his efforts. 'General Goddard gave it to the French good and hard.'
WEOJ

'Dicky' Dare brought history to life. Florence Nightingale was not a Vera Lynn, nor was the Charge of the Light Brigade led by Errol Flynn.
JNB

I have a great admiration and the warmest regard for 'Dicky' Dare. He was, if no ball of fire as a personality, the effective teacher of history *par excellence.* JS

(And, we might add, a historian *par excellence* of Owen's School. Ed.)

He had a dry wit. I remember early on in the Lower Sixth he came into class when I was in the middle of some comedy routine or other. He shook his head, bemusedly, 'Fennomenal', he murmured. Many years later, at the 1979 Bedford reunion, he used the same gesture. He had heard from 'Gus' of my work in teaching cinema, the media, popular music and the performing arts. 'Has it ever occurred to you', he asked, 'that truancies and delinquencies of your youth have now been elevated to the status of academic disciplines and University Departments?'

I am immeasurably in his debt for, by example, he taught me my trade and convinced me that teaching was a fit occupation for a grown man. His lessons were always well prepared, well paced and well delivered. His comments were useful and illuminating. In fact, he taught Medieval History so well that I effectively had a term off as an undergraduate – and since it was in that term that I met my future wife perhaps I owe him rather more than a history degree and a future career. WFF

Attitudes to one of the staff were decidedly mixed.

'Flash' (Mr Hardwick) was the best teacher in the school. Strict but fair with a whimsical sense of humour. IA

Many felt the effect of the latter. Particularly Jewish boys.

On receiving his new form at the beginning of term he ordered all the Jewish boys to stand up so that he could see who they were.   GS

Anti-Semitism wasn't strong in the school.

The school had quite a cultural mix. A lot of my friends were Jewish and one or two came from completely different backgrounds. We all seemed to get on very well. We had one situation in the fifth form. There were two boys in the class – Mervyn Crossick who was Jewish and Doug Sutton who wasn't. When they finished their School Certificates they decided to leave and 'Flash' called out to Mervyn Crossick as he left the room, 'Cheerio' and then to Doug Sutton, 'Well I expect you want to be with your Jewish friend,' Doug said, 'Why do you think that, sir?' and Hardwick said 'Well you are Jewish aren't you?' And Doug said, 'No, I'm not.' Hardwick then said 'I have given you such a disservice my son, I always thought you were Jewish.'   BS

Not a gentle man... A Plymouth Brother who walked the Jewish boys on tiptoe by grasping and hoisting their ears. He called young Isaacs 'Ikey Mo'. Not very brotherly.   AJ

Why 'Flash'? I never discovered. He was anything but flash. The only thing flashy about him was his shining cycle clips which he wore back to front. Now I see the appellation was ironic. What was perverse about the man was his anti-Semitism. Pity the poor Jewish victim with the foreign sounding name.
So Bernard Schwachman, for example, had to suffer the indignity of having his name syllabically dismembered and expelled by 'Flash', his face screwed up in distaste. Schw-a-ach-man, the syllables were cast out one by one as if they were repellent insects that had crept into his mouth. Unfortunately for 'Flash', the name Mitchell, even with split syllables, always sounded like Mitchell. I think he held that against me and would often pick on me for being insolent, like the time he demanded that I wiped the smirk off my face which I did with my handkerchief, pleasing my fellow pupils and earning myself a detention.   MM

But most pupils paid tribute to his teaching success – if not all of his methods. Dennis Jones expresses the duality of our attitude towards him.

'Flash' Hardwick, he of stern visage, gammy leg, blue pinstripe, high laced boots and Plymouth Brethrenism, was one to be wary of if found capless, or after lock-up downtown. Spotted from his stately cycling position, this meant a tongue-lashing or detention. Yet, of all my instructors, I received most from dear old 'Flash'. Macbeth, Julius Caesar and Keats' Odes were most favourably imprinted, and my only School Cert. Distinction was in English Literature. DMJ

Although so stern and something of a bully, Hardwick was a good form master, instilling a real sense of the importance of the School Certificate. GCk

When acting as second master he had a small boy hauled in front of him for some offence in a Bedford baker's shop visited by Owen's boys during break. (Cakes were off ration.) He said, 'Do you mean you had the temerity to demand *four* buns? In cubic capacity that almost equals yourself'. WEOJ

Evacuation meant that boys met masters outside the surroundings of school and in different circumstances. As we've seen, Basil Leverton got to know 'Flash' 'more easily and at a more friendly level because of fire watching'.

G.A. Hutchings, however, was rarely off guard, always a strict disciplinarian whether teaching English...

A cold fish – eight column analysis in English grammar. DHS

... or commanding the parade ground as a Flight Lieutenant in the Air Training Corps.

Mr Hopkins was, according to Jack Levy, 'an excellent mathematics teacher'. Harry Cuming provides a eulogy.

I came under the influence of the best master I had the good fortune to be in contact with; Mr. Hopkins was a superb teacher. He had read mathematics at Cambridge. He was very interested in anybody who showed any talent for mathematics and was willing to work at it. Given those two conditions, he would spare no effort to prepare the person for a Cambridge Scholarship or Exhibition. In a way he was a father figure as well. He epitomised very good traditional values, very unflappable, very calm, methodical. Very good at encouraging you and in terms that were quite new. He came up with not just satisfactory but very satisfying proof of a set of reasoning to prove some proposition or another. He would use a phrase like 'that was very elegant'. I was already interested in the subject but he opened up a whole new vista, added dimensions after dimensions to it. When I was about fourteen that was the most important influence as far as I was concerned. HCu

B.L.Vulliamy came to Owen's in February 1941 some months after the occupation of Dinant in Brittany where he had been teaching. An evacuee himself, he soon established a rapport with the boys. A Francophile, often mistaken for French, he was nicknamed 'Bon Bon' (his frequent utterance). He started the Philatelic Society, endured gardening and rather enjoyed fire watching.

> A thoroughly Frenchified Englishman in ginger Harris Tweed jacket with elbow patches, he instructed directly rather than grammatically. The recalcitrant received well-aimed chalk, or cuffing to the point of tinnitus.   DMJ

> He would constantly remove and replace his spectacles. 43 times was the highest I recorded in the lesson.   AJ

The Reverend R.H. ('Tubby') Turner contributed to the school, one son (Russell) and an intimate pre-war knowledge of Bedford, the latter greatly facilitating our smooth transition in September 1939. His links with the town were maintained after the war. He became a governor of the Harpur Trust and had a building in Harpur Central School named after him.

> It was '44 in the Liberal Club and 'Tub' was on patronymics in the Religious Instruction (RI) lesson. He explained that 'Bar' was often a prefix in Jewish names e.g. 'Barjona' meant 'son of Jonah' and that sometimes 'Bar' was used twice, extending to the grandparents. Someone asked what happened if a son left home and didn't want it known who his father or grandfather was. An anonymous voice said 'it would be bar, bar, blacksheep then'.
> 'Tub' initially threatened to 'sock' the joker, but soon dissolved into laughter with the rest of us.   WEOJ

> 'Tubby' Turner wore a clerical collar and shared my early interest in naked women. By which, I mean, he saw me skulking at the back of the Royal County theatre during a Phyllis Dixey performance. Phyllis Dixey stood motionless, as the law required then, with one hand demurely covering her pubic area – I'm not sure that legally she was obliged to do so – while a male artiste knelt submissively at her feet, I left abruptly and to this very day feel thwarted. With a little more self-confidence, I would have stayed. After all, what was *he* doing there?   MM

One of the School's few failings was in athletics and field sports. In 1941 'Taffy' Lloyd left Owen's for a headship in his native Wales and left Owen's without an effective gymnastics teacher.

Gymnastics thus stopped. With the exercise we got by cycling, climbing trees and generally being active, and with a lack of rich food occasioned by rationing, we did not grow fat and lazy, but we remained unskilled at athletics, until the appearance on the staff in the last year of the war of Mr R. Tricker, who had played for Arsenal. On seeing our general state of inadequacy, he instituted 'standard times', where boys were expected to run 100 yards in 15 seconds and in doing so would earn a point for their houses in the school house system. This stimulated an amazing latent interest in athletics and brought out unseen talents in the most unlikely boys, as well as upsetting the order usually prevalent in the school house system.   AWL

This chapter ends with a montage of impressions of teachers, both in 'the body of the staff' and those in support, including surprisingly (for Owen's at that stage) women.

Pearce had a disconcerting habit of going up half an octave when he spoke in French. These days that trait would probably have got him suspected of smoking pot.   WFF

The master who impressed me most was Mr Cyril Le Min who taught physics. 'Butch' Baker the chemistry master read out his lesson from a text book which was open in the drawer of his desk behind which he sat.   JNB

One remembers with fondness Beatrice Cast who was never meant to be a teacher of VIth form French Literature, but made no bad fist of it; I am ever grateful to Mr Le Min who, at the crucial moment of my pre-Matric history appeared at Owen's to make clear to me, for the first time, the basic characteristics of Physics; MrTingay was a very efficient teacher of French, while Miss Lowe was not so efficient when it came to German, but was a disarmingly pleasant woman, while Miss Sherwen was simply a legend sent to warm, even of those who were never actually taught by her, all the cockles of our hearts.   JS

Miss Sherwen, despite our unruly classroom behaviour, coped valiantly with Latin. I particularly resented having to stop the subject at fourth form level.   DMJ

In retrospect, it would have been difficult for women members of staff. I was taught by Alice Sherwen. She had much bad behaviour to deal with but managed to bring Caesar's exploits and the *Aeneid* to life and to instil all those declensions and conjugations.   GCk

Being taught by Miss Baker, a very young pretty geography teacher, was the highlight of my day. She had everyone's attention and my interest in geography took me to 'A level' success and a school prize that surprised my family and me. I do not recall her staying at Owen's very long but she made an impact on my life.

I remember Miss Lowe for whom I had a great deal of sympathy and on whom I look back with sadness. She may have been a fine academic but she could not control Owenians. I believe taking a sleeve of her gown and jamming it between the desk and desktop was a frequent pastime. Throwing chewed pieces (sometimes soaked in ink) of paper at her and the blackboard caused her and me a great deal of distress. These memories were of use to me later in life. This was a terrible form of bullying which I cannot tolerate.

JWes

Miss Sherwen. Did she know what was going on in her class? Smoking — or am I wrong?

IW

John Salmond, who taught physics and was my form master in the third form, knew how to use a ruler... on one's knuckles. He brought magic into physics. With his celebrated Wimshurst machine he could get you to light a Bunsen burner by directing a spark at it from your pointed finger. I can't get anyone to believe me that this happened, not even John Salmond, at ninety!

MM

Mr. Marshall Palmer, whom we shared with Bedford Modern School, taught music. He would hurl music books at offenders. It was the books that suffered.

AJ

We had a biology mistress who must have been in her middle twenties and found us rather a handful. Whether it was because of us (who on one occasion arrived with 'apples for the teacher') or not, she left after the first term. We were then left to cope by ourselves.

BF

And cope they did. All of the biology group became consultants and/or professors of medicine. The wartime generation of Owen's by and large, prospered and think themselves fortunate to have survived the war and to have benefited from an education at times makeshift, in alien though friendly territory, and often uncertain but well founded and thoroughly professional.

24

Generous Auntie

Harmony with BBC fellow evacuees.

No account of life in Britain in WW2 is complete without mentioning the pivotal role of the BBC. For Owenians it has a special meaning. Not only did the BBC provide news, information and entertainment, it became a fellow evacuee and profoundly affected our lives.

When the war started, the BBC Music Department went to Bristol. The Symphony and Theatre Orchestras were based at the Colston Hall. Just over a year later Bristol was under air attack. By the end of July 1941 the department moved. Bristol had in fact seen its last raid but one. (Colston Hall burnt down one night from unknown causes after having safely escaped the raids.)

Sir Adrian Boult describes the search for a new location by the 'corporation emissaries'.

> *They went to eight or ten Mayors with the same question: 'Can you produce two hundred and fifty beds, forty offices under one roof, ten studios of various sizes, including two really big ones for orchestras?' Finally Bedford, already crammed with refugees [sic], gallantly said 'Yes', and set about the preparations. The adaptation of the studios presented problems but worst of all was the question of the forty offices. Two small residential hotels* [the Kingsley and Cavendish Hotels in Bushmead Avenue, near the Embankment — Ed.], *mostly filled by old people, were requisitioned by the Mayor, and I felt awful when I inspected them and wondered how the poor residents would find accommodation elsewhere.*[1]

Boult found Bedford very friendly and took comfort from the fact the 'place was so thickly covered with trees and mist that no invader would be able to find it'.[2]

The first public concert in Bedford took place on 17 September, 1941. Throughout their stay in Bedford, the orchestras gave both studio and public performances, the latter noted in the *Radio Times* of the period (at a weekly price of 2d, unchanged from its first issue on 28 September 1923 until November 1950, when it went up to 3d) simply as coming 'from a concert-hall in the South', presumably to prevent any German music lovers dropping in un-invited.

> The number of concerts, and indeed the amount of broadcast music, was quite remarkable. As well as regular lunchtime (unreserved tickets one shilling) and Wednesday evening concerts at the Corn Exchange, there were very many studio concerts either with no audience or with troops — or boys from Owen's school; some of them were as short as half an hour or 45 minutes. Bedford was so compact that on our bicycles we could get to either of the halls within a few minutes from anywhere in the town; so we went as often as we could.   VM

> The BBC Symphony Orchestra, conducted by Sir Adrian Boult or by his deputy Clarence Raybould, gave public and studio concerts in the Corn Exchange less than a minute's walk from Bedford Modern School.
>   JNB

> We could attend Sunday afternoon concerts from the Hall in Bedford School and there were fortnightly concerts from the Corn Exchange.
>   CL

It was a fast track musical education: informal rehearsals, record-ings, public performances reinforced by the radio and, when pocket money allowed, 78 rpm records.

> We used to wait every week until the *Radio Times* came out to see what was on, then pop round to the BBC offices in Bushmead Avenue and ask Mrs Beckett, Sir Adrian's secretary, for tickets for all the stu-dio concerts and recordings. And we would go five times a week, they were just round the corner, a short cycle ride away and they didn't cost us anything. We were always going, in fact. We had to be in the Corn Exchange before 4.15 and the school assembly did not finish until 4.30 so we used to walk out or not go to the assembly. The Headmaster got quite upset until he heard we were engaged in this cultural activity and then he said, 'OK you can go'.   VM

> The Monday afternoon concert at 4.15 was more alluring than Jewish assembly.
>
> JNB

We were star struck and simultaneously coming to terms with the fact that these celebrities were human, evacuees like ourselves.

> We took in as lodgers two members of the BBC Symphony Orchestra, Joe Young who played violin, and Jack Mackintosh who played the cornet.
>
> JA

Not everybody regarded BBC musicians on a par with Owenians, Ken Deadman's billet family for example.

> Ultimately they did get fed up with me and traded me in for a flautist.
>
> KD

That musician would have received a memorandum:

> *Do not confuse billets with lodgings. The lodger is desirous and desired. You are a billetee. You probably don't want to live in a billet. Remember that it is even more possible that the billeter doesn't want you.*[3]

Flautist Lambert Flack visited the school, played and discussed the flute. We benefited from having great performers in our midst. Julius Isserlis gave a piano recital just for us in the school hall. The orchestra also performed publicly, sometimes specifically for young audiences.

> I remember Malcolm Sargent appearing in front of the audience and explaining the individual pieces about to be played, giving a lively description of the storm in Mendelssohn's *Hebrides Overture*, which is still vivid in my mind – 60 years later!
>
> RD

Adrian Boult, in a typically friendly fellow-evacuee gesture, took a party of boys into a Bedford studio to hear records of *Peter and the Wolf* which the BBC Symphony Orchestra had recently recorded.

> *The charming manner in which we were introduced to each player as his 'piece' occurred on the records was a gesture we shall always remember.*
>
> *Arrow*, Lent '45

Dennis Jones and Alan Locke remember a roll call of musical talent.

Familiar musical faces included Sir Adrian Boult, Sir Thomas Beecham, Basil Cameron, Clarence Raybould, Stanford Robinson (BBC Theatre Orchestra's conductor), horn player Aubrey Brain, gurning bassoonist Archie Camden, clarinettist Fredrick Thurston, and Polish refugee pianist Leff Pouishnoff. DMJ

It was interesting to see the members assembling in the Corn Exchange, fresh from the golf course, like leader Paul Beard, or with pipe alight, like Arthur Gilligan, the tympanist. Sidonie Goosens, the harpist, was always smiling and well dressed. Clarence Raybould and Sir Adrian Boult undertook the bulk of the broadcast and public concerts, but there were lucky ones among us who saw Charlie Munch, Ralph Vaughan Williams and Sir Henry Wood conduct. AWL

And some of us saw and heard Ida Haendel, Myra Hess, Louis Kentner and Yehudi Menuhin. Menuhin came back to Britain in 1943 and 1944, 'hitching a ride in a bomber so that he could play for the people "when it was dark and there was nothing, no assurance, except their faith" '.[4]

Particularly remember Menuhin in 1943 playing Brahms's Violin Concerto and Geoff Rans and myself being completely bowled over by his performance in 1944 of what is now called the Second Bartok concerto. WFF

I shall never forget Yehudi Menuhin playing five yards away from me in the hall at Bedford School. ME

Walking home one evening I saw Leslie Orgel and Vivian Moses waiting in a queue outside the Corn Exchange. They discouraged me from waiting, 'you won't get in'. I thought if they are hopeful, I will also have a try. We all gained admission and heard the first British performance of Bartok's violin concerto, the soloist being none other than Yehudi Menuhin. I cannot say that I enjoyed it then – or even now. Nevertheless a great occasion. JNB

Being among musicians provided insights, particularly if they lived with you.

It was fascinating listening to them discussing the idiosyncrasies of their various conductors: Sir Henry Wood, Malcolm Sargent, Thomas Beecham and Adrian Boult, who was a great favourite. JA

Owenians studied them with deep attention.

We became familiar with the faces, names and individual eccentricities of the performers.   ME

Adrian Boult used his baton in very small movements that, I learned later, followed his teacher, the great Nikisch.   JNB

Nowadays we are used to studying a conductor's movements and expressions as the players might see them through the TV camera. But seated in the hall, one only saw Sir Adrian Boult's back. His military bearing betraying little emotion, or even motion, from behind, but he produced some wonderful responses from the players, particularly in pieces with firm meter. It would be true to say that he did not seem to like Delius! The way in which he removed his jacket was noteworthy. With his back to us, he would unbutton it and shrug his shoulders, so that it slid gently down his back, then just as you were expecting it to hit the floor he would half turn and catch it by the collar, then gently drape it over the rostrum, on his right side.   AWL

In addition to concerts by the full orchestra, there were chamber music recitals in Bedford School broadcast under the title *Music in Miniature.*

It was at one of these concerts that Adrian Boult first came over and spoke to us. After that I often greeted him while he drank a mug of Ovaltine in Woolworth's.   WFF

After performances he would relax with a cup of Ovaltine at the tea-bar that stretched across the end of the store in Woolworth's, where one particular lady, with a shine to him, would see his noble head, well above the flat hats, advancing through the crowd, and the steaming cup would be ready for him by the time he got there.   AWL

Many of the orchestral players lived centrally in the town and became faces we knew, even acquaintances.

Attended BBC orchestral concerts whenever possible partly because my billet was directly opposite the house used by both Sir Adrian Boult and Stanford Robinson and families during their stay in Bedford. I was suitably 'chuffed' to be addressed by my Christian name whenever we met in Waterloo Road.   DAP

I have other memories of the BBC and Owen's: of the queue outside the chippy in Denmark Street (or was it the one in the next street?) with Paul Beard and Marie Wilson immaculate in evening dress after their concert; of Sidonie Goosens at rehearsals, sitting at her harp and knitting; and of the time that the conductor Basil Cameron was standing on the steps of the Corn Exchange after a concert when a group of Owenians were coming out. As we passed him, one of us (was it Ken Deadman?) patted him on the shoulder, winked conspiratorially, and said, 'You can't beat the old tunes can you?'   WFF

Adrian Boult was easy to spot.

Once in a while I would see Boult, with his walrus moustache and wearing gumboots, walking through the Bedford streets.   JA

I shall never forget the sight of Adrian Boult cycling jauntily along Castle Road, dapper as always on his way to work.   ME

One day, when I was walking into town from the sickbay I was overtaken by a car and offered a lift. Seated next to the driver was Sir Adrian dressed appropriately in wellies. When I got in the back I found myself next to a man in American uniform I immediately recognised as Glenn Miller. The journey was all too short. I learned later that Sir Adrian sometimes dropped into the Corn Exchange to watch Miller rehearse.
                                                           WFF

As can be readily appreciated, the BBC were generous with their time. David Price, an accomplished schoolboy violinist, joined the local Bedford Orchestra. It received help from the BBC and from time to time Glenn Miller's drummer sat in. Adrian Boult conducted on occasions.

I was playing with the second violins. He had forgotten his baton but spotting my white bicycle pump asked to borrow it. I fear he found it too unwieldy! And after ten minutes simply used his hands.   DP

The BBC's effect on Owen's was intense - even more so...

... when things hotted up in London and the Promenade concerts came from Bedford.   CL

This season included one of the last appearances of the founder of the Proms, Sir Henry Wood.

We were enthralled not simply by the music and the performances but the professionalism of BBC broadcasting.

The timing of the broadcast was highly precise: at 4.14 the green light went on, and 60 seconds later the red light signalled that we were on the air. Clapping was not permitted. The programme was announced by Alvar Liddell who, once the music began, would walk out. We school-boys were fascinated by his 'brothel creepers' – brown suede shoes with rubber soles - so his steps were inaudible even with very quiet music. I remember being apprehensive that he might come back late at the end of the first piece; but 5-10 seconds before its completion he would creep back and calmly announce, 'You have just heard...' (whatever the item was), 'and in a few moments you will hear...' This was repeated till the end of the hour's programme; after the red light went off, we were allowed to applaud.   JNB

We were introduced to the standard repertoire – and beyond.

Scheherazade bowled me over, especially Paul Beard's violin obligato. I yearned for a 78 album of Rimsky's masterpiece on window display in the Arcade – well beyond my pocket money.   DMJ

I vividly recall symphonies by Bizet which I believe were pioneered in this country by Adrian Boult.   JNB

I well remember the excitement of hearing brand new work by Bartok and Stravinsky both in rehearsal (Menuhin) and at the Corn Exchange concerts, sitting in the balcony for very little money. And the ersatz Proms. We received an excellent introduction to the body of European music. Most of us never forsook this tradition, or the BBC's honourable open-mindedness to new European and English music. Sometimes the experience would be overwhelming: to hear, say, Kathleen Ferrier, early in her career, singing Dvorak's *Stabat Mater*. For all that, I'm forever grateful.   GR

The school owed much to the BBC. At the end of February 1945 one Owenian, Henry George, helped to repay the debt.

I was in Bedford School and noticed a fire in one of the rooms. The fire brigade was called and while they were on their way I got BBC's instruments out of the room.   HG

The Bedford School's magazine, *The Ousel*, devoted four pages to the event without ever mentioning Henry George's contribution. It congratulated members of the school and other helpers for not just waiting 'to see what would happen'...

... before the water could get to it, everything of value that could be moved, had been moved to safety: the records and papers from the Office and Bell Room, the books and furniture from the Head Master's study, the instruments and apparatus of the B.B.C., including two grand pianos, from the Hall, the pictures from the galleries, the form libraries from the classrooms. All this was saved by bands of masters and boys: and your correspondent noticed parents, Old Bedfordians, and friends of the School among the helpers.

The Ousel, 4 April '45

One Old Owenian provided hands-on help in another way.

Recently we have had the added pleasure of hearing the B.B.C. Theatre Orchestra under the baton of one of our Old Boys – Mr Lionel Salter – who after a wide experience of conducting in North Africa and Italy has now joined the B.B.C. in Bedford. His Music from the Footlights *programmes, given a hall so acoustically perfect as that of Bedford School, have been some of the high-spots of our musical experience.*

Anon, *Arrow*, Lent '45

The musical experience of others hit highs in this period. Grant Woodruff of BMS was also an avid attender of rehearsals.

The BMS head of music, Mr Colson, was very close to the evacuated BBC and those of us school choir members sang in an end of war celebration concert. I think one of the works was Vaughan Williams' *A Song of Thanksgiving* for soprano, speaker, choir and orchestra (which VW composed in 1944). The BBC Symphony Orchestra's later 'farewell concert' conducted by Adrian Boult was an emotional occasion to savour. I seem to remember that Ravel's *Bolero* was one of the works performed. GW

Shortly after VE day there was a broadcast Victory performance from Paris of Sir Adrian Boult conducting Beethoven's Seventh symphony. DMJ

We appreciated our good fortune, then and now.

What extraordinary luck it was to have their concerts on our doorstep and to have easy *entrée* to their rehearsals and studio broadcasts. ME

In Spring 1945 the *Arrow* gave voice to our appreciation in a piece headed 'Thanks to the B.B.C.'.

There was one particular privilege for which we are supremely grateful – the opportunity of hearing the B.B.C. Orchestras. We little thought that the reception area to which we had been so summarily dispatched in 1939 would by good fortune become the Mecca of the musical world. The arrival in town of the musical section of the B.B.C. provided an unrivalled opportunity of hearing the finest music performed by first-class orchestras, and we would like here to record our sincere appreciation of the generous freedom with which the B.B.C. has allowed us access to their concerts.

... It will be a sad day in one sense when our school has to return to Islington, and we have to bid goodbye to our friends in the B.B.C. Orchestras and to the B.B.C. Commissionaires. But we sincerely hope that when they too return to their own abode in Broadcasting House, we shall be able to renew the contact which has brought us so much pleasure and musical education during our exile. Our thanks are warmly accorded to Sir Adrian Boult, Mr. Clarence Raybould, Mr. Stanford Robinson, and Mr. Lionel Salter and their respective secretaries for the generous manner in which they have granted our persistent requests for 'passes'.

Anon, *Arrow*, Lent '45

A final, *Farewell to Bedford,* Concert was given by the BBC Symphony Orchestra at the Corn Exchange on Monday, 16 July 1945 and then they packed up and went back to London. Some in the BBC no doubt thought they were rid of us with our endless requests for passes but little did they realise that we, too, were going back to London and some of us had had the foresight to ask Mrs Beckett for her London telephone number. So there we were once more, on Christmas Eve 1945, in the No. 1 Studio at Maida Vale for a performance of Rimsky-Korsakov's *Scheherazade...*

That apart, contact was never physically renewed but many Owenians retain a warm regard and a sense of belonging whenever the BBC broadcasts classical music.

The comparative ignoramus was initiated; the beginner had his horizons broadened.

The BBC Symphony Orchestra was a great help to me. Although my family were very musical, it was great that the BBC orchestra had moved to Bedford and we were able to go and listen and see. The first time I went Paul Beard was conducting and Moiseivitch was playing Rachmaninoff's 2nd, a very popular concerto. It was wonderful. Leon

197

Goosens stands out with his clarinet. It gave me a musical background that I will never forget and in later life is a source of satisfaction.   BS

The gramophone and live performances at the Corn Exchange laid the foundation for my love of classical music, going to opera, symphonic and later chamber concerts after returning to London; so much so that at the age of 32, for the first time in my life I started to play a musical instrument, the cello, which I do – badly – in the London Medical Orchestra.   JNB

Martin Mitchell sums up how we benefited and adds a post-war postscript.

Auntie's generosity in letting us attend rehearsals turned us into music lovers. In 1945 when I was living at home, my brother and I would listen to Alec Robertson's music reviews each Sunday morning. My brother, thirteen at the time, wrote an adulatory letter to the renowned critic, who promptly invited him to tea. Such a wonderful opportunity had to be shared, so I invited myself and Nat Solomon along. My mother was very excited and thought this historic occasion should be celebrated with one of her delicious apple cakes to be presented to the broadcaster. Alec Robinson was very touched, helped himself to a slice, and not sure of the protocol on such an occasion, I carefully wrapped the remainder of the cake in its covering and after we had talked about music, took it home. 'Did he like the cake?' my mother asked nervously. 'Oh, yes, but he only ate one slice,' I said as I handed the remainder to her. She found it hard to forgive me.   MM

25

Radio Times

Listening - link, linchpin, lifeline.

The billet was full of silence for the news.   IA

Radio was a lifeline. The set was a focal point. Everyone – parents and children, hosts and evacuees – sat around the set to hear the news at six and nine in the evening. It was a ritual.

There was a powerful family feel in the billet of always listening to the evening news together.   BL

The wireless was at the centre of our home life. Many times I had to hurry to pick up the charged (wet) battery if there was a special programme to be broadcast that evening.   JS

Not everyone had mains receivers (80% in urban areas but only 60% in rural). Those who didn't had trouble finding batteries and getting them charged. Those who did still found it difficult to replace valves and have their sets repaired. Nevertheless, the wireless remained on much of the time.

Mr and Mrs Fowler had the radio on almost constantly during the war and so I was well indoctrinated in current affairs.   AWL

Mrs Smith let me listen to the one radio in the house more or less when I liked.   DEB

The radio was on most of the time, even in the Boarding House.   MM

We were all very keen listening to the radio and some of us had hobbies making amplifiers. We eventually, using very ancient apparatus, made a single amp amplifier crystal set and were able to listen to the BBC long wave, to *Saturday Night Theatre*. There were six of us in the dormitory and we had six sets of earphones. Mr & Mrs Baker didn't like this but we used to smuggle batteries in and listen as much as we could. We placed aerials in obscure places such as under the floor, so we couldn't be discovered. For some of us this hobby eventually became a hobby for life.   BS

Surprisingly, my new home did not possess a wireless despite Robert's best efforts to persuade Mrs Sutcliffe to buy one. So he enrolled me in a plot. I was to tell her that in my previous billet they had replaced their old wireless set by one of the new utility heterodyne sets and that they were amazed at its superb reception. I don't think for one moment that Mrs Sutcliffe fell for the ruse but continual pressure from both of us won the day and she finally succumbed. I don't know who got the most pleasure from the set but she thoroughly enjoyed listening to *ITMA* and the obligatory nine o'clock news.   NC

If people were glued to the radio, the radio enabled them to be glued to each other. George Orwell caught the mood in 1941 when he wrote of Britain's 'emotional unity, the tendency of making all of its inhabitants to feel alike and act together in moments of supreme crisis'.[1]

Listening to the radio was a shared experience. We knew that our parents, miles away, were listening too, simultaneously.

We were in bed by 7.30 every evening but could hear the wireless from downstairs and later when the air raids started it was a relief to hear 'Hi Gang! This is Ben Lyon speaking to you from the heart of London'. When we heard this we were assured that all was well.   CL

Hi Gang! was the only major comedy show to be broadcast from the heart of London at the time though Conrad Lynn also remembers a minor one *Helter Shelter* apparently broadcast from the London Underground shelters.

The news, of course, was not always reassuring.

Delivered in measured tones were nerve-wracking bulletins of initial disasters: the Nazi occupation of France, the Low Countries, Denmark and Norway and the evacuation of Dunkirk, and in the same measured tones, the great successes; El Alamein, Stalingrad, D-Day, Hitler's death and the German capitulation. Most riveting and fraught were the bul-

letins of losses and wins in the Battle of Britain and the devastation
caused by the Blitz.   MM

Every few hours there was a drama of the news, with armies advancing, armies retreating, convoys attacked, battleships sunk; the long-
drawn-out excitement of the sinking of the *Graf Spee*; the bombings
and casualties in London, Coventry, Berlin and incredible day-by-day
accounts of the Battle of Britain with details of planes shot down like
massive football scores: the ups and downs of the Desert Army; the
insane attack of the Germans on Russia; the advance to and defence of
Stalingrad.   JA

The news was read throughout the war from London. After
Dunkirk, with the fear of invasion, of German parachutists taking
over Broadcasting House, the announcers told us their names:
Stuart Hibberd, Alvar Liddell, Bruce Belfrage, Joseph McCleod,
John Snagge, Alan Howland, Freddy Allen, Frank Phillips and, as
an exception to 'Received Pronunciation', the northerner Wilfred
Pickles.

'This is the BBC. Here is the news and this is Frank Phillips reading
it.' This gave me an idea. I would run a book on the announcers. Not
strictly a book, more of a lottery. I'd pair the announcers' names for the
two bulletins including 'x' for a new announcer. My pals would buy a
ticket for a penny. The winning ticket scooped the pool.   DEB

Immediately after the 9 p.m. news three nights of the week there
was a dramatised documentary. *Into Battle* lasted fifteen minutes.

There was a signature tune, an old march, *Liliburlero* which remained a BBC feature for some fifty years, at least in the World
Service.

On 19 May 1940 Winston Churchill gave the first of thirty-three
speeches broadcast to the nation. They were full of what we now
call 'soundbites', sentences that we could easily remember, recall
and comfort ourselves with. The words were inspiring, the delivery heroic. It was the most memorable radio of the war.

Once in a while when the situation looked blackest, we would hear the
rumbling voice of Winston Churchill injecting us with adrenaline.   JA

The most dramatic moments, equal to any great theatrical perform-ances, were Churchill's speeches with their stirring rhetoric.   MM

When Churchill remarked[2] that he wasn't the British lion he simply provided the 'roar', he might have added it was the wireless that brought the roar home.   JS

The wireless also brought home the V sign which Churchill ges-tured. It originated with a Belgian BBC programme organiser. V was the first letter of Victoire and of the Flemish word Vrijheid (freedom). It became a symbol of resolution, visual and aural, the sound – three shorts and a long – of the Morse code for the letter V. The opening bars of Beethoven's Fifth Symphony were harnessed. V for victory. The sound and symbol spread through occupied Europe. The V sign featured on school walls, in our day books and on satchels. And we tapped the tattoo on our desks.

But, as the BBC told us of the war, it also took our minds off it. Joss Ackland recalls two half-hour shows with names which were often confused.

Workers Playtime with artists such as the great Robb Wilton, Sandy Powell, Tessie O'Shea, Issy Bonn and Elsie and Doris Waters, and the appalling *Works Wonders* from factories 'somewhere in Britain'. The most untalented collection of artists ever to appear before a radio au-dience referred constantly, it seemed, to the factory foreman, thereby causing ensuing gales of laughter from his colleagues in the audience. Now I can only remember it with affection.   JA

Works Wonders depended on talent from the shop floor. All of them could sing along to a third programme, *Music While You Work* with its distinctive signature tune. No lyrics were ever broadcast because, allegedly, the Government were afraid that war workers would stop to write them down.

Work and music could go together whether listeners were in a factory or at home (though not it would seem in school). We could all, in Herbert Morrison's phrase, *'Go to it!'*

Monday Night at 8 o'clock (Oh can't you hear the chimes?) had be-gun before the war. Its producer was Ronnie Waldman, who left Owen's in 1932 and was the older brother of the school goalkeep-er and rugger advocate. On Valentine's Day 1940, with the Soviet Army breaking through the Finnish lines but its navy icebound in the Gulf of Finland, Ronnie Waldman came to Bedford to tell of his work at the BBC.

He began by describing his first moments in Broadcasting House spent watching a **Band Waggon** *'sit round'... Through a haze of tobacco smoke in a small room at the top of many flights of stairs, he saw 'Stinker' Murdoch lying on the floor trying to blow bubbles with a cigarette holder, Arthur Askey sitting on a waste paper basket saying, 'You must make my combs out of the carpet', whilst 'Bishop' Pepper, Gordon Crier, Vernon Harris were sitting around altering scripts and scores. Mr Waldman explained that* **Band Waggon** *was always produced almost impromptu at these 'sit rounds'...*

Then followed a technical but by no means uninteresting description of transmission. The lecturer explained that bad reception since the war was owing to 'overlapping' as all the transmitting stations were used to prevent direction finding by the enemy. It was explained that the revenue from licences was three and a half millions annually, but that expenses had risen because of the war. As an example, Mr Waldman said that 1,500 were employed on foreign news broadcasts alone.

B.A.L.Rust, *Arrow*, Lent '40

Ronnie Waldman let the audience into broadcasting secrets. Syd Walker was not really a rag and bone man and cards telling the audience when to applaud were not generally used. Bernard Fox remembers another revelation.

At the time there was a programme called *Penny on the Drum* and I suspect this was one of the first quiz programmes. The realities of life were revealed when he told us that this apparently spontaneous quiz was heavily rehearsed. I still retain my cynicism for quiz programmes.

BF

Radio stars were as popular as film stars – but more approachable, more immediate (television with its audience of 25,000 shut down the day we left London). Ronnie Waldman became head of variety (not entertainment which came later). And variety there was. We craved humour and we got all kinds.

The wireless was a great joy, laughter all the way. JA

There were lots of catchphrases, 'Take it away Ramsbottom'. 'Mind my bike!', 'I thang yew', 'Let me tell you', 'Not you Momma, sit down', and all those in *ITMA*.   DEB

We had Gillie Potter at Hogsnorton ('speaking to you in English'), Jeanne de Casalis as Mrs Feather, Murray and Mooney, Clapham and Dwyer, Albert Whelan whistling, Teddy Brown on the xylophone, Ethel Revnell and Gracie West as the long-and-short-of-it, Frank Randle, Albert Modley, Billy Bennett, Troise and his mandoliers, Nat Jackley, Western Brothers, Albert Sandler at the Palm Court, Harry Hemsley with Winnie and Horace, Carrol Gibbons and more.   DMJ

Mr and Mrs Fowler liked variety programmes such as *Music Hall* which was broadcast every Saturday evening and featured mainly northern comics and singers. They also let me listen to programmes they did not like such as *ITMA, Happidrome* and *Danger Men At Work.*   AWL

I bet if this moment you began singing *'We three in Happidrome'* any Owenian my age would immediately sing the subsequent lyrics *Working for the BBC, Ramsbottom and Enoch and me.* The tune was the Ink Spots favourite *My Echo, My Shadow and Me.*   DEB

Clay Keyes with his *Penny On The Drum* game; Arthur Askey and Richard Murchoch in *Band Waggon*. Jack Warner in *Garrison Theatre* with his catchphrase 'Mind my bike' and his 'Little gel'...   JA

... *The Old Town Hall* and individual artists, Robb Wilton, Suzette Tarry, Elsie and Doris Waters (Gert and Daisy)...   JS

And so the roll call continues. Noel Coward (providing nostalgia and an undercurrent of sentimental sadness), Max Miller, Stephen Potter...

Laughter and absurdity filled the airwaves. ('Ladies and Mantelpieces!' – Max Bacon. What superb idiocy! Every public speech should start like that.)   MM

The pinnacle of insanity was *ITMA - It's That Man Again.* Not one of our contributors recalls it without affection or respect for its breaking the bounds of radio and the boost it gave to morale.

ITMA, with Tommy Handley, was our weekly radio treat, half an hour of riotous pre-goon humour, with Jack Train's characterisations, Funf,

Mrs Mopp (Can I do you now, sir?) and a light orchestral interlude arranged and conducted by Rae Jenkins. DMJ

ITMA with Jack Train as Colonel Chinstrap and *Funf* the German spy, Dorothy Summers as Mrs Mopp, Horace Percival selling dirty postcards and an absurd submariner who would appear anytime, anywhere, with his 'Don't forget the diver'; and of course the incomparable Tommy Handley holding the lunacy together. JA

Tommy Handley gave a new dimension to radio. *ITMA* was a wonderful propaganda weapon for energising the home front with humour. It lampooned the ridiculous posturing of Hitler and Mussolini. It created a world of surreal people like Mrs Mopp, Colonel Chinstrap ('I don't mind if I do'). Tommy Handley's quick firing repartee was convulsive. Traditional BBC propriety was demolished. MM

The audience grew to sixteen million. It was invited to contribute.

In (I think) 1942 the BBC invited listeners to write a ten-minute programme using the *ITMA* characters. Alan Locke and I wrote a sketch which had us in stitches, but apparently nobody at the BBC. DEB

It was the age of the big bands – Harry Roy, Roy Fox, Henry Hall, Nat Gonella, Geraldo and Ambrose with their girl vocalists.

Vera Lynn perpetually singing *We'll Meet Again* seemed cloying to a young sophisticate like myself until my brother, home on leave on a thirty-six hour pass, gently rebuked me with 'Sentimental it may be, but – you'd be surprised it can mean a lot to us.' JA

Anne Shelton was always regarded as number two. Arguably, she was as accomplished a singer and when the American Army Air Force band broadcast from Bedford it was she, rather than the 'forces sweetheart', who sang.

She emerged from the rehearsal wooden building for a breath of air where I was standing listening. She gave me her autograph and we talked about London. Fifty years later I told her of the occasion. She was charming and pretended to remember. DEB

As already mentioned, the American contribution to our radio enjoyment predated Glenn Miller.

We had a number of American radio shows as part of Lease-Lend and were introduced to American humour which was very much more situation-based. We had the Jack Benny, Fred Allen, and Charlie McCarthy shows, all of which were accompanied by various American bands with their own singers. This stimulated the BBC to greater efforts in producing their own imitations such as *Hi Gang!* with Bebe Daniels and Ben Lyon. Their daughter Barbara Lyon later married an Owenian, Russell Turner, whose father, besides being a staff member at Owen's, had in pre-war days, been the Minister at Bunyan Meeting Church in Mill Street Bedford. AWL

Joss Ackland enjoyed the US imports.

American comedy shows with Jack Benny and Rochester, Bob Hope and Edgar Bergen and Charlie McCarthy were brilliant, but the funniest comedy show of all from abroad was the nasal Lord Haw-Haw broadcasting from Berlin each day and telling us our position was hopeless. JA

William Joyce, previously a pupil at Bedford School and later executed as a traitor, spoke to us in a weird and easily imitated accent. 'Jairmany calling, Jairmany calling', from Bremen and Hamburg.

I listened to Haw-Haw. I don't think I was ever taken in. Nor do I remember it being discouraged at school. DEB

But the Minister of Information wasn't best pleased. People turned to Hamburg because they wanted a change and in the very early days of the war, the news was limited and dull – simply the Home Service. Even when it was joined by the Forces Programme (a pair known universally as the 'Foam and Horses') the audience for Haw-Haw reached six million. What worried the authorities were the occasional nuggets of fact which, allegedly, could be verified and therefore implied credence for the falsehoods.

I had always been very interested in boxing so it was quite a thrill to go to Cardington aerodrome to a boxing match, which was put on in one of the old airship hangars. The hangars were camouflaged to look like rows of houses. Lord Haw-Haw in one of his broadcasts, to which we often listened, pointed out that the 'houses' on the Cardington hangars did not have any chimneys. This made one think! BF

This, however, was a popular myth, or so Kingsley Martin as-

1. (Chapter 1) In the foreground are new boys looking undaunted at the prospect of leaving home. In the background are the two masters, Dixon and Cumming, wearing obligatory armbands, responsible for supervising the school's evacuation. Herbert Morrison, leader of the London County Council, announced that London's children were naturally cheerful and so would cope well with evacuation, a view confirmed by the Owen's schoolboys pictured here, including three of our contributors: David Bernstein (second from left), Ron Coyte (fourth from left) and John Webber (fourth from right, back).

2. (Ch.1) Here are two streetwise Owen's boys emulating Drake's spirit at Plymouth Hoe playing pontoon (?) just before the order to evacuate.

THE DANGER OF WAR.

SCHOOL CHILDREN BEING EVACUATED.

Precautionary Action By The Government.

IT was officially announced yesterday afternoon that, purely as a precautionary measure, the Government had ordered the

3 (Ch.2) Purely 'a precautionary measure' the Government declared on 31 August. (Report in the Hackney Gazette 1 September.)

4. (Ch.2) This poster, appearing in most streets, meant much more to people, even in Bedford, after the Blitz began.

AIR RAID WARNINGS

Warnings of impending Air Raids will be given by

A fluctuating or "warbling" signal of varying pitch

or

A succession of intermittent blasts sounded by hooters and sirens.

5. (Ch.4) In this poster the little boy is clearing up the wreckage after an air raid The warden gently admonishes him:

"LEAVE THIS TO US SONNY — <u>YOU</u> OUGHT TO BE OUT OF LONDON."

Warnung

Großbritannien an das Deutsche Volk.

Deutsche,

Mit kühl erwogenem Vorsatz hat die Reichs-regierung Großbritannien Krieg auferzwungen. Wohl wußte sie, daß die Folgen ihrer Handlung die Menschheit in ein größeres Unheil stürzen, als

6. (Ch.4) The message on this leaflet (see p. 35) blames Hitler for the war.

'...The assurances of peaceful intentions the Führer gave to you and the world in April *[i.e. after the annexation of Czechoslovakia Ed.]* have proved as worthless as his words ... "We have no more territorial claims to make in Europe." '*[Chamberlain, infamously dismissed German claims on Czechoslovakia as 'a quarrel in a far-away country between people of whom we know nothing' Ed.]*

The leaflet ends with with the dire predictions:

"... Despite crushing taxation you are on the verge of bankruptcy. ... We are too strong to break by blows and we would wear you down inexorably."

7. (Ch.6) The Ouse in one of its many moods.

8. (Ch.9) Boys and staff alike began to make their way to every corner of Bedford and beyond. Masters, who had not ridden a bicycle for thirty or forty years, could be seen scorching from one end of Bedford to the other in their eagerness not to waste a moment between lessons. The boys, however, seemed quite content to walk at a steady two or three miles an hour.   H.K.Olphin (Diary)

9. (Ch.9) Lower sixth studying cheek by jowl in two of our many borrowed rooms. Mick Hooley (bottom left), Jack Levy (centre) and Jock Mackay (right).

10. (Ch.10) As time went on it became increasingly difficult to find homes for all of the boys. The town's population increased by 50 per cent and it was a heavy strain to have houses overcrowded for years on end. A School Boarding House *[at 48, Kimbolton Rd. ed.]* was therefore started to cope with our needs.

H.K. Olphin (Diary)

11. (Ch.11) The boys themselves could meet and recount to one another the last story.
H.K. Olphin (Diary)
This is the BMS quad where the boys were showered with leaflets by incipient in-surrectionists demanding that the Head allow weekend travel to London in term time.

12. Soldiers in the making. The Owen's Army Cadet Force on parade. Spot the lad not looking to the front!

13. (Ch.13) The Troop grew to 140 members and eight King's Scouts, including Bill Whitebread (holding the banner).

14. (Ch.12) On the extreme left is Alan Locke with a battery terminal. Behind him is Mick Horkins. Second from right a cadet clicks an Aldis lamp.

No. 2986

BOROUGH OF BEDFORD
FIRE PREVENTION ORDERS.

This is to Certify that

Name...M.R....Cook....... N.R. No...DPCD. 64/5~

Address ...3 . Glebe Road Bedford.

A member of the Fire Prevention Service under :—

The Fire Guard (Business and Government Premises) Order 1943.

~~The Fire Guard (Local Authority Services) Order 1943.~~

Performing duties at (Premises) Harpur Trust Buildings

Sector No...117 .

has completed the statutory Course of Training.

Course No.....70 .

Date of Completion of Course.......15 . 12 .'43

Fire Guard Training Officer.....B. Loverly..... Fire Guard Officer...A. L. Luelelle

---

15. (Ch.14) Geoff Cook's firewatching certificate. You could enrol in the Service at the age of sixteen.

16. (Ch.15) A Government poster.

17. (Ch.15) Owen's response was to form a Gardening Club. There were 70 members.

18. (Ch.18) Farming camp. Volunteers can't wait to start...

19. (Ch.18) Facing reality.

20. (ch.16) When we arrived at Bedford it is doubtful whether many of the boys could be trusted in the most modest Tub Pair. When we left, rowing had taken its place as a major sport... there is a future rowing blue in this eight.

H.K. Olphin (Diary)

[The future Oxford blue is, of course, Jock Mackay - Ed.]

21. (Ch.16) Chatterji who won every flat race from a 100 yards to a mile.　　H.K. Olphin (Diary)

22. (Ch.17) We were fortunate to be able to use the Meltis Chocolate works ground for many of our sports.

23. (Ch.21)
Oliver Worden Mitchell
Headmaster 1939 to 1948.

24. (Ch.21) The Head with second master Dixon and prefects in 1943, including Frank
Fenn (third from right back row) and Jock Mackay (first on left front row).

25. (Ch.19) *Brains Trust* at the Friday Evening Club. On the extreme right is the Head; in the middle is 'Dicky' Dare, and below something different ...

26. (Ch.19) ... a variety turn. In this jolly troupe are 'Mick' Hooley, far left, and Geoff 'Flooge' Rans far right.

27. (Ch.30) Frank Fenn is Cyrano de Bergerac and bending forward anxiously is Barry Skeggs, whilst looking on philosophically is Max Eckstein (second left).

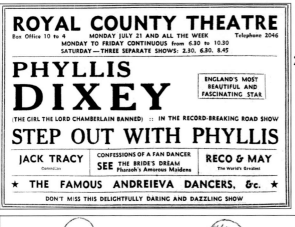

28. (Ch.29) / 29. (Ch.24) Sometimes others entertained us. The titillating artiste Phyllis Dixey, and the BBC Symphony Orchestra's Adrian Boult, no mean stripper himself, even whilst conducting.

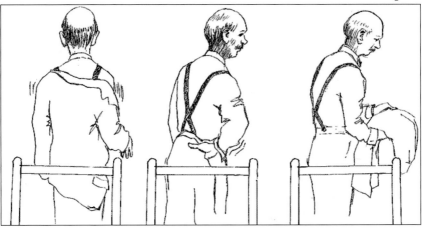

(Ch.31) Two familiar wartime characters.
30. Official: The Squander Bug, the National Savings bogeyman.
31. Unofficial: Chad, chalked on walls and bemoaning shortages.

32. (Ch.34) Wings for Victory, one of the 'Weeks' which endeavoured to make savings fun – and rewarding.

33. (Ch.33) An early announcement of scarcity.

34. (Ch.33) However, some goodies were never rationed.

35. (Ch.33) The exhortation to housewives became a popular song.

36. (Ch.31) Blackout was either a potential hazard or a minor irritant.

37. (Ch.31) Note the masking of lamps in the BSA bicycle strip cartoon advertisement.

38. (Ch.27) In 1939 Owenian cartoonist J.J. Hume forecast a war in which bikes played an important part. So did he. He was killed at Monte Cassino in 1944.

serted, on 8 June 1940.

> *There is scarcely a district in the country where it is not commonly believed that Lord Haw-Haw has tried to frighten the population with ... remarkably accurate details of the countryside and possible objectives ... We now know that no such threats have ever come from Lord Haw-Haw and all the stories about his uncanny knowledge of places ... are untrue.*[3]

On the day war began Dr Goebbels made it a crime to listen to foreign broadcasts, even those of Germany's allies.

In occupied Europe you would suffer imprisonment or worse if you were caught listening to the BBC. In Britain there was no punishment for tuning in to the enemy. You could, however, suffer a hundred pound fine and possible imprisonment for uttering 'any report or statement relating to matter connected with the war which was likely to cause alarm and despondency'.

In November 1939, Murphy, the radio manufacturer, even encouraged such listening. In an advertisement in the *Daily Express* headlined 'Freedom to listen!' pictures of Hitler, Stalin and Mussolini were featured with copy praising 'liberty to speak... liberty to listen to both sides of an argument... guard this freedom to listen – and use it'.[4]

We were not restricted to BBC transmissions though some of us missed the pre-war commercial stations, Normandy and Luxembourg. Vivian Moses was 'indoctrinated' by German broadcasting.

> I listened day and night to music, a lot of it from Germany. There was a programme from Germany every Sunday evening called *Unsterbliche Musik Deutscher Meister*. I remember hearing the second act of the *Flying Dutchman* and I have been a dedicated and convinced Wagnerite ever since.　　　　　　　　　　　　　　　　VM

Towards the end of the war, we tuned in to the American Forces Network. AFN had been set up with the BBC's help in 1943. 'It was made up of several low powered transmitters dotted around the country wherever there were concentrations of American troops'[5] which meant that reception in Bedford was far superior to that which we got back in London.

Subsequently we tuned in to AEF. This was the Allied Expeditionary Forces programme, an idea of Eisenhower to bind together the American, Canadian and British troops. The headquarters were at Broadcasting House. The setting up was hush-hush. 'BBC staff recruited to the network were not told why they were wanted.'[6] One recruit was Reg Perrin whom we last met in the billiard hall and who was now working in the Variety department in London.

> It was all very secret. I was an effects boy and I wondered what on earth I was wanted for that could be so hush-hush. No one would tell me any-thing when I reached BH except that I was to spend the night sleeping in the basement.[7]   RP

The next morning he was woken early, taken to a studio and presented with an 'enormous mountain' of 78 rpm records. From 6am his job was to play music for the invading forces and the reinforcements waiting their turn to cross the channel.

At the end of July 1945, the AEF programme was closed down and the following day the Light Programme began transmission.

We would also listen to the more serious programmes of the BBC.

The *Brains Trust* was required listening for the upper school. A group of intellectuals – Cyril Joad, Julian Huxley, chairman Donald McCullough *inter alia* – plus the ebullient Commander Campbell would answer spontaneously unseen questions from the public. The format was copied throughout the country – and by the Friday Evening Club.

> Other serious broadcasters were Charles Hill, the radio doctor (prunes were 'black coated workers' and carrots 'the No. 8 batteries for your body') and even Mr Middleton, who must have enjoyed the greatest following a gardening correspondent ever had.   JS

John Stockton refers also to J.B Priestley's 'thoughtful contribu-tions'. Priestley gave some of the early postscripts which were introduced in February 1940. These five-minute talks were meant as an antidote to Lord Haw-Haw. Priestley stressed the future, the upside of the conflict, the fact that life had a meaning and that we were all joining in 'a noble and common purpose'.

The BBC contributed to this.

The BBC brought the nation together like no other medium.   MM

Let's acknowledge that in inspirational, entertaining, strictly informative and purely distracting terms, the radio – especially the BBC – played in wartime civilian lives a greater role than any other form of media and overall, superbly so.   JS

26

'This Is Where I Came In'

The lure of the picture palace

The war opened and the cinemas closed. So did theatres, sporting venues, any place of entertainment that might attract a crowd. As E.S. Turner observed in *The Phoney War*, 'Notoriously, the only places of public resort permitted to stay open were the churches and the public houses.'[1]

One day into the war, Bernard Shaw wrote to *The Times*. 'We have hundreds and thousands of evacuated children to be kept out of mischief and traffic dangers. Are there to be no pictures for them?'[2]

Theatres and cinemas re-opened on September 14, and, though there is no record of any Owenian thanking GBS, we were delighted. The cinema, or as we called it, the pictures, was/were part of our life. Ken Deadman's Bedford Diary puts firewatching third, cinema visits second preceded by football and cricket results.

> I must have done rather well for pocket money as I'm pretty certain I went to the pictures two, three or four times a week, especially when back home in Islington.   KD

Back home we had developed the habit. Everybody went to the pictures — or so it seemed. Officially, only three-quarters of the adult population were cinemagoers but these fans made up for the missing quarter. 'Picture palaces' were comfortable, luxurious and sometimes magical places. Where was the competition? Home, or the pub if you were of age.

The queues at Bedford cinemas were full of Owenians, Bedfordians of all ages and GIs. Cinema was the most popular form of entertainment.

MM

It was particularly popular if you had a girl friend.

The parents of the girls in Goldington were tolerant towards us to the extent of going to the cinema together.   RC

The cinema was both an escape from drab wartime life and a window on the world. There cannot have been many weeks when I did not go. The films were a constant topic of conversation among schoolmates.

JL

I was a film fan and reasonably knowledgeable. I knew which studio made which film and when a star moved (or was lent) to another studio. I knew the names of most of the supporting players. I sent away to Hollywood for signed photographs. Most stars replied.   DEB

Cinema-going in the thirties and forties was different from today, particularly if your time wasn't your own. It was common for audiences to arrive and leave piecemeal, and to attempt to pick up the storyline in the middle of the action and then to leave when their initial scene came round again. 'This is where I came in.'

Other things were different. There was fug. Most of the audience smoked and many Owen's boys joined in. Who could catch you?

During sing-song intervals usherettes dispensed choc-ices, tubs and cornets from their trays.   DMJ

And the show was longer than today

A picture programme could run over three hours. Feature, B film, news and a cartoon.   AJ

And if your time *was* your own you could sit the show round twice. Always assuming you would be allowed in in the first place.

Films being graded U (kids) A (adult) and H (horrific), it was sometimes necessary to ask an obliging adult to purchase our tickets for Frankenstein and the like. For me this was a bad idea. At night I imagined Boris Karloff clumping up the stairs.   DMJ

Passing yourself off as an adult was difficult. It took more than the removal of your school cap unless like Don Curtis, you had been in Newmarket.

> There, because of the average height of the jockeys, us 12 year olds could easily be mistaken for 18 year olds. DC

Young children had their own film shows at regular cinemas in irregular hours.

> The Granada also ran a 'Saturday Morning Rush', the children's cinema club where I was able at the age of thirteen to catch up with the last few episodes, interrupted by the outbreak of war, of *Buck Rogers*, a serial based on the American comic strip. By the age of thirteen I could really appreciate the cardboard scenery and rubber costumes for what they were, but it was an interesting experience.
>
> AWL

The Granada was one of Bedford's four cinemas and by far the poshest.

> The Granada, the Plaza, the Picturedrome were the unforgettable temples at which we worshipped the largely black and white films of those years. JS

The Plaza screened *Of Mice and Men*. Joss Ackland saw it eight times in one week and decided to become an actor.

> The Plaza and the Picturedrome on opposite sides of the River Ouse and the little cinema directly opposite the school, which changed programmes twice a week and which we fondly called 'the bug house'. JA

It was actually called the Empire and Joss Ackland's fond memories are shared, as we shall see later. Alan Locke retains a soft spot for the Picturedrome next to the Boat Club.

> ... a delightful little cinema seating about three hundred. AWL

Frank Fenn has a favourite memory of the Picturedrome.

> One afternoon after school, when some of us had been sitting public examinations, a group entered as the second feature was playing. It was a deathbed scene and, as we sat down, there was an enormous close-up

of a grieving mother. 'Don't worry, mum' said Mick Morris, 'I can take it again next year.'   WFF

It was generally agreed that the Plaza along the Embankment opposite and, of course, the Granada in St. Peter's Square, showed better class films. There is a difference of opinion as to which of the commissionaires of these two cinemas was first to be subjected to what became a classic Owenian (i.e. London cheeky) ploy.

> Bedford played host to many foreign servicemen and women in strange uniforms. Frank Fenn went up to the Granada commissionaire, resplendent in a mauve overcoat with epaulets and braid, put his arm round his shoulder and said, 'Don't worry son, we'll get your country back for you.'   DEB

Frank Fenn, who should know, remembers things a little differently.

> It was of course, the blue-uniformed commissionaire at the Plaza who became the first victim. 'Are you on our side too?' we said. 'Don't worry son, we'll get your country back for you.' Members of the Town Band (green uniforms?) were also subjected to the same persecution.   WFF

However, Granada had more than a commissionaire. It had, in the words of Geoff Rans, 'a sub-tropical, open-air fantasy interior', and a restaurant, a large foyer, occasional live shows, an organ and an organist who became a slightly mocked but much liked icon for Owenians.

> I was always impressed with the Granada cinema and what a reception we gave Cyril Gell the resident organist.   KD

> The up-market Granada with its impressive Wurlitzer rising from the depths...   MM

> ... with a blaze of lights and crescendo of sound. There were even live acts, notably Mario 'Harp' Lorenzo, and probably Wee Georgie Wood, Ella Shields, Randolph Sutton and Hetty King.   AJ

Alan Locke, whose knowledge is matched only by his acute memory, recalls that

> Cyril Gell, son of the local bicycle shop owner, played the organ until he was called up for the RAF.

Moreover...

> Patrons were reassured by the air filtration system demonstrated in a window at the side of the cinema which was later covered up so you were not worried it was using precious fuel.   AWL

There was no filtration system at the Empire (more's the pity) but it retained our affection. Twice a week and with the cheapest seats and rarely a contemporary movie.

> Downmarket was the Empire. It was less salubrious. Some of the films were old though interesting (e.g. early thirties, Bela Lugosi, Boris Karloff, spy stories of the Great War).   DEB

> I must include the rather scruffy little cinema in Midland Road, where the offerings were usually horror pictures (Bela Lugosi, Peter Lorre) such as *The Mummy's Hand.*   JS

> Of Bedford's four cinemas, I favoured the ancient, rickety Empire in Midland Road, just round the corner from the fish and chip shop in Priory Road, where the blind lady handled salt, vinegar and cash with unerring accuracy, staring into the void.   DMJ

Frank Fenn seems to have spent most of his time in the cinema.

> Although I enjoyed many hours of pleasure at the Granada, the Plaza and the Picturedrome, my true spiritual home among Bedford's cinemas was the Empire. For the most part it lived off the leavings of the other three establishments. It was there, when the wartime film shortage was at its height, that I saw revivals of old 30s British movies ranging in quality from the original 1934 version of *The Man Who Knew Too Much*, through the prentice work of future famous directors like Michael Powell and Carol Reed, to now-vanished quota quickies and anthologies of performances by British radio and music hall stars. Since one in three of these films is now lost, I have become a walking archive and still receive requests for information about them. It was there, too, that I saw re-issues of classics like *Scarface*, many of the great horror movies including *I Walked with a Zombie*, *The Cat People* and *The Seventh Victim*, the first genuine Hollywood film noir *Stranger on the Third Floor*, and scores of Poverty Row B movies, most of them rubbish like *Hitler, Beast of Berlin* and *The Terror of Tiny Town*, (a repulsive Western which exploited a cast of midgets). But including films by future cult directors like Edgar G. Warner, Joseph H. Lewis and Bud Boettcher. And that is how I became a fully paid up member of the New

Wave ten years before Truffaut and his mates invented it. I think, too, that it was at the Empire that I saw (and re-saw) *Citizen Kane*.

WFF

Chas Baker was also an *aficionado*.

Draper and I used to take it in turns on Thursdays to buy *Picturegoer*. And then to the Granada on a Friday night. CB

On 2 June 1944 Philip Fawkes went to the pictures after a day of exams. There was a queue.

Two soldiers in front of me waited for about three quarters of an hour and then gave it up as hopeless. The film was very good, *You Were Never Lovelier* with Fred Astaire and Rita Hayworth - she will never make a better film. Lots of dancing and singing ... I see Bob Hope is in England. I hope we get a chance of seeing him in the flesh. PFa

(Hope, together with Crosby, did actually make it to Bedford, but no Owenian claimed to have seen them.)

The Jones brothers were keen students and eclectic.

At the Empire were enjoyed black and white Will Hay, Nat Jackley, Frank Randle, Ronald Shiner and Old Mother Riley (Arthur Lucan and Kitty McShane) movies, and never-to-be-forgotten *Hellzapoppin* (Mischa Auer, Olsen and Johnson and Martha Raye). At Granada and riverside Picturedrome and Plaza, technicoloured extravaganzas featured Betty Grable, Carmen Miranda and Maria Montez *Cobra Woman*. DMJ

Andrew Jones reels off the 'regular chief supporting players'

Eugene Pallette, Edward Arnold, Franklin Pangbourne, Gus Schilling Billie Gilbert, Billy Burke, Marjorie Main and Charles Winninger. AJ

... and a list of films remembered.

Hellzapoppin: Olsen and Johnson, Martha Raye, Mischa Auer, Robert Paige and Hugh Herbert tittering in the wings

My Friend Flicka: the immortal Roddy McDowell

The Spy in Black: Conrad Veidt, Valerie Hobson

Scarlet Pimpernel: Leslie Howard, Francis L.Sullivan
Cover Girl: Rita Hayworth
Miracle of Morgan's Creek: Betty Hutton giving multiple births, Eddy Bracken
All the King's Men: Ronald Reagan, Robert Cummings, Anne Sheridan
Blood and Sand: Tyrone Power, Linda Darnell.
Road films, *Stage Door Canteen, Showboat, Confessions of a Nazi Spy, Lady in the Dark, Sun Valley Serenade*, Shirley Temple, Andrews Sisters and Ink Spots, *Getting Gertie's Garter*, Bowery Boys, Huntz Hall and Leo Gorcey, and Tarzan, *Sanders of the River, Flying Down to Rio* with Carmen Miranda, *Dumbo, The Lady Vanishes*, Lena Horne sang *Stormy Weather* in *Green Pastures* (I met her 20 years later; she was tiny and vital).   AJ

My recollection is not particularly of war films but certainly of the best of Hollywood's Fritz Lang and similar directors' works. The incomparable *Double Indemnity* (never another film which matched its eroticism with so little sex) spring to mind – and stay there! The British films were for me mostly enjoyed in the forms of Will Hay, the Crazy Gang. But there were 'giants' too. I saw *Stagecoach* during the war and *Gone With The Wind* and naturally *Henry V*. Not overlooking the musicals – seeing *Cover Girl* at the Plaza with Gene Kelly and Rita Hayworth and a Jerome Kern/Ira Gershwin score was a high point in my cinema career. *In Which We Serve*, several Disneys; *Fantasia* (this was the only film which O.W. Mitchell, speaking in morning assembly, went out of his way to recommend to be seen) all these come back to one as sources of such deep, if quite different kinds of pleasure, distraction, excitement.
                                                                JS

Particularly memorable were *Yankee Doodle Dandy* with James Cagney's nifty footwork, Chaplin's *The Great Dictator*, Welles's *Citizen Kane* and the splendidly rotund Sidney Greenstreet and hapless Peter Lorre in Huston's *Maltese Falcon*. But the one best suited to a callow youth's unsubtle sense of humour was the manic *Hellzapoppin*. I'd love to see it again and revel in its lunatic humour and Cab Calloway's 'Hi-di-Hi' and respond with 'Ho-di-Ho'.   MM

I remember being entranced with Disney's *Fantasia*, falling in love with Rita Hayworth in *Cover Girl* and being excited by a thin and gawky crooner whom most of my pals felt it *infra dig* to admit they liked. *Come out, wherever you are!* was almost an invitation to own up to liking Sinatra.   DEB

We were in Hollywood's thrall. It may have been pure escapism for our elders but for us it was an alternative reality. It was reassuring. It reconfirmed our belief that we would win the war, that good would triumph over evil. As Koppes and Black say in *Hollywood Goes to War*, 'few pictures dared breathe what everyone knew but found hard to voice aloud - that death was random and success only partly related to one's deserts'.[3]

Hollywood and, to a lesser extent, British movies, made many of us romantic. In the movies sex wasn't real: the Hays Office saw to that. It was difficult to reconcile our adolescent fumblings with the assured behaviour of the stars. We tried to imitate them, to purloin gestures and phrases.

And if sex was romanticised, then war was sanitised. The majority of war movies were gung-ho adventure yarns. We viewed death scenes but little of the obscenity of killing. The cinema was a place of entertainment. *Verité* hadn't yet happened.

> One matinée – early in 1940 – at the Granada I was watching a news-reel of soldiers training and I suddenly realised that the whole object of that training was to equip the soldier to kill another soldier and that the Germans were simultaneously involved in equipping another soldier to do likewise. Did, I wondered, the soldiers in the audience realise this?
>
> DEB

Occasionally films got closer to reality. They were mostly British and documentary in feel. Not the sentimental *The Way to the Stars*, or *The First of the Few* or even

> ... stiff upper lip war films like *In Which We Serve* with, of all people, Noel Coward playing the gallant captain buoying up the spirits of ship-wrecked survivors adrift in the ocean. MM

Rather, *Above Us The Waves* (submarines), *The Way Ahead* (army)

> ...and *San Demetrio, London* about a crippled oil tanker, at first abandoned by its working class crew and then re-boarded by them against great odds and brought to port in Scotland. MM

There were others almost didactic in tone. *Next Of Kin* was anti-careless talk; *Fires Were Started* celebrated the courage and resourcefulness of the Auxiliary Fire Service. In 1940 we were warned of imminent invasion.

There was one film that taught us to trust nobody.

I still recall the impact of *Went the Day Well?*   JS

The cinema played a key part in our lives. It made us think as much as it made us forget. And, *pace* Bernard Shaw, it did more than keep us out of mischief and traffic danger. But this is where we came in.

27

Bikes

They bring us closer – and let us escape.

In the early weeks of the war, fifth former A. E. Bedwell wrote a short piece for the school magazine entitled *'Cycling and the war'*. The war, he maintained, would prove the cycle's worth. He noted the fully equipped bikes stationed outside air raid posts, praised the French Government for commandeering civilian cycles for military use and advocated equipping parachutists with them.

> *In Bristol, since the outbreak of war, the rate at which bicycles are selling is already 500 per cent above normal.*
>
> *The supply of car parts will become scarcer as the war goes on, and a bicycle will last years without needing any replacements unless damaged.*
>
> *There is no doubt that there will be a terrible slump in cycle manufacturing after the war but at least the cycle will have done its 'national service'.*
>
> *Arrow*, Michaelmas '39

There was an accompanying cartoon. The editor chose to dissociate himself from the ideas expressed and admitted to an inability to 'suppress the impulses of the magazine cartoonist upon such occasions'. The cartoonist, J.J.Hume would be killed in action at Monte Cassino in 1944.

Most Owenians would, over the years, agree with the prescient views of Bedwell. The bike showed its value in many ways. Geoff Cook, who learned to ride a bike in Bedford, had an allotment and played sports.

> The bicycle was, of course, essential in getting to and from Barkers
> Lane. The Meltis and BMS sports grounds became conveniently near
> and many worthwhile visits to surrounding villages and towns were
> possible.   GCk

Few of us had been cyclists before the war. Even those who had
cycles would have used them less frequently, around their homes
and not for travelling to school. In Bedford, however, the cycle
became in John Stockton's words 'almost a corporeal extension'.

To be without a bike, worse still to be unable to ride one, put you
at a practical, social and often economic disadvantage.

> During the holidays I did a newspaper round. The distance I had to
> cover was over six miles and I dared not tell the newsagent that I did
> not possess a bicycle at that time or I would never have got the job. So
> I am afraid some unfortunate householders did not receive their papers
> until the afternoon. It was weeks before my pretence was discovered
> and I lost the job.   JA

To own a cycle was to gain the freedom, not only of the town, but
the surrounding countryside.

> I travelled around the radius of Bedford and could go up to 120 miles a
> day. So within a 60-mile radius of Bedford I got to know the towns and,
> of course, the traffic was much lighter. It was very satisfying getting to
> know the places. It had a practical value as well, because as you headed
> north east towards the Fen country there were some absolutely superb
> orchards and the entrepreneurial spirit is always in the front of every
> Owenian. Just like a squirrel, a modest winter stock.   HCu

The further you travelled, particularly in the winter, the more you
had to consider the encroaching blackout. Cyclists were particularly affected by the battery shortage. Prior to the war, though a
front cycle lamp was necessary, a reflector on the rear mudguard
was sufficient. On the day war broke out rear lamps also became
compulsory.

These new enthusiasts had taken up the hobby at a period when,
given the comparatively empty roads, cycling had seldom been so
enjoyable. Bikes became a preoccupation, a cult, and an obsession.

How involved one became with gears and dynamos and fixed or free
wheels.   JS

If you couldn't afford a standard new bike there was always the
chance that an old, little used model lurked in your billet. Though
a few Owenians were somewhat reluctant to be seen astride a
ladies' cycle, particularly of the upright variety and adorned with
a basket (though baskets were more practical than saddlebags
for holding schoolbooks). One such had been dormant in Ray
Coombes's billet.

> I felt very elated when I reintroduced Evelyn (Auntie Tev by now) to
> cycling on her 28" bicycle that I had rescued from the garage loft. From
> hermit to Hercules as it were, but she was a joy to behold as I cycled
> beside her on Sunday mornings.   KRC

> I had lessons at most locations and a bike was essential. I never had one
> in London and I was given a second hand one with home made brakes
> which went on when going round corners.   KD

Of course, we all wanted to graduate from a second hand status.

> There was something of a cycle cult at school and we looked quite care-
> fully at what others were riding and what the latest models were in the
> shops.   JL

> I got a 639 Raleigh. It was called that because it cost six pounds, three
> shillings and nine pence.   KD

> I did an awful lot of cycling, on my own usually. I had two bicycles. A
> real old-fashioned Hercules roadster, sit-up-and-beg-and-last-forever
> sort of thing. As a reward for passing the matriculation in '43 I really
> had a super duper slim one with drop handlebars.   HCu

> My father was a keen cyclist and when my first bicycle arrived on the
> train life really began. It was a hand made Macleans with dropped bars
> and a free wheel was not allowed.   RN

Ron Nash owning a Maclean was the source of much scholarly wit.
Maclean toothpaste's pre-war advertising campaign continued
throughout the war with its famous slogan *Have you Macleaned
your teeth today?* This was addressed to Ron Nash with certain
variants e.g. *Have you gnashed your teeth today?*

One boy and his bike became notorious.

> Mickey Malz arrived with a brand new golden Raleigh with bright
> chromium plated dropped handlebars, cable brakes, and a Derailleur
> gear on top of a four-speed hub. These remembered details reveal the
> depth of my envy. I can see the bike now as clearly as I can see carrot-
> topped Malz draped over it. He had a hard time with us on account of
> the bike, not because of his red hair. DAMM

A cycle was a link to London. You knew that, if you had to, you
could get home at little or no cost. Ivor Walker cycled to London
just before the Battle of Britain with his great friend Donald Hall.

> I can recall that we broke our journey in the region of Potters Bar for
> refreshments where conveniently Donald had an aunt. IW

Jack Levy had a particular reason for cycling home.

> My longest cycle journey was one summer holiday when I made the
> 50 miles back home to London so that I could have the use of the bike
> during the vacation. JL

Alan Locke, *en route* to London by bike, popped in to see one of
the masters, Jesse Smith.

> 'Where are you off to?' he asked. 'London' I replied. 'Then you'll need
> these'. He gave me a tube of Smarties. They'd all gone by Cardington.
> AWL

> I cycled to London for the weekend, getting completely lost and being
> unable to sit comfortably in class the following Monday morning.
> DAP

Apart from masters arranging rides for boys spending holidays in
Bedford, there was little organised communal cycling. Then there
appeared a letter from the Old Owen's cycling club in the *Arrow*
in summer 1941. It was addressed to the editor.

> *While the school is at Bedford, we shall arrange to meet boys for*
> *tea on Saturday afternoons and sometimes accompany them from*
> *Bedford. It is proposed to hold a further Boys' Invitation Run towards*
> *the end of July and we hope a considerable number will turn out...*
> *Yours etc., J.F. Richardson (Hon Sec and Treas.)*
> *Arrow*, Trinity '41

A school club was formed the same year. It worked in conjunction with the Old Owen's club. An *Arrow* report in Spring 1942 told of 'enjoyable afternoons up the road'.

> *Hexton, Hitchin, Biggleswade, Baldock, Castle Ashby, Woburn Sands and Newport Pagnell were among the places visited. We only had one all day run, and on that occasion we met the Old Boys at Luton and had our sandwiches under a haystack on the road leading to Hitchin.*
>
> A.R. Mann, *Arrow*, Lent '42

Subsequent reports reflect a diminishing interest in communal cycling. Not that the report writer helps his cause by retailing the truth.

> *We had our share of rain (I recall vainly trying to keep dry whilst eating tea in a cramped up position beneath blackberry bushes) and blackout punctures also came to irritate us.*
>
> D.A. Cameron, *Arrow*, Michaelmas '43

You did not need to join a club to suffer mishap or discomfort.

> The misery of cycling in the rain and wind with books and gas mask case and 'chapped' thighs is a painful memory. RN

> Once a tyre burst in my face from over-inflating, ears ringing for several days. DMJ

> My free-wheel ceased to function. So Alan Locke towed me. We had travelled barely a quarter of a mile when a gust of wind blew my hat directly into my path. There was no way of swerving as I wasn't in charge. So I ran over my own, school-issue straw hat. It would be forty years before I bought another one. DEB

> My great problem was how to carry the satchel which, slung on the crossbar, insisted on clashing with each pedal at its uppermost position. JS

One boy carried personal belongings on his cycle with fatal results.

> Cycling back from football one day, Donovan had his boots on the handlebars. The laces caught in the wheel. He was thrown into the path of a lorry and was killed. This had a traumatic effect on the school. HG

The Spring 1945 *Arrow* carried an obituary.

It is with very great regret that we have to record the death of one of our own scholars – C.J. Donovan of Remove B on March 14 1945, while cycling along St. Mary's Street, Bedford, on his way home from the Meltis Sports Ground, where he had been playing football. He came into collision with an Eastern National omnibus and received fatal injuries. At the inquest two days later, the Bedford Coroner recorded a verdict of Accidental Death.

C. J. Donovan, who was thirteen years old, was the son of Mr and Mrs Donovan of Collie Street, King's Cross, London and was billeted with Mrs Allen of 62 Wellington Street, Bedford. He was one of our most promising pupils and very popular with everyone. His form master Mr B.L. Vulliamy writes: 'Donovan's form Remove B has been from the start, a very happy family and for that reason we cannot afford to lose one member – especially such a personality as Donovan. He was not only a steady worker – he was top of the form – but no one was ever able to accuse him of anything underhand or mean. He was everybody's friend – nobody's enemy. He had all the markings of a fine citizen.'

This is the first fatal accident that the school has suffered during its long evacuation in Bedford, and it is natural that the whole school feels the tragedy very keenly. A shadow fell across all our work and play during that week. But our first thoughts must go to his father, mother and sisters in their terrible loss, and we would ask them to accept our heartfelt sympathy at this sad time. We want them to understand that, just as they have lost a dearly beloved member of their family, so we too have lost a real 'pal.'

Arrow, Lent '45

Owen's cycling was mainly a solitary activity. Boy communed with machine, the 'almost corporeal extension'. He might explore the countryside with a friend but not in a group. Nor was cycling a school sport, though we did have among us a champion race cyclist, Ken Parker. He too was a solitary figure. The loneliness and self-sufficiency was caught in this verse by thirteen-year-old R.A Tyrrell.

THE CYCLE RACE
As I go tearing down the hill,
With cool wind blowing in my face,
My feet are working with a will,

My legs strive hard to force the pace.
Past window-box and window-sill,
While dust is blowing in my eyes,
With twirling feet and hands held still,
I'm out to win that golden prize.
Down hill and dale and round the bend,
The final lap is now begun,
Past flag and stands that mark the end,
The race is over – I have won!

Arrow, Trinity '44

28

Boys and Girls

The park, the river and other erogenous zones.

Boy met girl in Bedford, desire stimulated by availability. A recurrent dominant image of Bedford life is 'girls on bikes' and, concomitantly, glimpses of stocking tops.

Loud, Betjemanesque, burly biking girls at the teacher training college in Lansdowne Road. AJ

... the girls in Russell Park chatted up for hours straddling the crossbars of our bicycles. CL

I was pubescent, communist, and infatuated with Rowena Buncombe, a blonde girl cyclist I used to cross paths with on my way to school. Nothing there but food for fantasy. GR

Older Bedford girls who were of working age went either into the three services or were in reserved occupations attached to companies manufacturing munitions. The arrival of the US Army Air Force at Thurleigh cut a swathe through these and the prettiest, best endowed and tallest were featured in the weekly crops of wedding photographs in the *Bedford Record* before being shipped off as GI Brides. AWL

The girls who interested us were somewhat younger and still at school, Bedford Modern girls, Bedford High and, two years into the war, King's Warren evacuated from Plumstead via Maidstone. To Alan Locke they all seemed beautiful and well educated.

... And, in spite of school uniform, they added their own touches of individuality in the way they put tucks in the school regulation velour hats. AWL

226

They remain individuals two generations later.

Availability is one thing, opportunity another. If Russell Park had not existed would we have been able to find another location?

> Russell Park … Russell Park! The mere mention has almost assumed mythical proportions symbolising raffish enjoyment but I wonder whether memory embroiders the actuality. However, I was not one of those closely involved so maybe there was more going on than I realised. Certainly though, I enjoyed the freedom of occasionally riding around the park on a fine evening and meeting other boys and girls.
>
> JL

> Girls in Bedford were synonymous with Russell Park. This was a great meeting spot but unfortunately I lived at the other end of town.   GS

Russell Park was a rectangle fringed by the embankment and fed on the opposite side by parallel rows of working class streets of terraced houses two up and two down. However, at the two ends of the rectangle were bigger, more substantial middle class residences.

> Russell Park was the open stretch of green bisected by a line of bumps and ditches erected to prevent the landing of enemy aircraft (!) that became the meeting place for Owen's boys and some of the Bedford girls, where we demonstrated cycling skills in the 'Valley' – an uncultivated area of bushes and shrubs, by riding no-hands, three-a-bike, riding backwards, sitting on the handlebars etc. Refreshments were provided by 'Smokey Joe' Lightfoot whose café, in a keeper's lodge in the South West corner, boasted 'Tea, Coffee, Cocoa and Oxo on sale' in white plastic letters on a blackboard. His forbearance of rowdy Owenians showed in his face. He would much preferred to have been managing The Swan Hotel.   AWL

> Russell Park, especially the secret 'Valley', was the venue for our meetings with the Bedford 'Spice Girls'. It is rumoured that BMS boys were unaware of the 'Valley' though many of their more attractive and adventurous girl friends did and seemed to enjoy the experience.   DAP

> In Russell Park several of us queued in the bushes for a first real kiss from an obliging King's Warren girl.   DMJ

> When I was fifteen we would spend our evenings in Russell Park. It was the social centre. We met local girls and London girls.   VM

A nice pastime was chasing girls into the bushes. I was a good chaser but poor concluder. I can't even remember snatching a kiss. Other Owenians boasted of the most lurid sexual encounters in the bushes; one even came out waving a bra but I doubt it had ever been worn.

MM

When I had a bicycle and dusk had fallen I would ride up to Russell Park with other boys and we would grin sheepishly and make remarks at giggling clusters of schoolgirls until gradually we found our partners and walked off together, pushing our bikes, chatted, kissed and cuddled surreptitiously and then rode off home.

JA

The objects of all this activity, at least in their tranquil recollections, seem to have enjoyed it.

The favoured meeting place was, of course, Russell Park where the sun always shone.

J & MH

... After Sunday school was over we lingered a while with a small group of Owen's boys who had somehow gathered outside the church hall. George Gobey, Doug Young, Alan Locke, Clive Schroder and others. We became quite a band and for the next couple of growing up years met regularly in Russell Park.

PF

My third Bedford billet, with a kindly elderly couple, was conveniently only yards from Russell Park where various pupils of the two London schools met and milled around on their bikes at every free moment.SB

For boys and girls not conveniently placed, the problem could be overcome – with a cycle and the passage of time.

It took time for Russell Park to become the meeting place not just for the boys living nearby but also for boys like myself living out at Goldington or along the Clapham Road.

WFF

There were other less populated and indeed less notorious locations.

For Russell Park, read Goldington Green for some of the Owenian element in the village. It was the social centre on the long summer evenings.

RCo

But Russell Park, the easily accessible billets and houses of friends, had no real competition.

My happiest memories are of being in Russell Park with 'the boys' and several of them coming to our house in Castle Road. I think my mother used to give them cocoa and jacket potatoes, in return for which they did odd jobs for her. Alan Locke painted a mural on our dining room wall of a scene on the River Ouse!   MH

Russell Park had other attractions for schoolboys.

We played football in Russell Park on Saturdays and some early autumn and late spring evenings. The star was Leslie Williamson who became a distinguished all round sportsman and Cambridge soccer blue. We played five-a-side – with a tennis ball. We called it smallball and split into teams. On two occasions we held representative matches. RAF versus England (i.e. those of us in the Air Training Corps against those of us who weren't!). The rules were basically those of professional soccer with necessary amendments. The goalkeeper could not throw the ball. There was no offside. And – after Martin Pratt had rounded off a spectacular solo effort with a hotly disputed goal – you were not allowed to pick the ball up with your teeth.   DEB

Gerry Shaw, we know, lived at the other end of town.

However, I did bus over on Saturday mornings for five-a-side football on a full size pitch, which made me so exhausted that I could not cope with girls in any way.   GS

We had our own programmes for these matches – and a regular publication called *Russell Park Gazette* full of gossip. Most of this was unprintable, which was just as well as the scandal sheet wasn't printed but handwritten. Old jokes were updated and, where possible, names of Owenians and their friends substituted.

> *Upon being asked if he got his red hair from his father, Clive Schroder replied that his mother said he never took his hat off.*
> *Russell Park Gazette,* 7 June '44

> *Maggie: If you try to kiss me, I'll show you your place.*
> *Leggy: Don't worry, I'll find it myself.*   *RPG,* 24 May '44

> *Then there was the land girl who was expecting a happy event because she didn't keep her calves together.*
> *RPG,* 29 June '44

The one copy was passed from hand to hand.

We would read the current issue of the *Russell Park Gazette*. We understood that the authors were able to get a free portion of chips from the Bay's Fish and Chip shop proprietor if he was allowed a pre-issue read! We wonder if such wonderful chips have ever been made anywhere else. J & MH

Serving fish in the shop occasionally was Chris Lovell, Bedford's ex-heavyweight boxing champion whom the *Russell Park Gazette* accused of 'tipping the scales at lightweight'.

The lure of Bays Fish and Chip shop captured all including, as we have seen, the BBC Symphony Orchestra. Chas Baker recalls being part of a group passing the summer evenings on the park swings and roundabouts.

Somebody would suddenly shout 'vinegar'. We'd all make a mad dash to the fish shop in York Street to make sure we got some for our chips. CB

We cycled its circuit, often late into the night, without lights. There was a convenient shelter for close contact, also unlit.

It's where we learned to smoke. I was very sick after my first attempt and haven't touched one since. BS

We learned from each other. Ron Coyte remains grateful.

In Russell Park between games of football, or at night, senior boys would discuss films, politics and books. Indeed, I believe much of my knowledge did not come from the school but from these discussions and the public library. My happiest memories of evacuation were standing in the blackout listening to endless discussion and then walking down to the fish and chip shop. RCo

Some of us learned about life indirectly or directly in Russell Park.

We loved the informality of Russell Park which was also a place of assignation ... I did yearn after one or two out-of-reach girls during puberty, and enjoyed (suffered) the pleasures (pains) of sexual fantasy. I suspect there were very few of us who 'broke our duck' before leaving school. (Percy Richer claimed to have been initiated at a brothel by his father.) Some lucky few must have done so, but, notwithstanding the occasional free-spirited girls and the pandemic young male lust, inhibitions were still quite high. Nobody enjoyed the free sexual activity boys and girls enjoy today; I envy them for it but in an odd way, fear for them.

GR

My first lesson in serious snogging occurred in the 'summerhouse' in Russell Park early one evening. I eventually went back to my billet and boasted about it to Mrs Smith who was stoically unimpressed.   DEB

Others did not have to go to the park, or even out of doors, let alone leave their billet.

Mr Humberstone had a number of vivacious sisters-in-law (sisters of his unfortunately deceased wife) and the youngest of these, an attractive seventeen year old, taught me how to kiss.   JL

Mervyn Crossick recalls an initiation near the adjacent river.

There were three of us and we were due to meet S by the Ouse. S was known to be fairly liberal in her outlook and possessed a body that could be described as bountiful. I was the novice, a beginner; the other two already had carnal knowledge. It was agreed that we should spin a coin for body areas and a deal was struck. I got the right breast. Dusk had fallen when S arrived. We sat around in a circle and talked. I eyed the swell of the right breast under her blouse for which I had assumed proprietorial rights and wondered when the true purpose of the evening was to begin. I took for granted the disparate conversation was what they called foreplay. It was A who made the first move and began to unbutton S's blouse. At last I could finally take possession of the breast I'd won. After about fifteen minutes my erotic anticipations were definitely waning. My side was numb, the grass felt damp and my nose was running. I wasn't really certain what I should be doing with the right breast apart from holding it. I would have liked to have visited other areas but I knew these to be fairly crowded and after all a deal is a deal.
When we finally broke up we each thanked S for her generosity. It wasn't until afterwards I ruminated that I would probably have got more pleasure from playing football or looking at pictures in *Health and Efficiency*.   MC

Whether 'S' attended King's Warren, Mervyn Crossick is too discreet to say.

It would be invidious, indiscreet and possibly indictable to go into specific, individual comments, but one can express a particular gratitude to King's Warren and the particular joys that our association with that school provided. Contacts with King's Warren could be described as frequent, intimate, endearing, and, in some instances, ultimately fruitful. My own comment could be summed up in two cherished words: May Angus. (I suppose I cannot forbear from repeating dear ol' Winnie's whispered resort to Shakespeare, in my ear, concerning 'the darling buds of May...')   JS

(Dear ol' Winnie was a form mate, David Winton.)

One of the great pleasures of the recent re-union was to see Tilly Tysoe after so many years. She had been such a great friend of so many of us and was really, like Aileen Smith, a sort of unofficial Owenian. I particularly remember her at a school dance working really hard dispensing refreshments.   WFF

Eileen Farmer-Wright (aka Tilly Tysoe), born in Bedford and a pupil at Bedford High, herself recalls another gathering.

Something I have never forgotten was being asked to a party and being told firmly 'no'. Bert Seaborn and Nobby Madden looked at each other got down on one knee and sang 'Moonlight becomes you Mrs T', mother melted, changed her mind and said I could go if they promised to look after me – which they did! And I went to my first party.   EF-W

Sally Beecham (née Saunders) was in York Street.

One Owen's friend, David Bernstein, lived next door to me in the terrace of small houses. The party wall between his bedroom and mine was thin enough for me to hear and enjoy the selection of classical records that he would play on his wind-up gramophone. No trannies in those days!   SB

Dennis Jones gave up queuing for kisses.

I graduated to Iris Oakins and her friend Thelma, trysting behind the Eastern National Bus Station.   DMJ

Another group of girls had Bedford High in common. Pauline Fowler was one of them.

When my brother reported to my mother, 'she's standing on the corner with lots of boys again', my lovely mum would say, 'There's safety in numbers'.   PF

'Ultimately fruitful' was John Stockton's description of the contacts between Owen's and King's Warren.

> My first girlfriend was at King's Warren School, part of a group which resulted in two marriages, the Beechams and Wrights.   DDW

Eileen Card became Mrs Wright; Sally Saunders, Mrs Beecham.

Henry George 'hung about Bedford Park'.

> I didn't find out about Russell Park until fairly late in the war. I didn't find out about girls till fairly late in the war either. Became very friendly with a King's Warren schoolgirl. One day I was whistling. Two girls were standing nearby. Josie Ames said to Sally Saunders 'Who's that?' 'Oh that's Henry George'. My fate was sealed. We've just celebrated our 50th wedding anniversary.   HG

Martin Mitchell frequented Russell Park.

> In that park was a girl of my own age. We may or may not have met, but given the after school *mêlées* of Owenians, King's Warren and Harpur Street girls in the park, our paths, must have crossed at some time. Some ten years later I married this unknown girl.   MM

Lily Mitchell had been evacuated with Richard Cobden School of Camden Town.

Barbara Richardson was a Bedfordian. Her father had been killed in the crash of the R101 airship.

> My brother, Tom Dimmock married a Bedford Modern girl Barbara Richardson and, after a working life, retired to Pavenham in Beds. GD

Though few Owenians chose to live in or around Bedford after the war, many visited it and continue to do so. And virtually all wartime schoolboys' memories of town and the people remain green. Mick Hooley is particularly grateful.

> My own personal activities included learning to ballroom dance. Thank you to Bedford Girls Club for the opportunity. There is still a wave of nostalgia, when I hear Deanna Durban and *Waltzing in the Clouds*. We even had an end of school year dance.   FVH

It was the first ever. the *Arrow* devoted a whole page.

The dance had been heralded by a great deal of publicity, which had been greeted in many quarters by a certain amount of speculation and trepidation. 'Would it be successful?' the pessimists had asked. 'Would it show a profit?' the financiers had cried. 'Would the band be any good?' the dancers had demanded. Their fears were banished on the night itself...

When the prospective 'rug-cutter' and his partner arrived at the Girls Modern School, a trio of smiling faces, the stewards, in other words, Messrs Cowling, Seaborn and Fenn, greeted them. These guardians of law and order gently but firmly led the client to the paybox where D.O. Jones, resplendent in yellow gloves, pink carnation and other weird accessories, delivered him either of his tickets or his money ... These formalities having been concluded, the dancer found himself and his partner, if all went well, in the hall dancing to music played in an attractively straightforward manner by a seven piece ensemble of boys from the school, led very capably by D.J. Marshall, to whom the credit for the band's formation must go. Later on in the evening music was also provided by a three-piece orchestra consisting of piano, piano stool and F.V. Hooley, playing romantic waltz medleys.

W.F. Fenn, *Arrow*, Michaelmas '43

That same Mick Hooley asks today, 'would this have happened in London?'

29

The Songs We Sang

Other people's words but our emotions.

It may be a trick of memory, an example of remembering only the happy times, but we seem to have spent a lot of the war singing. The words are etched into our long-term memory, associated inextricably with important events, personal and national.

We were evacuated singing. There were the popular songs which we sang together to cheer worried onlookers. *Under The Spreading Chestnut Tree, Roll Out The Barrel, The Lambeth Walk* (a pity there was no north London equivalent), *Run Rabbit Run.*

The first few nights some of us sang ourselves to sleep, silently in strange rooms connecting with the life we had left. We in our turn were being sung at and thought of with a saccharine lyric based on the sign-off line of Uncle Mac on BBC Radio's *Children's Hour.*

> *Goodnight children everywhere*
> *Your Mummy thinks of you tonight*
> *Lay your head upon your pillow*
> *Don't be a kid or a weeping willow ...*[1]

We were all kids but how many were weeping willows was hard to tell. None of us confided in others with expressions of loneliness, fear or desperation. 'It would be over by Christmas' optimistic parents or foster parents assured us. This despite most of us knowing that similar nostrums were mouthed in the Great War and that had lasted over four years.

Songs reinforced the optimism. We knew all the words to *The Siegfried Line.*

We're going to hang out the washing on the Siegfried Line
Have you any dirty washing mother dear?
We're going to hang out the washing on the Siegfried Line
If the Siegfried Line's still there.[2]

It would be there all right but that was an encounter four years later. Meanwhile there was another line.

After all, the Maginot line was invincible – the Germans would never get through it. We were right - it was strong enough but not long enough. The Germans quietly slipped around the side and pushed the French and English back towards the sea.   JA

But in 1939 there was a sense of a job that had to be done – and got over with as quickly as possible. Alan Locke recalls a song which traded on a pre-war favourite, desperately trying to wring as much sentiment out of the wretched lyric as possible.

Goodbye Sally
I'm saying goodbye
Goodbye Sally
I don't want you to cry
I want to see that smile
That wonderful sign
That's going to cheer me on my way
Right through the Siegfried Line.[3]

It finishes *So long it won't be long.*

It might not take long but it was taking a while to get started. Evacuees were returning to London, some schools were re-opening. Owen's stayed put. The longer the phoney war continued, the more hope arose. Horrors were distant or unreported. The British Expeditionary Force ('our boys', ex-Owenians among them) seemed to be doing little more than reconnaissance patrols. Alan Locke recalls a Denmark Street pot boiler to boost the morale of the BEF.

If a grey haired lady says
'How's your father?'
That's Mademoiselle from Armentières [4]

There was little front line activity to write home, let along sing, about. Had Hitler made a major strategic mistake? One popular song encouraged us to think so.

> *Adolf you've bitten off*
> *Much more than you can chew*
> *Come on – hold your hand out*
> *We're all fed up with you*
> *Adolf you toddle off*
> *And all your Nazis too*
> *Or you may get something to remind you*
> *Of the old red , white and blue.*[5]

'The people of Britain' were, according to an American historian, 'largely unaware of the dangers that faced them.'[6] The ignorance was reflected in the press, and newspaper coverage was found wanting.

In May 1940, according to a Gallup Poll,[7] only 3% of the British people believed that they might lose the war. That month Chamberlain's confident assertion that Hitler had 'missed the bus' was the signal for things to change – for the worse. The war-related songs, which outlived the phoney war, were few. *God bless you Mr Chamberlain* died the death. One triumphed. *There'll always be An England* became an unofficial national anthem, as *Land of Hope and Glory* is today. It ended with

> *There'll always be an England*
> *And England shall be free*
> *If England means as much to you*
> *As England means to me.*[8]

Boys would sing it lustily but a few subversives substituted the end line with 'as the bottom of the deep blue sea'. It was one of the few examples of overt anti-patriotic sentiment that I encountered in the war.   DEB

Of course, putting new words to existing 'official' lyrics is a common schoolboy activity. The chorus of the school song ends with

> *Never let your ardour cool*
> *For the honour of the school*
> *On Owen's to the fray.*

This was invariably substituted by a significant minority of the assembly with

Never let your trousers fall ...etc.

And the habit was common, too, among our elders. We soon adopted the re-cycled versions of popular choruses and military tunes as we marched with the Cadet Forces.

> *Stand by your beds*
> *Here comes the Air Vice-Marshal.*
> *He's got four great rings*
> *But he's only got one arsehole.*

The anti-authority sentiment engendered a distinct frisson. Another, more popular, anatomical marching song (to the tune of *Colonel Bogey*) was directed at the enemy.

> *Hitler has only got one ball*
> *Goering has two*
> *But they're quite small*
> *Himmler has something sim'lar*
> *But poor old Goebbels*
> *Has no balls*
> *At all!*

Whoever composed that lyric must have saved the Government's propaganda machine a considerable fortune. Popular tunes, of course, reflected the mood of the times. Occasionally one wondered if there was a conspiracy.

> I helped in National Savings campaigns selling stamps. We used to sing...
> DEB

> *Save a little sunshine for a rainy day*
> *It's easy if you try*
> *Save a little sunshine*
> *And those clouds of grey*
> *One day will soon roll by.*[9]

Songwriters were quick to pick up a phrase and turn it into a patriotic ditty.

> I remember hearing the Home Secretary Herbert Morrison encouraging housewives to put aside all their scrap so that useful material could be recycled. He came out with an exhortation *Up Housewives and at 'em.* Sure enough this became a popular song.

Up housewives and at 'em!
Up housewives and at 'em!
Save your paper
And keep your eye on
Rags, bones
And any old iron.
Up housewives and at 'em!
We'll soon tit-for-tat 'em,
So save up all the junk you've got
To help to win the war – so it's
Up housewives and at 'em![10]

Looking back it seems appropriate that the initiative received help from Tin Pan Alley!   AWL

Our war leader's words did not inspire songwriters until soon after Pearl Harbor when Churchill made two rousing speeches in North America. A clever lyricist took soundbites from both the Ontario speech (*Some chicken. Some neck.*) and that delivered in Washington (*What kind of people do they think we are?*) and stitched a patriotic hands-across-the-sea ditty.

Some chicken. Some neck.
Some chicken by heck.
What kind of people do they think we are
When we've got Winston and FDR?[11]

A popular broadcaster's soundbite was also turned into a song.

I was allowed to stay up to listen to the nine o'clock news and also the postscript that followed it. This was given by the novelist J.B. Priestley. He didn't sound like the rest of the BBC, he was more a man of the people and would often talk about how things would be different, better, after the war.   DEB

In one of his postscripts, Priestley came up with the line *let the people sing*. This became a song, which in turn became the signature tune of ENSA.*

Priestley, of course, wasn't alone in looking to a brighter future.

---

* Entertainments National Service Association. ENSA organised shows in camps at home and abroad.

> Most of the songs we sang were about tomorrow. There would be *blue birds over the white cliffs of Dover* (that was written by an American in 1940) or we'd get drunk: *I'm going to get lit up when the lights go up in London.*
>
> JS

John Stockton is right. When things are tense move into the future tense. The principle applied to both British and American lyricists.

> *There'll always be an England,* of course; *When the lights go on again all over the world; Till the lights of London shine again; We'll meet again; I'll be around; I'll be with you in apple blossom time; It's a lovely day tomorrow; When they sound the last all clear.*
>
> AWL

We were always encouraged to look, not simply forward, but upward.

> *It's a lovely day tomorrow*
> *Tomorrow is a lovely day*
> *Come and feast your tear-dimmed eyes*
> *On tomorrow's clear blue skies.*[12]

A more immediate, though no less optimistic, note was struck by American gung-ho songs.

> *Off we go into the wide blue yonder.*

Flanagan and Allen reassured us that

> *Blue skies are round the corner.*

And though it pre-dated the war, *Over the Rainbow* expressed the mood perfectly.

The deprivations of forces' life echoed our own. We too could say

> *Ma I miss your apple pie.*

The song lists other examples of Ma's culinary prowess, comparing it favourably with non-home cooking.

Though in many cases Bedford foster mothers cooked better. We could also identify with the sentiments of lovers on parting. The lyrics of *I haven't said thanks for that lovely weekend* resonated with those of us who were granted a forty-eight hour pass to London, particularly the description of the last few hours.

> *Your kit to be packed*
> *The train to be caught*
> *There was so much to say ...* [13]

There were American songs neatly fitting into our life, like ... meeting girls

> *This is a lovely way to spend an evening*

... breaking up

> *I couldn't sleep a wink last night*

... being lonely

> *Don't get around much any more*

... joining the forces

> *This is the Army Mr Jones.*

Most of us knew all of the words. Many of us still do. No television of course. And the radio switch was generally controlled by our billet parents. Some of us had wind-up gramophones though a record would cost a week's pocket money. We may have been introduced to some songs at the cinema, occasionally by forces' bands (a lucky few hearing Glenn Miller), by outfits playing in the parks during holiday-at-home events. Some of us went to the County Theatre.

> ... With its live touring shows, saucy shows, variety shows, reviews, melodramas and Phyllis Dixey,   JA

Phyllis Dixey obsessed us. She was an artistic stripper, famous for her long-lasting statuesque poses.

> My father used to commute to his work in London every day by train from the Midland Road Station. I would go to meet him sometimes

if Phyllis Dixey was appearing at the theatre near the station and her picture was outside.

In those days Lord Chamberlain ruled that nudes must not move.

> A great attraction for us boys was when Phyllis Dixey 'the girl the Lord Chamberlain banned' appeared. I am well qualified to discourse on this subject as I wrote to her and got a signed photo of the lady in typical stage pose. I do recall at one performance seeing a certain master (a gentleman of the cloth) in the audience but needless to say we totally ignored each other. GS

Runner up to Miss Dixey was Andrée, the occasionally undressed half of Gaston and Andrée. There were other double acts such as comedians Murray and Mooney and Morris and Ford. Clearly we rarely went to the County Theatre for the songs, or indeed the drama, though there would be occasional melodramas featuring Tod Slaughter, as in *Maria Marten or Murder in the Red Barn*. Our dramatic needs were satisfied elsewhere – in London and by our own endeavours – as we shall see in the next chapter.

30

Theatre of War

Dramatic Improvement in Owen's Performance.

The war years were a high watermark in the history of school theatricals. Why should this be? Luck, as usual, played a part: a cast of talented, extrovert, versatile show-offs coinciding with the presence of an inspiring teacher, the indefatigable 'Gus' Cumming.

Two other factors contributed. One was the need to keep occupied. The war years represented a high also in staff productivity. A teacher was rarely off duty. He or she ran clubs, associations, cadet forces, sports teams — and dramatic societies. Teachers and pupils were never busier. There were few idle hours to tempt the devil, to encourage thoughts of separation and loneliness.

The other factor was the generosity of our hosts. We were, after all, lodgers with, at best, a borrowed authority to request, never command, help. A school play in London would be performed in the school hall. Where else? But we were a school without a school. Then a few months into the war, Mr Liddle, the Head of the Modern School gave permission for our first production to be performed in the school hall. Moreover, members of the Modern School prepared the stage for use by Owen's. A rehearsal room was needed and the authorities of St. Paul's Moravian Church in the centre of town placed their hall at our disposal. (It would later stage a distinguished Owen's production.)

The first production was *You Never Can Tell* by George Bernard Shaw performed on the evenings of 9 and 10 March in 1940.

> *Both nights the performance played to full houses, indeed on Saturday night the hall was so crowded that it was necessary to find seating accommodation in the gallery.*
>
> A.R. Jonas, *Arrow*, Lent '40

Female roles were taken by boys and duly praised in the school magazine, as was the performance of Peter Senn as the romantic lead, Valentine.

> *Indeed he was excellent in the romantic moment, despite the fact that his embrace was somewhat reminiscent of the rugby training he has been putting in this year.*
>
> A.R. Jonas, *Arrow*, Lent '40

The second performance closed with a speech of thanks by the Headmaster followed by *God Save the King* upon which 'the audience departed into the blackout'. The cast, however, on returning to their dressing room were 'regaled with a sumptuous feast thoughtfully provided by the Headmaster'.

In the same issue of the *Arrow*, 'Gus' Cumming details his future plans. His colleague, Mr Smith 'has carried on the play reading circle while I have gone on with the rude mechanics of the game'.

> *Here we were lucky in many things. Finding every blacked out hall in the hands of the A.R.P., I pursued more devious routes and persuaded the Trades Club to let us have a couple of rooms where no-one would object to our cheerful noise. Only once were we asked to be a little quieter. Trade unionists are very patient mortals.*
>
> H. Cumming, *Arrow*, Lent '40

'Gus' Cumming's resourcefulness and industry meant a more ambitious programme for the following Christmas. Instead of the usual prefects' variety show, there were performed three one act plays. The following year the players gave the English premiere of a tragedy

> *... The Nuremberg Egg by Walter Harlon, a minor German poet and playwright, who for his beliefs was expelled from his native land and died in exile a few years ago. The theme of the play revolves around the invention of the lever watch called 'an Egg' from its shape which, on account of its novel mechanism can be used in nautical navigation and whose invention conferred an incalculable benefit upon the*

mariners of that adventurous era.

P.D. Lee, *Arrow*, Trinity '41

'Gus' had conceived of this play 'based on the discovery of the pocket watch' as 'very appropriate for Clerkenwell (near the Angel), which is still the centre of the English watch trade'. However, given the story of its author, performing in wartime presented a different set of resonances.

Later that term, the school players 'chose a play *(The Private Secretary)*, learnt it and performed it all in the two and a half weeks between the end of exams and the end of term'.

The following Michaelmas saw an innovation, a contemporary nativity play, *Christ's Comet* by Christopher Hassall. 'Gus' wrote:

> *It is non-liturgical in setting and deals with the story that there were four not three Wise Men who set out to find the child Jesus. It will be performed during the last week of term in the Moravian Church in St. Peter's, the home of Owenian drama in Bedford.*

H. Cumming, *Arrow*, Michaelmas '41

The school magazine gave it a mixed review.

> *... memories of a play that had many weaknesses together with flashes of high drama; one that was surprisingly moving due in no small measure to the singing of the choir and the playing of Mr Marshall Palmer.*

Anon, *Arrow*, Lent '42

The author, invited to critique the production in the same issue, compared the staging favourably with its previous production at Coventry Cathedral, praised the lighting (ingenious) the costumes (appropriate) and above all the tempo and 'the confidence with which the actors forged ahead towards the quiet conclusion'.

Major productions were interspersed with occasional performances where boys could try their hand at production — from upper, middle and lower school. 'Gus' was forever experimenting rather than relying on plays 'established in popular favour'. The 1941 Christmas production was an English version of a little-known French romantic comedy, Alfred de Musset's *On ne badine pas avec l'amour (One must not trifle with love)* — but the translator trifled with the title, renaming it *Silken Dalliance*.

> *Mr Cumming this time shared the honours as producer and translator and displayed his usual sure hand at both. His translation of de Musset's French was straightforward and in simple English which provided excellent material for the actors who did it full justice.*
>
> 'Old Stager', *Arrow*, Lent '43

The *Arrow* critic praised Frank Fenn's drunkard (played 'with the skill which has now become a tradition in the Owen's players') and especially the 'females'.

> *Mr Cumming was most fortunate this time in his choice of girls. Physically they were two of the most attractive and convincing young ladies the school has produced for some time. Their acting too was of a high standard. L.G.A. Horton was well contrasted as Rosette the pretty village maiden, and, indeed, one rarely sees many such pretty village maidens these days.*
>
> 'Old Stager', *Arrow*, Lent '43

In the next year's production, *Cyrano de Bergerac,* there was no trifling with gender.

> *One novel aspect of the play was the introduction of King's Warren schoolgirls to fill the female roles. This contributed a great deal to the success of the venture for they were able to bring that touch of realism to the character that is impossible with an all-male cast.*
>
> G.A. Goold, *Arrow*, Trinity '44

Frank Fenn faithfully embraced the many roles of the main character.

> *... A really superb performance. He played the extremely difficult part with the assurance and skill, which is perhaps unequalled in the annals of the dramatic society.*
>
> *Arrow*, Trinity '44

Cyrano himself wrote in the same issue of 'the unfailing good humour and patience of our leading lady'.

> *The leading female part of Roxanne was played by Jean Wilton with a direct simplicity which was very effective. ... Iris McNamara... was a very convincing character.*
>
> W.F. Fenn, *Arrow*, Trinity '44

King's Warren had become in effect our wartime sister school.

Their staff had tribulations over and above ours for they had been evacuated twice, first to Maidstone and the Battle of Britain. Josie George (née Ames) appreciates the workload half a century later.

> How little we realised the strains and stresses of our teachers who, in addition to the school curriculum, managed to produce *Trial by Jury*. Some of our sixth form girls joined Owen's boys for a memorable production of *Cyrano de Bergerac*.   JG

Memorable indeed. Those who witnessed or took part felt at the time that Owen's dramatic history was being made. Enchantment was there before distance and time lent more.

> *An old lady leaving the hall after the play was heard to remark 'It was beautiful. I felt as if I wanted to cry at times'.*
> G.A. Goold, *Arrow*, Trinity '44

Players and spectators both knew who was responsible.

> *How this feat was accomplished is a secret known only to Mr Cumming, the only producer we know who combines the patience of a Bedford housewife queuing for strawberries with the ability to act a complete cast of thirty-four off the stage.*
> W.F. Fenn, *Arrow*, Trinity '44

and the *Arrow* critic concluded with

> *A tribute to the great amount of hard work done by Mr. Cumming. His work was behind the scenes and few people knew much about it, but it was he who laid the foundations for the success of the play.*
> G.A. Goold, *Arrow*, Trinity '44

'Gus' left the school that term and no report of drama is covered in the remaining year of the war. Those who came in contact with 'Gus' were infected by his enthusiasm. To a generation of Owenians he bequeathed a sense of self-belief, a quality vital in wartime.

31

'Darkness Visible'

Surviving the blackout.

Churchill had his own name for the phoney war. He termed those first eight months 'the twilight war'.[1] Had his countrymen known this, they might well have disagreed. The most immediate impact of going to war was the blackout. It began on September the first and our first night in Bedford. It ended just over five years later.

Collisions of people and vehicles were frequent. By the end of 1939 four thousand had died in road accidents. (Civilian deaths outnumbered military deaths then, through the Blitz and the greater part of the war.) In the first four months of the war there were 1700 more casualties than in the equivalent months of 1938.[2] The press recognised the dangers less than a week after the outbreak of war. The *Daily Express* in a leader urged the Government to modify the blackout.[3] But to no avail. The Government had a term for the effect it was trying to achieve: 'subdued moonlight'.

Street lighting was radically reduced. Traffic lights became slits and, later, half moons. Car lamps were masked. Car bumpers were painted white. Pedestrians were encouraged to wear white.

> In the early days of the war we bought luminous buttons and armbands. I don't think they did much good. DEB

Kerbs were painted white. So were front steps. They were normally red and carefully polished with Cardinal whose manufacturers opportunistically introduced a white powder 'for safety during blackout'. Familiar landmarks suddenly disappeared. Care had to be taken opening doors. Torches became crucial – as did the manner of their concealment.

At the beginning of the war, my Dad bought a large sheet of thick, green cellophane and proceeded to insert discs of the stuff in all our torches. It dimmed the brightness all right but it suggested green-for-go and was therefore banned (as was red) and torches and lamps had to be opaquely covered except for slits.   DEB

Masked torches weren't very efficient and during an alert you had to switch them off.   MM

Unfortunately, the need for torches generated a demand for batteries. Particularly scarce was the versatile number eight.

The No.8 battery and torch became almost fondly treasured companions for evening outings.   JS

Harold Caplan remembers using dim lights on his bicycle. A fading battery in an otherwise unadjusted cycle lamp could just about pass muster. Dennis Jones was even more resourceful.

I experimented with an oxyacetylene lamp, fuelled with lumps of calcium carbide, which released inflammable acetylene on contact with water.   DMJ

But cyclists and pedestrians gradually grew accustomed.

When there was neither starlight nor moonlight, and with virtually unlit street lamps, you could often walk into a tree, fall off the kerb, or collide with another pedestrian. Otherwise the blackout was no problem.   MM

The Government-imposed blackout of all street lights and house lights and the reduced level of lighting on cars, although there were very few of these, was to ensure that German aircraft could not see us from above. It was vigorously applied by ARP* wardens and the Police. But we were usually safe in walking about because we knew where we were and there was very little traffic on the road to be a danger to pedestrians.   AWL

We became accustomed to stumbling through dark streets at night. Fear of mugging was not on the agenda.   DMJ

---

* ARP Air Raid Precautions, subsequently called Civil Defence.

The blackout is remembered, strangely, as no great inconvenience, except in the tedious business of having to mask windows effectively every night.   JS

I believe we quickly got used to such things as gas masks, blackout, rationing.   DPe

We got used to the dark, to feeling our way, to listening acutely though, as Martin Mitchell comments, 'infra-red eyes would have been most useful'.

We read *Paradise Lost* as a set book. Dicky Dare would extract 'gobbets' of text which he'd chalk on the blackboard. One of these came from Milton's description of a dungeon in hell: *No light but rather darkness visible.*[4] It was a good description of the blackout we got to know. DEB

But what about strange places which you hadn't got to know? Visits often necessitated relearning the art of blackout survival. Even returning to a once familiar location, namely London, proved unsettling to Owenians. We were allowed home at weekends during the phoney war. One sixth former related his experience.

I caught the train and arrived at St. Pancras at dusk. I expected London to be as I had always found it at night... the slight mist made to feel homely by the ruddy glow of neon signs; the brightly lit shops; the friendly populace; the roar of the buses and tubes. These were the things which had endeared the Town to me and which I felt I needed as I stepped from the train.

On the platform I looked about me in wonder. The station, always large and rambling, now seemed vast and ghostly. Blue lights shone down, the roof seemed like an immense vault, a cave.

The general bustle of the station was gone, gone with the lights and the taxis. It was not entirely changed, however. Somehow, the station seemed only to be sleeping, or just dreamy. There was the same friendly noise, but subdued. The sounds were familiar, but hushed. The station had put on the garb of strategy, and thought it wiser rather to hide its welcome behind a mask of darkness than expose itself to the dangers of a silent death.

I stepped into the street and paused. There was the mist, and the slight cold; but no lights. The neon lights could no longer blaze their friendly greeting. Instead, it was as if wraiths were moving in the

streets below me. The dim outlines of the buses; the softly moving forms of the pedestrians; the subdued hum of a city disguised.

Thus I had come home and found it all so changed. Everything at first seemed different. The things I was looking for were there and yet they were not.

I descended to the street, and then the explanation for my queer feelings burst upon me. London was disguised. Down in the street the Londoner was the same; in fact his personality shone through the encircling gloom more strongly than ever. It was London and all that London means to a Londoner, but it had hidden itself under cover of darkness, and I could not help feeling that underneath its mask it was laughing and bubbling with good humour at the tricks it had played on its potential attacker.

What a surge of thankfulness and emotion passed through me when I boarded a bus and heard the conductor's voice say, in the way that only London conductors can: 'Hold tight there! Fares please!'

Then I knew that the blackout had merely darkened the face of London but had left its soul as free as ever. I had come home ...
M.C., *Arrow*, Michaelmas '39

The blackout was a way of life, a new routine with its own rituals.

I was not allowed a light bulb in my room for fear of air raids and the routine of undressing in the dark 'last thing off being first thing on' in an emergency became a habit.   RN

Lighting a cigarette was performed inside cupped hands.   DMJ

The billet had wooden frames, covered in blackout paper. These were placed in windows, carefully, each night.   BL

The windows, of course, were criss-crossed with strips of adhesive brown paper. Bus windows were protected with toughened materials. So were London tube trains.

A rather smug character drawn by cartoonist David Langdon used to advise, even admonish, Londoners from posters. One tube card pictured a passenger removing the adhesive protective covering surrounding the small, framed diamond of permitted clear window. Next to him sat this Billy Brown of London Town saying

*I trust you'll pardon my correction
That stuff is there for your protection.*

Not long after, a graffiti artist appended a reply from the offending passenger.

*Thank you for the information.
I want to see the bleeding station.*

Fines were imposed on householders if blackout curtains were not properly drawn or screens ill fitting.

As dusk approached, curtains were drawn and blackout screens put up. You couldn't meet a more meticulous, law-abiding person than my billet lady, Mrs Knight. She was nearly brought to tears when a warden called at the door and almost accused her of colluding with the enemy because a chink of light was showing in the front room. It seems there was always a warden about ready to swoop like a night owl looking for prey. MM

The cry 'Put that light out!' was heard in the land. It became a catch phrase. The warden, dressed in 'a little brief authority', a helmet and badge, was a figure of harmless fun, at best a necessary evil. He was the hero of a bathetic piece in the *Arrow* by G.A.Blundell (VA).

Collar turned well up and hat pulled down shielding the forehead and eyes, he stood crouching against the gnarled trunk of an old oak. ... For a while he remained there, straining his ears to pick up the slightest sound. But the only noise, which broke the uncanny silence, was the restless chirping of the crickets in the long grass around him. Then suddenly he stiffened and stood rigid for some seconds, his heart beating wildly against his breast, scarcely believing his eyes.

But no, he couldn't be mistaken, for there it was, sure enough, making its way out of one of the windows of the manor and creeping stealthily towards the place of his concealment.

By this time, however, he had raised himself up, his huge chest heaving with emotion. He clenched his hands and the veins stood out on his forehead like whipcords. Then, preparing for a great effort, he drew a deep breath and roared: 'Put that light out at once can't yer?' in a way, which only the most perfect air-raid warden can say it!!!

Arrow, Michaelmas '40

The blackout was a constant provocation. Here is Peter Provost recalling the start of the Blitz.

> The days of the phoney war were well and truly over. The blackout was
> blacker...   PP

Black was the obvious metaphor... death, despair, darkness. One longed for the opposite. Popular songs verbalised these longings. *When the lights go on again all over the world. I'm going to get lit up when the lights go on again in London.* Of course, not everybody needed to wait that long. The blackout encouraged a sense of adventure and hid indiscretion. The poet again got it right.

> *And when night*
> *Darkens the streets, then wander forth the sons*
> *Of Belial, flown with insolence and wine.*[5]

That was Milton. As for Frank Fenn

> I remember little of the blackout. It was too dark to see.   WFF

32

Life Was Full

How we earn money and spend our time.

There was an upbeat movie in 1944, thinly disguised propaganda featuring a host of Hollywood's finest. It was called *Thank Your Lucky Stars*. Few of us needed this encouragement. If we didn't know then how lucky we were, we know now. Safe, looked after, educated, entertained and busy.

Philip Fawkes writes in his diary on 22 June 1944:

> Went to butchers for Mrs Evans in Morning then school. 'Flash' for English, 'Dicky' for History; back to billet. Read a little of '*Gino Watkins*,' had dinner, stewing steak, new peas, carrots and potatoes - delicious! School in afternoon. Mechanics with 'Point' Clarke; French with Miss Cast & two periods of prep. Was let off A.T.C. to swot for exams which begin on Friday. Came home seeing one of Joe's girls, or so I believe, Margaret Baxter. Rather surprised — he already goes about with Barbara Richardson. Nothing on wireless. Went to get Mrs Evans' dentures after tea. Tried some of her new raspberry jam although she would not let me try the strawberry. The garden is looking well. Apple tree full of fruit, new potatoes nearly ripe, tomatoes, lettuces, beans & rhubarb all growing fast. Peas ripe.
> I have noticed that old people seem to become like children more & more as they grow older. I wonder if there is any similarity between their youth & old age?   PFa

Ron Nash summarises his evacuation.

> Life was full. I cycled, ran, swam, debated, marched behind the RAF band in Wings for Victory Week – saw Adrian Boult and listened to the concerts at Bedford School – learnt about jazz with the American Forces Network and heard Glenn Miller.   RN

There was a downside of course. We were worried about our parents in London and relatives on active service. There was uncertainty about our own future. There was occasional homesickness. But overall, for most of us, life was hardly miserable.

> It's curious that I didn't feel that life in wartime entailed great deprivation. Possibly the advantages of Bedford, for me, tended to balance the admittedly sad and constraining effects of family separation. Of course, sometimes one yearned for mum's style of food and for the unobtainable orange. I remember on one occasion I had a bad cold when my father visited me (which my parents did occasionally). He went out and brought back a life-saving – or so it seemed – bottle of Rose's lime juice. JL

Parents sent postal orders – small amounts frequently rather than, say, a pound to last a month. For many of us it was our first experience of real financial management.

Income could, of course, be supplemented. Billet parents might subsidise you with the occasional treat, bring you back something from the shop or pub. More satisfyingly, you could earn a few coppers running errands or silver doing jobs around the house, the garden or allotment.

> I had quite a few duties. I had to do all the washing up, making the fire and other chores, no real problem really.
> My strangest chore was meeting her at the Burns Club at 11 p.m. three times a week. I had to carry an Indian club to escort her home because a girl had been murdered nearby in a surface shelter. DHS

Shopping, since it invariably involved much patient queuing, was often entrusted to us. The more resourceful would sell their services to neighbours.

A very few chose to rob stores – more out of devilment than sheer need. Woolworth's and Boots neighboured the school building. They were officially out-of-bounds so there was a double danger in relieving them of merchandise.

> There were apocryphal stories of thefts from Woolworth's of sundry saleable goods but the consequences of being caught were too awful to contemplate. We were an indoctrinated, law abiding and conforming generation inculcated for the most part with a respect for authority. To

be caught by a policeman riding a bike at night without lights was a fate to be avoided at all costs.   MC

Bernard Fox rode a bike for profit.

I got myself a job at the local grocer delivering groceries with one of those heavy bicycles with a large basket in the front in which the groceries were carried. There was one lady who always gave me tuppence when I delivered her groceries. This helped to increase the spending money that my mother sent, I think, about every month. I also remember that she sent Mrs Bale some money to supplement the billeting money which was not very much.   BF

Ray Coombes got a Saturday morning job in Castle Road at a small grocer's shop and, more enterprisingly ...

I persuaded the man who owned all the rowing boats, canoes and punts to let me help him at weekends. His name, I believe, was Bryant and he lived in Castle Road also.

The pay was not spectacular but the tips were better; especially from the US servicemen who would often say 'Keep the change, boy'.

Bryant frequently left me in alone in charge for quite long periods with his 'Letting Book' and I took all the deposits and times of hire, etc. It was sometimes frantically busy and I once asked Bryant if he would allow one or two of my friends to help me – bearing in mind that I was all of thirteen years of age at the time.

His reply I have never forgotten.

'No! One boy's a boy, two boys are half a boy, and three boys are no boys at all.'   KRC

Fellow schoolboys were a source of income. Items unwanted by one had a value for another – comics, pens, souvenirs, shrapnel and signed photographs of film stars obtained, for the cost of a stamp, from British and US studios. Gambling kept the astute in pocket. Some boys made more money, via pontoon and solo in the evenings at farming camps than they did in the fields.

Very popular at the time was the 'football pontoon'. Members of works clubs, pubs and barracks put money in a kitty, drew a team and kept score each week. The winning team was the one that amassed eleven goals exactly. If the total was twelve it had 'bust'. Newspapers listed successive weeks' goal tallies. Mervyn Crossick worked out the mathematics and saw a potential goldmine.

The names of all the football teams in the various divisions were carefully written down and cut out. They were dropped in a school cap and for 3d participants drew blindly one team. The following week I would collect a further 3d for each team and the eventual winner would be the person whose team was the first to score exactly 11 goals. The prize was ten shillings. The average team score each week was between two and three and I calculated I needed to sell a minimum of 20 teams to break even after two weeks. After that it was bonanza time.

I was dazzled by the ease with which friends and acquaintances could be persuaded to subscribe. 28 teams were sold for a grand total of seven shillings. By the second week there would be a profit of four shillings. Saturday arrived and expectantly I sat in front of the wireless to listen to the football results. 2-1, 1-0, even a 4-3. It was then the thunderbolt struck. When I die, engraved across my chest will be the words Tranmere Rovers. The opposition on that day I don't remember. But how could I ever forget that on that fateful Saturday Tranmere Rovers scored 11 goals. My business empire had collapsed with this freak result. I read the name on the winning ticket. My heart became heavier. BC, a burly child in the form above mine with an acned complexion and a reputed short fuse was the winner. I knew instinctively that he would demand his pound of flesh. I was right, the only compromise was that the balance of three shillings missing from the kitty could be paid off at a shilling a week – or else.   MC

It is worth mentioning that Bernard and Nicholas Coral – of the bookmaking family – were not involved in any gambling enterprise. They chose a less exciting but more reliable route to supplementing income, delivering newspapers in Biggleswade before coming to Bedford.

We had the longest paper round in Biggleswade; the whole of London Road before seven o' clock.   NC

Wartime memories of early rising are always associated with darkness. Double summertime made our evenings long and our mornings dark.

I'd dress quickly and warm, pick up my torch and run down the road, turn the corner to the newsagent. The papers would have arrived. I'd take my card with its list of addresses and titles and assemble, in order, the papers (no more than six pages in each, later four). They would have come up by train the fifty miles from London. Occasionally one title would be missing, but bombing rarely stopped us from delivering. I'd put the papers in a canvas sack but not before I'd read the headlines, skimmed the news stories and checked any results in the minuscule sports section.

I got paid three shillings a week. When another evacuee (from the endangered Sussex coast) shared my billet we shared the round – one and six each!   DEB

Mervyn Crossick was still in debt to BC when he read a sign in a newsagent. A bright and willing boy (political correctness was a long way off) was required.

He went inside.

Mr P, the proprietor, told me to report to the shop the following morning at 6am. I left my billet that first day of gainful employment on my bike at quarter to six on a cold winter's day in wartime, blacked-out Britain with little enthusiasm. It was a new and depressing experience and it was only the image of the podgy form of BC stabbing his fist in my direction and demanding his money that provided the spur.

The top newspaper would have written on it a house number and the name of the road. Following that there would be written numbers. They were not in numerical order but were fashioned to enable me to proceed up the road crossing from one side to the other. When I reached the end I would begin afresh with a new road and number set out on a paper followed just by numbers.

On that first morning I needed that extra half-hour. The advantage a newsboy had during the war was the slimness of the newspapers we were delivering. Paper was severely rationed. It was, therefore, no problem tucking my allocation of papers under my arm. The downside was the blackout. Even with a torch, locating house numbers was a seriously difficult problem followed by the search for the letterbox. Each was sited differently, some horizontal, some vertical, some high, some low.

I still had two roads to do when I ran out of time and had to get to school. I decided hopefully that if my customers hadn't thrown away yesterday's paper there might still be bits they hadn't read and I would complete my round at midday. Miraculously, nobody complained to Mr P and I finished my deliveries during my lunch hour.

It wasn't until the fourth day that the matters went seriously wrong. It was raining when I started. By this time I had obtained some familiarity with the houses, their numbers and the location of their letterboxes. Despite the rain, the delivery was going smoothly. I had discovered short cuts between houses. It wasn't always necessary after delivering a paper to retreat down the path. All the metal gates and railings had been removed to support wartime demands for steel. It was an easy matter to jump over low brick walls that formerly had been proudly adorned with railing superstructures ...

It was such a wall that was to prove my undoing. I had delivered to about six houses when I leapt over a low wall. I slipped on the wet pavement as I jumped, the heel of my shoe caught in a section of the old railing still embedded in the wall and I went flying in one direction whilst my papers went slithering in a confused mash across a lawn and flower bed. I slowly got to my feet and looked with horror at my very personal disaster area. Clutched under my arm were a few copies, the rest were sprawled lying under and on top of bushes, herbaceous plants and lawn. The extent of the problem gradually dawned upon me. The numbering system was now entirely out of sequence.

I sat on the wall in the rain and dark desperately shuffling and trying with only the light from a small torch to resolve my predicament. I wiped my muddy hands on my trousers and decided that I was faced with unreasonable odds. My dilemma was that I didn't have time to return to the shop to get them sorted nor was I inclined to face the wrath of Mr P.

I would carry on delivering, guessing where they might belong.

I wasn't able to complete my deliveries before school began. I still believe that when I delivered some of the balance at lunchtime and the remainder after school in the evening that I had made a reasonable fist of the problem. Unfortunately Mr P appeared to think otherwise when he confronted me the following morning. Unmindful of the problems I had experienced, he was concerned only with the complaints he had received. Wet, soiled newspapers, some not delivered, others delivered wrongly and, probably the most cardinal sin of all, I had delivered to Councillor Y a *Daily Herald* whilst Mr T, a well-known local union organiser, had received *The Telegraph*. I was fired on the spot.

It was not being sacked by Mr P that upset me so much as confronting BC whose first shilling was imminently due. I was left with no alternative. My days of independence were over. A phone call home and a clean breast elicited a postal order for three shillings by return. BC was finally placated.   MC

The Headmaster was not pleased to learn that boys were delivering papers. Whether he was concerned about safety or sleep deprivation was not made clear. In any event, he banned the practice.

I was delivering Sunday papers to a house near the river when the door was opened by 'Flash' Hardwick then deputy Headmaster.

I was quaking and rooted to the spot by his frightening stare, but he simply took the papers and firmly shut the door. There was no castigation or punishment and 'Flash' never mentioned it again during any necessary contact we had in class from then onwards.   DAP

The ban was more honoured in the breach than the observance. Once the round was learned, the delivery was routine. On the walk there was time to think and the contents of one's sack provided food for thought.

> One day, as I was walking along Castle Road with a sack on my back, I engaged in a philosophical discussion with myself. There had been some particularly bad news. This presumably meant that the ultimate victory would be delayed. But, I argued, there is a definite date at which the war will come to an end. Nobody knows it of course, but it's there nevertheless and that hasn't changed so we are one day nearer than we were this time yesterday (i.e. before the bad news). When that day eventually arrived – at least in Europe – I was delivering papers. For the only time in my paperboy career I banged on each door and shouted the news.   DEB

There was a different sort of newspaper. Its tone and ethos can be discerned by recalling Don Curtis's recollection of 1 September 1939.

> Twelve-year-old boys do not cry (having been educated by the *Boys' Own Newspaper* and Kipling).   DC

Not that you would find many copies of the *Boys' Own Newspaper* circulating in the quadrangle. It was, however, permitted reading in the classroom, though not part of the curriculum as was the *Children's Newspaper* for those of elementary (primary) school age. These publications were serious attempts at stealing the ground from the truly popular media. Why should the devil have all the best tunes?

Comics still cast their spell today, not only for Doug Wade.

> My 'aunt across the road' brought me a subscription to my favourite comic the *Beano* as a going away present. In Calgary now I meet some friends for coffee every Saturday at a Café Beano, which until a recent renovation, had some old copies of the comic printed on the wall. It was nice to renew acquaintance with Lord Snooty!   DDW

But gaining entrance to a grammar school meant graduation in more ways than one.

I was not a great comic reader; I left that behind at primary and junior schools. I read *Armchair Science* (sixpence per month), *The Hotspur* and *The Wizard* and later I was a regular buyer of *Aeroplane Spotter* which stimulated my interest in everything aeronautical. AWL

Dennis Jones's delights are more eclectic.

Comics. I enjoyed *Beano, Dandy, Film Fun, Magnet, Rover* and *Wizard*. Their characters included Billy Bunter, unshaven Desperate Dan, Lord Snooty and his Pals and Wilson the wonder athlete. DMJ

Wilson ran the mile in three minutes. Other heroes had their followers.

I was devoted to *The Wizard – Six Bullets for Abdul the Cruel*, The Fiery Cross of Texas, Joe Cover, the unplayable bowler, Clicky Ba, the beat-up cricket bat used as a weapon by, inevitably, a totally loyal non-white hero who would never be allowed in a politically correct publication. These are some of the persistent memories I have of this 'tuppenny-blood' whose Friday appearance was the high point of my week. I also occasionally read *The Hotspur*. During the war I gradually lost interest, even in *Six Bullets for Abdul the Cruel*, until I eventually discovered John Buchan (largely because *The 39 Steps* was among the first films I ever saw). JS

I was hooked on two 'tuppenny bloods'. Initially the *Champion* and later *The Hotspur*. (Strange, since I was and still am an Arsenal supporter.) Soon into the war, paper was rationed. Comics became fortnightly not weekly. My hero in the *Champion* was Rockfist Rogan who was a pilot-cum-boxer in the Great War. A few weeks into World War Two there he was with all his mates in the current conflict – not a day older.
  DEB

Rogan outflew, outgunned and downed the Huns. The Germans of better class were further humiliated after crash landing, taught a lesson and brought firmly to heel by his teasing left and crushing right before stumbling away to incarceration. Queensberry rules always applied on the British side, war or no war. Gentlemen behaved as such, British and Boche. AJ

Andrew Jones and his brother shared John Stockton's affection for another hero, Chang.

Chang was far from the Orient but a staunch supporter of the Raj. He cracked the skulls and put down the wily and rebellious Parathions of the Northwest Frontier with his 'Clicky Ba' of trusty, English willow, wire-bound and well bloodied.   AJ

There was a definite upper class touch to the stories and mores. The schools featured were public schools, most famously Greyfriars in the *Magnet*.

> I seemed to have a fixation on the *Magnet* to such an extent that I used to play a secret game, identifying Greyfriars Remove characters with Owenians. It was obvious who was Hurree Jamset Ram Singh (Peter Senn or R.B.Chatterji), and the unflappable Harry Wharton had to be Alistair Mackay. Billy Bunter really did exist and often propelled you backwards across the quad with his aggressive stomach. As for the misanthropic master, Quelch …   MM

The *Magnet* itself closed down in July 1940 but Billy Bunter *et al* lived on in paperback form.

Though frowned on by the teaching staff, 'tuppenny bloods' did encourage reading and formed a step on the way to the appreciation of better writing.

> Yes, I did read 'tuppenny bloods' quite avidly. Looking again at one recently I was struck by the quality of much of the story writing, so maybe they weren't as bad for us as our parents sometimes feared. However, I soon graduated in Bedford – via the library – to *Just William* and Agatha Christie and subsequently to W.H. Auden and Christopher Isherwood and *Penguin New Writing*.   JL

33

We Never Went Hungry

Getting round rationing via ingenuity and artifice.

Rationing would be a fact of life in wartime. This we knew from our parents and from the newspapers. We would have guessed that ration books had already been printed. (The Ministry of Food was set up five days after war was declared.) Items became difficult to get through actual shortage or fear of shortage.

> My first errand – on the second day of the War – was to get a tin of tomatoes before they ran out. I succeeded. It cost sixpence.   DEB

Queuing preceded rationing proper. From 19 September 1939 everyone had to register at a grocer and a butcher. Goodies first, then basics were available only to registered customers. You could not register at more than one outlet. The shop became more important than the customer. No question of the customer always being right. In October we collected our ration books. On November 28 we were told that rationing would begin on January 8. (It was not to end till 1954.) The weekly allowance of butter would be four ounces, sugar twelve and bacon or ham, four. Once rationing came in, the queues for those items diminished but the queues for off-ration items increased. Many Owenians had less spare time to call their own

> I used to queue regularly at Sear's the butcher next to the library for off-the-ration sausage meat.   KD

> On many occasions I would queue for hours on Saturday at the butcher's shop adjacent to the Bedford central library for half a pound of unrationed sausages.   BF

But none of our Owenians standing in line was ever to faint with hunger.

> Generally well-fed. KD

> Bearing mind the actual amount (of meat, butter etc.) allowed, I am amazed that I don't seem to have felt the deprivation more than I did.
> JS

> I never recall feeling hungry. RN

Meat was rationed (one shilling and ten pence worth per week) from 11 March 1940 but Bernard Fox isn't alone in remembering 'incredible Sunday lunches'.

> There was often a roast when it was beef with Yorkshire puddings, roast and boiled potatoes, large quantities of vegetables which mainly came from the allotment rented by Mr Bale. The plate which was a large one was piled high. BF

The bacon ration which had been increased to twelve ounces in January, reverted to four in June. In May, the sugar ration was halved to six ounces. In July, margarine and cooking fats were rationed, as was tea – two ounces per week and, as the posters advised, *none for the pot.*

Further rationing followed rapidly. In May 1941, the universal standby, cheese, was rationed, initially at one ounce per week. In June clothes rationing was introduced. In July, we were restricted to half a pound of jam or preserves per month. That summer, food stocks (we learned much later) would have lasted two weeks had the merchant navy not beaten the blockade.

Less troublesome for a schoolboy was the introduction in February 1942 of soap rationing – one pound per month.

April 1942 saw the demise of white bread.

FOOD IS A MUNITION OF WAR – DON'T WASTE IT said the posters. We were unlikely to.

> We all had our own small plate on which was placed at the beginning of each week our two-ounce ration of butter. When it was gone it was gone! Good training in self-restraint. DDW

The training left its mark. Our generation abhors waste and bores its grandchildren by equating the food they leave with the wartime weekly ration.

There were minor deprivations and difficulties, mostly surmounted.

> I was well fed and looked after under the circumstances and it could not have been easy for Mrs Hickson especially as I had been brought up as a vegetarian after my father. JL

> Becoming a vegetarian in rationing's latter years I received nuts and extra cheese in place of meat. DMJ

> I had sugar in my tea till Mrs Smith said she would make plum jam if she could find some sugar. I gave up sugar in my tea that day and hate it to this. But I enjoyed the jam. DEB

Sometimes the restrictions were felt only when we had the opportunity to live someone else's life, for example on an American airbase or, in the case of Harold Caplan, *en route* to air officer training in Canada.

> I remember when I first went to Canada and on the ship and in Canada itself, you had unlimited food. I remember enormous amounts of eggs, fruit and food and we made pigs of ourselves for two months. HC

There were plenty of opportunities to supplement official nourishment.

> Individual (how could it be anything else?) Lyons Fruit Pies in boxes, square with bevelled corners, sugar-crusted, with ventilation holes on top and filled with fruit puree. AJ

> The occasional Spam roll costing threepence from Marks and Spencer filled a gap. RN

> Spam, a processed, canned meat, arrived by the boatload from the United States. I remember the news on the radio. There was another product, very much like it, which arrived at the same time. It was called MOR. The announcer said, I'm sure unwittingly, 'so when you've tried SPAM ask for MOR'. DEB

Spam and Mor were rationed as were the similar Prem and Tang. They formed part of the 'personal points' scheme, an idea introduced at the end of 1941, which the Ministry of Food pinched from the enemy. Each of us had a number of points to spend per month and a selection of scarce goods on which to spend them. The number would change according to supply, as would the selection.

Geoff Dimmock found ways round rationing.

> There was always the fish and chip shop and Lyons tea shop.   GD

A pairing echoed by Martin Mitchell.

> The two most important, non-illicit sources for topping up rations were Joe Lyons and Bays fish shop. Joe Lyons did a roaring weekend trade in fruit pies. Owenians would swarm round the teashop like bees desperate for pollen.   MM

Bays was near Russell Park and off Castle Road and as busy as both of them. A piece of cod for threepence, a bag of chips for a penny and, for a treat, a potato fritter – more batter than spud.

> Bays would be thronged with a mixture of Owen's and the BBC Symphony Orchestra. A mere whiff of that pungent smell of their fish and chips, from even half a mile away, would set your heart thumping as you raced after your nose.   MM

You could, of course, also eat sitting down if your pocket ran to it. Apart from the reasonably priced Lyons tea shop, there were up-market restaurants and tea rooms, the Cadena and the Dujon (an abbreviation of Dudeney and Johnston, a rather posh grocers). There was also a milkbar next to the bus station.

> Welsh rarebit in the Granada cinema café.   CL

> A café near the swimming bath was also a favourite, my party trick being drinking the Worcester sauce with hot Bovril.   RN

> We used to eat often at the British Restaurant. The food was not marvellous but all right.   HC

> The British Restaurant, where many of us went daily for lunch, fed us with novel substitutes for meat, like Spam, an American sausage concoction, and whalemeat.   MM

British Restaurants were public cafeterias located throughout the country in existing buildings, such as local government offices, churches, schools and the Chinese galleries at the Victoria and Albert museum. Lord Woolton, the Minister of Food, proposed calling them 'Communal Feeding Centres'. Churchill was aghast. He sent this note to Woolton: 'I hope the term 'Communal Feeding Centres' is not going to be adopted. It is an odious expression, suggestive of communism and the workhouse. I suggest you call them 'British Restaurants'.[1]

The food was wholesome, the atmosphere friendly and the price reasonable: tenpence or a shilling a head, and one shilling and sixpence for a three course meal. By September 1943, over two thousand had opened serving half a million meals per day.

Of course, there were also private sources of supplementary feeding.

> Rationing was not heard of in our house, because 'Sir' was the General Secretary of the Bedfordshire and Huntingdonshire Farmers' Union.
> KRC

> The rigours of food rationing were not greatly apparent in many billets. Certainly not in the Tysoe household, especially since Mr T belonged to a 'pig club' with the result that we feasted on ham such as I have not tasted since.
> MJC

> Being billeted on a butcher with a sister-in-law who kept a dairy, I was never too aware of rationing...I lived with people who always had 'that little bit extra'.
> AWL

> Occasionally, a food parcel arrived from my father in India containing a fruitcake and other goodies – but most disappeared in the post.   DMJ

Make do and mend was a slogan to encourage improvisation. It applied to the cook as well as the seamstress.

We got used to substitute fillings. The Woolton pie (meatless and mainly potato and other available vegetables) made the Lord a household name. It was even served at the Savoy. Whereas back in Bedford, Ian Appleby 'liked the tomato filled sausages'. A small general store near Russell Park made ice cream from mashed potato. The Ministry of Food promoted a banana sandwich composed of parsnip and banana essence.

> Our meagre weekly food rations would barely do for one meal today but with reconstituted egg powder, dried milk, vegetables with curry powder or a three-penny piece of haddock, skate or cod and two penn'orth of chips we managed to keep healthy.   JA

Reconstituted egg powder? If your billet lady kept chickens you could have the real thing. (By 1943 a quarter of the country's eggs were produced by domestic hen keepers.) In the thirties the average Briton ate three eggs a week, in WW2 one a fortnight. You made do with the American dried variety. One packet equalled a dozen eggs and cost one shilling and nine pence – or a penny three farthings each. One level tablespoon of powder and two of water equalled one egg. And you were advised not to reconstitute more than your immediate need.

We had heard the word *ersatz* but that applied to the enemy who were allegedly drinking a 'coffee' made of ground acorns. We Britons were being innovative. The *Daily Telegraph* published 'readers' tested recipes' and claimed 'homes are now experimental kitchens from which dishes are being launched'.[2] We were realising the values of vegetables. A Ministry of Food war cookery leaflet told the housewife 'no country in the world grows vegetables better than we do' ... (Owenian allotment holders would nod to that.) '... and probably no country in the world cooks them worse'.[3]

Carrots, of course, helped you to see in the dark. The Government told you so.

> *The carrot is one of our most valuable root vegetables for it contains particular substances which increase our resistance to infection and help us to see in the blackout.*[4]

And Captain ('Cats Eyes') Cunningham the ace bomber pilot personally endorsed this. There was no reason not to believe it.

And carrots weren't rationed. No fresh vegetable was, though some of the tinned varieties were 'on points'. And bread was not rationed till after the war!

> Bread and potatoes were never rationed during the war and we were stuffed with carbohydrates.   PP

By 1943 consumption of potatoes was 40% above the immediately pre-war level. White bread was banned in March 1942.

> The greyish National loaf, part wholemeal and supplemented with vita-
> mins, calcium and iron was the only bread available.   DMJ

Harold Caplan and two others were sixteen.

> We didn't actually starve; I ate a lot of bread. I remember we could eat
> a whole loaf at one sitting.   HC

Sally Saunders, evacuated to Bedford with King's Warren School and soon after to marry an Owenian, Alan Beecham, recalls the challenge of finding foods that were off ration. Offal was one of these.

> My mother once sent a large piece of liver, well wrapped up, through
> the post, but it was green and very smelly by the time it arrived.   SB

Fresh fish was not rationed.

> The fishermen, who risked their lives even more so than in peacetime,
> were the unsung heroes of the war. We could not do much about the
> cod, but, at least, we were able to contribute to the chips as holiday
> farm workers.   MM

Dennis Jones did not risk his life when catching fish.

> We and our cat Chibby ate Ouse pike, but a large tench proved inedible.
> I recall selling chub and roach to the fishmonger for 3/6d a pound.
>   DMJ

Dennis also ate bought fish. Late in the war there arrived snoek from South Africa.

> Snoek helped maintain protein levels.   DMJ

Martin Mitchell remembers snoek as a *plat de jour* in the British Restaurant. Nick Coral enjoyed an altogether less restricted fish menu.

> With my usual good fortune I found myself living in the home of the
> manager of the local branch of Macfisheries. As a result, bearing in
> mind wartime rationing, we ate extremely well although unfortunately
> I never acquired a taste for fish cooked in bacon rinds.   NC

Fresh fish, like fresh vegetables, remained unrationed whilst the tinned varieties for instance, sardines, pilchards, salmon (if you could get it) and snoek were 'on points'.

In July 1942 the axe fell! Sweets and chocolates were put on personal points. The ration was eight ounces for a four week period. In October it was increased to twelve.

To Malcolm Campbell, and others, rationing had at last begun to bite.

> Throughout these years the dearth of sweets was powerful. Mars Bars were thinly sliced with a razor blade. MJC

(No mean feat when razor blades were like gold-dust.)

> We underwent agony when playing football at the Meltis Company's field at Elstow because the factory was still producing chocolate bars for Red Cross parcels for prisoners of war. AWL

Joss Ackland, looking back, finds consolation.

> I'm sure my generation benefited with strong, healthy teeth. JA

A few didn't really like sweets. They could sell their ration or benefit in other ways.

> I was never a great eater of sweets and invariably at the end of each month I had many more coupons still in my possession than many of my contemporaries. I gained some cheap popularity at times, I feel sure! JS

> I didn't have a sweet tooth and, accordingly, gained great popularity with girls. As a substitute and dietary replacement I developed to my great pleasure a taste for draught bitter. After all, our Governors were not the Worshipful Company of Confectioners. WFF

Later in 1942 the use of milk in chocolate manufacture was prohibited. Milk was not rationed but the Government believed there were better, more direct ways for citizens to benefit from it. Indeed, the consumption of milk, like that of potatoes, topped the immediately pre-war figure. In the case of milk by 30%.

So... no more milk chocolate. Rowntree's Kit-Kat was now plain

– in a blue wrapper.

> Cadbury's had already introduced a standard bar called 'Ration'. It was 2 ½d. They called it 'the Wartime stamina food'. One soon got used to it and later I found full cream milk chocolate sickly. I craved Ration for many years after the end of the war. DEB

The choice of confectionery – and with rationing there came choice – was difficult. Value for money was always a top consideration for a school child but what now represented value – taste or time?

> I stuck to fruit pastilles. They went further. IA

Your ration could go further when supplemented by off-ration items. If you looked hard enough, particularly in Bedford's back streets, you could find unfamiliar confections, rough 'chocolate' coated toffee bars, rolls of so-called fruit flavoured chalk, known as Swizzles, slab toffee which, in today's parlance, had passed its sell-by date and metamorphosed into a sort of fudge. All these merited no coupons and were, as we said at the time, 'cheap at half the price'.

> My Dad – then a precision tool engineer working in a factory in London's West End – had a source of supply, presumably black market, of some OK, but lesser known, confectionery which supplemented my legal allowance. DEB

Alternatives were sought. Lemonade crystals could be eaten if you didn't mind shredding your tongue. You could concoct a substitute sherbet by adding to it Andrews Liver Salts. Jean and Mary Hope, who entertained Owenians in their mother's Castle Road house, were more professional.

> We made chocolate truffles with cocoa and Shredded Wheat. And there were occasional biscuit-making sessions when rations would allow. J&MH

Sally Beecham remembers the restraints of wartime cooking.

> Domestic Science remained on the curriculum of my school, but cooking was severely restricted because of rationing. I learned how to make and toss a pancake. Only one egg could be sacrificed to a whole group

of girls, so having made the batter, we jointly cooked and then each, in turn, tossed the one pancake. SB

Sweet substitutes were discovered at the chemist's.

Ovaltine tablets and Lurie's Herbal Oblong lozenges – medicated so off ration. HG

Ovaltine and Horlicks tablets and even, I seem to remember, Meggezones throat pastilles were consumed as substitutes. MJC

At one time we discovered sulphur tablets, sold by Boots the Chemists. These came in convenient cellophane packs of two ounces and were the nearest thing to unrationed sweets that you could buy. Their purpose was to 'purify the blood'. In fact they created a foully fragrant flatulence, which was uproariously funny, until you got tired of it. AWL

Sulphur tablets from Boots came in several fruit flavours but the farts were indistinguishable. DEB

Cakes and buns were not rationed but demand exceeded supply.

When the news of doughnuts in the Co-op was heard, the classroom emptied. No jam inside and not much sugar. RN

Demand was equally ferocious at Sam Hester's bun shop. The cream was artificial, of course, and, to emphasise the fact, was gaudily coloured.

The sweet ration could be stretched by various substitutes such as soft rolls which is the best way of describing a currant bun with the currants taken out (dried fruit was rationed). AWL

The Scouts seem to have fared well. Just before Christmas 1939, the Modern School troop invited the Owen's School troop to join their party in the gymnasium.

Here we were provided with tea and cakes. The cakes were in plenty and of such a kind as boys dream of. Cream buns, jam tarts, chocolate eclairs and iced cakes full of raisins and other delectable fruit. We sat around a large, glowing fire, its comforting warmth an hors d'oeuvre, as it were, to the main dish. A number of our hosts waited on us, including the Scoutmaster, and weren't they kept busy replenishing our cups and plates! It would be interesting to know how many reached the schoolboy's state of perfection in being ill through an overdose of rich pastry.

T.A. Simmonds, *Arrow*, Lent '40

Rationing was generally accepted. It was seen as fair and less of a hassle than chasing items in short supply. Imported fruit was very scarce.

I remember a school friend complaining that his mother on a visit from London had spent half a crown (a fortune) on a single peach for him. He was angry. I think he ate it to please her, but he didn't enjoy it.

DEB

Of course, sometimes one yearned for the unobtainable orange.   JL

In Castle Road, my main artery to school, there was, at the junction with Bushmead Avenue, a small circle of grass and trees and benches. One day, in the middle, there appeared a black cabinet with a glass top with a small hole in it. Inside there was a lemon. Adjacent to the cabinet there was a box. A sign invited passers-by to put a coin in the box, which would permit them to sniff the lemon. All proceeds to the Red Cross, whose HQ was in Bushmead Avenue.   DEB

I remember once hearing a news flash on the wireless asking for a banana for a child in hospital with some rare disease, which could apparently only be cured by this unobtainable fruit.   JA

Rose hips, commercially gathered and made into syrup, were a valuable source of vitamin C, imported citrus fruit having altogether disappeared.   DMJ

Shortages had their own patron saint, Mr Chad, a cartoon character who would appear atop walls and say 'WOT NO (whatever)?' He was commemorated in the school magazine by K. Teacher, a fourth former:

A man whom everybody knows,
And always seems so sad,
With 'Wot! No this?' and 'Wot! No that?'
Of course it's Mr Chad.
He pops his nose o'er tops of walls,
And thinks himself a lad,
When holding on with both his hands,
Our famous Mr Chad.

> *The question mark above his head*
> *Is precious to this cad,*
> *Who says he is not bald: so keep*
> *Your hair on Mr Chad.*
> *To end the story of this man,*
> *Who's really not too bad*
> *We rub his face off tops of walls*
> *Then cry out, 'Wot! No Chad?'*
>
> K. Teacher, *Arrow*, Trinity '46

Cigarettes were so hard to get they were often sold singly.

> On the odd occasion rumours would go around that a particular tobacconist would have cigarettes, and early in the morning queues would grow in the hope that ten cigarettes would come their way.   JA

'Wot! no cigarettes?' 'Wot! no matches?'

> Queues everywhere and I particularly remember with pride one Christmas my present to my mother was the result of many hours of queuing over a period of three months – six boxes of matches.   JA

Fuel for cooking was not rationed but the country was urged to cut down consumption. A member of the public took the Ministry of Food to task.

> *Cooking potatoes in their jackets may be an economy from the point of view of food, but such cooking takes longer and is not therefore an economy as regards fuel.*[5]

> We survived shortages and rationing. Rationing concentrated on items such as meat, sugar, butter, cheese, eggs, tea and sweets – many now considered less desirable ingredients of a healthy diet.   DMJ

But in September 1941 Lord Woolton proclaimed that the nation had 'never been in better health for years'.[6] That was both ungrammatical and untrue. It was, however, better than 1938-9 and that was something. Moreover, as Professor Richard Titmuss wrote, the war brought with it 'full employment, food subsidies, "fair shares", price control and welfare food schemes'.[7]

Geoff Dimmock speaks for most of us.

I suppose life was hard but I cannot remember ever being hungry.

GD

We didn't do too badly.

34

The War Effort

Saving - money, scraps, salvage - to save the country.

The war has resolved itself into a question of Rations, War Savings and Allotments...

Arrow, Trinity '40

That comment appeared in what was to be called the 'Spitfire Summer' of 1940. In fact, the 1940 *Arrow* was quoting extracts from the *Arrows* of 1914-18. As the editor tacitly suggested, the preoccupations were identical in the later war though WW2 non-combatants were to feel that they were more closely involved. They were indeed *made* to feel that. The Government insisted, the Ministry of Information (MOI) insisted, that 'civilians should regard themselves as also serving in a front line.'[1]

'The thing which distinguishes this war from all previous wars,' said *Picture Post* in August 1940, 'is that today everyone is in it.'

The rhetoric became fact in the summer of 1940. An American, expressing concern regarding the morale of London's civilian population was told that in London there were no civilians.[2] That could never be said about Bedford.

That summer, Winston Churchill called the conflict 'a war of unknown warriors. The whole of the warring nations are involved, not only soldiers but the entire population men, women and children.'[3]

Mind you, patriotism had been fed us at elementary (primary) school. We were loyal to King and Country and proudly waved flags on Empire Day. A Ministry of Information booklet in the middle of the war reinforced the sentiment. 'Day by day, too, in the schools the courage and discipline of children and teachers alike have been helping to maintain steadiness of our national life'.[4]

Discipline by itself, though necessary, is a passive virtue. The 'war effort' demanded effort. War Savings could be regarded as passive – i.e. not spending. Indeed, the real though perverse *raison d'être* for War Savings was to combat inflation by reducing personal expenditure. But there were two other benefits – raising morale and keeping busy.

Linking saving with the war, and hence making it a key part of the war effort, was the job of the Ministry of Information. *Lend to defend the right to be free* – with its rhythm, rhyme and simple words – was very quickly learned, understood and acted upon. There was another, entirely monosyllabic slogan *Lend a hand on the land*. (Lend? Why not give?) There was an emphasis on 'defend'. The earliest savings certificates were called 'defence bonds'.

Then came Spitfire Funds. The money was given rather than lent. Spitfires – or parts thereof – were bought. Planes were sponsored. Initiated by patriotic individuals in the commonwealth, the idea was appropriated by Beaverbrook, the Minister of Aircraft Production. Price lists were printed. A complete Spitfire cost £5000, the brass tube of a machine gun cost fifteen shillings, but schoolboys could save up to purchase a rivet for sixpence. Many Owenians did so, some starting their own Spitfire funds. John Stockton added a refinement

> I ran my own form of 'Spitfire Fund' which offered a small prize as an incentive once a week. But it didn't take on, and I closed it. JS

An ex-Owenian on active service, Captain J. H. Lush, wrote to the editor of the *Arrow* in Autumn 1940 asking boys to write to him.

> *I can undertake, on production of identity cards, to retail State secrets at a reasonable figure, on the strict understanding that they go no further and that all proceeds go to the local 'Spitfire' Fund.*
> *Arrow*, Michaelmas '40

The Spitfire Fund had the effect of transforming national savings into an active movement – not so much saving as taking part. Each of the four subsequent years saw a themed week of activity.

It was a partnership. A poster featured a pilot and the caption: *I'll fly it if you'll buy it.*

> The regular National Savings campaigns were a feature of the town and a good excuse to have a lot of fun. There were exhortations from local dignitaries, visiting Cabinet ministers and members of the services to buy National Savings certificates and savings stamps to raise money for munitions and whatever. AWL

Individual groups, streets, and the whole town kept scores. The most common graphic representation of the amount raised was a thermometer with the target figure at the top.

> I would take part in the various weeks. At the time they were like street parties or village fetes. Looking back, they seem rather bleak boot fairs. DEB

But, no doubt, they engendered camaraderie. People who had kept themselves to themselves were associating in groups – fire watching or serving or saving. Sylvia Luckman (King's Warren) with prescience wrote to her father:

> Nobody will be so friendly after the war. SL

In 1941 there was War Weapons Week.

> I took part in a competition to produce models of tanks, lorries etc making a model of a DUKW, an American amphibious troop carrier, which won me half-a-crown and was exhibited in the National Savings office opposite St. Paul's Square. AWL

In February 1942, the Owen's National Savings Group was founded. (The National Savings Movement had been launched in November 1939.) It was run by the masters under the leadership of the tireless and versatile 'Dicky' Dare. The amount saved grew slowly but steadily each week. 1942 was the year of Warships Week – the events around the country did not take place simultaneously. Mr Dare reported on the group's success in the summer edition of the *Arrow*, and produced another incentive for taking part.

> *The Lower School has usually shown up to best advantage in this respect and the zealous efforts of Mr. Phillips in the Seconds and Mr. Tingay in the Thirds have combined to keep the Squander Bug*

at bay. The Removes too, under Mr. Vulliamy's guidance have done their part while the frequent visits by Mr. Dare to the Post Office testify to the regular purchase of Certificates going on amongst our more affluent members. We have topped the £150 mark and are now working hard for 'Wings for Victory' Week in which we hope to out-do our splendid effort for Warships Week last year. Intriguing badges, devised by the Bedford Committee, are awarded to really enthusi-astic members who contribute a good sum or secure a new member, and the numerous striking posters displayed in the class-rooms will do much to whip up the necessary keenness. The testing-time will come, however, when the spurt of this Week has slackened off, and it is the earnest hope of our Group leaders that the Owen's effort will continue and improve rather than decline. Apart from other objec-tives, it is one way of swelling the weekly Bedford total and thus doing something to show our neighbours how much we appreciate all that they have done for us during our long stay in the town. So 'Strive with a will, Owenians!'

R.A. Dare, *Arrow*, Trinity '43

One former Owenian was concerned with a somewhat larger contribution to Warships Week.

It is interesting to know that the £1,000,000 cheque, which was recently contributed by the Prudential Assurance Company to the Warships Week Fund, was handed to the Lord Mayor by an Old Owenian, Mr. P.C. Crump, who is secretary of the company.

Anon, *Arrow*, Trinity '42

The Squander Bug referred to in Mr. Dare's piece made his ap-pearance in 1943. He was a repellent character, not unlike cartoon representations of the cold germ generated in the contemporary anti-infection advertising (*Coughs and sneezes spread diseases*). In the same year the total of savings groups in the country reached 300,000 – and Wings for Victory weeks sprouted everywhere.

Wings for Victory week was marked by an hilarious incident one Sunday evening. Various decorated floats were lined up along the Embankment opposite Russell Park, some of them bearing local firms' 'Beauty Queens', ready to depart for a parade through town. As they took off, they were overtaken then integrated with at least a dozen fur-lough trucks from the American Air Force base at Thurleigh coming into Bedford for their regular night out. The resulting chaos with the trucks of GIs whistling furiously at the Beauty Queens and the person-nel on the floats was glorious to behold.   AWL

In 1944 came Salute the Soldier Week. According to Mr Dare, the Owen's group, a small but devoted band of enthusiasts, achieved a creditable performance. The Bedford week began on 10 June (D Day plus 4). Montgomery landed in France that day and the US troops from Omaha and Utah beaches linked up. By the time the week ended, the first V1 flying bombs had fallen on southern England. Meanwhile, Owen's was aiming to reach a target of £50. It was passed within the first two days and the limit raised to £100.

> *Thanks to the keen support throughout the School, and especially in the lower forms, this was also achieved with a handsome margin, the final total being £107. In view of the fact that we are an evacuated school, with few parents and relations to tap for subscriptions, this must be regarded as a performance to be proud of. Mr. Phillips, Mr. Vulliamy, and Mr. Smith became veritable stamp-machines during this period, so insistent was the demand for the familiar blues, reds, and greens; while Mr. Dare seemed to spend more time in the Post Office purchasing Certificates than he did in school, surplus wealth pouring in from all directions!*
>
> *This big step forward brings our evacuation total to nearly £400, and obviously suggests a fresh target for our efforts – to reach £500 before we leave Bedford. What about it?*
>
> R.A. Dare, *Arrow*, Trinity '44

Everything indicates that the sum was reached. The war effort manifested itself in other ways. The Scout troop trained in first aid and the *Arrow* report in Spring 1942 mentioned two further services.

> *National Service is being done in many ways, the most recent being the distribution of pamphlets for Warships Week. A concert was given in the Central Hall in aid of War Distress Fund for Scouts.*
>
> W.J. Whitebread, *Arrow*, Lent '42

King's Warren School participated in another charity event.

> At some point there was 'Allies' week for which we school girls were given the task of learning folk songs and dances from a variety of (mainly German-occupied) European countries. The performance took place in Bedford High School Hall. A snippet still lingers in my brain – 'Howling storms rage high, the Tatras peaks assailing ...' What was that about?   SB

Giving and saving of pocket money became, if not the norm, then at least as important as spending. And there were other things to save. *Turn this raw material into war material* commanded a poster. Beaverbrook made an appeal on 10 July 1940 for aluminium. 'We will turn your pots and pans into Spitfires and Hurricanes, Blenheims and Wellingtons.' *SEND YOUR PANS FLYING* shrieked a headline. 5000, the ad claimed, would make a fighter: 25,000 a bomber. Owen's boys responded by nagging and shaming their billet ladies; collecting unwanted saucepans and subsequently, encouraging the removal of railings.

> The metal railings around properties disappeared, probably a greater boost to morale than to the war effort – everybody felt that they were doing their bit. RSB

Bones also were needed. 'They make glue for aircraft' we were told. You formed a picture of a plane made from second hand saucepans held together with artificial glue. How did these collectors' items transform themselves into flying machines and weapons? Our predecessors must have asked similar questions in the Great War.

FROM THE 'ARROW' 1914-18

> *A ton of chestnuts has been collected by various members of the school in response to the appeal of the Ministry of Munitions.*
> *Arrow*, Trinity '40

In summer 1942 the magazine – in its *Without Offence* column – made a suggestion:

> *When you cannot produce your homework, it is a good idea to say that your hostess accidentally put it out for salvage.*
> Anon, *Arrow*, Trinity 1942

Books were saved for service personnel. Printed in your Penguin would be a request to leave it at a post office 'so that men and women in the services may enjoy it too'. Alternatively you could take it to the local Red Cross post for inclusion in parcels sent to prisoners of war. Old socks and outgrown woollen items were called into service. Your billet lady would recycle the wool to make socks for the troops, and pullovers for POWs. This activity was generally co-ordinated by the Women's Voluntary Service. Its motto was *If it should be done the WVS will do it*. Though they didn't decline offers of help.

> On Sunday afternoons I also went to the Corn Exchange to help my landlady with her WVS duties in providing refreshments to local troops.
>
> DPe

Discipline (as praised by the MOI) faced its earliest and severest test with gas masks. Owenians had collected these over a considerable period.

> We had all been issued with them in 1938.
>
> AWL

> A few days before the outbreak of war we were issued with the standard gas masks at school.
>
> DMJ

Gas masks came in standard, drab cardboard boxes. We were compelled to carry them at all times slung from the shoulder. They proved cumbersome and as the phoney war continued we were concerned not with the efficacy of the mask but the look of the container. Style over substance.

> Gas masks had to be taken with you wherever you went. We wrote our names on them, distinguishing them with designs or coloured string.
>
> DEB

> Cardboard boxes on strings. An aunt of mine made and sold covers.
>
> IA

The cardboard box was hardly a fashion accessory. In the early days of the war some shops sold cases to take unboxed masks. They were shaped to take the mask itself and looked like large camera cases. These cases were banned and for a period, personal cases had to cover the obligatory cardboard box.

> We carried them initially in Government issued cardboard boxes until it was obvious that the first heavy shower of rain on the boxes reduced them to pulp, whereupon enterprising producers began to market boxes and later cans in stouter material.
>
> AWL

Discipline was not exactly strict at school. We all brought our gas masks but did not carry them from class to class. However, that – and much else – changed on 10 May 1940.

'*NAZIS INVADE HOLLAND, BELGIUM, LUXEMBOURG*' read

that afternoon's *Evening Standard*. News of this, and a map, covered the whole front page save for a column on the right: *YOU MUST CARRY YOUR GAS MASK*, a warning from the Ministry of Home Security and a signal at a personal level that the phoney war was over, and that maybe we ought to reacquaint ourselves with the contents of the case we may have been carrying.

> Occasionally we were drilled in its use. I longed for the more dramatic version, as carried by armed forces and ARP wardens, with goggle eyepieces and corrugated flexible tubing. DMJ

> Gas would invade the eyes and nose. Those were just the orifices I had problems with. I had to take my glasses off to wear one and was blind as a bat. WFF

> I recall the whole household sitting peeling onions with our gas masks on for protection. GS

> Thank goodness I never smelt gas. Mind you the smell of the gas mask was bad enough. DEB

> I always kept a tube of Trebor mints in my desk to compensate for the nasty, rubbery smell it exuded during practice wearings. MJC

David Pratt remembers both nose and ears being affected.

> I remember in particular the gas mask drill in which everyone competed to produce the most thunderous farting noise with or without the use of additional equipment. DAP

That equipment itself was later added to.

> We all had our gas masks converted by the addition of another filter, which was strapped to the existing mask as a precaution against some likely newly developed gas, but after a few years they were put quietly away. AWL

It had become obvious that poison gas would not feature in this world war. Owenians remember gas masks as 'tedious', 'a nuisance', 'a bit of a joke'. As a contribution to the war, carrying them was a minor effort.

35

Holidays – in the War

Sharing the dangers of Londoners.

Bedford is fifty miles from London. It wasn't too much of a hassle going back home. It could be done in a day quite easily. Not that you were allowed to during term time. But boys did it. However, during vacations, half-term breaks and even weekends, we were permitted to visit London provided there was little danger and that we got written permission from our parents and from the school.

> It's irrational and very human that, even though we had been evacuated to escape the war, we were allowed to return to our London homes once a month.   DDW

Doug Pearce took every opportunity.

> The majority of holidays were spent at home in London. There are vivid memories of some of the Battle of Britain fights, the raids on the London docks, the drone of the doodle-bugs and waiting for their cut out, before they landed and exploded and, later, the explosion of a nearby V2 rocket. It was also the time when people were sleeping at night on the platforms of the tube stations or using Anderson shelters in their own gardens during air raids.   DPe

The Battle of Britain began on 13 August 1940. On 5 September the *Luftwaffe* dropped sixty tons of bombs on London. Two days later the Blitz began in earnest. Its initial phase lasted over seventy days. Its 'official' ending was 10 May 1941 after which Hitler turned his attention to Russia. There were intermittent bombings throughout the next four years, sometimes with the intensity of the initial Blitz.

In June 1944 the first V1s or 'doodle-bugs' landed, to be followed in September 1944 by the silently approaching V2s. Raids of all sorts ceased in March 1945.

None of this seemed to deter Ken Deadman among others.

> Throughout the war I made regular trips to London and can recall a reasonable time spent in the Anderson shelter*. Apart from the school holidays I used to nip home when my brother was on leave, either by bike, train or Birch bus.   KD

> As I got older I was allowed to visit home in London for the weekends and part of the holidays. Before we could go I remember we had to get a leave pass signed by our parents. I, like most other boys, forged our parents' signature. We used to get on the Birch bus (the slow route) or the train, somewhat quicker but more expensive, about three shillings and nine pence return on the Birch bus or five shillings and a ha'penny return on the train. I remember at end of school on Friday a gang of Owen's boys would be running hell for leather to the Midland Road station where we would catch the train by the skin of our teeth. The train was always crowded, standing room only.   DHS

We would be standing in the corridors next to servicemen. We felt we were nearer the real war. The feeling intensified as we approached St.Pancras.

> There was a sign chalked on a pillar at St.Pancras Station *This is not King's Cross*. Somebody— I like to think a porter – scrawled it to help travellers in the blackout and a strange location. King's Cross was adjacent and easy to confuse. Knowing what isn't is often as important as knowing what is. That became the subject of a television play I wrote – and the title was ready made.   DEB

The phoney war lasted almost a year.

The longer it went on, so historians assure us, the better Britain's chance of mobilising our and French economic strength. And, of course, Chamberlain hadn't entirely ruled out appeasement. Though London looked and felt different, there was no apparent danger. Christmas shopping went on with as great fervour

---

*The Anderson Shelter, named after the Home Secretary Sir John Anderson who was also Minister of Home Security, had to be erected by the householder. It consisted of thin corrugated steel screened with a mound of protective earth.

as pre-war. Parents were keen to make things feel normal and to compensate for our absence from each other.

> In the holidays at Christmas, Easter and summer, I almost always went home. At first this was to Brighton where my mother and father had taken a flat following our holiday there in 1939. The idea was to be away from possible air raids on London, but after Dunkirk they thought the coast would be more vulnerable so returned to our house. So during the 1940 bombing I was back in Stoke Newington and had to spend time either in our own strengthened cellar or in the local public shelter.
>
> JL

Jack Levy's family did not own an Anderson shelter. Two and a quarter million were given away free at the start of the Blitz and subsequently for seven pounds except for those on low income. A census in November 1940 showed that 9% of Londoners used public shelters, 4% the underground and 27% domestic shelters.

Until 7 September Goering's *Luftwaffe* had attacked RAF airfields. That afternoon it switched to London's docks and East End streets. That afternoon Owen's boys had been enjoying themselves.

> I remember standing in the front doorway sheltered by a concrete mantle above, watching the London docks ablaze. There was the sound of German bombers (we all knew the sound of their engines), anti-aircraft guns and the tinkle of shrapnel on roofs. DDW

> My parents shared a house with my grandparents. We did not have an Anderson shelter but when the sirens sounded we all used to sit under the stairs. It was a three-storey house and from the top rooms at the back we were able to see the fires burning some distance away in the London docks. So much for being evacuated but this was during school holidays! IW

> I was in London the day the Blitz began. The following morning I ventured east, not to the real East End, which had borne the brunt, but Dalston Junction where buildings were still burning. The next day the school rounded us up and we were soon back in Bedford. DEB

> Summer holidays: back to the familiar surroundings of Gunton Road. How I enjoyed that summer being with my parents and grandparents and two brothers. But early in September the Blitz struck. Gunton Road, not all that far from the docks was vulnerable.

The docks were ablaze. I could see the glow of fires spread across the sky from just outside the cellar door. We were sheltering in our reinforced cellar, my parents and brothers, one seven years old and the other a year- old baby. The London sky was overwhelmed by the drone of hundreds of German bombers, a pulsating brrmm, brrmm, announcing the impending terror of destruction, injury and death. The whine of falling bombs drew ever closer. 'Oh my God!' shrieked my mother. There was a loud explosion and the sound of shattering glass. I remember rushing into the toilet and being very sick. Apart from the emotional trauma, the tears and cry of heartfelt relief, we were all intact. (The bomb, we learned later, had landed on a house in the next road.)

The droning died away. Soon the all clear went. We rushed upstairs. The kitchen door was still in its frame but minus the glass panes which lay shattered over the floor. Sitting by the kitchen door calmly drinking a cup of tea was our Irish maid, Rose. 'Why didn't you join us in the basement?' asked my father incredulously. 'You could have been killed.' 'Oh, no. I knew Mary the Mother of God would take care of me', was her confident answer. That was the last night I spent in my childhood home in Gunton Road and the last time I saw Rose. The next night we all slept in an underground shelter, sharing the space with a mass of refugees from the Blitz. The day after I went back to Bedford.   MM

Though trips to London during the height of the Blitz were forbidden by the school, except in the most extreme circumstances, boys continued to visit parents thereafter. They became real Londoners again and shared the dangers and the stubborn lifestyle.

I often went home to London in the school holidays which often coincided with air raids. I spent many nights in air raid shelters with my family. We were very lucky in that, although there were bombs very close to our house, we were never bombed. By 1941 the air raid shelters were well organised so that one was able to sleep in relative comfort.

BF

Air raid warnings were an intermittent wailing; the all clear was a steady sound. I developed 'siren ears', a common complaint. We sheltered nightly under the stairway cupboard as the bombs fell, our cat Chibby joining us with her kittens. One grew able to recognise German bombers' characteristic thrumming. But the loudest noises were of anti-aircraft batteries on nearby Tooting Bec Common, blasting into the night skies swept by searchlight. We never got round to having an Anderson shelter in the back garden. Our parents must have been much more frightened than we were. Most streets had wrecked houses. Mornings were given to shrapnel gathering, streets daily swept clear of glass shards, and strategically located barrage balloons winched up and down. DMJ

I spent several breaks in London and remember something of the Blitz. Most vivid in my memory is my father's instructions to get into the air raid shelter as soon as possible after the warning. On the first occasion I was first into the shelter. My father was angry, he'd seen me scuttle down the stairs at a rapid pace with 'no regard for others' and told me I'd behaved cowardly. The next raid resulted in me being equally chastised because I had deliberately taken my time and my long absence had worried my mother. JWes

Being occasional and infrequent 'real Londoners' meant that we would notice the changes in central London and on the journey to our homes. There would be gaps instead of houses, buildings half destroyed revealing wallpaper and doors going nowhere and, as if compensating for the destruction, new buildings such as brick built surface shelters, ARP posts and emergency water supply tanks.

From the station I took the 73 bus to Newington Green. I'd get off the bus and walk up Green Lanes and turn into my road, Leconfield Road – and hope to see the flat whole. (The railings had gone of course to help build guns and planes – and to this day have never been replaced.) DEB

Not everyone found home 'whole'. In fact, by the end of the war only one London house in ten had escaped damage of some sort. Most of us were safe in Bedford when homes were damaged. Not everyone though.

When away from Bedford, London and home were the attractions. It was my misfortune to be at home when the house suffered damage from a nearby bomb, but the family escaped without injury. RC

Frank Fenn also chose an inopportune time to return to London. He was enduring a bad spell, unhappy in the fifth form and at odds with the form master.

It came to the point when I could not bear to be in his presence, a fact amply demonstrated by my attendance record in his classes. Matters came to a head and I foolishly did a runner to London largely to weep on the shoulder of a childhood friend. Both my parents at this time were on war service and away from home. Unfortunately, the house where

288

the friend lived was bombed, two people killed, and the friend and I escaped with what seemed to be slight burns. I concealed the damage on my return to Bedford, sat School Certificate, and promptly came apart at the seams. I developed a troublesome skin condition brought on partly by the physical and psychological effects of the bombing and the burns. WFF

I was at home when incendiaries landed in the yard of the pub my parents ran; they seemed harmless and some did not ignite – the event seemed exciting. It was the same night that incendiaries burnt down a store in Upper Street near the pub (our home). I remember the *quid pro quo* relationship amongst the traders – my father the source of scarce alcohol; the butcher, the baker, the candlestick maker, the sources of other scarce resources. I was never sure of the honesty of these barter transactions but would willingly benefit from them JWes

If John Weston found excitement in the early raids, Geoff Rowley discovered resolution.

It seemed strange that we went home to London for the holidays when the Blitz was at its height but we did and I believe that I grew up during the August and September of 1940 and the Christmas later that year. It is hard to describe but the experience of the Blitz – including losing the roof of our house and on one occasion being evacuated at 2.30 am because a land mine was hanging by its parachute from a chimney opposite – gave one a sense of confidence, a feeling that one could cope with life. GRo

And life was lived, as far as possible, as normal.

I used to go to the Hackney Empire for music hall and other concerts.I saw Stephen Grappelli, the jazz violinist, and George Shearing, the blind jazz pianist. The concerts continued during the air raids and we just sat through them with the concert accompanied by anti-aircraft gunfire. BF

The V1 and the V2 may have generated fear but not panic.

Bay windows were criss-crossed with tape. The V1 flying bombs often droned by and a V2 rocket fell near Bounds Green Station one morning. RN

V stood for *vergeltungswaffen*, i.e. retribution weapon. The V1 (or 'doodle-bug') flew at 400 miles per hour and carried one ton of high explosive. Only 72 reached London. The V2, a twelve ton rocket, flew ten times faster – and 500 hit the capital One's reactions to the two Vs – bomb and rocket – were understandably different. Their mechanisms were different, as were the noises they made.

> The vibration of doodle-bugs caused the windows of our house to rattle. A sound I've never liked since... the sound of the V2 was that of a tornado. Since then I've never liked high winds. JWes

> I had returned to London in the summer of 1944 and experienced both the V1s (doodle-bugs or buzz bombs – it was more like a sputtering growl than a buzz) and V2s which struck without warning. There were two ways of responding to the V1. As long as you could hear it, you were safe. Only when the sputter stopped would you dive for any available cover: a shop doorway, table, Morrison or Anderson shelter, the Underground, or whatever was at hand. With the V2 there was no warning other than the flash of its rocket and whirr of its descent. There was usually no time to take shelter. It was as casual as that. MM

> I was in London when there were raids with the V1 (doodle-bugs) which were particularly frightening as one waited for the engines to cut out knowing that they were soon to land and explode. During the day you were able to see them – once they passed over you could relax. The V2 rockets were much less frightening because once you heard the explosion you knew it was all over. BF

> My experiences in London included some near misses by flying bombs. The first one to cut out over our head paralysed me with fear. The V2 rockets were less frightening, for you only heard the double bang after it landed. DHS

The double bang was first, the explosion and then (strange to relate but even stranger to experience), the sound of the approaching rocket. Reason: they flew faster than sound. We would hear this frequently during our vacations in the six months of the V2 raids. Many Owenians were near the scene of the action.

> At the end of my street, Compton Terrace disappeared with a V2. I helped pull a lady from a wrecked house. She ticked me off for her stockings were damaged. IA

One that landed near the Carlton Cinema in Essex Road gave me my first experience of seeing bodies being carried out of the wreckage.

DHS

A V2 landed nearby in St John's Way, Upper Holloway. It landed on a home hosting a birthday party killing all the children and other inhabitants. To feel the V2 land and seconds later hear the sound of it coming was frightening. The impact was so great that I watched a moving double-decker bus sway to the extent that I expected it to topple over.

JWes

This incident was also the occasion of a lucky escape for Doug Wade and John Stockton in July 1944.

I had Peter Huntingford, John Stockton, Bill Wright, and Geoffrey Dimmock at home in Fairbridge Road for my birthday party. Shortly after my mother had called us to come for tea from the front room to the kitchen at the back of the house, a V2 rocket struck a house in St John's Way close to the Archway Tube station, about 400 yards from us. The blast blew in the windows at the front of our house. The room which we had just vacated was covered in splintered glass.   DDW

We saw the huge column of black smoke rising above the house, but we were totally unscathed, although there were heavy casualties in the row of houses on which the rocket had landed.

JS

The birthday party carried on. Life carried on. David Bernstein frequented the theatre. He was at a matinee performance of a revue, *Flying Colours* at the Lyric on 8 September 1943 …

Just prior to curtain up, the theatre manager appeared in dinner jacket and announced that Italy had surrendered unconditionally. The orchestra played the national anthem and we belted it out. In the revue Douglas Byng in drag was playing a blowsy middle-aged lady. He inserted a line, 'Unconditional surrender? I was surrendering unconditionally all the time'.

DEB

The following year there was another matinee, at the cinema.

I was at the Finsbury Park Astoria watching a war film. The hero and heroine were in a London nightclub. In the film a siren went off announcing an air raid. The scene was taking place earlier in the war. We no longer heard sirens since V2s gave no warning of impending attack. Suddenly, in the real world, there was a massive explosion. A V2 had landed nearby. Immediately on screen the hero said, ' that was close'. The theatre fell about. Nobody left.   DEB

There was nothing you could do about a V2 except leave town – for Bedford perhaps where masters spent time and energy providing diversions and the municipality arranged entertainments for evacuees and Bedford citizens alike. They were called *Holidays at Home*. The Government discouraged travel and, as preparations for D-Day began, visits to within ten miles of the coast from the Wash to Land's End were banned.

We remember a performance by the Ballet Rambert to Ponchielli's *Dance of the Hours* on the very uneven grass of Russell Park. Brave dancers.   J&MH

And then, of course, there was the Town Band. I remember one Sunday afternoon they gave a concert from a raft moored in the middle of the river. When the raft began to take water, we approached the man with the collection box and requested *Nearer my Lord to thee*.   WFF

Though if London was dangerous, the coast prohibited, and too much of Bedford a bore, there was, for some, another option – going on holiday with your billet parents.

On the first Xmas away from home we went to Mrs Bale's sister in Kettering, where we played Newmarket. I loved this game as it appealed to my gambling instincts. Mrs Bale's brother-in-law drove a refuse truck and he took me on his rounds and regaled me with all the intricacies of refuse collecting and how important it was to examine the rubbish after dumping it at the tip as it was not uncommon to find watches, jewellery, etc.   BF

But for the majority of us there were short breaks in safe areas with one or even both of our parents. We managed.

36

1940

Dunkirk and the Battle of Britain.

On 20 May 1940, three days after the fall of Brussels, the German army reached the Channel coast. The British Expeditionary Force (BEF) troops in France 1939-40 were cut off.

The troops were making for Dunkirk. Among them was Alfred Hughes who had left Owen's in 1933. He had to help defend a canal before heading for the beach. He had left his pack in a barn.

> *"As darkness fell, I set out to retrieve it. On opening the barn door I tripped, shone a torch and saw a dead body of a soldier lying across my blood soaked pack. The body was that of an Owenian a form above me at school. I never knew his name."*

As the Germans swept towards the Channel I was billeted with a woman whose husband was in the BEF and was in fact taken prisoner. Before his capture, he had written to his wife, telling of the constant strafing and Stuka dive-bombing of the British troops.   JS

By Monday 27 May about half a million Allied soldiers were trapped 'in an area no bigger than Greater London'.[1] By the night of 3-4 June, 366,131 troops had been rescued by what the *Daily Express* called at the time 'History's strangest armada'.[2] It was hailed as a miracle.

One night, Mrs Headland burst into the bedroom I shared with her son (who was later killed in battle) to say that she'd heard they'd rescued thousands of British troops from the beaches.   JS

Churchill, who had replaced Chamberlain on 10 May, was relieved but sanguine.

It was not to be confused with victory. 'Wars are not won by evacuations.'[3] Bedford, in common with many towns in the southern half of the country, received new evacuees. Chas Baker remembers talking to them in Russell Park. They were exhausted.

> One vivid memory was seeing soldiers in ragged clothes and torn uniforms lying along the pavements in the town; there seemed to be hundreds of them. All the ladies were making tea and feeding them – they were the survivors of Dunkirk. DHS

> The Black Watch was billeted in Bedford. I remember the look of the men marching along Bedford streets, unshaven, eyes tired, their uniforms stained, the gait less than parade ground. DEB

> The troops slept in the streets after they had escaped from Dunkirk. RN

> You would see them sitting wearily on benches around the town, plied with refreshments from WVS canteens. It was after Dunkirk that one began to worry about possible defeat. But the very nature of the rescue, the hundreds of little boats that risked destruction from German bombs, the courage shown by ordinary people, turned the rescue into a victory. MM

Martin Mitchell was not alone in disobeying Churchill's admonition. *Picture Post* at the time also considered the deliverance a victory. 'To the British, the Finest Hour is not the last battle which we always win but the first which we always lose.'

> Next day, we went down into town and I remember seeing and talking to Scottish soldiers who were gathered in one of the buildings near the Corn Exchange. The troops were resting on blankets and 'biscuit' mattresses on the ground. I was interested to learn that among the 'Little Boats' that went to Dunkirk, had been the Thames paddle steamer 'Royal Eagle' on which my mother, my sister and I had gone to Ramsgate for our summer holiday in 1938. JS

Joss Ackland had gone to the to the Plaza to see *The Wizard of Oz*.

The projector of my mind whirred on through the night and in the morning when the bell rang. I raced downstairs with the film still playing. There, at the door, was my father, messy, dusty, unshaven and fatigued. 'I've just come from Dunkirk', he said. After days on the beach and hours in the water he had been picked up by a fishing boat and brought back to England. My mother helped him off with his clothes, laid him down on the bed and fed him some soup. 'I've had an exciting time, too', I said, and I proceeded to tell him the story of *The Wizard of Oz* shot by shot. He sat up in bed, smiled and for one of the few times in his life listened avidly with total concentration.

JA

Dennis Jones in South West London

… saw a trainload of bedraggled troops. Dunkirk survivors shouting and waving crossing a bridge.

DMJ

Ian Appleby

… saw the sad faces of the Dunkirk survivors as they passed through Bedford.

IA

Frank Fenn is hesitant about offering the following anecdote because he cannot remember the names of the two Owenians involved.

I was standing in an almost empty BMS playground. Into the playground comes a former pupil in bedraggled Army uniform. He looks battered and extremely weary. A contemporary, still at school, says to him
'Hello! Where have you been?'
'Dunkirk', says the soldier.
'Fine bloody time to take a holiday.'
They hug one another. These days you call that sort of thing psychotherapy.

WFF

Meanwhile around Bedford

… the Black Watch sat around in the parks and squares. We spoke to them and asked for souvenirs. I got a plastic gas shield. That afternoon in assembly the Headmaster told us not to pester the brave soldiers.

DEB

Peter Provost recalls O.W. Mitchell saying something else to the whole school. After the disaster/miracle of Dunkirk, Mitchell gave us all a pep talk and told us to concentrate on our studies and not worry about the gloomy war news.

'We will win in the end and I will tell you why - because we are British!'
It was good advice and he was right on both counts.   PP

We could, with a little selective perception, actually witness the
British winning. On 13 August the Battle of Britain began. We had
expected an invasion by land. We would know when it came by
the ringing of church bells. Precautions had been taken. Signposts
had been removed (which made cycling trips more adventurous).
If your billet parents had a car (unlikely) with a radio (even less
likely) the latter had to be dismantled and removed whilst the
former, in the event of invasion, would in all probability, be commandeered. But the invasion never happened and the Battle of
Britain was aerial.

> We know now that we were on a knife-edge. Had they failed, Britain
> would have been invaded. But who were they? Many were youngsters,
> in their early twenties, not long out of school, possibly some out of
> our school – there were some ten ex-Owenians serving in the RAF in
> 1940 – and many other schools like ours. They became the legendary
> 'Few'. 'Never... was so much owed by so many to so few'. Churchill knew
> exactly the words that inspired national pride and stiffened national
> resolve.   MM

Owenians showed that resolve. Joss Ackland found that it was
proving more and more difficult to concentrate on schoolwork.

> The sixth formers were going straight off into the forces and when the
> Battle of Britain started they queued to get into the RAF. All too often
> only a few weeks after they had taken off their school caps for the last
> time the Headmaster would read out their names among the latest
> casualties.   JA

The heroics could be witnessed from the safety of *terra firma*. A
thirteen-year-old describes an aerial battle in the *Arrow*.

> *One day I was cycling in the country. It was a fine day, with hardly
> any clouds in the sky. I set off about eight o'clock in the morning and
> had been about an hour on my journey when suddenly I heard the
> sirens in the distance. I went on, but soon I heard the drone of aircraft
> high in the sky. Immediately I dismounted from my bicycle and ran
> to the top of a little hillock by the roadside. For some time I could not
> see the aeroplanes. Then three British Hurricane fighters came out of
> a cloud. They were not going very fast, but they circled round as if on
> patrol, weaving a pattern in the sky. Then I heard the deep, irregular*

drone that is characteristic of German planes. Soon eighteen specks appeared. Simultaneously, three more Hurricanes dived through the sky at terrific speed. The eighteen specks I identified as twelve Heinkel 112 *fighters and six* Dornier 17 *bombers, the much-vaunted 'flying pencils.'*

The British fighters instantly attacked, three from above, three from below. The Nazis were taken completely by surprise, and before they could reply to this sudden onslaught a Dornier *was spinning down with a thin streak of smoke trailing out behind it. At this the Germans were thrown into complete confusion.*

The Heinkels *tried to form a protective circle round the bombers, which jettisoned their bombs. These fell with a deafening roar in some fields about a mile away, causing no damage.*

By this time, the British fighters attacked again. A dogfight ensued and the outcome of this was that a bomber was lurching badly, two enemy fighters were falling in flames and another was badly damaged. Two Hurricanes, however, were in difficulties and they disappeared over the trees getting lower and lower.

J.J.T. Dumbrill, *Arrow*, Michaelmas '40

Barry Skeggs was interested in aircraft.

We made all sorts of models with something called Frog kits which was just like Airfix today. This was a great hobby. BS

It came in handy that summer at farming camp in Haxey in Lincolnshire.

We looked up into the sky and saw a plane and one of us said it's one of ours and I said 'Rubbish it's a *Dornier*. Everybody lie flat.' We all lay flat on the earth and the plane dropped bombs about five fields away. A terrific noise. It seemed as if the pilot just wanted to drop his load and get back to where he came from. It was a good lesson in plane spotting. We used to get *Jane's* flying aircraft and plane spotting magazines and spend enjoyable times recognising the planes from the silhouettes in the magazine. It was a good game testing each other. We used to spot aircraft flying out or coming back from over East Anglia and you could tell if the plane was crippled by the funny noises it made. BS

Bill Whitebread was a member of a party sent to a 'safe' area in the heart of Kent …

... with the battle of Britain raging overhead! With the traditional East End of London hop-pickers, we frequently sought shelter in appropriate ditches.
WJW

Another exciting experience, during farming activities near Dover, was reported in the *Arrow*.

> *I heard the whistle of bombs and the next thing I knew was that my knee was bleeding, having been cut by a bomb splinter... The next morning I heard the rattle of machine gun fire and the bullets just missed my right arm. I dived straight into a ditch and stayed there till all was quiet.*
>
> I.E. Smith, *Arrow*, Michaelmas '40

That summer, with about ten other boys, Peter Provost cycled to Kent to assist in the fruit and hop harvest.

> I count it a privilege to have witnessed at close hand the battle of the 'Few' against the Nazi hordes. I particularly remember a Saturday, 7 September. We were playing at the top of an old chalk quarry. What at first seemed like a flock of birds on the horizon grew into an armada – the sky seemed full of German planes, the bombers flying in formation with the protective screen of fighters wheeling and weaving above. Against this force of several hundred, a flight of just three Spitfires roared up from below, straight through the invaders. Almost at once, one of theirs and one of ours crashed towards earth in a stream of smoke. The remaining two of ours sped away... Courage, heroism, and the responsibility to do as much damage as possible and get away to fight another day.
>
> PP

Even if you weren't an actual spectator, the battle was still a spectator sport, though the scores were revised years later.

> We were very aware when the Battle of Britain started, keeping score of the German planes being brought down. I remember August 15 was one of the record days (about 140 shot down) as it was my eleventh birthday.
>
> DHS

For Goff Baker one spectator sport replaced another on 7 September shortly before 3pm.

> My father and I were standing on the terrace behind the goal at the south end of White Hart Lane, not to watch Spurs but the alternate weekly game played by Arsenal. The siren began to wail and an an-

nouncement was made that the game was to be abandoned. We left the ground and stood in Tottenham High Road. We were disappointed and my father was annoyed that no gate money was refunded. Several other spectators were lined up along the pavement. Looking northward, we watched several squadrons of the *Luftwaffe* following the A10 or the A1010 southward. Clearly they had bought the London *A to Z* and thus proceeded over Stamford Hill, Stoke Newington and Shoreditch into the City and turned left for the docks.

Whilst, over our heads, the enemy were engaged by some RAF fighter planes and by anti-aircraft gunfire. At the height they were flying, just above the barrage balloons, they seemed to fill our sky but I cannot remember any sense of fear nor any panic among the supporters around us.

We must have walked home to Stamford Hill since buses stopped running during the daylight raids. GB

That night – and it followed the afternoon when he had witnessed the Few in action – Peter Provost from Kent saw in the northern sky

> … a blaze that looked like a haystack fire in the next field – it was that bright. Next day we learned that it was not a haystack fire in the immediate vicinity but six miles of London Docks were ablaze…
>
> Virtually every day we witnessed the continuing battle. From personal observation it seemed that the honours were about even, and I wondered about the accuracy of the more favourable reports in the wireless news. Eventually, it was revealed from German records that the British claims were exaggerated – but Dowding and his fliers did do enough.
>
> PP

On 7 September, provoked by an RAF raid on Berlin, 375 German planes attacked London. There were 2,000 casualties of which 430 were fatal. It was the start of the Blitz which continued for 76 consecutive nights with one exception, 2 November. By the end of September 5,730 had been killed and over 10,000 injured. German priorities had shifted. On 5 September, Hitler's 'Sealion' invasion plan was indefinitely postponed.

During the Battle of Britain, Basil Leverton's brother (DW) who was in anti-aircraft (ack-ack) defence at RAF Wittering came over to Bedford to take him to lunch at The Swan.

> I went back with him to see his troop HQ. There was a pilot there, Cardnell, an old Owenian who had been in the same form as DW and

had taken him up on flights. One had been planned for the following day but had been cancelled due to new orders against passengers. Sadly Cardnell was killed the same night.   BL

The RAF was the glamour service. Soldiers referred to airmen as 'Brylcreem Boys'. They 'could get lifts from cars and free cups of tea much more easily than brown jobs.'[4]

37

War Once Removed

Vicarious experiences on the sidelines.

I t was death at a distance, adventure second hand.

It was easy to forget there was a war on in the relaxed atmosphere of Bedford.   KSK

On the one hand we were living here in Bedford, and, on the other hand, a series of fearful events told about on the wireless news or newsreels.   GR

Bedford was bombed but it was nothing to write home about and home was really being bombed.

Occasional visits to London provided indelible pictures of German bombers making the first daylight raids on the city, the burning city, and then the waste land of bombed buildings. The nights there were filled with noise and sudden flashes of light. Bedford seemed something like a sanctuary from all that.   ME

Death was not an ever-present topic of conversation though it was a lurking thought, especially for senior boys such as Basil Leverton.

Our home and our family firm were near Euston and too near King's Cross and St. Pancras railway targets. I recall commenting to Mrs Ralph, my billet lady, what would happen if my family were wiped out. Mrs. Ralph, daughter of a Leeds solicitor, was very sensible and straightforward. Just said she was sure everyone would 'rally round' and wisely didn't pursue the subject. Never occurred to me who would do the rallying.   BL

Doug Sutton's parents were also vulnerable.

> Dad gave me a sealed envelope to open if anything happened to them, as he put it. I kept the envelope for six years, but fortunately never had to open it to read what was ever inside. I burnt it in 1945.　　DHS

> I was approaching John Bull's passage and met, unexpectedly, my parents (phones then were rare). We knew from newsreels of the London bombings. And I assumed, correctly and tearfully, that we had been bombed out. After the loving embraces (mum wore a hat!), Dad remonstrated with me that the vital thing was that we were all alive.　GR

Donald Mackay witnessed death and destruction in both Bedford and London.

> War didn't really touch us. Yes, there were rations and coupons and Utility clothing, and a great shortage of torch batteries, but at our age there was little excitement about war. I remember a group of us took bicycles to see a site up near Kimbolton where a German bomber had crashed with its bomb load. It was just a field with a large crater, and two engines mostly buried in the bottom of it. There was nothing else to see except tiny unrecognisable scraps of clothing hanging from the hedgerows, and one sheepskin flight boot. There was, however, a highly characteristic smell I can never forget of burnt cordite and burnt flesh. The crater was fascinating; the flight boot with something in it was repulsive. If anything brought home war to us, that was it. My second cousin, Hamish Mackay of the Seaforth Highlanders was killed at St. Valéry after Dunkirk, but that was a disappearance, a loss not to be felt until I went to Ross-shire and found no one to help me launch a boat into the Dornoch Firth. Death was distant except when you stood at the edge of a crater and smelled it.　　DAMM

Donald Mackay doesn't recall any bombs in Bedford but he left in the middle of the war and there were plenty in north London.

> ... where I kept a map in my room marked with the various kinds of bombs that fell nearby. A land mine took out a block about a half-mile away, and ordinary bombs took out two houses across the road and cracked our windows and ceilings, but somehow death and destruction were divorced. Only in that crater in the field near Kimbolton did they come together.　　DAMM

Of course, we all lost people we knew – if only slightly – when masters and senior boys were reported killed or missing (see chapter 40). We also had fatalities nearer home. John Stockton had a good friend at his elementary school, Walter Grant.

> He had a six-year-old brother who was a delightful child but had given Walter and me difficulties when we took him, on only one occasion, to church. This child was usually at home with parents in Warren Crescent, not far from where I lived, in Upper Holloway. In October 1940 a bomb fell onto the LMS sidings alongside Warren Crescent. The explosion lifted a freight wagon full of coal clear above the ground and dumped it right on top of the Anderson shelter in which were sheltering, and in which were killed, both of Walter's parents and his small brother.   JS

About that same time, E.Hyde in form IIA wrote a contrasting piece for the *Arrow* entitled *Air Raid.*

> *It was Saturday afternoon. The town was crowded with shoppers. The Square was a mass of pushing people and shouting stall-owners. Then, suddenly above the noise of the market and traffic, there arose a loud wailing. Most of the people took no notice of it until it stopped. Then there was a big rush for cycles, cars and shelters. Special policemen rushed to their posts. Wardens ran here and there telling people to get under cover.*
>
> *At the bus station the empty buses were pouring in to 'stay put' until the 'all clear' went. In the shelters at the factories the men and girls who work on Saturdays and Sundays were singing and playing cards or darts to pass the time away.*
>
> *Arrow*, Michaelmas '40

We had a war to help us pass the time away. We were playing the Germans.

> It was like a football game. They scored. We scored.   DAMM

We had won the previous time. Indeed, at the start of the war, in that unreal twilight, one of the opposing team, a spy no less, named von Rintelen visited the school and gave us a diverting speech. He was later interned.

Donald Mackay recalls having no kind of animosity to the Germans – and none towards a fellow Owenian.

George Webb I remember feeling somewhat sorry for since his mother was German (his father had been in the British Occupation Army of the Rhine after the Great War) and I thought – without really knowing – that he had to have a problem with divided loyalties.

But we all did to some degree. Those of us who were classmates of Karl Lohmann (or his younger brother Claus) knew they were enemy aliens, but it didn't matter. They were good friends and I for one was genuinely sorry when Karl left us for internment on the Isle of Man the day he became sixteen. DAMM

Two years later another German arrived.

Then around 1943 a German boy, Gunther Dorzbacher, joined our class. Where had he come from in the middle of hostilities, with his smart continental-style suit and large leather briefcase shaming our shabby satchels? Curiously, as far as I knew, nobody asked him (good manners or sheer lack of interest meant we seldom enquired about other boys' home backgrounds). The obvious solution would have been that he was a refugee, probably Jewish, but again, matters of doctrinal allegiance were splendidly irrelevant at Owen's, so I couldn't say. There must have been an interesting story Dorzbacher could have told, but he kept it to himself. We accepted him as one of us, and never made fun of his heavy German accent. MJC

Though some of us may have gone along with the belief that the only good German was a dead German, we could probably make the distinction – necessary much later – between Germans and Nazis.

We knew which side we were on, that this was 'total war' and there could be but one goal – 'unconditional surrender'. The end would justify the means.

I remember a physics lesson when a large contingent of US bombers flew overhead. The master, 'Fishy' Salmond, paused to mutter a regretful comment about terrible death and destruction they were about to wreak across the Channel. We boys were quite unmoved – killing the enemy could only be a *good* thing. It took a few years for some of us to accept that there might be a moral downside to the wholesale destruction of cities, even those inhabited by German women and children. MJC

One of our masters registered as a conscientious objector. When the news broke I and others would not take his subject seriously, paid little attention and failed the exam, miserably. I am not proud of this but it reflects the 100% concentration on the war.   GRo

The longer the game went on, the more permissible were the dirty tricks - and after all they had started it. We would win the game of course.

I had a naïve kid's view that England was best and that England would make it and the fact that the Germans were across the Channel was a small difficulty that we would overcome.   VM

I never doubted that we would win. I got depressed occasionally when ships were sunk, battles lost, parts of Europe occupied, but never for a moment did I doubt that final victory would be ours. I felt that I was not alone in this. I can't recall any friend having a different opinion.   DEB

They might be ahead now, but in the end we knew we would win even as they proved to be tough opponents. Even in the days when invasion seemed likely, I had no worries. We were in the Cadet Corps. We would get rifles (if only 303s chambered for .22 bullets), we would withstand the paratroopers and the tanks, and we would win. Oh, the blissful ignorance of youth!   DAMM

The young weren't alone in their ignorance. Not many ordinary people – civilians or military – appreciated the abyss beneath us in 1940.

According to Angus Calder, 'by the end of the year the proportion [of Britons believing we would lose] was so small that it could not be measured'.[1] We had faith and the media reinforced it.

Propaganda ensured that things weren't going so badly during the desperate years 1940 to 1942.   KD

On 2 February 1943 the Germans were defeated at Stalingrad.

I believed that this was a blow from which even the German Army could not recover– maybe for the first time, a conviction that we were actually beginning to win the war.   JS

The victors of Stalingrad were, of course, our allies. But it hadn't started out that way. The early months of the war were confusing

to young watchers of world affairs. The USSR had signed a non-aggression pact with Hitler eleven days before the war started.

> Early in the war, those of us who had Communist sympathies were puzzled. There had been a Nazi-Soviet pact. This made the Russians our enemies. In November they invaded Finland and bombed Helsinki. The papers were full of stories of brave Finns all in white on the snows beating off the aggressors. Then that war was settled. DEB

The settlement on 12 June 1940 ceded some land to the Soviets. It might have been more had the Finns' resistance been less. The following year...

> 22 June 1941 – the day Stalin's dalliance with Hitler ended: the day the Nazis invaded Russia and the day pro-Communist Owenians felt relief because the slate had been wiped clean; the Non-Aggression Act consigned to oblivion. Stalin would now be canonised as Uncle Joe; the Russians welcomed by Churchill as our close allies and no longer did the school Stalinists have to wriggle in embarrassment in defence of their idol. MM

> Suddenly the Soviet Union was our ally and we would revert to our earlier feeling of solidarity. 'What does it mean?' we asked our form master. 'It will halve the number of days of the war', he said confidently.
> DEB

> My father had left-wing inclinations and although he was anti-Stalinist, but being Russian by nationality and having in fact been there in Soviet times, he must have had an emotional attachment to the Russians, some of which transferred successfully to me. So, although he and his friends knew how wicked the Stalinists were, the fact that the Russians were on our side was an enormous benefit. Everybody welcomed that. Indeed, I remember the speech that Churchill made the night that the Germans invaded Russia and we expected him to say, 'hard luck, we sympathise with you but you are not our friends', but he didn't. He said, 'anybody who is an enemy of Germany is a friend of ours'. And that also made a very great impression, so we had solid friends. Had I been older in 1941, I might have had a more acute sense of our isolation. VM

Mrs Churchill headed a committee to raise funds for Russia. It was hard to reconcile one's feelings. Enemy turned ally.

W.E.O. Jones was billeted with a middle-aged couple who followed the news regularly.

We discussed the war a lot. At that time Russian successes, e.g. Stalingrad, hit the headlines. The billet people were, however, working class Tories and virulently anti-Communist. Whatever one's pleasure at the German reverses, one mustn't say anything remotely in praise of Soviet Russia – a strange attitude. WEOJ

Many of us were praising the Soviets. It was like praising British triumph with the added ingredient of class warfare.

The victorious Soviet generals became popular heroes, their names bandied about as if they were football or cricket stars. One was Timoshenko; it was rumoured by a pro-Soviet Welshman that he had a Welsh ancestor whose name was Timothy Jenkins. MM

Russia took the brunt of the war. Britain provided help, mostly by sea in bitter weather and extreme danger. There was a nominal contribution of aircraft and pilots.

In the newspapers it said that the RAF had sent a wing to Russia. A wing was less than a squadron. I drew an amateurish cartoon. One military character is saying to another 'I see we've sent a wing to the Russians'. The other gent says 'Port or starboard?' DEB

There was agitation for a second front.

I remember going to a mass meeting in London to hear Michael Foot and the Dean of Canterbury dressed in gaiters (and for whom Stalin was the near equivalent of Jesus) demanding that the second front be opened, accusing Churchill of unnecessary delay. MM

Agitation stopped on 6 June 1944. Ken Deadman can't understand why his diary is blank on D-Day.

I was in a classroom (above the Liberal Club) when, somehow word was brought of Eisenhower's announcement. We all cheered and then, I think, the lesson went on. The event had been 'imminent' for so long we were able to take its announcement quite calmly. JS

When D-Day came it was business as usual for P.H. 'Flash' Hardwick. The son of a member of staff arrived late, explaining that his mother had said he should stop and listen to the wireless. 'Flash' said 'at home, do as your mother tells you, but the school rules say you must be here at 9 o'clock – late class tonight'. This met with general satisfaction! Masters' sons were seldom popular! WEOJ

But generally masters encouraged us to follow the war. During the summer term of 1943, G.W. Baker allowed W.E.O. Jones to go into his study to listen to Churchill's account of the German attack on the Italians. The Headmaster invited old Owenians and others in uniform to address the school.

> I remember Harold Moore standing on the school stage to tell us of his naval experiences and on other occasions we were addressed by military gentlemen obviously looking for recruits. RN

Occasionally, the Headmaster himself spoke of the war's progress.

> The Headmaster impressed on the school that the fall of Tunis in May 1943 was a fact of contemporary history that we should remember in later years. He obviously saw it as a major turning point. WEOJ

But we would also teach ourselves.

> I used to make model battleships of the Royal Navy and one after the other my model battleships were getting sunk. I remember the day the *Hood* was sunk and the *Hood* was my biggest battleship so I got affected at that level. VM

We followed the war with maps. Every newspaper featured them. Some published more permanent versions. We would flag-pin advances and retreats. Place names formed a litany: El Alamein, Sidi Barrani, Tobruk. On the eastern front: Odessa, Minsk, Rostov, Vitebsk, Kharkov, Kursk.

> We had large war maps on the living room wall and we stuck flags in them, particularly on the Eastern Front. We listened to Radio Moscow every night to the communiqués, both when they got bad and more enthusiastically when they got better. The war in the Pacific was more remote to us. By the time the war in the Pacific got started we already had friends in the world. The Russians and Americans were on our side and the threat was not local. VM

We would also practise aircraft recognition especially in the Scouts and ATC. It was important to distinguish ally from enemy shapes. Some of us read *Aeroplane Spotter*.

> Combative aircraft were recognised from the Players cigarette cards series. DMJ

> On Saturday evening (14 November 1940) many Owenians stood and watched what seemed to be hundreds of German bombers flying in the same northwest direction. The next morning we heard of the horrific devastation inflicted on Coventry. DAP

The war became real at moments like this, what Malcolm Campbell refers to as 'intimation of greater things'.

> Soldiers in Bedford and back from Dunkirk and watching aerial dog fights. The church bells ringing out after El Alamein. MJC

Very occasionally an air raid siren would sound in Bedford.

> In school we used to go down to the cellars and we discovered that this is where Bedford Modern School tuck shop was and I hate to think what we consumed in the half hour that we spent there. BS

We followed the war and we followed other things – as indicated by this doggerel in the school magazine.

> *IGNORAMUS*
> *I'm filled with apprehension*
> *At Einstein's Fourth Dimension;*
> *And Roosevelt's fight with Dewey*
> *Completely sends me screwy,*
> *I think it pretty beastly*
> *To censor J.B. Priestley,*
> *But I begin to feel good*
> *At 'Hamlet' with John Gielgud.*
> *I've read of delegations*
> *To Spain and the Dalmatians.*
> *I've heard of Mona Lisa,*
> *The Leaning Tower of Pisa,*
> *Of Rome and its Colossus,*
> *And Japs who try to boss us.*
> *I've studied every war front,*
> *I know we've crossed the Meuse,*
> *But please won't someone tell me*
> *Who's keeping goal for Spurs?*
> D.E.B., *Arrow*, Michaelmas '44

W.E.O. Jones viewed the war with more intensity and application. The palm for understanding war strategy must go to him and his good friend Keggie.

Throughout the period I discussed the war endlessly with Peter R.Keggie (1940-51). He was most knowledgeable and had an understanding of the technical side of warfare that was denied me. It is remarkable that, when we were in Form RA in 1943, we picked on the Cherbourg Peninsula as a good site for the Allied invasion of France.

WEOJ

Owen's had a small part to play in that invasion.

In the run up to D-Day the whole school was engaged in packaging small items of military hardware - we called it 'pistol packing' but there seemed no resemblance to parts of a firearm and we would not dare to ask their purpose.

MJC

Dennis Jones remembers packing

... military parts in wax paper in the gymnasium.

DMJ

Whereas another recalls

Packing hundreds of little boxes of springs and nuts and bolts, etc.

DHS

Ron Nash is more specific.

We packed spare parts for Bren guns in the gymnasium.

RN

John Stockton remembers his fellow packer, a future eminent physicist.

I was seated next to Leslie Orgel. He devoted quite a lot of time as we wrapped the bullets in waterproof material, in extolling the virtues of science as a course of study,

JS

The majority of us got no closer to the battlefield but we became more conscious of war's bloody downside. A poem called *Night Patrol* contributed by a fifth former to the Christmas 1944 *Arrow*, despite its patriotic sentimentality, grasped death's nettle in a way that the earlier *Air Raid* did not.

Camp at last; are we glad?
Rest our feet; have a fag;
Clean equipment, wash and shave,
Hand of poker – lose our pay.

Can you wonder what it's like?
Prowling round at dead of night?
Then it comes – that sudden whine,
Staccato sound – machine gun's sign.
Men fall wounded, many dead,
Bullets whistle past my head.
Bayonets gleam; a sudden thrust;
All this for a madman's lust!
A man bobs up, I run him through,
Pull out my weapon – that makes two,
Then back we stagger, yard by yard,
Bayonets ready at 'On Guard,'
Still retreating, fighting ever,
Praying wildly, now or never
Then we make our final stand,
Nearby batteries lend a hand;
Jerry yields! – the battle's over,
Thoughts wing to the cliffs of Dover.
Yes, my homeland, how I miss you!
Lest I die, I say 'God bless you!'

D.H. Briggs, *Arrow*, Michaelmas '44

38

Closer Quarters

The war hits Bedford – and the school in Islington.

Many Owenians got to appreciate what their parents were enduring only on those rare occasions when bombs fell in Bedford. When incendiaries sprinkled Russell Park one night, killing nobody, it was almost an enjoyable adventure. But when more heavyweight merchandise landed the effect was different.

> There were two landmines, one at Kempston and the other on the waste ground at Queens Park. No one was injured. I lived near the one at Kempston and was quite shaken by the experience.   DHS

For those whose London homes had luckily escaped damage finding themselves attacked in a designated safe area had a certain irony. In 1941 John Stockton's mother and sister (whose City employers had been bombed out) moved to Bedford to join him.

> The first night of their moving to Bedford coincided with the first air raid on the town and they spent the night crouching under the stairs, in Queens Park, with their landlady who wore a tea cosy throughout the raid, which, I remember, hit Laxton's, the seed company, and killed one of the Laxton family.   JS

Conrad Lynn remembers the raid.

> Brookfield Road had houses only on one side. On the other side was the ditch, which separated it from Laxton's Nurseries. On one of the rare occasions when the air raid siren sounded in Bedford, Mr Huckle rapidly packed some valuables, money, deeds of the house, insurance policies, etc into a small attaché case, rushed it out of the house and hid

it in the ditch for safety. It took a direct hit from one of the few incendiary bombs to drop on Bedford and went up in flames! CL

Two years later Ron Coyte, for whom war brought tragedy, experienced 'a strange twist'.

People providing shelter to myself were victims of a bombing attack. The house in which I lived (15 Irwin Road) was hit by an explosive incendiary bomb wounding my host and his son. Two of the few air raid casualties suffered by Bedford during the war. RCo

Bombs on nurseries, parks and residential areas were random. Most were a result of what the Anderson Committee had forecast - German aircraft releasing unused explosives on their way home. Near the station (on the London, Midland and Scottish line) were a theatre and a hotel. There was a daylight raid.

I was living in Phillpotts Avenue. I heard a strange sound. I saw a German plane coming out of the clouds. A bomb fell in the station area near the County Theatre. IW

A lone German bomber was heading for home with the RAF in hot pursuit and jettisoned its bombs near the railway station. This was about 9a.m. It might have been aiming for nearby Allen's Engineering works but its bombs straddled the railway, hitting the coal dump and a small hotel in Alexander Road where several people were killed. AN

One Owenian, however, was nearly hurt. The 'danger of war came very close' to army cadet Bernard Fox when he went to collect his uniform from a building near to the railway station.

I arrived early and so decided to cycle around a bit and whilst cycling along the road which ran parallel to the station, I noticed an aeroplane high up in the sky over the station. I remember thinking I will not go any further but will turn around and go back to get my uniform. As I turned around I heard a colossal explosion - a bomb had wrecked the hotel near to the station and on either side there were people leaning out of windows looking to see what had happened. It was extremely surreal. I cannot remember what I thought or felt at the time but later realised that if I had not turned around I would probably have been killed. BF

Though civilian fatalities in Bedford were very few, damage was done to premises. Geoff Cook's billet parents were among the very few Bedfordians who suffered directly.

> It was at breakfast time (in spring 1944, I think) that we heard a thud and shortly after there was a telephone call to Harold Garlick to say that the premises in Prebend Street had been damaged. He ran a wholesale sweet and confectionery business and acted for his widow's sister-in-law in a monumental masonry business housed in adjacent quarters. There was significant damage, mainly broken windows and doors, fortunately no staff were present at the time. GCk

Military casualties in and around Bedford were confined to crashing planes. We would cycle out to the scene but, apart from Donald Mackay's encounter at the crater, (see chapter 37) incidents in the surrounding countryside presented no evidence of human loss.

> One Sunday afternoon, on a blackberrying expedition, we witnessed a small RAF aircraft crash in a field nearby. When we arrived at the scene one of the aircrew had gone off for help, while the other was fending off souvenir hunters. MJC

When a plane crashed in the town itself, reality was nearer. Ivor Walker did occasional work at a small department store, E.P. Rose, on the High Street. It had a tower.

> I used to go up it when US bombers were flying. One day I saw an Airacobra come down. IW

> Looking from a back window on a sunny, soundless afternoon we saw a US Airacobra plunge down into the streets across Bromham Road, a couple of hundred yards away. Miraculously, no civilians died. AJ

Henry George has a reason for Andrew Jones's miracle.

> I remember seeing a plane doing aerobatics. It was an Airacobra. I didn't realise it was out of control. It came down in Priory Road. No civilians were killed because it landed between the houses. The pilot was killed. The engine of the Airacobra was behind the pilot. He stood no chance at all. HG

Alf Nunn adds further detail.

> Airacobras were rear-engined aircraft and, when under stress, the engines sometimes broke loose from their mountings and in a dive

would slide forward and crush the pilot. It was assumed that this was the cause of this crash. The aircraft was in a steep dive and the engine was screaming. It seemed ages before it actually crashed and I remember that we were running towards the spot where it seemed likely to fall. Consequently, we were at the spot very shortly after the crash. By good fortune, the aircraft had fallen into a small back-yard just off the Midland Road and so damage to property was minimal. Unfortunately, the American pilot was killed outright. AN

Alf Nunn and his colleagues, especially those in the Air Training Corps, were cognisant of aircraft and intrigued by anything strange or unrecognisable.

Bedford was not far from Hatfield, the home of the De Haviland Aeroplane Company and I can clearly remember a day in early 1942 when Bedford was beaten up by two prototype Mosquito bombers blatantly stunting all over the air above the town and delighting us all because nobody knew what they were.

They were not the Hawker Typhoons, which we had heard of, because they had twin engines, but all was to be revealed within a few weeks when they accomplished their first daylight raids. They were built of a sandwich of balsa wood between two layers of plywood, were incredibly light and strong and gave employment to all the otherwise unemployed woodworkers in and around High Wycombe.

Summer camps took place at RAF aerodromes and I remember one held in 1944 at Bircham Newton in Norfolk. This was a strange grass airfield with no actual runways and thus suitable for only light and communications aircraft. Quite what went on there I do not know, except that in one hangar there was a Mosquito bomber fitted with a 75 mm cannon in a gondola under the fuselage. AWL

The Mosquito – precision bomber, fighter, photo-reconnaissance plane – flew at over 400 miles per hour, the fastest until jets appeared. Over 8000 were built.

Direct experience of the war was minimal for most Owen's boys but not Owen's School. In the spring 1941 issue of the *Arrow*, Mr Vaughan, the beadle of the school building, reported comprehensively on *Owen's in the Blitz*. He and his wife had volunteered immediately on war's outbreak for Civil Defence as Air Raid Wardens. The school dining hall was converted into a public shelter; the playground was dug up to provide two more and various rooms were transformed into a first aid depot. The first bomb in the immediate neighbourhood fell in late September 1940.

We could see a lot of people lying on the pavement outside Burton's shop, and you can appreciate our sighs of relief when we found the 'people' were dressed tailor's dummies, flung out of the window by the blast. They went back into the shop front just as fast as they came out! Actually, the bomb exploded on some dwelling houses, wrecking a number of them, and damaging the school.

We put up four 'refugees' in the school that night. All they had was a handbag and a comb — plus about half a hundredweight of brick dust. This raid foreshadowed several more visitations from Fritz...

During a night raid in October, Jerry dropped a load of incendiaries locally. We had two through the school roof (over rooms 17 and 18), one in the Cloisters, another on the florists' roof overlooking the school and a fourth in the back garden by the Assembly Hall back staircase...

The night raid in the middle of October was our worst. Soon after 8pm several high explosive bombs were dropped very near the school. Unfortunately one fell directly on the Girls' School opposite and completely demolished the main building. Another bomb fell just outside the Boys' playground right in front of the Girls' School. Two more bombs landed a hundred yards away, and a delayed action one came up to rest not far away. Although there were some casualties among the public in the Girls' School shelter, the number would have been far greater if the bombs had fallen on the shelters in the centre of the Boys' playground.

We were at the opposite end of the street when the disaster occurred. What a crash! Our Warden's Post was notified at once, and although many Wardens' Rescue Squads, etc were soon on the spot, it was difficult to do very much as the building had collapsed on the basement shelter. The bomb on the playground had made a huge crater, so we went around the back of the Girls' School to try and help rescue someone. The playground was a mass of floating coke. The situation was almost as bad at the back. The only door left standing was soon disposed of with a pickaxe, but the room behind it had been blocked with fallen concrete. After hours of work it was agreed that the Rescue Squad should await a crane at daylight to lift some of the debris, and, feeling nearly exhausted, made a move towards home. As we got back, we were astonished to see Mr. Burley, the Girls' School Beadle, being dragged out of a pile of bricks. He was badly shaken but not injured. He said that a wardrobe had hit him on the back and knocked him under the stairs, thereby saving his life. On top of this he was forced to knock a hole through a wall to allow the water to run to a lower level. He and others were in great difficulties, and had doubts about getting out at all. Mrs. Burley did not fare so well. She was pinned down by a heavy chair, and it was some hours before she was rescued. I understand they are quite all right now. It was twelve days afterwards before their pets, a dog, parrot and cat were rescued alive from the wreckage. They are still alive and well. A Warden from our post was killed outside the Girls' School.

(Mr Vaughan details more minor incidents and closes on a personal and confident note.)

Finally, we are looking forward to the day when masters and boys return. We have seen so few of them. Many thanks to the Headmaster for his kind letters giving us some details of the school's 'doings' in Bedford, also for the words of cheer during our 'isolation'.

With best wishes to you all at Bedford -and 'Cheerio! We shall win!'
W.A. Vaughan, *Arrow*, Lent '41

Henry George, not yet an Owenian, spent the first year of the war in London.

We lived near King's Cross station. We were lucky apart from a window frame being blown in, the ceiling coming down and an incendiary in the garden. Our Anderson shelter filled with water so we went underground — Green Park station but that was bombed so we tried Piccadilly Circus. Claustrophobic. HG

His schooling was interrupted. Before schools reopened, masters taught him in his own parlour. Then, no sooner had his school reopened...

On two successive Sundays there was a time bomb near the school. It meant a week's holiday each time while they defused the bomb...
During daylight raids we went to the shelter. Sometimes eight times a day. HG

Bob Beecham had been evacuated to the Bedford area with his brother. Alan joined Owen's. Bob's education was suffering and his parents decided he should return home despite being 'at great bodily risk from the enemy'.

In this London interlude I witnessed the fires of London from the vantage point of Alexandra Palace, lived through the height of the V1 doodle-bug, heard the thud of the V2 and the rocket arriving, the rattle of the windows as the nightly AA barrage went off, thanking God for the protection of a terraced house, not receiving a direct hit, survival in the 'Morrison'* shelter from extensive blast damage on several occasions choking in the dust from the lath and plaster walls and ceiling as they collapsed, enjoying the relief as the dust settled. The daily routine stuttered but did not stop. Occasionally at the school roll call a name was unanswered and the next day a chum was mentioned in our prayers at assembly.   RSB

As we have seen, some boys experienced bombing whilst briefly on vacation. Basil Leverton was round the corner from Mornington Crescent and a bus on its side, the photograph of which went round the world.

Conrad Lynn had been granted leave to stay with his aunt in relatively safe Edgware.

I had an arrangement to meet my father the next morning in his office in St.Paul's churchyard. That night there was an air raid and next morning I got as close as I could to St.Paul's to find the whole area one of smoking rubble, with firemen and their hoses all over the place. Only the cathedral was left intact, everything else had gone including my father's office.   CL

Of course, there were Owenians who experienced bombing once they had left school. Jack Levy was one.

I had left Owen's in 1943 and in the summer of '44 after first year university, was on vacation industrial training at the engine works of AEC in Southall and living near there. It was the time of the V1s and for some reason I telephoned my home where my father was living and working having re-established his business on a small scale at home after his small factory in Holborn had suffered serious bomb damage. There was no answer to my call and the line appeared to be dead. Worried, I telephoned the local police station and the sergeant on duty asked me where I lived. 'Number 7 Clissold Crescent' I said. There was a pause and then he said to me, 'You'd better go home'. I did, and as I came down Albion Road an hour later on a 73 bus I saw my house in

---

* Named after Herbert Morrison, the new Minister of Home Security, the Morrison Shelter (unlike the Anderson) could be erected indoors. It was 82 cms high with a steel plate on top. Its sides were of wire mesh.

complete ruins. It had taken a direct hit. Fortunately, my father, who was alone in the house at the time, extraordinarily was unhurt apart from shock. When he heard the V1 engine stop he had gone down into our cellar which the council had strengthened to be a shelter. Here he had kept a whistle. In the adjoining cellar our neighbour had similarly escaped but all the exits from both houses were blocked with debris. 'Blow your whistle, Mr Levy' she called through a brick hole between the houses. 'Blow your whistle'. He did and was heard by the air raid warden. Later, my cousin, John Slater, the actor and author, wrote a short story entitled *Blow Your Whistle, Mr Levy*.   JL

Many sons were not so fortunate. The Coyte brothers were bereaved.

My father was in the RAFVR (balloons) and in the spring of 1940 our parents decided to transfer me to Owen's. I soon settled down in Bedford and remember vividly the wonderful summer of 1940 and for a brief period of that time Dad was on a course at RAF Cardington and came down to Bedford on numerous occasions to see us when we would stroll along the Embankment just across from the Swan.

The start of 1941 however, was a dreadful time for me. I can still see Mrs Perkins (the billet landlady) reading from a letter sent by my mother to say that my father had been killed on January 6th. He was blown up in the Thames Estuary taking supplies to RAF colleagues who were stationed on balloon carrying Merchant Navy Ships.

My father was buried at Manor Park Cemetery and after the funeral Ron and I returned to Bedford. Most certainly Bert Seaborn knew what had happened since we lived next door to each other in Windsor House, Wenlock Road but I don't recall telling school friends of our tragedy.

Mitchell saw both of us in his office on our return around 11 January 1941. He was probably more ill at ease in his attempt to give us words of comfort than we were in receiving them.

Other Owen's boys must have lost relatives and close friends in the WW2 but I can't recollect any mention of such in the three years I spent at the school.   PCo

There was reticence as there was loss. Terry Eyre was evacuated with the school on day one. His little sister Pauline accompanied him. She felt they were 'the luckiest evacuees' because their mother had joined them.

She had taken a flat in Castle Road and we would spend every weekend with her. My father had opted to stay in London and joined the

Auxiliary Fire Service - he was too old for the Services - but insisted on helping his country. The Hobkirk family thought he was wonderful, when he visited us and told them tales of terrible raids and fires that he and his mates were facing in London and on 8 December 1940 my father lost his life with seven other firemen. They had national coverage of their funeral in the Press. They were buried together and their names are commemorated on that statue to London wartime firemen which stands in the shadow of St. Paul's Cathedral.   PF

Basil Leverton's older brother, Ivor, who had left Owen's in 1929 was also in the Auxiliary Fire Service, having been deemed medically unfit. His other parallel job was in the family funeral business. He went through the Blitz, was injured in 1941 and, in both occupations, had to cope with horrors - death and bereavement ('some including several from the same family'). He was also involved in the famous decoy later celebrated and filmed as *The man Who Never Was.* A body was selected, uniformed, filled up with secret plans to mislead the enemy and dumped at sea ...

The ploy helped move German troops from Sicily to Sardinia and from the Russian front two German divisions were moved nearer to the Balkan/Greek theatre of war. Ivor recalls his very difficult and secret removal during night of a body from St. Pancras Coroner's Court Mortuary to Hackney Mortuary (within the same Coroner's jurisdiction) under a cover story .The success of all this may well have saved old Owen's casualties in Sicily, including our own brother.   BL

Barry Amiel left school in 1939. A year later he wrote a letter to the Headmaster. O. W. Mitchell read it in assembly.

It included a poem of Amiel's which has been anthologised since, most recently in the *Faber Book of War Poetry*. I remember being deeply moved at the time   WFF

BARRY AMIEL

Death is a Matter of Mathematics

Death is a matter of mathematics

It screeches down at you from dirtywhite nothingness
And your life is a question of velocity and altitude,
With allowances for wind and the quick, relentless pull
Of gravity.

Or else it lies concealed
In that fleecy, peaceful puff of cloud ahead,
A streamlined, muttering vulture, waiting
To swoop upon you with a rush of steel.
And then your chances vary as the curves
Of your parabolas, your banks, your dives,
The scientific soundness of your choice
Of what to push or pull, and how, and when.
Or perhaps you walk oblivious in a wood,
Or crawl flat-bellied over pockmarked earth,
And Death awaits you in a field gray tunic.
Sights upright and aligned. Range estimated
And set in. A lightning, subconscious calculation
Of trajectory and deflection. With you the focal point,
The centre of the problem. The A and B
Or Smith and Jones of schoolboy textbooks.

Ten out of ten means you are dead.[1]

Frank Fenn wasn't the only one to have been moved.

39

Yanks

Starry-eyed London kids meet GIs–and Glenn Miller.

In 1942 Bedford began to look different. In the previous November, the Japanese had bombed Pearl Harbor. It was a Sunday, what Roosevelt termed 'a day which will live in infamy'. Great Britain too had gone to war on a Sunday. On 26 January 1942, the first American troops landed on British soil in Northern Ireland. In 1944 one and a half million were stationed here, many around Bedford, on airfields.

We were glad to see them in the war and our midst. If any of us had harboured doubts about the outcome of the conflict, this friendly invasion dispelled them. We spoke to the GIs unasked. Why did we shed our normal reserve with American forces? Did we feel a duty to make them feel welcome? Maybe, but our hello was soon followed by a spoken or tacit request, 'Got any gum, chum?'

> Yanks were unavoidable. Not that one wished to avoid them. They were always good for chewing gum.   MM

Conversation was interesting. We discovered different meanings for the same word, different words for a shared meaning. Occasionally there was mutual incomprehension.

> I remember a cartoon in *Punch*. A GI is standing by a river asking a local fisherman if he had caught anything. 'I haven't caught a sausage,' he replied. 'Maybe', says the Yank, 'you ain't using the right bait for sausages'.   DEB

Grant Woodruff of BMS was confronted by an American serviceman.

The biggest indignity was when challenged by a United States soldier stationed in the area. He likened our Eagle (on all our cap badges in those days) with the German eagle. I had no idea what that looked like and I was not quick enough to say the American eagle was probably nearer in design to the German one.   GW

Frank Fenn encountered a similar lack of comprehension in Bedford's one and only milk bar close to the bus station.

After the fashion of the day, it served a beige, milky liquid masquerading as coffee. The process involved a lot of steam and some jiggery-pokery with a machine that looked like a prototype of the FA Cup but without the gilt and baroque adornments. One afternoon I watched an American GI attempt unsuccessfully to get a cup of black coffee from the machine's operator. 'Could you not,' he asked, 'arrest the process at an early stage?'   WFF

Their sports were different.

When the Americans came into the war, some of them in Bedford introduced us to baseball. I remember watching them playing in Bedford Park and two balls came flying over into the road and we took them. Later we got them autographed and I have them to this day.   BS

Their uniforms were different. So were the things they consumed.

They were friendly. They had exotic cigarettes that tasted sweet and some of chocolate or so it seemed. They chewed gum and gave us some. One tasted of toothpaste.   DEB

They were generous - especially to kids. (They were generous to young women also, but in our case we could offer little in return.) Schoolgirls, friends of Owen's boys, remember innocent experiences. One was Mary Hope.

American forces sometimes opened their camps near Bedford, picked children up in the Market Square and took them in lorries to Chicksands and Thurleigh. They fed us, played games with us and brought us back, each child clutching a sweetie bag.   MH

Alan Locke benefited indirectly.

The arrival of the Americans in 1942 certainly made us realise what we were missing because some of our billet ladies got part-time jobs serving in the American Services Centre in Bromham Road or the American Officers Club in Goldington Road, and would come home with chewing gum, doughnuts and Hershey bars, all of which tasted wonderful. Mrs Fowler came back from the American Services Club with a ten shilling note, the only paper she had on her at the time, autographed by Broderick Crawford, who was then serving with the USAAF and who was later to become Sergeant Dan Matthews of *Highway Patrol*.

AWL

Sally Beecham (*née* Saunders) had moved into a new billet near Russell Park.

My young billet lady's many friends included some of the US servicemen from nearby Thurleigh. One of these, a chef, hearing that I was to be allowed to hold a party for my birthday, made a huge and most delicious Devil's Food cake for the occasion and supplied many other goodies unheard of in the days of rationing. This excellent fare was the talk of the Fifth Form for the rest of that term and got to the ears of the school staff. Consequently, I shortly afterwards found myself in yet another billet - the powers-that-be had decided that, however innocent, any association with American servicemen was not wise for a schoolgirl. SB

There was no directive against fraternisation for Owen's boys. Had there been, it is doubtful if it would have been honoured, the attractions being so substantial.

We had visits to an American airbase and were so well treated – ice cream and foods that we'd not experienced before. JWes

The Americans I will never forget. They even found time to take some of us to Thurleigh to look over a B17 followed by donuts and Coca-Cola during a lull in proceedings. RCa

Quite a number of Owenians did more than 'look over'.

When the US Army Air Force arrived, the 306 Bomber Group were posted to Thurleigh, not far north of Bedford, and on several occasions I cycled out there with a couple of chums, through the gate receiving a salute and to the crew room where we would scrounge a flight on a training trip. On one occasion we were offered a trip 'abroad' but declined. KD

One of my group had an American cousin in the USAAF based a few miles from Bedford and a few of us hitched a lift and visited the base on a Saturday afternoon. We were treated very well to tea and in conversation, we said that we were in the Army Cadets and ATC. They said that if we had our parents' permission they might be able to arrange for us to have a flight. That was enough for us! We all wrote letters purporting to come from our parents giving permission for us to fly and, donning our various uniforms, again went out to the base the following weekend to meet our American friends. True enough, a Flying Fortress was laid on and we went for a flight for about thirty minutes in an operational plane. We could not believe our luck. Needless to say, our parents never knew what we had been up to.   GS

John Stockton, whose mother had moved to Bedford, had a closer association with the American Army Air Force and as a result, feels unable to speak about 'Yanks' as an 'impersonal phenomenon'.

My sister became engaged to, and eventually married, a Master Sergeant in the USAAF 8th Air Force, providing me with six much-loved nieces and nephews.   JS

Sixty thousand British women became GI brides. Many more became involved.

Doug Sutton's billet lady's husband had been captured by the Japanese in Singapore.

Our regular visitor was an American airman, Eddy. I learnt a lot about life there. I find it difficult to condemn her for I don't know if she ever heard from her husband again.   DHS

Pavements, doorsteps and the banks of the Ouse became literally festooned with US issue 'evidence of summer nights' – to use T.S.Eliot's prim phrase. Once, fishing at Batt's Ford where Charles Wells' brewery discharged warm hop-laden water into the river, attracting vast shoals of fish, I did actually hook one with a bleak struggling inside.   DMJ

It made an equally memorable impression upon Dennis Jones's brother, Andrew.

By the riverside and in the roads, the used souvenirs of GI recreations drifted and tangled... one good yank and a lot came down.   AJ

Frequently, a US Army truck would saunter down the High Street on its way to a recreation centre, stopping to pick up 'dancing partners'.

> Yanks were a major attraction to the local girls. I never tried to compete. I would have been out for a duck. Even in Minehead, Devon, where the family went on holiday, there were Yanks and one stole my holiday girlfriend and left me with mixed feelings about them. On the one hand, they were allies; on the other hand, they purloined our girls; an unresolvable dilemma. MM

Whether they were 'our' girls is another matter. Maybe in the future tense. Nevertheless, real or imagined, this reason for our lack of success with girls did create some resentment.

> The Americans created a great deal of animosity with their money and extrovert ways - especially with the men because of the Americans' success with women. JWes

> Very unlike our soldiers, the doughboys were everywhere, flashing cash and getting the girls. DMJ

Juliet Gardiner recounts that GIs used to leave copper and silver change on the counter whilst British troops always counted every penny. She quotes one Tommy, ' "I wish I could afford to get drunk", a British soldier said wistfully as he watched two legless GIs being evicted from a dance hall in Bedford'.[1] No doubt by military policemen who, in their white helmets, were known as 'snowdrops' and drove around Bedford in jeeps.

> Tradespeople – of all sorts – relished this new and wondrous source of custom.

> On a visit to the barber, my haircut was interrupted by a US soldier's entry. I was waved aside, and the anticipated heavy tipper instantly tonsured. DMJ

They even looked different.

> They had very smart uniforms. The ordinary soldiers (enlisted men) wore material equivalent to British officers. None of that rough khaki which some of us knew from within. DEB

> Better clothed, shod and paid, they had little competition. DMJ

Not that any animosity on our part became physical. Though Ian Appleby was attacked by a bemused GI in St. Peter's Green.

> But lucky for me I had just come back from a PT course which included a lot of dirty tricks unarmed combat.   IA

Real fighting was not far off. On Independence Day in 1942 the American air force attacked occupied Europe for the first time, joining an RAF strike on Dutch airfields used by the *Luftwaffe*. On 27 January 1943, a year and a day after the American arrival in Great Britain, the USAAF flew its first mission to Germany. The target was Wilhelmshaven. Thereafter, the two airforces would alternate.

> The USAAF would fly out by day and bomb Germany. At night RAF Bomber Command would do the same. The sound was reassuring. Very occasionally in Bedford the sound of the bombers was intermittent not continuous. This meant that Germans were overhead. A siren would of course, have sounded. That too was intermittent. And when the raid was over and/or the bombers had passed, the all clear would go – and that sound was continuous.   DEB

The bombing of Germany and occupied Europe was a constant accompaniment to our lives. The crews were not much older than us. The targets may have been known to them. As the American poet Randall Jarrell wrote:

> *In bombers named for girls, we burned*
> *The cities we had learned about in school.*[2]

We were witnesses to destruction.

> The war became very close and, on occasion, the morning air would be shattered by a huge explosion which could only mean a B17 Flying Fortress must have crashed on take-off fully laden with bombs at nearby Thurleigh airfield and again in the late afternoon seeing the 'lucky' ones return with their damaged aircraft. Holes seemed to be everywhere. An engine would be stopped, a tailplane missing and Very lights being fired to let the field know the state of the aircraft and crew.   RCa

For Doug Sutton and his friends, fireworks enthusiasts, opportunity beckoned.

Gerry Shaw, Derek Angier and myself made some pretty impressive bangs, especially when we got cordite out of the 5 mm shells from the crashed American bombers.   DHS

Others were less dispassionate.

I remember one sunny summer's afternoon three or four of us cycled up to Thurleigh airfield north of Bedford. Several Flying Fortresses were parked round the perimeter. We got chatting to a rear gunner who gave us some M/G bullets 0.5" dia. Mid-afternoon a droning heralded the return of the squadrons from bombing Germany. They came in desultory fashion, some with rudders shot away, great holes shot in the fuselage and wings. Some of the fuselages stained red! This brought home the horror of war into our own backyard and showed us that the Americans were shedding their blood in our war. Some years after the war, a film called *Twelve o'clock High* starring Gregory Peck was made which captured the atmosphere of those times very closely.   PFa

Although we were in the safety of Bedford, it really brought home to me the bravery of those very young Americans and the terrible losses they sustained. It did my heart good to see them arrive every night in town to enjoy themselves ... while they could ... At night Bomber Command would take over and we would see them on their way to bomb Germany.   RCa

I have a recollection of seeing an American B29 coming in to land, where the crew parachuted out leaving the pilot to land with a bomb carriage jammed by a bomb. On landing it exploded and the pilot was killed. My admiration of the Yanks, who had come to our aid changed dramatically. Their cheek became friendliness; the signs of wealth became signs of generosity.   JWes

John Stockton's admiration has been steadfast.

I was very much aware of the heavy casualties that my prospective brother-in-law's 8th Army Air Force suffered, especially in the initial daylight raids over Germany. My brother-in-law himself completed over fifty such missions.   JS

Dennis Jones remembers

... a sadder occasion when a Greek tailoress with a shop in Bromham road, a friend of my mother's, became highly indignant on finding a pack of 'unmentionables' in the pocket of a US Air Force pilot's uniform she was repairing. He never did call for it, being lost over Germany.

DMJ

One American serviceman, later to be lost over the Channel, made a deep impression on all of us.

> I had been to London for the weekend and on returning to Bedford was informed that, guess what, Glenn Miller and the Band of the AEF were in Bedford.
>
> GS

Bedford was their main base from which they travelled to other bases giving no fewer than 71 concerts.[3]

> I recall the long queue in the covered alley next to the cinema to see Glenn Miller's band. The wait was worthwhile as we heard all the number familiar from records.
>
> AD

> I listened to the Glenn Miller band at the windows of the US Officers' Club.
>
> ME

> I was billeted in Queen's Park and the band rehearsed in a nearby timber-framed hall. We would go down and listen outside whenever possible and the musicians would chat to us boys when they came out for fresh air.
> This was a real thrill for me as I was a Miller fan. I can still recall seeing these great musicians queuing up for fish and chips at Bridgman's the corner fish shop. Unfortunately, we only got brief glimpses of Glenn Miller himself, as he appeared very much aloof.
>
> GS

One Owenian found him not so much aloof as diffident. Frank Fenn, you may remember, shared the back seat of Adrian Boult's car with Glenn Miller in a journey that was 'all too short'.

> He was rather terse and laconic but responded in an amused but dismissive manner when I told him that, in addition to the records of his own band, I owned early recordings of him playing with Mound City Blue Blowers and the Louisiana Rhythm Kings. He was rather more forthcoming when he answered my query as to whether he had organised and played in Ray Noble's first American band.
>
> WFF

Another boy shared Glenn Miller's staff car with his sergeant.

> There was a major AEF concert being broadcast by the BBC from the Corn Exchange. I got there early with my autograph book. I waited

329

an hour. Glenn Miller came out of his staff car to rush up the steps. I interposed my book. 'After the show son', he said. Another two hours to wait, one of which was spent listening to the live broadcast in his car on the radio with his sergeant. There was a crowd by the steps. I was in front. At last, Glenn Miller came down with a British major. I went forward. The major brushed me aside. Glenn Miller tapped the major on the shoulder and said, 'I promised the kid'. The kid still has the auto-graph.   DEB

A few weeks later, Joss Ackland was at a cottage where the orches-tra's piano player was a frequent guest.

I remember saying goodbye to him when the orchestra was flying off. 'Is Glenn Miller going with you?' I asked.
'No', he replied, 'he's gone ahead.'

That day, 15 December 1944, Ron Nash and Alan Locke were fly-ing with the Air Training Corps at Twinwoods airbase.

It was the day the USAAF orchestra took off for France in a Dakota - but Glenn Miller who'd left the day before was lost elsewhere.   RN

We were very sad when he was killed in a plane crash, and all sorts of rumours went around.   GS

Many more Americans were to die in the five months before VE Day. John Stockton is reticent about his reactions — then and now — to the familiar sneers.

'Over sexed, over paid and over here' mouthed by many who never heard a shot fired in anger throughout the war and who gave the impression at times that they thought it was the British and not the American tax payer who provided their forces' remuneration. It is, to put it mildly, interesting to recall that on the night of VE Day all the airmen (who'd survived) in the 8th Army Air Force at Thurleigh were confined to barracks, almost in punitive style, while the town gave itself over to celebration.   JS

40

On Active Service

News from Owenian fighting men – and of those who don't return.

At school it was proving more and more difficult to concentrate on work. The sixth formers were going straight off into the forces and when the Battle of Britain started they queued to get into the RAF. All too often only a few weeks after they had taken off their school caps for the last time the Headmaster would read out their names among the latest casualties. Peter Senn was a tall Anglo-Indian and although I was a junior when he was a sixth former he was always friendly and treated me like an equal. It was not long after his leaving school that I saw him back in Bedford, elegant in his officer's uniform, covered in plaster and walking on crutches. His Wellington bomber had been hit and crashed. Luckily for him he was in the correct crouching position when the plane hit the ground, was thrown clear and was the only survivor.   JA

The future would be something like this. Fifth form: General School Certificate (with Matriculation exemption if possible). Sixth form: Higher School Certificate (with good enough marks to warrant a university place – or, if you were really bright and conscientious, a scholarship entrance). Call-up and one of the services, probably immediately, but if you were selected for officer training you might go to university on a short course paid for by that service. Then active duty, and possibly combat, glory, death.

The stages were all recorded in the *Arrow* in letters, in news items of honours, medals, visits to school and in obituaries.

The letters told of training, of boredom, of meeting up with other Owenians and of adventure.

I feel very glad and lucky that I am able to write to you, for as you know, I was on the M.S. Domala *when she was bombed and subjected to a murderous machine-gun attack. It is a marvel to me that I am alive to tell you the tale. In writing this I would like to mention the marvellous rescue work which one of H.M. destroyers performed. The task was made doubly difficult by the cold weather and the rough sea. The sea was so rough that when the raft to which I was clinging rose on the crest of a wave, I was actually looking down upon the destroyer's deck. Yet in spite of these hardships the commander was able to rescue a large number of survivors; and when we arrived on board the sailors were wonderfully hospitable to us. Some of them gave away every stitch of clothing they had to spare.*

I owe a great deal to Mr. Lloyd who taught me how to climb a rope at school and I used one of his patent grips when I climbed down onto the raft. The rope was fixed to the raft and I felt that I was clinging to a piece of elastic, since when the raft was on the crest of a wave the rope was slack and I found myself right under the water; and when the raft was in the hollow of the waves the rope would snap tight and then I found myself quite a distance above the water. After two months leave I am glad to say that I am able to join another ship and I am looking forward to this very much indeed.

In conclusion, I would like to wish every success to all the Old Owenians at present serving in the forces and those Owenians who will shortly be called up. I sincerely hope that they will come through unscathed.
Yours, etc. S.F. Cooper   *Arrow*, Trinity '40

Another Owenian naval type, H.A. Moore visited the school to tell of the sinking of his ship *HMS Eagle* – then followed up with a letter in which he added a footnote to the story.

Perhaps some permanent record might be made of the achievement of a certain 'Tiny', who swam to safety still wearing his size 13 boots, because he feared the difficulty of getting them replaced. Also it seemed to me that I put in less enthusiasm swimming for the nearest destroyer than I used to put into swimming for Hermitage – possibly because school-galas were never conducted in oil fuel ...

Owen's leaves a deep impression on one's mind. In fact I have never been more grateful than in the Navy for my Owenian education; the philosophy I acquired in the school library has been invaluable; particularly so the degree of self-confidence which Owen's gave me: for here, perhaps more than elsewhere, one tends to be accepted at one's true value, and the higher that is the better; here humility is no virtue and the meek do not inherit.

Arrow, Michaelmas '42

The letters which don't mention actual activity (and censorship might well preclude that) compensate by being informative and appreciative of the character of the reader. L.S. Bill wrote from an RAF camp in Norwich early in 1940.

My work in the R.A.F. is entirely connected with the weather, but let me add at once that I am in no way responsible for it. You have probably realised after reading about the war in Finland and about the hardships suffered by our soldiers in France during the past month, that the weather has a very powerful influence on the activities of the men on the ground and it is easy to imagine how important it is to the man in the air. Naturally, we cannot control the weather, but we can take advantage of its moods and although our pilots are prepared to face anything from **Messerschmidts** *to ice accretion and thunder, they like to be warned about the last two.*

The gunners are interested in the winds, temperature and humidity at various heights, because they all affect the trajectory of a projectile, and if we are unfortunately compelled to resort to chemical warfare we shall have to be careful that we do not suffer the disastrous consequences of an abrupt change of wind direction.

Arrow, Lent '40

Peter D. Lee was an RAF cadet on a short course in Durham...

No one can deny the grim charm of the colleges and city grouped around the Castle and Cathedral on the hill. We cadets have little time to admire the view, however, being pre-occupied with work of both scientific and aeronautical nature. Our hours are spent in studying physics, navigation, signals and all the other requirements of the Air Force, in energetic physical training and games, and leavened by the hilarious life of the Common room.

Arrow, Michaelmas '41

Life was less hilarious for Private Hoyle whose address was 'Number X bomb disposal section. Somewhere.'

At present I sit in a pool of oil beneath the bowels of a three-ton lorry thinking-

1. How am I to understand aforesaid bowels sufficiently to maintain aforesaid vehicle?
2. What is this sticky substance upon which I sit?
3. Why did I ever leave school and go into the Army?
From all this you may gather that –

a) I'm learning to be on Motor Transport
b) I've spoilt a beautiful pair of overalls
c) I still think of school, but am 'happy in my work.'

If you can gather anything from the address you may realise that I'm supposed to be disposing of bombs. We have seen a few bombs (dud) and have even dug some holes searching for 'real' ones. The first try was on holes made by bombs already exploded: the second attempt turned out to be a well, dug by an ardent allotment-holder for the good of his crops: the third shot had to be lucky, so we dug a shaft and lowered an ancient 1,000kg bomb into it. There couldn't be any mistake this time ...

Taken all round the Army's fine – try it sometime (you'll have to soon anyway ...)

Arrow, Trinity '42

J.E. Williams tried it a little later that year and was thankful for the physical training he had received in the school gym.

The mounting and manning of a tank can only be compared to that of the submarine, for this rumbling, cramped vehicle requires both skill and stamina. I, as a wireless operator and loader, must fling shells into the breech with the mechanical accuracy and repetition of the business end of a sausage machine.

Arrow, Michaelmas '42

F.W. Draper pays the Royal Navy a sincere compliment.

Navy life is grand. My great fear on leaving Owen's was that my future surroundings could never recapture that certain something, that esprit de corps perhaps, which permeates the school. But life in the Navy approaches this spirit much more than I had thought possible, and this, in a rather backhanded way, is the greatest compliment I can pay the Service.

This ship, at the moment, has a decidedly Owenian flavour evenly spread – if a mixed metaphor may be permitted – in the divisions.

There is Johnny Cornwell in Tops, Howland, who left at the outbreak of war, in Foc's'le, and myself in Quarterdeck.

Arrow, Lent '43

In the same issue, Peter Senn, on flying training, dropped an idiosyncratic line to the editor, L.W. Madden.

You, yourself, are going in the army soon, I believe, so I hope my tale of woe doesn't depress you. However, you need not worry; there are plenty of compensations. It's true you will probably have to peel potatoes; that you will have to scrub a very great number of floors, that you will line up for breakfast by moonlight, with the wind blowing about your ears: you will, as I had to, sort out pig's swill (personally, I thought it carrying democracy a little too far – giving pigs hand-picked swill): but whatever you have to do you will certainly meet some interesting people. In my room, for instance, is an ex-detective who used to be the Duke of Windsor's personal bodyguard, a former naval officer from Jersey who has been sunk three times, a high-spirited young Irishman with a law degree and a chap from the Isle of Man, who acts as the universal provider. The only really annoying feature is the discipline ... At the moment I am on a charge for losing a pair of socks.

Arrow, Lent '43

Brian Chapman joined the Navy, trained as an officer, saw active service. His two letters to the *Arrow,* both combined joy and sadness.

Since leaving my ancient domicile of learning last summer, my main feat has been the great extension of my vocabulary – but that, they tell me, is what the Navy does to you ... they have given me a commission after the most fearful headache I have ever had in my life, trying to remember all the maths I so thankfully forgot in the Fifth form. Like most sailors, I have sailed, and I also have been given a glimpse of infinity which Coleridge, who never sailed but once in his life, so aptly described.

I have told you of myself: now I will tell you of yourselves. The saddest thing is the number of my contemporaries who have died. When first, I came to the school, the 'Arrow' had a 'Valete' for those who were leaving. It always seemed a rather melancholy time and, having been told that you have begun the practice again, may I tell you that only too often it is 'farewell' indeed.

Arrow, Trinity '43

L.W. Madden did, as Peter Senn predicted, join the Army and wrote from a primary training centre.

> *I feel like an old 'Sweat' already, and if knowledge of Cookhouse fatigues qualifies me, then I am a Sweat of Sweats indeed ... Rifles, bayonets, grenades and machine guns, and then finally to our Corps, which will be anything from the Pioneers to the Tanks, for no one is sure. That is definitely boring. Anything of interest I could tell you would be banned either by the Censor or the Lord Chamberlain ... once this spell is over I shall be well on my way – where, only time will tell. Till then, about two months hence, when I hope to have some leave, I must remain your degenerate friend.*
>
> *Arrow*, Trinity '43

P.D. Lee wrote again, this time from an RAF course in Canada. Already a fully qualified air bomber/air gunner, he was training to be an observer.

> *We get plenty of flying and I don't get on too badly in the air except that my astro-work is pretty poor. My second navigator swears that he looked over the side the other day and saw little black boys running around but although I've invaded the States a couple of times, I think he was exaggerating.*
>
> *Arrow*, Trinity '43

David Pratt wrote a virtual recruitment advertisement for the RAF, which he joined after a short course at St. Andrew's.

> *I have already begun flying – a thing I would rather do than anything else. Yes! Even than playing soccer – and that, as you know, is saying a lot! The planes we fly are rather primitive but believe me, at this stage of training it is best to pay the deepest respect to them.*
> *Drill, signals, airmanship and air recognition are what we fill our time with when we are not flying. Our instructors are the best in the world ...Naturally, there are things that stick in my mind more than others. For instance, the exhilaration of my first slow roll; the thrill of my first parade and, lastly, the embarrassing but nevertheless pleasant experience of being dragged on to the stage by a pretty* ENSA *showgirl amid the sighs and whistles of the other pupils.*
>
> *Arrow*, Michaelmas '43

Service food was mentioned often. If they never went hungry as evacuees, they were rarely less than full as servicemen.

> *The food I love, as only an epicure can. I realise that a Navy chef's imagination is the most wonderful mind in the world – he can serve 'toad-in-the hole' under nine different names and can still escape lynching.*
>
> G.E. Huggins, Arrow Michaelmas '43

The chef at Magdalen College Oxford, where Dennis Robinson was combining studies with training for the University Air Squadron, was also single-minded.

> *If I have not eaten a ton of fish I am a ' soused gurnet.' Even at the thought of fish my stomach gives a flick of its newly grown tail and attempts to make off. Fish together with suet roll (which I am told has been almost used up so that only half a mile now remains) forms a large part of our college diet; but, seriously, I cannot complain in any way.*
>
> Arrow, Trinity '44

Meanwhile, from what he regarded as a superior university, where he was training for the Senior Service, Nat Solomon told readers that he had become ...

> *fairly adept in tying knots, rowing in massive whalers, and all the other less glamorous aspects of naval life.*
>
> *When we first arrived here the CO warned us, rather mysteriously, not to enter the Wrens'* room without his permission, as some 'trouble' had arisen on the last course. Needless to say, since that day the Wrens' room has been as crowded as the prefects' room during break ...*
>
> *I will give three weighty and rational reasons for any Owenian joining the Navy. They are: -*
>
> *a) it is permissible to grow a beard (what a boon!)*
> *b) tobacco and cigarettes are cheap (ditto)*
> *c) 'all the nice girls love a sailor' (ditto).*
>
> Arrow, Trinity '44

E.H. Burden wrote from, and of, India.

---

*Women's Royal Naval Reserve

> *The thing that impresses me most about this country is the amazing fertility and increasing energies of the insect population.*
>
> *Arrow*, Michaelmas '44

G.E. Huggins wrote from, and of, a beach in Sierra Leone.

> *... Clustered around is a collection of native girls selling bananas, pineapples and occasionally, coconuts. The recognised price for bananas is two a penny. Pineapples are about sixpence, and jolly fine they are, too – luscious juice running down your chin ...*
>
> *Arrow*, Michaelmas '44

And P.D. Lee, in a third letter, wrote from somewhere in West Africa of another beach ...

> *where there are long stretches of good sand and grand bathing. You can lie around there for hours, and native women come and sell you bananas at fifteen for a shilling! If you are not too lazy you can just pick them off the trees.*
>
> *Arrow*, Michaelmas '44

Brian Chapman's second letter, dated 20 January 1945, tells of the deserts, of volunteering for Anzio.

> *... a few madcap jeep rides at night with James Barrie's nephew, since killed ... Naples, a rest, Cassino, and off via Rome to Civitavecchia ... a hectic month as First Lieutenant at Santo Stefano.*
>
> *Received a letter from Waldman today, and I discover he is within striking distance of here. I hope to take advantage of his invitation – or threat – to sample RAF hospitality soon.*
>
> *I hear that, in addition to Jonas, Norregaard has been killed. The toll mounts, I fear, and the names are all familiar. It seems to have hit my period very hard but was inevitable, I suppose. The world is poorer.*
>
> *Arrow*, Lent '45

We all lost people we knew. Friends or friends of friends.

Peter Provost in September 1939 shared his first billet with three others.

> The third boy, Joe Hume was the oldest, aged 17, who was to join the sixth form. I had just passed my fifteenth birthday and started in the

fifth form. Joe Hume was sadly killed at the battle of Cassino, an officer in the Royal Fusiliers. His name is recorded on the Cassino memorial but he has no known grave. PP

Cassino began in January 1944. The year before, the North African campaign was raging. Doug Pearce remembers...

the shock felt when Mr Mitchell announced during assembly in the school hall that Mr H.C. Swift had been killed in action. He had been my form master in 2b during my first year at Owen's, at Islington in 1938-1939. DPe

Hedley Charles Swift

It can only be with pain and sadness that one writes of the death of this gallant young member of the Staff, so loved and so much esteemed by all of us at school. He visited us as recently as last December and died in action on 26ᵗʰ April in North Africa. His ways and his nature were those of a man of peace, of culture, and of friendliness. He might have been thought too gentle and too modest to be a schoolmaster, were it not that he had just that appeal of men for men whereby small boys and sixth formers and other masters alike listened eagerly to him and smiled with him, and loved him. He had joined the staff in September 1938, played a great part in our evacuation and helped very much to establish the school in Bedford. For some time he acted as senior English master; then after being called to the Colours and serving in the ranks for a period he was commissioned in the Royal Artillery. As a soldier and an officer he was as successful and as greatly followed as he had been at school; and his Commanding Officer wrote of him in terms that we well understood. They too had loved him.

This has been a personal blow to all of us; and our sympathy with Mrs Swift is deep. We know what she has lost because it is our loss as well.

Anon, *Arrow*, Trinity '43

Honouring the dead began with the *Arrow* of Christmas term 1940.

The first name on our Roll of Honour of Old Boys who have fallen in the war is T.C. Prescott. He was at the school from 1923-1930 and is remembered by older members of staff as a quiet and lovable boy. He was a Pilot Officer in the Volunteer Reserve of the Royal Air Force in 1937, became a sergeant pilot in the R.A.F. when war broke out and was awarded a commission as Pilot Officer in the R.A.F. for gallantry and good work. He took part in many raids over enemy territory, was reported missing in June 1940 but later was definitely reported killed in action.

Letters show what fine work he had done, and how much he was appreciated; it is a great pity that a full account of his flying career cannot be given. But we are proud of such an Old Boy and we send our sincerest sympathy, mingled with pride, to his family in their sorrow.

Arrow, Michaelmas '40

Two more names were added the following term.

Pilot Officer C.F. Cardnell, was killed while on operational duties over this country. He was born in 1917 and joined Owen's school in 1928. He was in the school for five years and gained the General School Certificate in the summer of 1933, after which he left. His R.A.F. record was good and we wish to record our deep sympathy and pride.

In the early hours of one morning in January, R.H. Freeman met his death while returning from operations over enemy territory. Richard Freeman joined the Volunteer Reserve of the R.A.F. in 1938 and on the outbreak of war began serving with the Bomber Command as a Sergeant-Observer. He was remembered at school as a boy of sunny temperament and was only 20 years of age when he met his death.

Anon, *Arrow*, Lent '41

In the following issue, coupled with the announcement of an annual prize in memory of T.C. Prescott, was published a letter to his parents from a fellow sergeant of the young man whom the *Arrow* called 'the first Old Boy to give his life for England'. At the time of writing, 25 June 1940, Prescott's death had not been confirmed.

Tom, you probably know, is my best friend and I told him that should something of this nature occur, I would write to you and endeavour to give you all the facts I could.

Last Sunday he took off at 1.30pm to make a lone raid somewhere in the Ruhr Valley. He returned some two hours later owing to unsuitable weather conditions. At 5.30pm he was instructed to try again, and told to make use of cloud cover in the North of Holland. This cloud unfortunately evaporated some two hours later, leaving no cloud protection whatsoever. I can only assume that Tom managed to get into enemy territory using cloud to hide in, and was left stranded in a clear sky over there when the clouds suddenly evaporated and was consequently forced down by enemy action and had to make a landing in Holland.

Firstly, may I say that Tom was the most liked man in the Squadron. He was admired tremendously for his courage, good sense and devotion to duty. One of the many incidents when these qualities were really shown was when he was struck in the face and neck by shrapnel, and had his helmet shattered by the explosion; this did not deter him and he pressed on with his attack and said nothing about it.

While with the Squadron he has made a tremendous number of operational trips, particularly since the big push in France started: he must have done well over 100 hours operational flying. He was often doing two trips a day during the evacuation of Denmark and Norway and since the big push in France, Tom has been almost continuously over Holland, Belgium, France and Germany and accomplished tremendously valuable work for the country. The country should be proud of Tom as we are in the Squadron, and he really earned the Commission he has just been given.

Dick Miller, *Arrow*, Trinity '41

The following term's issue briefly listed three dead.

OBITUARY

We regret to announce that three Old Owenians have been killed whilst on active service:

R.F. HUBBARD
R.J.B. EVANS
J.F. RIMER

Arrow, Lent 1942

The reporting rate accelerated.

We regret to announce the death of the following, and express our deepest sympathy to their bereaved relations

ARTHUR ROBERT HULLS

Sgt. Pilot R.A.F.   At school Sept 1926 – Dec 1933
Hulls was a school prefect, was keen on shooting, tennis and river

sports. He was first pilot of a Wellington shot down over Holland September 29th 1941.

ROY WALTER GEORGE STEVENS
Sgt. Pilot R.A.F.   At school April 1932 – April 1935
Stevens, during his short time at school, made many friends. He flew a Coastal Command Beaufort and was killed in an accident March 8th 1942

J.A. GROOM
Air Observer R.A.F.   Left school 1936
After obtaining his Higher School Certificate, Groom entered the L.C.C. In August 1939 he volunteered for the R.A.F.V.R. and was called up in 1940. He flew a Whitley bomber and just before his death he had been recommended for Flight Lieut. Commission. He was killed on his 17th run over Germany and is buried in the Garrison Cemetery at Kiel.

D.E. SMITH
Smith will be remembered by many present Owenians as a high-spirited boy who left school since we have been evacuated. He was killed in action in South Africa.

L. LUCK
At school 1933-36
Luck was a very cheerful boy who was very popular in the school. He was a 1st XI Football Cap, had his 2nd XI Cricket Colours and was in the school shooting team. He was killed in action.

J.H. WISHER
Wisher has been reported missing.

Arrow, Trinity '42

We regret to announce the death of the following Old boys and express our deepest sympathy to their bereaved relatives –

Sgt. HENSTRIDGE T.G.   R.E.
ALDERTON A.F.
COUCHMAN R.   Aust. Army
LT. BALCHIN R.F.   Royal Naval Reserve.
BAMBER R.C.   R.A.F.
Cmdr. REDMOND L.C.   R.N.
Sgt.Pilot DOWLING A.   R.A.F.

Sgt.Obs. FREEMAN R.H.   R.A.F.
Arrow, Michaelmas '42

Perplexingly, no obituaries are recorded in the following (Lent 1943) issue but under *News, Notes and Notices* there is a poignant account of the doings of three ex-members of school, of whom two were to be killed.

> *J.J. Hume is now a subaltern in the Royal Fusiliers serving overseas. And finally, Mr Swift, a master whom we can all remember scoring the winning goal for the Masters in 1940, has sent us a letter from distant lands where he is now putting in harder shots.*
>
> *Arrow*, Lent '43

J.F. Fisher had been reported missing in April 1941 but was not officially recorded as 'killed at sea by enemy action' till the summer of 1943 issue of the *Arrow*.

> *Going abroad in August 1940, he accompanied General Wavell's force to Benghazi in command of a light field ambulance. Returning to Cairo, he again volunteered for Field Service and went to Greece as Medical Officer to a regiment of Royal Horse Artillery. It was during the evacuation from Greece that the transport he was on was bombed and sunk, there being only four survivors. His gallant behaviour right to the last earned the highest praise from his Commanding Officer.*
>
> Anon, *Arrow*, Trinity '43

Other deaths were recorded in the same issue.

F.E. WARE
Corporal, Middlesex Yeomanry
Killed April 1941

J. H. WISHER
Pilot Officer, R.A.F.
Killed. Buried in Hamburg.

P. MILLS
Sgt. Gunner, R.A.F.
Missing after last raid over Stettin.

A. NORREGAARD
R.A.F.   Lost while guarding a convoy in the North Sea.
Arrow, Trinity '43

We deeply regret to have to add further names to the growing list of Old Owenians who have laid down their lives for their country. Our deep sympathy is extended to their relatives and friends.

L.W. BALDWIN (left school 1936)
Flt.Sgt. Pilot R.A.F.
Missing from night operation over Tunisia, April 1943.
Presumed killed.

A.E. REES
Sgt. Pilot R.A.F.
Buried in Mannheim.

Arrow, Michaelmas '43

A.R. JONAS
Flying officer R.A.F.
Lost in the Channel after operation, 1944.

J.J. HUME
Lieut. R.A.
Killed in Italy 1944.

Arrow, Lent '44

R.A. ULPH
Lieutenant, Essex Regiment
At school 1931-34
Went overseas, June 1942 with English Army from El Alamein.
Killed in Italy, March 1942.

JOHN WHITEBROOK
Lieutenant, King's Shropshire Light Infantry
At school 1936-39.
Killed, June 1944.

W.F. CROWTHER
Acting Leading airman, Fleet Air Arm
Lost at sea, December 1942 or January 1943.
Officially declared lost, July 1943.

Arrow, Trinity '44

R.C. WILSON
(left school 1939)
killed on operations over Berlin.

M.H. FELDMAN
Flight Sergeant, South African Air Force
and
GORDON STEPHENS
Leading radio mechanic in the Fleet Air Arm,
have both lost their lives.
Also
A.J. EDE
Flying Officer R.A.F.
and
BASIL PURKIS
Pilot Officer R.A.F.
are both missing.*
Our deepest sympathy is extended to their relatives and friends.
Arrow, Michaelmas '44

We regret to record the following:-

J.G. KEMP
Capt. Royal Engineers.
Died in India

W.T. O'BRIEN
Pilot Officer R.A.F.
Killed

A.G. REEKIE
Major R.A.
Killed in Burma

A.J. STIFFEN
2nd Lieut. Royal Corp of Signals
Died in India.

R.J.T. YARDLEY D.F.C.
Flying Officer R.A.F.
Killed.

H.A. BENNETT D.F.C
Flying Officer R.A.F..
Killed returning from Germany.

* Their deaths were subsequently confirmed.

R.D. OVIS
Sgt. Pilot R.A.F.
Missing over Germany.

A.W. HICKLING
Pilot Officer R.A.F.
Missing over Germany.

Arrow, Lent '45

In this same issue the editor chose to print a tribute to one of the Owenians killed in action 'as typical of the noble sacrifice they have made and of the high praise which they have gained in every field'.

IN MEMORIAM
Lt. JOHN WHITEBROOK King's Shropshire Light Infantry
born November 20, 1922, was killed on June 6, 1944 at the
Normandy invasion of that day.

He had left Owen's at the time of the evacuation of the school, and thereafter passed a year of useful experience in boating and sailing that qualified him for the Admiralty permit to navigate the lower reaches of the Thames.

After one or two rejections due to his youth – he was only seventeen – he was accepted by the King's Royal Rifle Corps. Later he was transferred to Sandhurst, from where on May 2, 1942, he was commissioned and shortly afterwards seconded to the Hallamshire Regiment for service in Iceland. From here he returned to Scotland and England and was then shipped by way of London and Durban to Egypt, which he reached just before the El Alamein offensive. He volunteered for command of an anti-tank platoon with the Dorset Regiment and followed the desert journey to Tunis, and thence to Sicily and the mainland of Italy. A period of leave was necessitated by malaria, and during his stay in England he utilised the time to qualify as a student of the Inner Temple. Then he returned to the Dorsets in Scotland and was soon selected as officer in charge of one of the largest convoys that ever moved through England to the South. On May 18 he had his embarkation leave, and just over a fortnight later took part in the Normandy landings being killed a few feet from his surviving commanding officer. No finer tribute from the military point of view could be accorded than that then inscribed 'A fine soldier and a man of blameless honour'. It omits only what those who knew him best in civilian life perceived, a principle of freedom that was the passion of his life and the justice that dominated his performance of duty to God and men.

Anon, *Arrow*, Lent '45

One entry only appears in the next issue and that for a death two years before.

ALFRED BURGESS – Sergeant observer, R.A.F. Killed over Essen on the night of January 9-10 1943. He had had a very distinguished operational career. We extend our sincere sympathy to his mother and friends.

Anon, *Arrow*, Trinity '45

No magazine appeared at Christmas 1945. A double issue came out in Spring 1946 and with it a late record.

TERENCE H. ABRAHALL

Drowned after his ship was attacked and sunk, December 1942. He was going out on behalf of his employers, Cable and Wireless.

Arrow (double issue), Michaelmas '45
Lent '46

Also recorded was the passing of R.J. Triggs (at school 1887-9) composer of the music for the Owen's Football song. The last war obituary notice appeared in the summer of 1946.

Although the war is over, we deeply regret to have to record the belated news of a further loss among our Old Boys. Our heartfelt sympathy is extended to his parents, relations and friends. R.E. DAVENPORT (left school 1941) Pilot Officer R.A.F. Killed in operations over Chemnitz, Germany 1944.

Anon, *Arrow*, Trinity '46

Throughout the war the *Arrow* kept the school posted with awards for bravery, occasionally accompanied with details of the action.

Congratulations to Captain J.T. KEEPING of the Royal Army Pay Corps for having been awarded for his gallantry with the Military Cross. Details are yet unknown.
Pilot officer R.A. LARGE for gaining the Distinguished Flying Cross (D.F.C.) for his daring bravery during a Fighter sweep. It is said, in connection with this, that Pilot Officer Large became aware that one of his comrades had received hits and had been obliged to come down in the Channel. Immediately he made for the nearest refuelling sta-

tion and sailed out to do what he could. For a long period he alone held off the enemy attacks around the downed plane until help could arrive for its occupant.

Anon, *Arrow*, Michaelmas '42.

P.E. WILLIAMS awarded the Military Medal.
F.A.V. SALMON awarded the Distinguished Flying Cross.

Arrow, Lent '44

Congratulations to MAJOR J.R. CUTHBERTSON who has been awarded the Military Cross for his work in Normandy on 'D Day'.

Anon, *Arrow*, Michaelmas '44

The following have been mentioned in despatches: -
L. AMSWYCH Major R.F. 'for gallant and distinguished services in the Middle East'.
S.D. WALKER Lt. R.A.M.C., for gallant and distinguished services in Italy'.
.

Arrow, Lent '45

Squadron Leader BARRY PAYNE was awarded the D.F.C. in April 1945.

Arrow, Trinity '45

W.A. KING – Flight Sergeant R.A.F.V.R. – awarded Distinguished Flying Medal after 59 operational flights with Pathfinders.

Arrow (double issue), Michaelmas '45
Lent '46

News of Old Owenians was regularly featured in the magazine.

We hear that Captain M. Poad attached to Allied Military Government has had a private audience with Pope Pius XII. He was very much impressed with the personality of the Pope and with the cordiality of his reception.

Arrow, Michaelmas '44

The following Old Boy has also paid us a welcome visit this term. S. BRONKHORST, 2nd Lieut. Recce won the 'Belt of Honour' at Sandhurst last year.

Arrow, Lent '45

In the same issue the editor recorded 'activities of Old Boys in India' including this piece about two of them.

H.C. HASTINGS (1918-25) has been promoted to Major and is now Adjutant to Col. B.S. Sowton, OBE (1907-1915).

Arrow, Lent '45

The main source of news was, of course, the visiting serviceman on leave before and/or after combat duty.

JONAS. A.R. (R.A.F. – flying Typhoons, and recently wounded in the foot).
LYNCH A.C. (now in Bedford after recovering from serious wounds in the North African campaign).
SHERWIN B. (R.N.V.R. home after convoy duty).

Arrow, Michaelmas '43

We were glad to welcome back to school three of our Old Boys wounded in recent operations. L.W. MADDEN (seriously burned in Normandy), P.D.R. SENN (injured in a flying crash) and FRANK TAYLOR (shot in the arm during heavy fighting on the Rhine). We wish them a speedy recovery.

Arrow, Lent '45

The previous term's issue had carried a note about Madden.

We are very glad to hear that L.W. MADDEN (Royal Corps of Signals) is making a good recovery from the severe burns he received during the Normandy campaign. He is modestly reticent about his actual mishap and only regrets that he was in France for so short a time.

Arrow, Michaelmas '44

There were frequent such notes.

A.E. BEDWELL R.A.F. (happily not 'missing')

Arrow, Michaelmas '43

We are glad to hear that H.W. CANTLE, who has been a prisoner of war, has been repatriated.

Arrow, Michaelmas '44

R.G. WASH, a private in the Royal Fusiliers, who was wounded at Anzio, spent 15 months as a P.O.W. at Dresden, but is now back in England.

Arrow, Trinity '45

S. DUGGAN is back in England after some hair's breadth escapes with the S.A.S. in North Italy and Germany during which he was severely wounded.

Arrow, Trinity '45

A. GREER, R.N.V.R., in the Trieste region, after a fortunate escape after striking a mine in the Adriatic.

Arrow (double issue), Michaelmas '45
Lent '46

For most contributors to this book our fortunate escape was being just too young to have fought in World War Two, to have been, in a sense, spectators.

One such, Dennis Jones, pays tribute in a poem in honour of Owen's dead.

DOGFIGHT 1941

From Pulloxhill on looking south one war time June day,
Briar roses pinked the hedgerow. World War seemed far away.
Above the Hiz stream valley, white cloud on cranesbill blue,
Black specks became two aircraft, engaging as they flew,
Encircling, manoeuvring, guns' rattle I could hear,
An orange yellow tulip flash; grey smoke blowing clear,
And he who was victorious swung off and droned away,
The other spiralling down, onto Barton-le-Clay.
At school prayers were remembered late sixth-formers we knew,
Students strapped in aeroplanes. Our Roll of Honour grew.
Warring elders recognise for courage there's a fee.
Lollipops proffered were Iron Cross and DFC.
Time-tunnelling to those days inevitably grieves,
Youth was harvested for war like summer's golden sheaves.

Abrahall, Alderton, Balchin, Baldwin, Bamber, Bennett, Burgess, Cardnell, Couchman, Crowther, Davenport, Dowling, Ede, Evans, Feldman, Fisher, Freeman, Groom, Henstridge, Hickling, Hubbard, Hulls, Hume, Jonas, Kemp, Luck, Mills, Norregaard, O'Brien, Ovis, Prescott, Purkis, Redmond, Reekie, Rees, Rimer, Smith, Stephens, Stevens, Stiffen, Swift, Ulph, Ware, Whitebrook, Wilson, Wisher, Yardley.

41

Victory

VE celebrations in Bedford – then goodbye.

On the afternoon of 7 May 1945 a group of boys were listening to a radio beneath the partly erected stage in the school hall.

> We heard that Nazi Germany had probably broadcast for the last time. With this news circulating, how could a master expect a show of work? [Just after four o'clock] perhaps the most memorable, certainly the strangest, assembly started. After prayers, it was announced that our VE holiday would last just over forty hours if the news was declared that night.
>
> R.S. Beecham, *Arrow*, Trinity '45

Later that day, Ray Castle was walking with some friends near Russell Park.

> We heard Mr Churchill's broadcast coming from a nearby house. The lady of the house saw us trying to listen and immediately opened the window so we could hear the marvellous news.　　　RCa

VE (Victory in Europe) day was confirmed. Nearby in Castle Road

> ...I remember mother sending me round to the caretaker of Goldington Road Girls' School to ask if it would be open on VE Day. It would not, so I was allowed to go to Russell Park and into town to join in the fun, but I would have to be home by 10pm.　　　MH

Nat Blau doesn't seem to recall much fun on the day itself, 8 May 1945.

352

The end of the European War was celebrated by us having a day off school and walking along the riverbank, nothing as glorious as the VJ celebrations in London later that year. Nevertheless, we were confident that VE day heralded the end of evacuation. JNB

Nat would have had a very different day had he left the riverbank for the town centre – or perhaps, stayed out longer. Ray Castle remembers that VE day itself started slowly.

So slow in fact that I went to the dear old Picturedrome with some friends. I can't recall the film but I can the thunder-flash going off causing much amusement. Any other time it would have been a serious offence. It made the man who opened the screen curtains jump. He used to open and close them with what appeared to be a mangle handle, at the start and end of the film.

Lots of happy people greeted us when the show was over. As if by magic, coloured lights appeared on the River Bridge and people were literally singing and dancing in the streets. RCa

Girls joined in, notably those from King's Warren.

While we fifth formers were awaiting our School Certificate results, VE Day was declared. What joyous celebrations! Dancing in Russell Park, then we joined the procession towards the Swan Hotel and along the road leading directly to John Bunyan's Statue. JG

What happened next is etched on many minds.

We assembled and one of the boys put a straw hat on John Bunyan's head and a bottle of beer in his arms, and we all sang. JG

The *Arrow* carries prominently a photograph of the banner-waving column of Owenians who marched, many abreast, from Russell Park to Bunyan's statue, in quite an extraordinary spontaneous demonstration that began, one knows not clearly when and how, and culminated as it did when one member of the column (the writer, in fact, it must be admitted) received warm cheers from the mob of marchers and, later, the reproaches of many local inhabitants, when he climbed John Bunyan's statue to place an empty whisky bottle in his hands. JS

The accounts don't exactly tally but John Stockton's catches the spirit.

A more lofty report of the events appeared in the *Arrow*.

And it came to pass that there was peace in the land, and on the eighth day of the fifth month the Chief Minister, Win, spake unto all the people, yea unto Bedf itself, saying, 'Thou shalt not work.' And the people of Bedf rejoiced with exceeding great joy.

And the same night all the people of Bedf gathered themselves together in a great multitude in the plain of Russ and the valley that is beyond, and every man waxed happy and bowed down in homage that peace had shone forth upon the land.

And there came unto the plain of Russ a band of brothers giving forth triumphant music unto the host. And the leader of the tribe was named Lew and when he did both speak and chant the assembly did clap their hands and hail him. And Lew spake unto them saying 'Thou dost the Hoaqui Koaqui and thou turnest round.' And all the people obeyed him `... and the host arose and departed from the plain of Russ and the valley that is beyond and came unto the banks of Ooz which floweth nearby. And they travelled for part of the night until they reached the way which is called Hi and they halted at the graven image of Bun and did festoon it with garlands and did pay homage unto him. Then the night being far spent, they returned unto the banks of the Ooz and rejoiced together in the plain of Russ and the valley that is beyond, from whence they departed unto their own shacks which are called billets.

DEB, Arrow, Trinity '45

An adjacent piece in the school magazine by Russell (son of 'Tubby')Turner served as an antidote. It was headed *VE Day in a London suburb.*

The merry month of May, peace in the air, a glorious sun overhead. I walked through our flag-decked London suburb. The brave show of flags, some of them as old and threadbare and torn as parts of England, was gallant and touching, as well as gay. It seemed to suit the strange mingling of sorrow and joy in all our war-torn hearts. Every patch, every hole, every faded glory spoke eloquently of the years of Britain's great trial.

I could have pointed out that many of the Union Jacks were upside down: I could have remarked that most of the people who hung up this motley collection could not have told which country they represented. But I could not – the spirit of it was too tense, too real ...
People were dancing round the flood-lit bandstand: the searchlights flashed and exploded all around us. An old man came up to me and

said, 'Now I can sleep without listening for the siren! Now I can go to bed on earth without expecting to wake up in Heaven!' ...

The real spirit of England was obvious in these days of rejoicing, and our nation can look forward to the future with confidence and faith in our destiny.

The lights shone on, all the world was rejoicing. The national anthem sounded majestically over the midnight air. As Big Ben sounded out the hour, all the searchlights swept across the sky and came together to form - a Cross.

R.L. Turner, *Arrow*, Trinity '45

Some decided that London, not Bedford was the place to be and central London of course.

On VE Day I assumed that the school would be cancelled for the whole day in celebration and set off with two Owen's friends to cycle down to London, where we joined the festive crowds until the small hours, snatching a couple of hours' sleep at the Edgware Road home of one of my companions, before returning to Bedford the following day. I got a severe wigging for bunking off school (I should have turned up for registration before taking the day off) and I cannot recollect whether I told my form mistress exactly where I'd been.   SB

On VE Day Clive and I got on a 33 Birch Bus (3s. 9d fare) and went home and that day helped Dad to take the Anderson shelter to pieces. Then I went up to London and joined the crowds.   DHS

I celebrated VE with thousands of others, civilians and Forces personnel in Trafalgar Square. It was impossible to get into the Mall. The palace was mobbed. The crowds were screaming for the King and Queen. My republican sympathies scorned such a display. There was a marvellous spirit in the Square. People were climbing up on the lions, jumping into the fountains, hugging and kissing each other. It went on all night, a great mass exhilaration; an explosion of six years' pent up yearning for victory and a celebration that at last it was all over and the future had arrived.   MM

Home to London on VE night with the celebrants in Russell Square, the first kiss from Lydia, then back to Balham.   AJ

Bob Gould, Ray Schwalb and I anticipated VE Day and went to London. We were in Piccadilly Circus and spent most of the day there for some time perched on the top of one of the shops, I think Dolcis.　　　BF

Ron Nash had left school and was already in London awaiting call up.

Finally the searchlights formed victory cones all over London. The war was finished – without me.　　　RN

We referred to the following day as VE+1 (as with D-Day+). The *Arrow* recorded that too. Tony Stone lived in a country town where it apparently took till VE+1 'before the fact that the war was over really sunk into their minds' – and then not properly till after tea when 'things livened up a little'.

A worthy band of townsmen, dressed up in an assortment of old German uniforms, portrayed the whole Hitler gang and a few other assorted Nazis. They were marched through the town and then 'shot' by some soldiers stationed there. After this they were all thrown onto an old cart and taken to the yard of the 'Two Brewers' where doubtless they were suitably consoled for their bruises.

When it was dark a few buildings were floodlit. 'Fairy lights' appeared in windows and a V sign in red, white and blue was to be seen in the window of the local caterers. We walked the streets glumly, letting off thunder-flashes with nostalgic, if vague, memories of Coronation and Jubilee nights in London.

We wandered aimlessly around, listening to the shrieks of local damsels, who were accompanied by the inevitable 'swains' in the inevitable condition. Finally I returned home and went to bed feeling that this was a fine way to celebrate the conclusion of the greatest conflict in history.

A.T.R. Stone, *Arrow*, Trinity '45

On VE+1, 9 May 1945, weather forecasts returned. They had been banned the day we left the Angel. It would soon be time for us to return.

But there was one more victory for some of us to celebrate before we departed. On 5 July the country voted. A general election – the first since 1935. We gained our first experience of electioneering, meetings, canvassing. We were too young to vote but we could observe and help.

Bedford was a seemingly impregnable Tory bastion.

At that time I was a convinced Socialist (an affiliation I discarded totally during National Service), but, apart from my hopes of a Labour win, I had a gut feeling that we would get one. This intuition that a great change was in the air is difficult to explain completely. However, I came from a left-wing household where I was taught to think politically from an early age and it seemed to me inevitable that working people, having endured so much before the war, would insist on something very different after it.

In the Boarding House I was in a minority of one. The staff and other boys were true blue, and I spent hours arguing about such subjects as nationalisation, the record of the parties in the 30s and the schemes of Sir William Beveridge. There was much confusion among my opponents, few of whom seemed to realise the extent to which the Tories had already accepted the principles of the 'welfare state' e.g. the NHS. Moreover, it seemed to my contemporaries unthinkable that the electorate would reject Churchill. We had several old boys who had become officers coming back to tell us that the Service vote would be solidly for Winston. They could not have been more wrong. I was, incidentally, reported to the Headmaster for stirring up trouble in the house and promoting noisy political argument. This may not have been entirely unjust. But those in authority at No.48 were undoubtedly biased. Churchill could be heard on the wireless but not Attlee. I studied the Gallup polls published in the *News Chronicle*. No one else seemed to notice them.

Polling was on 5 July but there was a three-week delay, in order to take account of the Services' overseas vote, before results were announced. On 26 July the Labour landslide was duly proclaimed. I can see the headline in the *Evening Standard* now – 'Socialists in, 26 ministers out, London and Birmingham captured'. In Bedford, the Conservatives lost narrowly (by 288 votes) and their celebration dinner that night had to be cancelled. Members of staff who seemed pleased by the result were H.K. Olphin whom I saw the next day and R.A. Dare who, I understand, was a strong supporter of Skeffington-Lodge the successful Labour candidate in Bedford. On the other hand A.J. Hopkins, G.W. Baker and Ralph. H. Turner thought it disastrous.

Never very charitable, I made a point of ringing up several Boarding House Tories in order to crow over them. I was owed eleven shillings through bets taken on the result, and I collected these to the last penny, even boys who had left and come back to see us the following term.

WEOJ

The following term we were back in London and life had changed. Not just for us but, though few of us appreciated it at the time, Bedfordians.

When the war ended our house seemed much too quiet..   EF-W

Owen's school returned to London and we lost some very good friends. Our mother greatly regretted their departure. With their good humour and terrible jokes they had helped the Hopes through a very bad time and, with their going, life would never be the same again.   J & MH

Nor would it for Bedford Modern School and Grant Woodruff.

The addition of afternoon school on two or three days a week after Owen's return to Islington was a great imposition and without compensation for shorter mornings, if I remember correctly, we were very sorry to see them go.   GW

We were sorry too in a way. Six years. The Headmaster reviewed them at the last Bedford Visitation Day, with what the *Arrow* called the 'bird's eye view of the whole of our evacuation experience'.

> *'Owen's'* he said, *'is like a ship which after some very stormy seas is reaching port, battered but safe.' He turned in gratitude to those who had helped us come safely through. First to our Bedford hostesses. 'We were homeless, and you took us in,' said the Headmaster, with obvious emotion, 'and this will never be forgotten by the boys of Owen's School.' Nothing could have been finer than the generosity and kindness they had shown.*
>
> Anon, *Arrow*, (double issue) Michaelmas '45
> Lent '46

He then paid tribute and made a presentation to his opposite number Mr Liddle and his wife. Mr Liddle, in his turn, donated, and Mrs Liddle presented, a prize to be awarded each year for the best contribution to the school magazine.

Later that day, BMS and Owen's held a dinner in the hall attended by the dignitaries of the town and the 'governors and staff of both schools with their ladies, and the two head boys' (as the *Bedford Record* put it). Sir Richard Wells, chairman of the Harpur Trust, in proposing a toast to Owen's School, 'pointed out ... that in spite of the hazards of the experiment the general standard of work had been improved rather than lowered.'

The boys returned to London to prepare for a new term in a new (old) school building. War in Europe was over but not in Japan. Then came the atom bomb. The Japanese surrendered on 14 August. Next day was VJ day.

> VJ was spent in much the same way as VE, but, with the horrors of Hiroshima and Nagasaki fresh in our minds, there was this uneasy feeling that, despite victory, peace was somehow tarnished and the world less safe. MM

> Mass necking in Trafalgar Square and the Mall ending with a mass demonstration outside Buckingham Palace plus royal appearance. DMJ

John Stockton was still in Bedford staying with his mother and sister.

> Peter Huntingford was staying there with me when we learned of the Japanese surrender. So he and I took a train for London to be among the celebratory crowds around Piccadilly Circus etc. We called first at Pete's home before heading, at his mother's clear consternation, for the West End where, we hoped amenable taxi-drivers and similarly well-disposed Wrens would be awaiting us. I do not remember when and how we got back home. JS

> VJ Day I celebrated in London. A few of us decided to meet outside the Hippodrome, Leicester Square. This was the real thing. We went to Piccadilly Circus. We were an infinitesimal part of a national, a multi-national, largely uniformed gathering. It felt important. I met Sylvia. We still see each other. DEB

For others, serving Owenians, VE and VJ Days represented but short pauses during active service ... of sorts.

> I left school in autumn '44. I was staying at the Grand Hotel, Torquay, courtesy of the RAF on VE Day and was in Ilminster, Somerset on VJ Day. KD

I think I was stationed in Harrogate and we seemed to celebrate every day, as there was little to do. We drank a lot, so the celebration of VE Day wasn't very different. HC

Basil Leverton, after a spell in the Home Guard, was in the Army from 1943 to 1947.

Had married Joan (she was in the ATS) 25 April 1945. Newspapers recorded that as the date when US and Russian Forces met on River Elbe near European War's end. In autumn '45 I sailed East from UK and was involved in Japanese War Crimes Investigation and Trials. BL

It was a time of mixed emotions – joy, relief, pride... guilt? Most of us were too young maybe. Most of our seniors had seen too much.

I think on VJ Day I encountered no sense of horror, guilty regret, among the heartily relieved and thankful population, at the manner in which the Japanese were brought to surrender. JS

Dennis Jones remembers his uncle imprisoned in Changi jail Singapore for the duration.

When liberated by the Allies they had drowned the worst of their Jap guards by dangling them head down in latrine pits. With scarred back and emaciated with beriberi, he wept when reunited with his bombed out parents, who were more or less camping out in the least damaged section of their south west London house. DMJ

For another, older Owenian, the news from the east was even-worse and the celebration of VE and VJ Days 'seemed unreal'.

Within the family there was a great sense of relief, a time to reflect and pick up the pieces. My uncle did not return from the Japanese POW Camp. The horror of Belsen and of war generally seemed to overcome my parents. They seemed exhausted, their war time responsibilities and their inbuilt sense of commitment to the cause had stressed them to breaking point, as I am sure it had proved to be for huge numbers of ordinary citizens. WFF

If we could, we would have waved flags at half-mast.

42

Back with a Backward Glance

A bitter sweet reunion with our school building in a fragmented London.

School in tired and shabby Islington would not start till September, six years after some of us had set off from the place, not knowing where to. David Price was one of a few volunteers who helped clear the building beforehand. As was Ray Castle.

> The big clear up began. The School had to be sorted out. Although the advance party headed by 'Pop' Dixon had made a start before we returned, much had still to be done. RCa

As Doug Sutton found.

> It seemed to me to be a grimy old-fashioned place, for it had not really been cleaned up. The gym was full of dirt and boxes. When I looked in some of the boxes, they were full of teeth in racks; I suppose they were from a bombed dental factory. DHS

Ruins were all around...

> We returned to London to see the piles of rubble, from bombed buildings and the spaces where the remains of people's houses still stood. ME

Houses were sliced, their windows long gone. But faded wallpaper and mantelpieces clung to the walls. Tarpaulin served as a roof. Bricks sprouted colourful weeds and bomb sites were home to allotments.

What a sight! That was my first impression of Owen's Islington. What should I expect, the place had been through a war. We were lucky that it wasn't bombed like the Girls' School which caused so much loss of life.   RCa

The ruins were a reminder of what we had missed.

An awareness of the terrible bomb damage in London and the time it would take an exhausted country to recover.   DPe

Two years later, Basil Leverton returned from service in the Far East.

I was startled by a large sign at Southampton as our troopship docked: *We work or want.* The country seemed grim. Rationing was as fierce as wartime. Worse even – bread was rationed.   BL

Rebuilding and restoration in 1945 involved further demolition.

The Quad had a large underground air raid shelter beneath it, so when the pneumatic drills arrived on the scene to demolish it, there were lots of willing 'would be' drillers to be had!   RCa

The physical exercise would have been welcome.

Owen's at Islington was not much fun. Trying to keep warm in rooms with nothing more than a stinking Aladdin stove.   AJ

As the year went, and the days got colder, we shivered over oil heaters, as the central heating wasn't working. The surprising thing was that everybody was cheerful and pitched in to make the school habitable once again.   RCa

The return to London and starting school at the Angel was amazing. The most striking thing was that the school was so cold; we were freezing. At first there was no heating whatsoever. However, we soon started working and it was not too long before the chemistry laboratories under Mr Baker and the physics laboratories under Mr LeMin were back in working order.   BF

School lunches were an innovation in which the masters shared tables with the pupils. Mr Mitchell was frequently at the table with the upper sixth.   BF

If school was different so was the relationship between school life and home life.

> The impact of going home to a completely different sort of life was such a contrast. BS

John Weston had to make a personal adjustment.

> My welcome home by my parents was unforgettably happy. However, my brother Doug had been effectively an only child for some years – suddenly there was competition. It was not easy for either of us.
>
> JWes

We had looked forward to returning to the Angel – even those of us who had never known pre-war Owen's. But we found the journey and the school building depressing.

> How Dickensian the building looked! KD

> A long trip to the Angel on the Northern Line. AJ

> We were missing the compactness of Bedford, and the cohesiveness of the town itself and, of course, of our inner society. London evenings were different. I knew a few people who lived nearby but there was no sense of that unity which evacuation forced upon us, a displaced community in a strange town. DEB

> The return of Owen's to London after the war, despite the excitement of occupying our own school buildings, represented quite a culture shock in that, for me, many aspects of school life changed dramatically. I went to school and back on a number 35 tram instead of a bicycle. We stayed for lunch at school whereas at Bedford I used to cycle home for lunch. The difference was in the whole sense of comradeship, both during school hours and outside, that we all enjoyed at Bedford, which was exchanged for a more impersonal existence. DB

> At the end of the school day in London, we dispersed over a large city, making our own personal arrangements. In Bedford we stuck together – well we had to – and were better for it. FVH

Many of us maintained an association with, if not the town (though two Owenians Peter Senn and Reg Chapman lived there for a while), then those we had been close to.

I kept in touch with my first billet at Goldington for fifty years and they were guests at my wedding in 1952. Sadly they are now 'evacuated' themselves. KD

I remained in touch with, and visited, the Goodmans until their deaths, attending both funerals. Their expressed wish to adopt me never came to fruition, but I shall always remember them with gratitude and affection, God bless them. KRC

I kept in touch with Mrs Smith. We corresponded regularly, if infrequently. In 1947 I joined the RAF and the following year was posted to nearby Cardington. Sue and I married in 1961 and became parents three years later. Mrs Smith knitted a baby suit for our first-born. Mrs Smith died of cancer in 1965. DEB

I returned for Ouse fishing holidays. Staying with the Oakdens at Landsdown Road. DMJ

I kept in touch with the Garlicks and the Fowlers by mail and occasional visits, right up to their deaths in the 1970s. Mrs Garlick even left me a small legacy in her will. AWL

I kept in touch with the elderly couple in my last billet, and visited them just once, but by then the old lady was in her last illness and there was no response to subsequent letters. Many years later, my husband Alan and I passed through the town and made a sentimental tour of Russell Park and other favourite locations, but so much time had gone by and there were no townspeople who would have recognised us. SB

I was extremely fortunate with my billet in Bedford. They were very good to me and we corresponded and met up (not enough) until they both passed away. I am, however, still in touch with their nephew in Bedford. GS

Mother was asked to look after Malcolm Campbell who had experienced a very unhappy time – he became my younger brother until the school returned to London, he was very much part of the family and contacted my parents until their death, which was thoughtful of him.
EF-W

Derek Ball had arrived in Bedford as an eight-year-old with several other children from his area of North London. His mother visited him soon after and was unhappy.

She walked the local streets for a sympathetic ear and found one round the corner in London Road. I was promptly moved into this new foster home where I was treated as one of the family, stayed with them throughout the war years, and have maintained contact to this day.

DB

King's Warren School was also returning to London – but south of the river and that was another world to Islingtonians.

We said *au revoir* to many friends. Some we never saw again. Others we have remained in contact with over the last fifty years. Some of these were Bedfordians who were kind and welcoming to us during the war. From our school, Sally Saunders, Eileen Card, Beryl Logan, Betty Baker and I all married Owen's boys.

JG

The Hope sisters, who with their mother, played host to the Russell Park gang, and regretted their going, knew...

...we were parting with good friends, and it is a measure of affection we had for each other that, sixty years later we are still in contact and still concerned for each other's welfare.

JH

Four decades after the outbreak of war, Owen's 'boys' returned to Bedford for a celebratory lunch and promenade. The event was repeated in 1989. And in 1999 the Owen's School Orchestra held a sixtieth anniversary concert jointly with the Bedford Town Band and the BMS Orchestra. This was the first occasion since the war in which the two schools had co-operated. Owen's had since moved from Islington to Potters Bar and become co-educational. BMS had also moved – to the edge of town. However, the façade of the original building remains, facing the library and now brandishing a plaque from Owen's boys thanking the people of Bedford 'for putting us up and putting up with us'. The plaque was unveiled at the 1989 event. Ten years earlier we had thanked the town with a poem.

> *TO BEDFORD 1939 – 45*
> *You taught us to row*
> *To swim in the river*
> *To wear straw hats.*
> *The war taught us rationing*
> *But you taught us to share.*
> *Your school building was ours in the afternoon*
> *And yours in the morning*

When we learned in, and of, strange halls,
Co-operative, Liberal, Oddfellows.
You taught us to skate
That early unreal winter
When the Ouse froze.
We had arrived with gas masks,
Rucksacks, tinned salmon,
Biscuits and a label.
We had assembled on Goldington Green
Were taken in dozens
Down streets of neat dwellings
Past neat detached faces
Behind curtains, and stopping
Where a number on a gate
Matched a number on a list
And alone, or in pairs, were
Pointed to, picked, ushered and welcomed.
What futures were decided then
What memories determined
What friendships forged
What knots untied
Opinions etched.
The evacuee is father to the man.
You opened your doors
Your spare rooms
And, mostly, your hearts.
You lent us your fields
Smelling of Autumn
And one smelling of chocolate
Where we played football.
You taught us to row
To swim in the river
To fall off a bike.
The country was full of villages,
Woods and blackberried lanes,
Strange giant sheds
Where airships were said to be housed,
Assemblies of soldiers
Apprenticed as we were.
We kept our identity
Whilst grafting another.
Russell Park, Bedford Park, Queens Park,
Kimbolton Road,
Ampthill Road, Bushmead Avenue,

Castle Road. And streets
Of tight packed, squat backed houses
Denmark, Dudley, Bower, York.
You taught us to row
To swim in the river
To play fives.
By the time school started
That first first term (the war was phoney
but life was real)
The new boys were already
Part of the school
And the credit for that –
You may not have known it –
The credit for that was yours.
All of us were one
Being strangers, together.
You taught us a school is not a building.
We carried two passports,
Held dual nationality.
Aggressively Londoners,
We were conspicuous
Playing a role.
One hour from Saint Pancras
And parents in peril.
Down by the station
The Royal County Theatre
Murray and Mooney
Morris and Cowley
And for Sixth Formers with long trousers
Nerve and some guile
Immortal, immobile Phyllis Dixey.
You taught us to row
To swim in the river
To neck in the park.
The girls from South London,
The wounded from Dunkirk,
The Yanks from the airfields,
Sir Adrian Boult and the BBC Symphony.
Corn Exchange concerts incredibly free,
The Glenn Miller Orchestra.
Ask us what happened
A decade ago
We'll mumble some answer.
But test us the war years

We've total recall.
We lived at the summit
Where things were clear-cut
We knew where we were.
You – in loco parentis –
Taught us values.
You taught us to grieve.
You taught us to celebrate.
We delivered your papers,
Polished your floors,
Washed down your windows,
Weeded allotments
As some form of payment.
Maybe we realised
What you'd taken on
Taking us in...
And what did we call you?
Not Mother or Aunt
But Missus,
Billet Lady.
We waved flags on VE Day
And also goodbye.

Did we ever say thank you?

43

A Character Forming Experience

What evacuation did for us.

D oug Pearce sums up the evacuation

In retrospect, an immensely important and potentially damaging period of development but instead it turned out to be very character forming.   DPe

The Chief Inspector to the London County Council reached the same conclusion many years before. In a report, dated 17 December 1941, he regretted that evacuated children may have missed certain amenities and some variety of curriculum but continued:

> *On the other hand, in the bigger and more lasting matters, like experience, breadth of outlook, contact with different types of community life and so on, they certainly received valuable contributions to their general education which they could not have had in London.*[1]

Owenian evacuees by and large agree.

Evacuation formed my character and made me independent.   RN

The Bedford experience made me more self-reliant than I otherwise would have been and, I am sure, developed a sense of values.   JL

My experiences, although very upsetting at times, cured my food fads and made me self-reliant.   DHS

Cut off from parents and home life, it nevertheless taught self-reliance and many other qualities which have been useful in later life.   DPe

Away from immediate parental discipline and in a more permissive billet environment, some boys blossomed.

How much freedom we had to do our own things. I cannot remember having to account for where I had been. This freedom in my adolescence shaped my later life. Life would almost certainly have been different if I had been with my family in London. BF

Evacuation thrust 'independence' on us, like it or not. We learned self-reliance, how to take more care of our clothing and belongings, how to budget on the pocket money we received from home, or earned by doing paper rounds, how to respect our billet parents and their property, bearing in mind that most were couples without children or experience of the disruption that children could cause. AWL

Being an evacuee from the age of ten to sixteen years greatly benefited my personal development, in that I learned self-reliance and self-control – no surly teenage temperament could be indulged when living under a stranger's roof. School friends became the siblings that I never had. I suppose being away from home for such a long time at an impressionable age did make for a degree of independence but there is no place like home. GS

Evacuation was an amazing experience particularly in the earlier years. The enormous freedom and responsibility you were given. If I had to now contemplate a grandson or grand-daughter going away without even knowing where they were going, who was going to be responsible for them, what the lines of communication were, I think I would be prematurely aged by the experience. I would find it very frightening. Looking back on it, I wasn't frightened but I think my parents must have been. The experience certainly encouraged independence. How independent would I have been in normal circumstances? I, of course, don't know. It encouraged you to stand on your own feet and do your own thing. Now more with satisfaction than with pleasure, but at the time that was also true but it was interspersed with periods of homesickness and feeling very lonely. HCu

One is tempted to feel sorry for a child shoved from pillar to post in other peoples' homes for a period of five years or so. But, on the whole, I think it was a beneficial experience and, together with the bleak early post-war years of youth hostelling, it was a fair preparation for the later rigours of National Service. Perhaps we became better equipped to appreciate the other person's point of view, accept different lifestyles and withstand the inevitable buffetings of adult life with a degree of composure not always given to those who have had it cushy throughout.

MJC

There were instances of evacuation aggravating a domestic problem.

My mother never lost her natural jealousy of my hosts and regretted our missed years together.   RN

Indeed, it must have been difficult for some parents to sense, on each visit to Bedford, that their children were growing up without them – and, maybe, growing away from them with new interests and new adult influences.

Sometimes evacuation eased a problem.

Just being away from home removed me from a domestic situation that I found it hard to cope with – i.e. father gone, mother with new (resented) partner.   SB

If loneliness was a problem, it was confined mostly to night time. School fellows bonded (though we'd never heard of that word) both in and out of school.

There was camaraderie... unlike other years at the school. They were the Bedford years.   HG

There have been programmes about evacuation recently and clearly some people had a very rough deal. I suppose there might have been some boys, even in our school, who didn't have it particularly good, but I don't remember anyone like that. By and large I think it was pretty good. I think a strong sense of community helps and we were a lot of streetwise London kids in a provincial town and nobody interfered much with us in the town.   VM

The presence of the school in an unfamiliar – one hesitates to say 'alien' – environment served, most importantly, to foster among the school members an immediate sense of closer community, kinship even ... I experienced the most rewarding years and deepest friendships, some of which still enrich my life today.   JS

There were other benefits.

Tolerance. You had to get on with all sorts of people who were completely different, boys with different backgrounds sharing billets with people who had a different standard of living. BS

Our horizons were broadened. RCa

It enhanced and complemented my parents' guidance ... tempered the foundation upon which all else was built and *en route* I added the country outlook to that of the town-dweller. RSB

I feel that the Bedford experience was worthwhile as it gave us another dimension. We encountered small town types who were vastly different from our Cockney relatives and neighbours in their outlook. The pace of life, even in wartime, was a lot slower and we were made aware of rural life through our excursions into the countryside. AD

I have never thought of the Bedford experience as a disadvantage. On the contrary. I had so many billets of different backgrounds I can mix with anybody. Meeting new people has never held any fears. JWes

Owen's boys, *force majeure* perhaps, were adaptable.

Without realising it at the time, we just carried on, coping with the changes, overcoming difficulties and turning them into opportunities.
FVH

The result.

I had a whale of a time. JL

The sunny days seem more numerous than the rainy days. DHS

I wouldn't have missed it for the world. JS

I remember Bedford and the war with affection. It was a comfortable time in my life. My evacuation was a great success. I don't think I know anybody who was harmed by it. Nobody was isolated. There was no blatant hostility. HC

It was really a happy and carefree section of my life. I had been at the school for two years and had a circle of friends and was never homesick to any degree. Happy memories have been recaptured by frequent Old Owen's gatherings. I can't recall any desperately unhappy events, even when I lost my two front teeth denture in Newnham Swimming Pool and spent an hour or so with about 30 other youngsters groping in the muddy bottom of the pool looking for it.   KD

Some children, of course, <u>were</u> desperately unhappy. John Stockton has told of ten and eleven-year olds setting off to walk from Bedford to London. There were frequent, though mostly short, sad times when a now familiar environment would suddenly implode. A billet lady would need to house bombed out relatives or circumstances in the household would change and the evacuee would be taken in by new strangers.

I do remember how despondent my brother and I felt when we were told that Mr Jackson, who was a bus conductor, had been called up and that Mrs Jackson was going to take his place on the buses.   NC

The saddest of Bernard Fox's otherwise 'life enhancing' days with Mr and Mrs Bale was the very first.

Our first night was memorable. The Bales had a pet rabbit which usually lived indoors. As they were going out for the evening they thought that we could not cope with the rabbit so it was outside in the hutch. Unfortunately, it was a very cold evening and by the time they came back the rabbit was dead! Not the most auspicious start to our stay.

BF

Unhappiness was the result largely of separation, rejection and loss.

My unhappiest memories are really of the tearful times when, by myself, I felt the wrench of separation from my family. It seemed to take an age to get used to it.   DBa

Seeing the defeated troops returning from Dunkirk. Seeing the red glow at night after heavy raids on London. The main sadness was losing my father.   IA

Unhappiest memories are of the billets where I wasn't wanted (all of them but one) being told by Mrs Wright that I was wicked for being Jewish, the death of Jonas, lost over the North Sea in 1943. I knew him for only a few hours when he found me a billet with Mrs Knight. So why was there so many years after his death, a minor but persistent grief?

MM

In 1940 at Assembly, Mr Mitchell reported the death of Ron Coyte's father in the RAF.

AD

Death seemed nearer when it embraced those Owenians recently departed for the Armed Forces.

There were some boys who left and joined the Forces and were killed and that had an effect on us. Even kids of my age knew some of the older boys by sight and to know that some of your school colleagues had been killed made a big impression. Like Jonas who was a fighter pilot and got killed.

VM

For Mary Hope, like her mother an evacuee in Bedford, the saddest moment was the return of 'the boys' to London. We did not appreciate that the end of the war was as much of a wrench to many of our hosts as the beginning had been to our parents.

I was indeed very fortunate to be looked after by a couple who were very caring. At the time, none of us liked being away from home and could not wait for an opportunity to get back to London. However, after all these years I now realise in hindsight how Mr and Mrs Spreckley must have felt. My mother had knocked on their door out of the blue and persuaded them to take in two young boys. They did not have any children and, after looking after two boys for five years, they were suddenly on their own again. It only came to me at our recent reunion that they indeed must have felt a terrible sadness at suddenly losing a family. What a shame I didn't realise it at the time.

GS

John Webber, whose time in Bedford was a 'surprisingly contented one', has similar regrets.

Mr and Mrs Allen, a middle aged, childless couple, took on an outcast from London and made a home for me. I feel guilty ... I didn't keep in touch with them.

JW

Alan Locke is exceptional. He cites among his happiest memories

... sharing life and experiences with my billet ladies, and, even then, appreciating the sacrifices they made in allowing boisterous lads into tidy homes in exchange for ten shillings and sixpence a week, later fifteen shillings, to cover food and laundry, with only a few chores in exchange.

AWL

Nick Coral took a little longer fully to appreciate their sacrifices.

> Writing this small memoir not only brings back memories but also reminds me of the enormous debt that is owed to the numerous women who so unselfishly took evacuees like myself into their homes. I was saddened to read a short while ago an article concerning itself only with the bad billet ladies and stories of abuse. Of one thing I am glad, that I lived my early life in a society that, at the outbreak of war, could innocently entrust so many of its young boys and girls to the care of complete strangers without any thought of evil consequences – today's army of social workers neither could, nor would, allow a similar happening now.
>
> NC

The billet lady stars in this idyllic cameo.

> Spring was always brilliant. Mr Smith used to bring home new potatoes and in the summer there were all shades of currants. Mrs Smith made delicious puddings and pies. She also managed a chocolate pudding – cocoa was off ration. She was a miracle worker with the bare essentials. Cheese I loved but there was only a two ounce ration per person. She spun it out by making cheese fingers. I can't remember a Sunday when we didn't have a roast for lunch (called dinner). Cold on Monday and braised on Tuesday with potatoes tasting quite different in the braised gravy.
>
> DEB

For Henry George his time in Bedford was 'the happiest four years of my life'.

> If there'd been no war I'd have failed the eleven plus exam. I'd have left school at fourteen, probably gone into a dead end job and led a life nowhere near as good as I did have. From a slum area to a pretty country town, a river, parks to play in. If anything had happened to my parents in the war I would have stayed in Bedford ...
>
> Unfortunately, Mr and Mrs Davis died soon after the war at a young age. But I still have three sisters in Bedford. I regard them as my sisters. We're still in regular contact.
>
> HG

Peter Provost married his host's niece. Ron Nash learned later from his parents that in the event of their death in the Blitz, his billet couple would have adopted him. For him, for most of us, Wartime life was full.

Happiest memories boating on the river on a nice summer's evening, having at long last got a date with a certain school girl – nearly as good as leaving to come home to London once the war had ended, nearly as good as making a 35 break at snooker!   GS

Was Owen's evacuation a success? It maintained its numerical strength and improved upon a creditable record of academic achievement.

Bedford Modern School provided us with a building and never made us feel interlopers. Credit must go to all manner of people – but most of all to the staffs from both schools which, in the early weeks of the war, whilst we were playing by the river, exploring the parks, making new friends, were tirelessly engaged in putting in place a system of accommodation which stayed in place, virtually unchanged, for the duration. Not many boys complained, let alone left to go home.   DEB

There was a peculiar symmetry about the two schools. Each had a 'patron saint' with the same forename. Dame Alice Owen and Dame Alice Harpur. We were born within some fifty years of each other – in 1561 and 1613. Fifty years after the war we were both to move from the centre of town to suburban premises. Ten years later we were to join in a commemoration concert.

That the Bedford experiment would be a success can be gauged from a letter received in September 1939 by the parents of potential Owenian, Peter Provost.

Mr Mitchell, the newly appointed Headmaster, said that everything was fine, accommodation and billets were excellent, arrangements had been made with Bedford Modern School – another foundation grammar school – and 'Peter's education could be continued in a favourable environment with masters and fellow students known to him'.   PP

Contributors to this book are virtually unanimous in declaring the evacuation a success.

A large number of boys, removed from London and given shelter by strangers for four or five years, coupled with a solid educational experience without much in the way of delinquent behaviour, must be judged as successful.   RCo

Yes, on reflection, I have no doubt. The fact we are sitting here wanting to record it. The very fact we had these gatherings over the years.

I am not aware that other schools did similar things. So many going to university. I think Bedford might have been a particularly welcoming society. There was a good relationship with the host school. I do have fond memories of growing up in Bedford.   AH

I would rate the Owen's evacuation as extremely successful and to quote from Dare's book: 'The friendly relationship between BMS and Owen's carried us to a point where we became one of the few schools which carried through that remarkable experiment for the whole of the time demanded of it, not returning to London until July 1945 with numbers little diminished'. To quote from the school *Arrow* magazine of 1945, 'It was a brilliant success'. I reiterate that remark now and add that the great success of our evacuation to Bedford constitutes our own little corner of achievement in World War Two history.   JL

The school did a marvellous job in very difficult circumstances. Everything was a compromise, in terms of academic schooling, sports and social activities but the majority of pupils were reasonably happy (or uncomplaining?) with their lot.   DPe

Owen's evacuation success can be attributed to the assistance given to us by BMS, our own determination to continue our studies regardless of the environment in which we were taught, our sporting achievements which moulded us together and, of course, the foster parents and the inhabitants of Bedford who put up with us.   JW

Evacuation a success? Yes, several times over. Why? A natural discipline, carefully fostered by a high quality dedicated staff under a new Headmaster (but who was an old Owenian), who was a martinet and not popular with his staff, but a leader and skilled politician. I think that we pupils realised our position keenly as strangers in a strange land. 50 miles then felt like 500 miles today. We were better fed and fitter than our peers in London and we had escaped the air raids, night bombing and disruption to examinations and were immeasurably strengthened as a school.   AWL

Take numbers. In 1939 there were 430 pupils. In the first year of the war, they had fallen by nearly 100 but began recovering the following year and by 1946 had risen to 443. In terms of academic standards, a useful guide is the achievement of the Upper Sixth in passing the Higher School Certificate, the nearest equivalent to today's A levels. In 1939 it was 60%. By 1946 it was 82%. This is certainly success.   MM

The school returned to London with its academic record intact, with many new achievements (rowing especially) to its credit and with a reputation in Bedford which was tarnished, as I recall, by few serious misdemeanours. The key was that stable numbers were maintained; disintegration would have made a post-war renaissance so difficult.

GCk

As Dare writes in his history of the school, scholarships and awards continued to be won with commendable regularity:

> *In fact, with the newly-instituted State Bursaries in Science, the Short University Courses (for Commissions in the Services), the University Air Training Scheme and the Teachers' Training Scholarships, more boys were getting university education than ever before.[2]*

Not long after the war and National Service, John Stockton went to Oxford.

> I did so in the company of no less than six of my contemporaries. And, of course, awaiting us were to name but four, Frank Fenn, Alistair Mackay, Leslie Orgel (already a Fellow of Magdalen, I believe) and Peter Senn. This is not to mention (a) the many at Cambridge, London and other universities, nor (b) the additional many who had been up and come down in the years preceding. My point, obviously, is that only a most successful evacuation experience could have yielded academic success of this level.
>
> JS

Academic success occurred early in the war. Ansel Harris, a realist, wondered how much was due to the raw material or the moulding of the school. Both presumably – and the environment in which we lived and worked.

> The evacuation went very smoothly from the pupils' point of view and this must be due to O.W. Mitchell who had only recently been appointed and several stalwart masters, not forgetting mistresses who, in effect, were on active service continuously 1939-45. The success can also be measured by the turnout for the 40, 50 and 60 year anniversaries and odd ones in between.
>
> KD

> A more subjective measure of success is the lasting sense of community that so many of us still share at our annual and decennial events commemorating our evacuation.
>
> MM

Talking to many others after the war, who had gone to other secondary schools, it was clear that we had had a very good time of it and our evacuation was a very successful one. I think it is visible by the affection that the remaining old boys hold for the school. The turn-out at the reunions is not inconsiderable. We have remained a remarkably strong community, that is those boys who were in Bedford during the war. I don't know if other schools or other cohorts have that sense of community; maybe they do and we are in no sense remarkable. But I suspect we are.   VM

Sylvia Luckman, evacuated to Bedford late in the war, was introduced to Owen's at a dance in 1945.

Having been to five schools in six years and nine billets, experienced the mini blitz, the V1s and V2s in London, what struck me that day was the sense of stability, the cosy camaraderie and the easy togetherness of you all.   SL

Nat Blau suspects...

evacuation taught us more about life than we would have learnt in Islington and living at home.   JNB

For Donald Mackay evacuation was a 'transforming and unifying experience'.

Company psychologists and job counsellors have seized on evacuation in 1939 to explain the many idiosyncrasies that surfaced later in my professional life. Too cool, too self-contained, too unemotional, too judgmental, too self-assured, too everything of attributes that are, and were, for me always considered matters of pride. I felt sorry for the warped psychologists who were convinced evacuation had warped me. Sure there were problems, but one grew up fast. As far as I could see, evacuation was a good thing – good for me and very good for the school.   DAMM

At the end of the School's six-year exile no less than nineteen boys were still with their original 1939 householders, seven had been in the same billet for over five years, thirteen had five years to their credit and fifteen had four years or more. Such was the pluck and determination of Owen's schoolboys and the patience and friendliness of the householders all over Bedford and no tribute could do it justice. It is also pleasing to record that some boys who were at school during this period kept up their contacts with their former hostesses long after the return to London. There was actually one case of full adoption.[3]

'Mick' Hooley has the final word.

We made the best of it and shaped it to our ends and, in its turn, evacuation shaped us.   FVH

Appendix A

Owen's School: A Brief History
1613 - 1945

Dame Alice Owen's School is like many other endowed grammar schools: a product of the Tudor merchants' beneficence. On the dissolution of the monasteries, the State had taken over many of the church's functions. The relief of the poor was left to private charity. According to the historian, Christopher Hill:

> The charitable ... were overwhelmingly merchants (especially of London) and the Puritan section of the gentry. They established schools, alms-houses, credit for apprentices, etc.[1]

Dame Alice Owen, the founder of the School, thrice a widow, was one such benefactor, though of the established church. According to the school's cherished legend, Alice Owen had a miraculous escape from injury or worse when a stray archer's arrow penetrated her hat. As an expression of gratitude to the Almighty for her deliverance, she vowed to erect 'something' on the spot of the accident. The 'something' became almshouses followed by a schoolhouse, which opened to some thirty pupils in 1613. Under the terms of her will, the trustees were to be The Master and Wardens of the Company of Brewers of London.

Her three husbands, one a brewer, had predeceased her, leaving her a considerable fortune. The role of trustees as benefactors and governors was an important element in the future growth and educational development of the endowed schools. City livery companies were intimately involved in the foundation of many of today's grammar schools. (No foundation was ever established for a girls' school.) Owen's was fortunate in securing the commitment of the established Brewers' Company through the family connections of Dame Alice Owen. As governors, they provided valuable financial advice and support and played a major role in the type of school Owen's would become. In turn, the School proudly displays its historic link to the Brewers' Company: its 'corporate logo' is the Company's coat of arms. For hundreds of years Company and School have celebrated their association at annual Visitation with carnations and 'beer money'. The Visitation is a festive occasion. To quote from the school's brochure:

> *The original scholars collected flowers from the surrounding fields to make buttonholes for themselves and to decorate the school; the custom today is for the carnations to be worn by all pupils and to be presented to the governors at Visitation ... Today all Year 7 pupils receive one crown each at a ceremony held at Brewers' Hall, in the City of London, while other pupils receive a sum which rises according to their seniority.*

Legends, customs and rituals are important elements in sustaining the culture of an established institution. But these are at best only emblematic. They do not tell us Dame Alice's motivation in framing the Orders and Rules for the nascent school. It is not too fanciful to see the influence of Protestantism, the then dominant religion in England. Protestantism projected the belief in individual salvation (without the intercession of the priest) through personal endeavour: business and profits were thus respectable ambitions.

The early curriculum reflected the prevalent ethos. On the one hand is the prescription of the Bible (New Testament) and Church Catechism for English reading thus taking care of religion; on the other hand, Latin provided a 'training of the mind' and significantly, the equivalent of today's business studies was pursued in the 'cyphering and casting of accounts', perhaps in the form of early double entry book-keeping, which was then advancing in Europe alongside the rise of merchant capital and the need to keep ledgers for recording financial liabilities. The school historian, Dare, observes:

> *Dame Alice was obviously thinking of the big business and commercial opportunities of the neighbourhood or in nearby London.*[2]

At the turn of the nineteenth century, the curriculum, in keeping with that of many of the other so-called grammar schools, had been extended to more general subjects for which fees were being charged by opportunist Heads. Owen's now took in fee-paying scholars: the school was no longer just for the poor, as required by the terms of the endowment, but also for the rising middle classes moving into Islington. The middle classes set the pace of education reform in the nineteenth century. Greek and Latin teaching, in other than public schools, was surrendering to more practical subjects, such as languages, history, science, geography. The Grammar Schools Act of 1840 recognised the unofficial widening of the curriculum that was taking place. The Act also defined a grammar school as a foundation where Latin and Greek were taught. By this definition, Owen's was no more than an elementary school with a ' "progressive" and advanced curriculum' as indicated in the following summary of the 1863 Examination Report[3].

CLASS SUBJECT	1	2	3	4	5	6
Arithmetic	Money.	Reductions	Practice	Fractions	Decimals	Misc.
Algebra	-	-	-	-	Fractions	Quadratic
Reading	✓	✓	✓	✓	✓	✓
Grammar	-	-	-	-	-	Parsing
History	-	-	-	England	Rome	Greece
Geography	England	Asia	America	England	Russia	-
Natural Physiology	-	-	-	-	-	External Senses, etc
Spelling	✓	✓	✓	-	-	-
Church Catechism	✓	-	-	-	-	-

At the middle of the nineteenth century, the endowed schools of England... presented a picture of education in decay.[4]

For Owen's the rot had set in a century earlier. The school 'seemed to be decaying' according to the Brewers' Company minute books. The period (the mid-eighteenth century) was the 'nadir of Owenian fortunes', observes Dare after referring to 'The era of Whig complacency with the Church "belly full, soul dead", gin-drinking widespread, and other evils rampant, no doubt affected schools as well.'[5]

Over the next century, Owen's slowly improved its fortunes through the selection of competent and determined Headmasters. For example, one reforming Head stood out against the governors in opposing the monitorial system being introduced into elementary schools, a measure that might have undermined the school's claim to be a grammar school. The curriculum was modernised, premises extended, and numbers of scholars expanded. By the 1860s, the school was in a fairly robust position to introduce the improvements required by the Schools Enquiry Commission of 1864-68, better known as the Taunton Commission. Belatedly, compared with interventionist Germany and France, the British State was laying the foundations of a state led education system. It could not have been more necessary. The education system was chaotic. '... there were seven or eight hundred grammar schools... accompanied by a dense... thicket of private schools, and a staid and limited plantation of more promising proprietary schools.'[6] Each school varied in size, wealth and efficiency, and often succumbed to the market.

Once it had satisfied Taunton, Owen's leaped into the ranks of the fee paying secondary (grammar) schools. No longer was it a keeper of almshouses. No longer did a Head have to be concerned with welfare of ageing pensioners. If Tudor society was more inclusive, Victorian society was more focused. The almshouses were abolished, the pensioners pensioned off. Resources would now be concentrated on education and the school. The latter was to be enlarged, numbers increased to three hundred boys; the girls' school to be established for as many pupils. Apart from the fees, selection was to be based on a graduated entrance examination, initially with preference for boys from Clerkenwell and Islington. Annual examinations and annual reports were to be instituted; foundation scholarships established, half being eligible for candidates from public elementary schools and half open to any candidate. Exhibitions were to be made available, the curriculum to be extended.

> *Thus, in one mighty leap Owen's was to cross the great divide – to change from the comparatively small primary school with its limited range of subjects and restricted appeal to a modern secondary grammar school as we know it today [1976], with its larger numbers, wider syllabuses and horizons, opening out to the Universities and the world of business such as it had never had before.*[7]

Who, then, was to lead this exodus from the arid lands of the elementary schools to the fruitful pastures of the grammar school in a golden land to be known in years to come as Middle England?

> *The Joshua chosen to lead the Children of Owen into the Promised Land was Mr. James Easterbrook... [he] bestrode the little Owenian world like a Colossus.*[8]

We learn that he expanded the buildings to accommodate the wider, more demanding curriculum, particularly in science and mathematics. Under his regime, scholarships piled up and Oxbridge and London University distinctions showered on Owenians.

As a result of Easterbrook's leadership

> *Owen's was transformed from a small, comparatively insignificant grammar school to one of the most important and most perfectly-equipped secondary schools in the country, with a record of successes excelled by none.*[9]

Where Owen's fitted into the education system was determined by more than educational success. Rather, its educational success was partly due to the model it followed. The model chosen by the new grammar schools was the reformed and thriving public schools:

> *... the old grammar schools, very flourishing in the sixteenth and seventeenth centuries had declined, often to the point of extinction, in the eighteenth and early nineteenth.*[10]

And so we see Owen's adopting the trappings of the public schools based on meritocracy. For two short periods Owen's even became a public school by joining the Headmasters' Conference – in 1906 during Easterbrook's reign and then again in the 1940s.

A driving force of the public school reform was the religious revival of the nineteenth century in which Dr. Arnold of Rugby School played a significant role. For him the chapel was the centre of religious delivery, and in the grammar schools the Assembly Hall represented the chapel. For Owen's the quest for a purpose built assembly hall became an overriding objective. With a biblical flavour Dare chronicles the construction of the Hall:

> ... *at long last what had nearly developed into a 'baseless fable' actually came to pass and the cheerful noise of workmen at work was heard in the land. Gaunt girders soon straddled over the remains of the Lower School while the Manual, Lecture Room and the Gymnasium were invaded by the homeless hordes of the unfortunate erstwhile occupants of the demolished class-rooms.*[11]

Part of the significance of an assembly hall was to project the Headmaster's authority. With a capacity of 400 seats, the spaciousness of the new assembly hall and its display of the Owen's coats-of-arms lent an impressive dignity to the Headmaster as he praised, exhorted and cajoled the assembled scholars; and at his side the school captain (another public school invention) delivered the Lesson of the day, whereupon the air would carry upwards the swelling chorus of 400 voices, led by the Headmaster, lavishing praise on the Almighty. The occasion was essentially Christian, in line with Arnold's aspiration to create 'Christian Gentlemen'. Underpinning the Christian ethos of the School was the establishment of a Christian Union by the Head, the Rev. Asman, in 1930. Dare hails this as an 'essential organization'. However, it must not be thought that the School was exclusive to Christians. Far from it. The 1930s under the *aegis* of the then Head, Rev. H. N. Asman, saw the enrolment of an increasing number of Jewish boys. Possible reasons for this development are considered later.

Yet another significant innovation of the reformed public schools bolstered the authority of the Headmaster. This was the creation of a privileged sixth form from whose ranks prefects were drawn. Prefects were handed limited powers of discipline over the lower orders.

> I was chosen as a prefect and, in fact, was house captain of Colebrooke in my final year. This gave me an unhealthy taste for authority – no doubt engendered by the public school traditions to which we adhered and which has stood me in good stead ever since.   JL

Public school notions of leadership and team spirit were represented by the competitive house system. The four Houses are Cloudesley, Colebrooke, Myddelton and Hermitage* – there were originally six – all with historical connections to Islington.

The house system was bolstered by the acquisition of the school playing field. Inter-house rivalry, now taking place in a much larger arena, supplanted the previous narrowly based inter-form rivalry. Dare neatly sums it up:

> *corporate spirit would arise, one of the most valuable assets that a big day-school finds it hard to acquire.*[12]

But this wasn't enough for the competitive spirit. The curiously named 'Cock House' honour was awarded to the house that achieved the highest number of points in a range of sports including shooting and chess. The appellation Cock House may have been chosen to reflect the relentless fighting quality displayed by feathered combatants. In this extract from the school magazine the *Arrow,* house captain, Andrew Rothstein, addresses thus his house warriors in words suitable for a party rally or an Agincourt send-off.

> *Now is the time for resolutions. Let ours be to make a fresh start, to strive with all our strength to restore Cloudesley to its former high status. Let us set out to write new glorious chapters in the annals of our House, remembering that in a collective effort and co-operation lies that goal which we seek.*
>
> *Arrow,* Michaelmas '43

*Richard Cloudesley lived south of the Angel. At his death in 1517 he left considerable property to endow religious foundations. One of these was a Hermitage or chantry founded by the Knights Hospitallers – a priest's house and chapel near the corner of St. John's Street and Goswell Road. It was probably pulled down in the dissolution of the monasteries in 1541, leaving just the name Hermitage Fields.

Hugh Myddelton was responsible for bringing pure water from the springs of Chadwell and Amwell in Hertfordshire to London via the New River. On 29 September 1613 (the year Owen's school was founded) the New River was formally opened by Hugh's brother, Thomas Myddelton, who was that day elected Lord Mayor of London.

Sir George Colebrooke, banker and Lord of the Manor of Highbury, was deputy governor of the New River Company in 1770. He, or an ancestor, gave the name to Colebrooke Row. Colebrooke Cottage nearby became the home of essayist Charles Lamb.

In spite of its desire for independence, without adequate funding Owen's had no alternative but to turn to the developing state system for support. It was already subject to inspections by the Board of Education set up in 1899. The Education Act of 1902 created new Local Education Authorities. By 1904 the Education Committee of the London County Council had taken control of both primary and secondary education in Inner London. One advantage of this development was a reconstitution and strengthening of the School Governing Body by the addition of four outside governors, three being nominees of the LCC and an additional one nominated by the University of London. Another advantage was the provision of free places which grammar schools were required to make available through the LCC scholarship known as the Junior County, in effect the eleven-plus. The purpose of the scholarship was to provide a ladder of opportunity for 'bright' working-class children to progress upwards into secondary and higher education. Undoubtedly, it was elitist and meritocratic, and not all working-class children who qualified were able to take up the free places. Nevertheless, the growing number who did in the thirties enjoyed the prospect of a professional career which Owen's was well qualified to provide. Among these new recruits to the London middle classes were the sons of first and second-generation immigrants from Eastern Europe.

Owen's was not the only school chosen by ambitious parents. Grocers, Parmiters, the Davenant Foundation and Cowper Street were the popular schools in Hackney. It was inevitable that many of these boys, brought up in the politically charged areas of Stepney, Hackney, Shoreditch, Clapton and Dalston, would reflect and air their parents' concerns: recession, impending war, home grown fascism, anti-Semitism, concerns which are reflected in Chapter 3, Early Memories.

By 1939, Owen's had left far behind its earlier elementary status. It is not unreasonable to say it was a leading edge secondary school as near as it could get to being a public school. Its ethos was Christian but not narrowly so. It had no problem in accommodating other faiths and nationalities, even German. It had a fine record of scholarship – the academic staff were all graduates of Oxford, Cambridge or London Universities – and excelled in many sports. It could afford to be self-congratulatory. To echo Dare, its corporate spirit was strong; it needed to be to sustain the rigours and challenges of evacuation.

Although it was a fee-paying school – until the 1944 Education Act abolished fees – there was a significant number of Free Places. Of the 420 boys on the books in Bedford early in the war, 31 held Owen Foundation Scholarships and 13 Free Places were held 'in accordance with the terms of the Scheme by sons of inhabitants of the Ancient Parishes of Islington and Clerkenwell.' In addition, there were 251 boys holding Scholarships from the London, Middlesex and Essex County Councils, and from various foundations.

Throughout the war the average strength of the School was nearly 400 boys. Between them they achieved well over 100 Higher School Certificates (similar to A-levels) and 350 School Certificates (similar to GCSEs). Sixth formers won 34 Open Scholarships and Exhibitions, mostly to Oxford and Cambridge, and altogether between 75 and 80 boys gained admission to Universities and Medical Schools – the latter a great favourite with Owen's.

Finally, let the wartime Head, O.W.Mitchell, tell his own story shortly after the war ended.

> In the mighty effort of keeping this School together our own pride in it and our self-respect have played a great part; it must be stated that officialdom has not helped very much, though individual officials have often been sympathetic and kind and sometimes useful. Responsibility for our oft proclaimed 'successful evacuation' lies first with the Staff and their splendid efforts; second with the resilient London boy, the boy with the Owen's tradition of initiative, independence, and third with the parents, whose loyalty and confidence have survived the direst blows.
>
> If any proof were needed that a School is a living organism, with a distinctive and special character and life of its own and not a mere collection of administrative units, then here is that proof. And I pity the society that would treat its schools in defiance of that fact. For the society would not have long to live.
>
> I conclude by pointing out that Owen's School is a ship that has come through some very stormy seas, is reaching port (what sort of port?) and will be in need of careful and sympathetic shipwrights, with all their resources, for some time to come. Whatever lies in store, the voyage will be unforgettable – six years of struggle, yes, but six years of such comradeship and the fundamental harmony of a good ship's

company, as, please God, will never be lacking where Englishmen come together, bound by a worthy and adventurous cause.[13]

Appendix B

Evacuation Activities of the London County Council[1]

1. Arrangements for road transport for expectant mothers, blind persons and physically handicapped children.

2. The registration of expectant mothers at maternity and child welfare centres, the issue of permits for different types of transport, and the maintenance of a 'live' register of mothers within one month of confinement.

3. The enrolment and organisation of an adequate number of teachers and helpers to travel with the schoolchildren.

4. Advising all parents of the luggage and clothing to be taken by children.

5. Arrangements for assembly points, entraining and detraining stations, including the organisation of reception staff (with armlets).

6. The provision at railway stations and for the journey of water supplies and first aid and sanitary facilities. [Carriages were usually without toilets; accidents happened.]

7. The production and distribution by the London County Council of a complete terminology of evacuation issued to prevent misunderstanding.

8. The distribution by the London County Council of an evacuation pamphlet for mothers and children, including a number printed in Greek for Cypriots in Soho.

9. Arrangements for a special registration day in London for the Jewish community.

10. Rehearsals by London schools in methods of crossing roads (demonstrations of 'wave' crossing). [Children crossed roads in rows as opposed to crocodile fashion.]

11. Provision and distribution of emergency food rations (meat, milk, biscuits, chocolate and carrier bag) for forty-eight hours through the Food (Defence) Plans Department and the subsequent increase of food supplies in reception districts.

12. Arrangements with the police to control entraining and detraining at main stations.

13. Preparation of billeting forms and notices, appointment warrants, identity labels, final warning notices, telegrams, posters, wireless, press and cinema notices and arrangements for loud-speaker vans.

14. The organisation of petrol supplies for road transport at detraining stations.

15. Arrangements for the transfer and reception of the children and staff of day nurseries and nursery schools.

16. Arrangements with the British Medical Association for the medical treatment of children.

17. Provision of accommodation for handicapped children including the staffing and equipping of premises.

18. Provision of adequate nursing and medical services in the reception areas, including hospital address, accommodation, maternity homes and midwives and obstetricians for expectant mothers.

19. The purchase and distribution of camp beds, palliasses, blankets and rubber sheeting.

20. The appointment of billeting and reception officers and the organisation of their work.

21. Arrangements with post offices for the payment of billeting allowances.

22. Preparations for the appointment of tribunals in reception areas to hear appeals from occupiers to vary or cancel billeting notices.

23. Arrangements (including the opening of special offices) by the Unemployment Assistance Board to pay allowances to evacuated adults in need of temporary assistance.

24. The preparation of railway vouchers for helpers returning to the evacuation areas.

25. The printing and distribution of postcards for the use of evacuees to announce their safe arrival and address.

Appendix C

The Story of the Bedford Modern School – and another Dame Alice

During the Middle Ages, the monks of Newnham Priory ran a school situated somewhere in Mill Street (then called School Lane). Priory and school disappeared in the Reformation, so in 1552 the town council obtained letters patent to found a grammar school. Sir William Harpur, a Bedford man who became a Merchant Taylor and Lord Mayor of London, endowed the Bedford Charity to support the school and other benefits in 1566. Dame Alice Harpur, his second(?) wife, was a joint founder of the charity, whose income derived from 13 acres of farmland in the parish of Holborn, just outside the City of London.

In 1764, control of the Bedford Charity passed from the town council to the Harpur Trust, and a Writing School was established on the ground floor of the Grammar School (now the Old Town Hall in St. Paul's Square). Rapidly rising Holborn rents enabled the Trust to build new premises in Harpur Street to house the English (formerly Writing) School, an orphanage, a boardroom and a clerk's house, and the Elementary (later Harpur Central) School, all behind a splendid Tudor Gothic facade in Bath stone designed by Edward Blore in 1830. Meanwhile, the Grammar School stayed in the old building until 1892, when it moved to what is now Bedford School, north of St. Peter's Green.

The English School became the Commercial School in mid-century, and finally Bedford Modern School (BMS) after 1873, when a reorganisation of the Harpur Trust also provided for the High School and Girls' Modern School since renamed after Dame Alice Harpur (both opened in 1882). The first Harpur (elementary) Girls' and Infants' School (1840) later became the BMS physics labs, with art room above.

BMS flourished under Dr. R.B. Poole (Headmaster 1877-1900) who built the cloisters in the quad, provided science labs and electric light and started commercial and military "sides" (streams). The Old School Field was laid out in 1884.

C.W. Kaye (1900 -16) completed the quad and built a new gym behind the Blore facade. H. W. Liddle (1922-46) converted Kaye's gym into Big School (the hall) in 1929, and Poole's old hall, with honours 'boards' of painted plaster, became the gym. The Memorial Hall (1923) behind the tower commemorated the 166 OBMs killed in the First World War. A memorial alcove for the 126 OBMs who died in the Second World War, each of whom figures in a book of remembrance, was added in 1948. A covered swimming bath was built at the Old Field in 1935 and the New Field was acquired in 1938. During the war it was given over to growing vegetables.

Mr Liddle helped foster adult education and welfare programmes, admitted a number of Jewish boys fleeing Hitler's Germany, and was quick to offer to share BMS with Owen's School in 1939.

'Your School, your Foundation, and your Headmaster... have saved another School... by your hospitality, your kindness, and your forebearance.'

O.W.Mitchell, at the BMS Founders Day service, 21 November 1942

*Text provided by BMS for the programme of the 60th anniversary of evacuation joint concert of the two schools.

Contributors

AD	Alan Davis
AH	Ansel Harris
AJ	Andrew Jones
AN	Alf Nunn
AWL	Alan Locke
BC	Bernard Coral
BF	Bernard Fox
BL	Basil Leverton
BS	Barry Skeggs
CB	Chas Baker
CCo	Chris Coyte
CL	Conrad Lynn
DAMM	Donald Mackay
DAP	Dave Pratt
DB	Dick Burden
DBa	Derek Ball
DC	Don Curtis
DDW	Doug Wade
DEB	David Bernstein
DHS	Doug Sutton
DMJ	Dennis Jones

DP	David Price
DPe	Doug Pearce
EF-W	Elaine Farmer-Wright (Tilly Tysoe)
FVH	Mick Hooley
GB	Goff Baker
GCo	George Cowan
GCk	Geoff Cook
GD	Geoff Dimmock
GR	Geoff Rans
GRo	Geoff Rowley
GS	Gerry Shaw
GW	Grant Woodruff
HC	Harold Caplan
HCu	Harry Cuming
HG	Henry George
IA	Ian Appleby
IW	Ivor Walker
JA	Joss Ackland
JG	Josie George
JH	Jean Hope (Gray)
JL	Jack Levy
JNB	Nat Blau

JS	John Stockton
JW	John Webber
JWes	John Weston
KCS	Kevin Seeger
KD	Ken Deadman
KRC	Ray Coombes
KSK	K.S. Knowles
MC	Mervyn Crossick
ME	Max Eckstein
MH	Mary Hope (Barnard)
MHor	Mick Horkins
MJC	Malcolm Campbell
MM	Martin Mitchell
NC	Nick Coral
PCo	Peter Coyte
PF	Pauline Fowler
PFa	Philip Fawkes
PK	Peter Keggie
PP	Peter Provost
RC	Reg Chapman
RCa	Ray Castle
RCo	Ron Coyte
RD	Ruby Davis

Contributors

RN	Ron Nash
RP	Reg Perrin
RSB	Bob Beecham
SB	Sally Beecham
SL	Sylvia Luckman
VM	Vivian Moses
WEOJ	'WEO' Jones
WFF	Frank Fenn
WJW	Bill Whitebread
WT	William Tomaschoff

References

Chapter 1
1. Titmuss, Richard M.
   Problems of Social Policy (part of the Official History of the Second World War)
   HMSO and Longmans Green, London 1950
2, . Ackland, Joss
   I Must Be In There Somewhere
   Hodder & Stoughton, London 1989
   Note: All subsequent 'JA' contributions are from this source.
3. *The Times*, 2 September 1939
4. Quoted in Haining, Peter
   The Day War Broke Out
   W.H. Allen, London 1989

Chapter 2
1. Titmuss, *op cit*
2. Hansard, 10 November 1932
3. Titmuss, *op cit*
4. Titmuss, *ibid*
5. Titmuss, *ibid*
6. Titmuss, *ibid*
7. *Report of Committee on Evacuation.*
   Presented by the Secretary of State for the Home Department to Parliament by Command of His Majesty.
   HMSO, July 1938
8. Titmuss, *op cit*
9. *ibid*
10. Quoted in Jackson, Carlton
    Who will take our children?
    Methuen, London 1985.
11. *Bedfordshire Times*, 7 October 1938
12. *Bedfordshire Times*, 3 February 1939
13. *Bedfordshire Times*, 10 February 1939
14. Titmuss, *op cit*
15. *Bedfordshire Times*, 5 May 1939
16. *Bedfordshire Times*, 26 May 1939
17. *Bedfordshire Times*, 8 Sep 1939
18. *Bedfordshire Times*, 8 Sep 1939
19. *Bedfordshire Times*, 8 Sep 1939

Chapter 3
1. *R.M.Tinkler, bayoneted by the Japanese at Tientsin on 6 June 1939.* Quoted by Cosgrove, Patrick
  The Lives of EnochPowell
  Bodley Head 1989

Chapter 4
 -

Chapter 5
1. Isaacs, Susan (Editor)
  The Cambridge Evacuation Survey
  Methuen, London 1941

Chapter 6
 -

Chapter 7
1. Longmate, Norman
  How We Lived Then
  A history of everyday life during the Second World War.
  Hutchinson & Co, London 1971
2. Quoted in Croall, Jonathan
  Don't you know there's a war on?
  The People's Voice 1939-45
  Hutchinson Radius, London 1989
3. Martin, Kingsley
  Critic's London Diary
  Secker & Warburg, London 1960

Chapter 8
1. *Space supplement, The Guardian,* 8 March 2001
2. Gilbert, Martin
  An Atlas of Jewish History
  Routledge, London 1993

Chapter 9
1. Dare, Richard
  A History of Owen's School (1613-1976)
  The Barnet Press Group 1980
2. Dare, *op cit*
3. Calder, Angus
  The People's War, Britain 1939 – 45
  Jonathan Cape, London 1969
4. Dare, *op ci*
t

5. Harrisson, Tom and Madge, Charles (editors)
     Mass Observation
     War Begins at Home
     Chatto and Windus, London 1940

Chapter 10
1. Titmuss, *op cit*

Chapter 11
1. Gosden, P.H.& J.H.
     *Education in the Second World War - a study in policy and
     administration.*
     Methuen, London 1976
2. Hennessy, Peter
     Never Again - Britain 1945-1951
     Jonathan Cape, London 1992
3. Calder, *op cit*

Chapter 12
1. Fussell, Paul
     Wartime: understanding and behaviour in the Second World War
     Oxford University Press, London 1989
2. James, Anthony
     Informing the People
     HMSO, London 1996
3. Dare, *op cit*

Chapter 13
     -

Chapter 14
1. Calder, *op cit*
2. *ibid*
3. *ibid*

Chapter 15
1. Quoted by Longmate, *op cit*
2. Dare, *op cit*

Chapter 16
     --
Chapter 17

Chapter 18
     -

Chapter 19
1. Gosden, *op cit*
2. *ibid*
3. *ibid*

Chapter 20
1. *The Times*, 29 November 1941
    Quoted in Gosden, *op cit*
2. The Worshipful Company of Brewers
    Extract from *Minute Book*
3. Churchill, Winston
    The Second World War
    Volume one: *The Gathering Storm*
    Cassell, London 1948

Chapter 21
    -
Chapter 22
    -
Chapter 23
    -
Chapter 24
1. Boult, Adrian Cedric
    My Own Trumpet
    Hamish Hamilton, London 1973
2. *ibid*
3. Quoted in Hickman, Tom
    What Did You Do in the War, Auntie?
    BBC Publications, London 1995
4. Hickman, *op cit*

Chapter 25
1. Orwell, George
    The Lion and the Unicorn; Socialism and the English Genius
    Secker & Warburg, London 1941 (quoted by Hennessy, *op cit*)
2. Churchill, Winston
    Speech on his 80th birthday
    Westminster Hall, 30 November 1954
3. Martin, Kingsley, *op cit*
4. *Daily Express,* 9 November 1939
5. Hickman, *op cit*
6. *ibid*
7. Quoted in Hickman, *op cit*

Chapter 26
1. Turner, E.S.
   The Phoney War on the Home Front
   Michael Joseph, London 1961
2. *The Times*, 5 September 1939
   Quoted in Fussell, *op cit*

Chapter 27
-

Chapter 28
-

Chapter 29
1. Written by Gabriel Rogers and Harry Phillips
   Copyright Cecil Lennox Ltd c/o Kassner Associated Publishers Ltd
   and reproduced with their permission.
2. Words and Music by Michael Carr and Jimmy Kennedy © 1939
   Reproduced by permission of Peter Maurice Music Co. Ltd
   London WC2H OQY.
3. Words and Music by John Borelli and Arthur Riscoe © 1939
   Reproduced by permission of Francis Day and Hunter Ltd
   London WC2H OQY.
4. Words and Music by Ted Waite
   Copyright 1939 Ascherberg Hopwood & Crew Ltd c/o Warner
   Chappell Music Ltd, London W6 8BS
   Reproduced by permission of International Music Publications Ltd
   All Rights Reserved.
5. Written by Annette Mills
   Copyright Lawrence Wright Music Co. c/o EMI Music Publishing Ltd
   and reproduced with their permission.
6. Lukacs, John
   Five Days in London, May 1940
   Yale University Press, New Haven and London 1999
7. Quoted in Calder, Angus
   The Myth of the Blitz
   Jonathan Cape, London 1991
8. Written by Ross Parker and Hugh Charles
   Copyright Dash Music Company Ltd c/o Music Sales Ltd and
   reproduced with their permission.
9. Written by Ross Parker and Hugh Charles
   Copyright Dash Music Company Ltd c/o Music Sales Ltd and
   reproduced with their permission.
10. Words and Music by Clarkson Rose © 1939
    Reproduced by permission of Peter Maurice Music Co. Ltd
    London WC2H OQY.

11. Words and Music by Arthur Young and David Heneker © 1942
        Reproduced by permission of Peter Maurice Music Co. Ltd
        London WC2H OQY.
12. Despite the good offices of the Music Publishers Association, we are
        unable to trace the copyright owners of *It's a Lovely Day Tomorrow*
        (parkrussell@aol.com).
13. Words by Moira Heath. Music by Ted Heath.
        Copyright 1941 Chappell Music Ltd
        Warner Chappell Music Ltd London W6 8BS
        Reproduced by permission of International Music Publications Ltd.
        All RightsReserved

Chapter 30

-

Chapter 31

1. Churchill, Winston, *op cit*
        (Title of Book Two: *The Twilight War)*
        Cassell, London 1948
2.Titmuss, *op cit*
3. *Daily Express,* 9 November 1939
4. Milton, John
        Paradise Lost, Book One, 1667
5. *ibid*

Chapter 32

-

Chapter 33

1. Quoted in Fussell, *op cit*
2. *Daily Telegraph* 1944
        Suggestions for Wartime Dishes – a new selection of Daily Telegraph
        readers' tested recipes.
3. Ministry of Food, 1943
        War Cookery Leaflet No 6
4. Ministry of Food, 1943
        War Cookery Leaflet No 4
5. Letter to *The Times,* 5 October 1939
6. T*he Times*, 15 September 1941
        Quoted in Hennessy, *op cit*
7. Titmuss, *op cit*

Chapter 34

1. James, *op cit*
2. Gardiner, Juliet
        Pictures from the Past. The People's War.

Collins & Brown, London 1991
3. Churchill, Winston
Speech to the House of Commons, 20 August 1940
4. Ministry of Information, 1943
The Schools in Wartime
HMSO for the Board of Education, 1941

Chapter 35
-

Chapter 36
1. *The War Papers, Part 5*
Marshall Cavendish Partners, 1976
2. *Daily Express*, 31 May 1940
3. Churchill, Winston
Speech to both Houses of Parliament, 4 June 1940
Quoted in War Papers
4. Mass Observation Survey 1941
Quoted in Calder, Angus
The People's War

Chapter 37
1. Calder, Angus
The Myth of the Blitz
Jonathan Cape, London 1991

Chapter 38
1. *Poems from India by Members of the Forces*
Edited by R.M. Currey and R.V. Gibson
Oxford University Press, Bombay 1945, London 1946

Chapter 39
1. Gardiner, Juliet
Over Here – The GIs in Wartime Britain
Collins & Brown, London 1992
2. Quoted in Fussell: *op cit*
3. Longmate, Norman
The GIs – the Americans in Britain, 1942 -1943
Hutchinson, London 1975

Chapter 40
-

Chapter 41
-

Chapter 42

-

Chapter 43
1. Quoted in Titmuss *op cit*
2. Dare, *op cit*
3. *ibid*

Owen's School: A Brief History 1613 - 1945
1. Christopher Hill
   The Century of Revolution 1603-1714
   Sphere Books 1974
2. Dare, *op cit*
3. *ibid*
4. Gordon, Peter
   Selection for Secondary Education
   Woburn Press 1980
5. Dare, *op cit*
6. Allsobrook, David
   School for the Shires: The Reform of Middle Class Education in Victorian England
   Manchester University Press, Manchester 1986
7. Dare, *op cit*
8. *ibid*
9. *ibid*
10. Wardle, David
    English Popular Education 1780 – 1975,
    CUP, Cambridge 1976
11. Dare, *op cit*
12. *ibid*
13. Visitation speech, July 1945

Evacuation activities of the LCC
1. Quoted in Titmuss, *op cit*

Index

A

Abrahall, T.H. 347, 351
Abyssinia 20, 21, 22
Ackland, Joss
  Preface, 7, 27, 130,154, 158, 202,
  206, 212, 270, 294, 296, 330, 396
  Contributions (JA) 8, 26, 191,
  192, 194, 201, 202, 203, 204, 205,
  206, 212, 220, 228, 236, 241, 268,
  270, 273, 274, 295, 296, 331
Airacobra 314
Air Raid Precautions (ARP) 1, 11,
  13, 94, 106, 107, 249, 283, 288
Air Training Corps (ATC) 94, 95, 97,
  98, 102, 103, 107, 308, 325
Aldenham School 135
Alderton, A.F. 342, 351
Allen's Works 113
Allied Expeditionary Force
  (AEF) 207, 329
allotments 42, 116ff, 182, 361
American Forces Network
  (AFN) 207, 254
Amiel, Barry 320
Amswych, R.F. 348
Anderson
  Committee 13, 14
  Report 14
  Shelter 34, 284, 285, 286, 287,
  290, 303, 355
  Sir John 17, 285
Anderson, M.K.M. 54
Angel Islington 3, 7, 36, 45, 123, 128,
  245, 356, 362, 363, 387
Angier, D. 328
Angus, May 232
Anschluss 20
Anti-Semitism 25, 184, 388
Appleby, Ian 22, 267, 295, 327, 396
  Contributions (IA) 22, 33, 39, 62,
  75, 133, 181, 183, 271, 282, 290,
  327, 373
Armitage, G.H. 67, 117, 161, 174,
175, 177
Army Cadet Force (ACF) 94, 102,
  103, 104, 325
Arrow 27, 58, 68, 99, 102, 233, 273,
  278, 280, 296, 310, 315, 331, 353,
  377
  Extracts 1, 2, 3, 4, 5, 54, 59, 92,
  94, 95, 96, 97, 100, 102, 103, 104,
  105, 106, 107, 108, 109, 110, 112,
  115, 117, 118, 120, 121, 122, 123,
  124, 125, 130, 131, 132, 133, 134,
  136, 137, 138, 139, 140, 141, 142,
  143, 144, 152, 153, 154, 155, 156,
  158, 159, 173, 175, 176, 177, 181,
  191, 196, 197, 203, 219, 222, 223,
  224, 225, 234, 244, 245, 246, 247,
  251, 252, 273, 274, 276, 277, 279,
  280, 281, 297, 298, 303, 309, 311,
  317, 332, 333, 334, 335, 336, 337,
  338, 339, 340, 341, 342, 343, 344,
  345, 346, 347, 348, 349, 350, 352,
  354, 355, 356, 358, 387
Arsenal F.C. 187, 261, 298
Asman, Rev.H.N. 1, 68, 177, 386
Assembly 67, 74, 90, 91, 114,
  179,190, 216, 352, 386
Austria 20, 26, 28, 30
Auxiliary Fire Service (AFS) 320

B

Bailey, W. 155
Baker, A. 85
Baker, Chas 143, 215, 230, 294,
  Contributions (CB) 215, 230
Baker, Colin 79, 84, 85
Baker, G.W. 67, 71, 78, 79, 80, 82, 84,
  171, 187, 200, 308, 357, 362
Baker, Goff. 298
  Contribution (GB) 299
Baker, Miss 161, 188
Baker, Mrs 79, 80, 82, 200
Balchin, R.F. 342, 351
Baldwin, L.W. 344, 351

Baldwin, Stanley 12
Ball, D. 364
    Contributions (DBa) 47, 373
Bamber, R.C. 342, 351
Baptists 40, 64, 65
Barnett, D. 102
baseball 133, 323
batteries 199, 220, 249
Battle of Britain 94, 113, 201, 222, 247, 284, 293, 296, 298, 299, 331
Bays fish & chip shop 48, 230, 266
BBC 153, 189, 190, 191, 194, 195, 196, 197, 204, 205, 207, 208, 209, 235
BBC Symphony Orchestra 189, 191, 196, 197, 230, 266
Beard, Paul 192, 193, 195, 197
Beaverbrook 277, 281
Bedford 4, 5, 8, 13, 16, 17, 18, 33, 42, 45, 46, 47, 48, 53, 56, 57, 59, 66, 71, 77, 88, 116, 118, 148, 172, 189, 190, 207, 213, 219, 220, 226, 240, 255, 271, 280, 284, 288, 292, 294, 295, 301, 312, 363, 369, 371ff
Bedford Girls' Modern School 131, 393
Bedford High School 232, 393
Bedford Market 58
Bedford Modern School 5, 59, 66, 70, 71, 72, 73, 74, 75, 76, 85, 90, 91, 106, 108, 112, 113, 114, 123, 124, 125, 130, 132, 138, 175, 190, 192, 193, 195, 196, 206, 243, 272, 295, 309, 322, 358, 365, 376, 377, 393, 394
Bedford Park 108, 233, 323
Bedford Record 226, 359
Bedford School 55, 66, 74, 75, 125, 140, 393
Beds. and Herts. Regiment 97
Bedfordshire Times 18, 19, 61
Bedwell, A.E. 219, 349
Beecham, A. 56, 269, 317
Beecham, R.S. 317, 352

Contributions (RSB) 17, 281, 318, 372
Beecham, Sally (née Saunders) 232, 233, 269, 271, 324, 365
    Contributions (SB) 26, 228, 232, 269, 272, 280, 324, 355, 364, 371
Beecham, Sir Thomas 192
Bennett, H.A. 345, 351
Bernstein, D.E. 157, 232, 291,
    Contributions (DEB) 2, 4, 6, 22, 26, 33, 34, 40, 51, 58, 61, 62, 74, 75, 89, 93, 99, 102, 104, 144, 152, 156, 158, 168, 175, 199, 201, 204, 205, 206, 211, 213, 214, 216, 217, 223, 229, 231, 237, 238, 239, 248, 249, 258, 260, 261, 263, 265, 271, 272, 273, 278, 282, 283, 285, 286, 288, 291, 292, 294, 295, 305, 306, 307, 322, 323, 326, 327, 330, 359, 363, 364, 375, 376
Biggleswade 8, 223, 257
Bill, L.S. 333
Billets 36ff, 49ff
Billiard Hall 48, 62
Black Watch 294, 295
Blackout 1, 220, 248ff
Blau, J.N. 169, 352, 379
    Contributions (JNB) 8, 126, 128, 129, 169, 187, 190, 191, 192, 193, 195, 198, 353, 379
Bletchley 54
Blitz 13, 112, 201, 253, 284, 286, 287, 289, 299, 320, 375
Blundell, G.H. 252
Blythe, N. 55
Boarding House 66, 71, 78ff, 180, 264, 357
Boat House 114
Bomber Command 328
Boots 255, 372
Boston, Lincs 147
Boult, Adrian 189, 190, 191, 192, 193, 194, 196, 197, 254, 329
Bowers, Jack 128, 129

Boys' Own Paper 3, 260
Bradding, H.A. 83
Braggins 18, 152
Brains Trust 154, 208
Brewers Company – see Worshipful
    Company of Brewers
Brice, G. 134
Briggs, D. 146, 311
Brighton 7, 286
British Expeditionary Force
    (BEF) 236, 293
British Restaurants 266, 267, 269
British Union of Fascists (BUF) 24,
    25
Bronkhorst, S. 76, 97, 156, 348
Bunyan Church 5, 63, 65, 66, 206
Bunyan, John 57, 63, 64, 69, 353
Burden, E.H. (Dick) 337
    Contributions (DB) 28, 119, 170,
    363, 365
Burgess, A. 347, 351

C

Cakebread, A.A. 159
Calder, Angus 17, 88, 112, 305
Cambridge 60, 100, 163
Cambridge Economic Survey 37
Cambridge University 173, 229, 378,
    385, 388, 389
Cameron, D.A. 223
Campbell, M.J. 88, 270, 364
    Contributions (MJC) 4, 5, 38, 46,
    267, 270, 272, 283, 304, 309, 310,
    314, 371
Canada 55, 89, 108, 208, 265
Cantle, H.W. 349
Caplan, B. 84, 156
Caplan, H. 83, 163, 166, 249, 265,
    269
    Contributions (HC) 4, 23, 43,
    163, 165, 166, 173, 181, 265, 266,
    269, 360, 372
Cardington 16, 47, 88, 206, 222, 319,
    364

Cardnell, C.F. 300, 340, 351
Cashmore, P. 166
Cast, B.M.D. 74, 161, 187, 254
Castle, R. 229, 256, 260, 273, 352,
    353
    Contributions (RCa) 38, 145, 147,
    324, 327, 328, 352, 353, 361, 362,
    372
Castle Road 47, 104, 266, 271, 319,
    352
Chad 278
Chamberlain, Neville 26, 27, 32, 33,
    34, 87, 237, 285, 293
Chapman, B. 335, 338
Chapman. R. 363
    Contributions (RC) 22, 32, 45, 51,
    211, 288
Chatterji, R.B. 130, 131, 132, 262
China 21, 25,
Church of England 38, 64, 65, 66, 67,
    106, 164, 382, 384, 386
Churchill, Winston 28, 95, 136, 144,
    163, 201, 202, 239, 248, 267, 276,
    293, 294, 306, 307, 308, 352, 357
cinema 26, 210ff
Clarke, W.H. 67, 161, 176, 177, 254
Cloudesley (house) 120, 158, 387
Cohen, D. 155
Cole, Captain W.F. 67, 83
Colebrooke (house) 120, 158, 387
Communists 91, 158, 170, 181, 226
Cook, G. 6, 37, 64, 166, 219, 313,
    Contributions (GCk) 36, 42, 166,
    172, 185, 187, 220, 314, 378
Coombes, K.R. 221, 256
    Contributions (KRC) 41, 43, 49,
    117, 221, 256, 267, 364
Co-op 43, 272
Co-op Hall 66, 73, 74
Cooper, S.F. 332
Cope, G.W. 154
Coral, B. 257
    Contributions (BC) 38, 51
Coral, N. 257, 267, 375
    Contributions (NC) 52, 200, 257,

269, 373, 375

Corn Exchange, Bedford 58, 190, 192, 194, 197, 198, 294

Cornwell, J.

Couchman, R. 342, 351

Coventry 34, 112, 201, 245, 309

Cowan, G. 138, 182
   Contributions (GCo) 51, 54, 182

Cowling, D.W. 133, 234

Coyte, C. 319
   Contribution (CCo) 34

Coyte, P. 319
   Contribution (PCo) 319

Coyte, R. 82, 230, 313, 319, 374
   Contributions (RCo) 39, 82, 228, 230, 313, 376

Cranfield 16, 95

Cranwell 149

cross-country running 132, 133

Crossick, M. 43, 184, 231, 256, 258
   Contributions (MC) 38, 44, 50, 110, 231, 256, 257, 259

Crowther, W.F. 344, 351

Cuff, C. 66

Cuming, H. 140, 141, 142, 143, 149, 185
   Contributions (HCu) 40, 149, 220, 221, 370

Cumming, H ('Gus') 64, 65, 67, 126, 181, 183, 243, 244, 245, 246, 247

Curtis, D. 212, 260
   Contributions (DC) 3, 212, 260

Cuthbertson, J.R. 348

cycling 219ff

Cyrano de Bergerac 246, 247

Czechoslovakia 26, 28, 176, 194, 197, 198, 294

D

Daily Express 27, 99, 248

Daily Telegraph 140, 259, 268

Dam Busters Raid 150

Dare, R.A. 61, 62, 71, 122, 164, 169, 176, 182, 183, 250, 254, 278, 279, 280, 357, 377, 378, 382, 384, 386, 387, 388

Dash, T. 80

Davenport, R.E. 95, 112, 134, 136, 142, 143, 347, 351

Davies, D. 146

Davis, A.
   Contributions (AD) 22, 23, 32, 40, 61, 164, 329, 372, 374

Davis, Ruby.
   Contributions (RA) 36, 191

Davis 99, 100

Davison, J.A. 62, 105, 106, 107, 109, 110, 145, 147

D-Day 200, 292, 307, 310

Deadman, K. 113, 125, 132, 191, 194, 210, 285, 307
   Contributions (KD) 7, 39, 45, 60, 62, 102, 114, 130, 149, 191, 210, 213, 221, 263, 264, 285, 305, 324, 359, 363, 364, 373, 378

Dell, E. 27

Dimmock, G. 84, 117, 266, 291
   Contributions (GD) 9, 233, 266, 275

Dimmock, T. 146

Dixey, Phyllis. 186, 241, 242

Dixon, H.G. 137, 147, 161, 165, 173, 174, 175, 177, 361

Donovan, C.J. 223, 224

doodle bug 290

Dorzbacher, G. 304

Dowling, A. 342, 351

Draper, F.W. 154, 334

Duane, M. 179, 180

Dudeney and Johnston (Dujon) 58, 266

Duggan, S. 350

Dumbrill, J. 297

Dunkirk 200, 286, 293, 294, 295, 309, 373

E

Easterbrook, J. 385
Eckstein, M.
  Contributions (ME) Foreword,
  47, 114, 192, 193, 194, 196, 301,
  329, 361
Ede, A.J. 345, 351
Education Acts 388, 389
Education, Board of 151, 388
Eisenhower, Dwight D. 307
El Alamein 200, 308, 309, 346
Elizabeth, Princess 92
Ellis, B. 84, 166
Elston, D. 55
Elstow 64, 149, 270
Embankment 213, 319
Empire Cinema 212, 214, 215
E.N.S.A. 239
evacuation areas 14
Evacuation Committee 11, 14
evacuation planning 5, 11
Evans, R.J.B. 341, 351
Evening Standard 283, 357

F

Farmer-Wright, E. 232
  Contributions (EF-W) 232, 258,
  364
farming 140ff
Fascists 23, 24, 25
Fawkes, P. 72, 215, 254
  Contributions (PFa) 72, 98, 99,
  215, 254, 328
Feldman, M.H. 345, 351
Fenn, W.F. 61, 63, 77, 139, 154, 155,
  156, 157, 161, 168, 174, 181, 212,
  213, 234, 246, 247, 253, 288, 295,
  321, 323, 329, 378
  Contributions (WFF) 25, 40, 61,
  62, 63, 76, 77, 156, 158, 161, 168,
  169, 174, 175, 177, 179, 180, 181,
  182, 183, 187, 192, 193, 194, 213,
  215, 228, 232, 253, 270, 283, 292,
  295, 320, 329, 360
Finnish War 306, 333
fire watching 112ff
Fisher, J.F. 343
fives 123, 130, 133
Flack, Lambert 191
Fleet Air Arm 345
Flying Fortress 101, 325, 328
football 125, 134ff
Foss, Brigadier 103
Fowler, Pauline (née Eyre) 33, 232,
  319
  Contributions (PF) 34, 228, 232,
  320
Fox, B. 126, 127, 134, 256, 264, 313,
  373
  Contributions (BF) 33, 107, 114,
  119, 134, 143, 146, 188, 203, 206,
  256, 263, 264, 287, 289, 290, 292,
  313, 356, 362, 370, 373
France 219, 280, 285, 293, 333, 384
Franco 20, 21, 23
Freeman, R.H. 340, 343, 351
Friday Evening Club 81, 153, 157,
  159, 182
Fussell, Paul 93

G

gardening 116ff
Gardiner, Juliet 326
gas masks 282, 283
George, H. 149, 195, 233, 314, 317,
  375
  Contributions (HG) 9, 55, 56, 63,
  74, 127, 147, 149, 195, 223, 272
George, Josie (née Ames) 233
  Contributions (JG) 247, 353, 365,
Germany 20, 21, 26, 28, 29, 32, 34,
  35, 120, 304, 305, 327, 328, 384
GIs 69, 211, 279, 322, 326
Gobey, G. 228
Goebbels 29, 168, 207, 238

Goering 158, 238, 286

Goldington 5, 6, 7, 38, 46, 49, 54, 67, 116, 153, 182, 211, 228, 324, 352, 364

Goold, G.A. 158, 247

Gould, R. 356

Government 1, 10, 11, 12, 13, 14, 15, 16, 78, 86, 91, 92, 202, 248, 268, 270, 276, 292

Grammar Schools 383

Granada Cinema 212, 213, 214, 215, 217, 266

Great War (1914-18) 6, 11, 28, 29, 87, 89, 174, 214, 235, 261, 281, 304, 394

Greer, A.E. 350

Groom, J. 117, 154, 156

Groom, J.A. 342, 351

The Guardian 57

H

Haile Selaisse 21, 22

Hall. D. 102, 222

Handley, Tommy 204, 205

Happidrome 117, 204

Hardwick, 'Flash' 68, 183, 185, 259, 307

Harpur Central School 186

Harpur, Dame Alice 375, 393

Harpur Trust 186, 359, 393

Harris, A. 69

Contributions (AH) 21, 69, 70, 114, 163, 377

Hastings, H.C. 349

Hatfield 315

Haxey 147, 297

Henlow 16

Hennessy, Peter 88

Henstridge, T.G. 342, 351

Hermitage (house) 120, 387,

Hickling, A.W. 346, 351

High Street, Bedford 49, 58, 120, 314, 354

Highbury County School 144, 180

Hitler 1, 18, 21, 20, 23, 26, 29, 87, 158, 200, 207, 237, 238, 284, 306, 289, 299, 306, 356

Hollywood 216, 217, 254

Home Guard 51, 94, 95, 112, 115, 144, 160, 360

Hooley, F.V. 154, 155, 156, 159, 233, 234, 380

Contributions (FVH) 159, 171, 233, 363, 372, 380

Hope, Jean 271, 365

Contributions (JH) 228, 230, 271, 292, 358, 365

Hope, Mary 271, 323, 365, 374

Contributions (MH) 228, 229, 230, 271, 292, 323, 352, 358

Hopkins, A.J. 6, 165, 166, 185, 357

Horkins, M. 35

Contribution (MHor) 35

Horton, L.C.A. 246

Howard, John 57, 64

Howland

Hoyle, T.O. 333

Hubbard, R.F. 341, 351

Hudson, J. 6

Huggins, G.E. 337, 338

Hughes, A. 293

Hulls, A.R. 341, 351

Hume, J.J. 219, 338, 339, 343, 344, 351

Huntingford, P. 291, 359

Hutchings, G.A. 95, 102, 185

Hyde, E. 303

I

Imperial Defence Committee 11

International Brigade 23

Islington 48, 123, 358, 361, 362, 363, 389

Italy 12, 20

It's That Man Again (ITMA) 155, 204, 205,

J

James, Anthony 94
James, D.H. 68
Japan 25, 26, 82, 325, 359
Jarrell, Randall 327
Jewish Assembly 90, 164
Jewish Centre 69, 70, 89
Jews 11, 21, 24, 25, 29, 63, 68, 386, 394
Jonas, A.R. 50, 244, 338, 344, 349, 351, 373, 374
Jones, A. 56, 62, 314, 325
  Contributions (AJ) 49, 56, 58, 62, 143, 147, 171, 176, 182, 184, 186, 188, 211, 213, 215, 216, 226, 261, 262, 265, 314, 325, 355, 362, 363
Jones, D.M. 60, 144, 163, 184, 191, 232, 249, 261, 269, 295, 310, 325, 328, 350, 360
  Contributions (DMJ) 18, 29, 41, 46, 47, 58, 60, 64, 103, 120, 125, 126, 128, 144, 145, 150, 164, 185, 186, 187, 192, 195, 196, 204, 211, 214, 215, 223, 227, 232, 249, 251, 261, 265, 267, 269, 273, 274, 282, 283, 288, 295, 308, 310, 325, 326, 329, 359, 360, 364
Jones, D.O. 121, 122, 234
Jones, P. 84
Jones, W.E.O. 65, 68, 78, 82, 85, 306, 308, 309
  Contributions (WEOJ) 22, 23, 68, 79, 80, 82, 83, 85, 183, 185, 186, 307, 308, 310, 358
Joyce, William (Lord Haw-Haw) 25, 207

K

Keeley, J.C. 132
Keeping, J.T. 347
Keggie, P.R. 309, 310
  Contribution (PK) 168

Kemp, J.G. 345, 351
Kettering 4
Kimbolton 302
Kimbolton Road 84
Kindertransport 17, 30, 89
King, W.A. 348
King's Cross 3, 224, 285, 301, 317
King's Scouts 106, 107, 108
King's Warren School 74, 226, 227, 231, 232, 233, 246, 280, 353, 365
Kipling, Rudyard 3
Knowles, J.M. 68, 83, 145, 158, 180, 181
Knowles, K.S.
  Contributions (KSK), 42, 301
Kristallnacht 20, 30

L

land girls 120, 149
Langdon, David 251
Large, R.A. 347
Lauffer, D. 132
Lee, P.D. 245, 333, 336
Le Good, C.E. ('Leggy') 229
Le Min, C. 166, 187, 362
Leverton, Basil 42, 141, 185, 299, 301, 318, 320, 360, 362
  Contributions (BL) 42, 113, 119, 199, 251, 300, 301, 320, 360, 362
Leverton, D.W. 299
Leverton, Ivor 320
Levy, J. 72, 173, 185, 222, 286, 318
  Contributions (JL) 7, 72, 73, 75, 98, 119, 149, 153, 161, 165, 167, 211, 221, 222, 227, 231, 255, 262, 265, 273, 286, 319, 369, 372, 377, 386
library, Bedford 62, 105, 263, 365
library, school 164, 165
Liddell, Alvar 195, 201
Liddle, H.W. 71, 112, 243, 358, 394
Liberal Club 73, 186
Literary and Debating Society 164

Lloyd Williams, C. 97, 103
Lloyd, J.S. 126, 132, 186, 332
Locke, A.W. 6, 37, 42, 61, 64, 101,
116, 156, 162, 178, 191, 213, 222,
223, 226, 228, 229, 236, 323, 330,
374
Contributions (AWL) 2, 3, 5, 6,
24, 26, 33, 38, 40, 41, 61, 62, 64,
75, 76, 90, 91, 98, 101, 113, 116,
161, 162, 164, 172, 178, 179, 182,
187, 192, 193, 199, 204, 206, 212,
214, 222, 226, 227, 239, 240, 249,
261, 267, 270, 272, 278, 279, 282,
283, 315, 324, 364, 370, 374, 377
Lohmann, K. 304
London 1, 2, 3, 11, 12, 13, 15, 45, 46,
57, 75, 78, 88, 112, 134, 171, 174,
201, 222, 250, 251, 252, 257, 284ff,
293, 312, 355, 362
London County Council (LCC) 15,
78, 165, 369, 388, 391
London, Midland and Scottish
Railway (LMS) 303, 313
London North-Eastern Railway
(LNER) 3
London Passenger Transport
Board 13
London University 165, 179, 378,
385, 388
Low, David 21
Lowe, M.M. 83, 85, 187, 188
Luck, L. 342, 351
Luckman, Sylvia (née Colato) 278,
379
Contributions (SL) 278, 379
Luftwaffe 94, 284, 286, 299, 327
Lush, J.H. 277
Luton 4, 124
Luton Town F.C. 138
Lynch, A.C. 349
Lynn, C. 126, 166, 200, 312, 318
Contributions (CL) 43, 52, 54,
174, 176, 177, 190, 194, 200, 226,
242, 266, 312, 318

Lynn, Vera 205
Lyons (tea shops) 81, 265, 266,

M

Mack, D. 129
Mackay, A. 262
Mackay, D.A.M. 83, 84, 129, 139,
302, 303, 314, 379
Contributions (DAMM)
Foreword, 3, 79, 80, 84, 114, 139,
222, 302, 303, 304, 305, 379
Madden, L.W. 97, 124, 136, 137,
143, 154, 155, 232, 336, 349
Malz, M. 222
Mann, A.R. 223
Marks and Spencer 46
Marshall, D.J. 234
Martin, Kingsley 54, 206
Mass Observation 77
McNamara, Iris 246
Meltis (chocolate factory)
ground 46, 134, 135, 139, 220,
224, 270
Menuhin, Yehudi 192, 195
Merchant Navy 319
Methodists 64, 65, 66, 69
Meurice, J. 79
Midland Road 5, 74, 214, 241, 285,
315
Mill Hill 4, 6
Miller, Dick 341
Miller, Glenn 194, 205, 241, 254,
322, 329, 330
Mills, P. 343, 351
Ministry
Agriculture 116, 122
Aircraft Production 277
Food 263, 266, 267, 268
Information (MOI) 92, 206, 276,
277, 282
Supply 131
Mitchell, M 52, 63, 79, 128, 147,
154, 165, 169, 170, 198, 233, 250,

266, 269, 294
Contributions (MM)
Foreword, 8, 22, 23, 24, 26, 31, 35,
38, 45, 46, 47, 48, 50, 53, 72, 73,
74, 78, 79, 81, 84, 85, 86, 90, 98,
109, 128, 129, 148, 157, 165, 170,
182, 184, 186, 188, 198, 199, 201,
202, 204, 205, 208, 211, 213, 216,
217, 228, 233, 249, 252, 262, 266,
269, 287, 290, 294, 296, 306, 307,
322, 326, 355, 359, 373, 377, 378
Mitchell, O.W. 2, 7, 18, 65, 71, 77, 80,
88, 90, 91, 92, 105, 106, 112, 154,
157, 160, 161, 163, 168ff, 173, 175,
179, 224, 259, 295, 308, 317, 319,
320, 331, 339, 357, 358, 362, 374,
376, 378, 389, 394
Moore, H.A. 27, 308, 332
Moravian Church 64, 65, 66, 114,
179, 181, 243
Morris, M. 63
Morrison, Herbert 112, 202, 238,
318
Morrison Shelter 290, 318
Moses, V. 16, 192, 207
Contributions (VM) 2, 3, 5, 6, 9,
10, 21, 29, 33, 45, 48, 75, 91, 114,
161, 175, 179, 183, 190, 207, 227,
305, 306, 308, 371, 374, 379
Mosley 24
Mosquito fighter bomber 315
Munich 13, 14, 15, 20, 26, 27, 29, 173
Mussolini 21, 22, 207
Myddelton (house) 120, 129, 387

N

Nash, R. 65, 101, 126, 221, 254, 310,
330, 356, 375,
Contributions (RN) 7, 33, 40, 58,
60, 65, 101, 108, 113, 126, 127,
145, 146, 149, 221, 223, 251, 254,
264, 265, 266, 272, 289, 294, 308,
310, 330, 356, 369, 371

National Savings 277, 278
National Service 357, 371, 378
Nazis 23, 28, 29, 30, 31, 134, 200,
306, 352
New Statesman and Nation 54, 207
News Chronicle 357
Norregaard, A. 343, 351
Nunn, A. 133, 314, 315
Contributions (AN) 313, 315

O

O'Brien, W.T. 343, 351
Oddfellows Hall 73
Olphin, H. K. 48, 95, 116, 117, 118,
120, 121, 152, 153, 156, 158, 182,
357
Orgel, L. 192, 310, 378
Orwell, George 200
Ouse, River 33, 46, 47, 85, 100, 126,
128, 229, 269, 325, 364
Ovis, R.D. 155, 346, 351
Owen, Dame Alice 376, 381, 382
Owen's Girls' School 5, 316, 317, 362
Owen's School, history 381ff
Oxford 51, 100, 129, 180
Oxford University 169, 182, 337,
378, 385, 388, 389

P

Palmer, H. Marshall 188
Panacea Society 67
Parker, G. 79, 154, 155, 156
Parker, K. 224
Payne, B. 348
Pearce, D. 165, 284, 339, 369
Contributions (DPe) 166, 175,
179, 250, 282, 284, 339, 362, 369,
370, 377
Pearce, W.J. 96, 160, 187
Perrin, R. 63, 154, 156, 208
Contribution (RP) 208
Peters, M. 102

Phillips, W.E. 280
Phoney War 88, 210, 236, 250, 253
Picturedrome Cinema 212, 214, 215, 353
Picture Post 276, 294
Plaza Cinema 126, 212, 213, 214, 215, 216
Poad, M. 348
Poland 3, 30
Pope Pius XII 348
Powell, Enoch 26
Pratt, D. A. 55, 98, 138, 283, 336
    Contributions (DAP) 2, 4, 32, 52, 55, 75, 101, 113, 127, 130, 138, 147, 150, 193, 222, 227, 260, 283, 309
Pratt, M. 229
Prescott, T.C. 339, 340, 351
Price, D. 194, 361
    Contributions (DP) 9, 94, 179, 194
Price, J. 144
Priestley, J.B. 208, 239
prisoners of war (POWs) 281, 360
Propper, C. 59
Provost, P. 295, 298 ,299, 338, 375,376
    Contributions (PP) 7, 26, 34, 48, 50, 51, 127, 253, 268, 298, 299, 339
Purkis, B. 345, 351

R

R101 (airship) 233
radio 199ff
Rans, G. 84, 86, 127, 154, 166, 192, 213
    Contributions (GR) 2, 25, 29, 54, 94, 166, 171, 172, 195, 226, 231, 301, 302
rationing 263ff
Raybould, Clarence 192, 197
Reading F.C. 139
Red Cross 270, 273, 281

Redmond, L.C. 342, 351
Reekie, A.G. 345, 351
Rees, A.E. 344, 351
Richardson, Barbara 233, 254
Richardson, J.F. 222
Richer, P 230
Rimer, J.F. 341, 351
Riverside Club 73
river swim 126, 127
Robinson, D. 157, 337
Roman Catholics 23
Roosevelt, F.D. 322
Rosen, D. 126, 127, 131
Rothstein, A. 90, 387
rowing 127, 128, 129, 130
Rowley, G. 113, 153, 154, 156, 289
    Contributions (GRo) 28, 55, 60, 90, 113, 126, 135, 146, 153, 289, 305
Royal Air Force (RAF) 2, 35, 89, 90, 94, 95, 96, 98, 99, 102, 103, 149, 150, 158, 254, 286, 299, 300, 307, 314, 315, 327, 331, 333, 336, 338, 339, 340, 342, 343, 344, 345, 346, 347, 349, 359, 364, 374
Royal Air Force Volunteer Reserve (RAFVR) 319, 339, 348
Royal Artillery (RA) 344, 345
Royal County Theatre 186, 241, 242, 313
Royal Engineers (RE) 50, 345
Royal Fusiliers 339, 343
Royal Naval Volunteer Reserve (RNVR) 340, 342, 349, 350
Royal Navy (RN) 308, 332, 334, 337, 342
rugby 123, 124, 125, 134
Rugby School 130
Russell Park 40, 48, 50, 226, 227, 228, 229, 231, 266, 267, 279, 294, 312, 324, 354
Russell Park Gazette 229, 230
Rust, B.A.L. 203
Rye Grammar School 74, 95, 103,

135

S

St. Cuthberts 65, 135
St. Pancras 8, 250, 285, 301, 320
St. Paul's Cathedral 318. 320
St. Paul's Church 59, 64
St. Paul's Square 58, 60
St. Peter's Church 64
St. Peter's Green 327, 393
St. Peter's Square 213
Salmon, F.A.V. 348
Salmond, J.M. 68, 83, 188, 304
Salute the Soldier Week 280
Sargent, Sir Malcolm 191
Saturday Afternoon Club 152, 182
Saunders, P.J. 155
Schama, H. 6
Schroder, C. 228, 229
Schwalb, R. 74, 139, 159, 356
Scouts 105ff, 272, 280, 308
Seaborn, H (Bert) 6, 60, 137, 138,
    139, 232, 234, 319
Seeger, K. C. 84, 85, 144
    Contributions (KCS) 85, 144, 145
Senn, P. 99, 100, 141, 142, 244, 262,
    331, 335, 336, 349, 363, 378
Setford, D.G. 84
Seventh Day Adventists 64
Shaw, G. 146, 328
    Contributions (GS) 9, 33, 45, 62,
    103, 108, 123, 129, 143, 146, 181,
    184, 227, 229, 242,
    283, 325, 329, 330, 364, 370, 374,
    376
Shaw, G. Bernard 210, 218, 243
Shelton, Ann 205
Sherwen, A. 62, 161, 187, 188
Sherwin, B. 349
Simmons, T.A. 108, 109, 110, 273
Simpson, P. 76
Skeggs, B. 84, 132, 136, 297
    Contributions (BS) 8, 42, 57, 86,

102, 132, 136, 164, 176, 184, 198,
    200, 230, 297, 309, 323, 363, 372
Smart, A. 9
Smith, Aileen 232
Smith, D.E. 342, 351
Smith, I.E. 298
Smith, J. 161, 175, 176, 177, 222, 280
Smith, L.I.S. 84
Society of Friends 64, 66, 68,180
Solomon, N. 93, 154, 198, 337
Soviet Union 30, 91, 92, 171, 284,
    306, 307
Sowton, B.S. 349
Spain 21
Spanish Civil War 23, 88
Spiritualist Church 66
Spitfire Fund 277
Squander Bug 278, 279
Stalin 30, 207, 306
Stalingrad 144, 200, 305, 307
The Star 10
Stephens, G. 345, 351
Stevens, R.W.G. 342, 351
Stiffen, A.J. 345, 351
Stockton, J. 9, 88, 129, 133, 148,
    157, 208, 220, 233, 240, 291, 303,
    310, 312, 325, 330, 353, 359, 373,
    378
    Contributions (JS) 8, 9, 26, 29,
    34, 74, 88, 117, 118, 127, 129, 130,
    142, 148, 157, 158, 166, 169, 180,
    181, 183, 187, 199, 202, 204, 208,
    209, 212, 214, 216, 218, 221, 223,
    232, 240, 249, 250, 261, 264, 270,
    277, 291, 293, 294, 303, 305, 307,
    310, 312, 325, 328, 330, 353, 359,
    360, 371, 372, 378
Stoke Newington 286
Stone, A.T.R. 356
Sutton, D.H. 160, 162, 165, 184,
    302, 328, 361
    Contributions (DHS) 10, 29, 32,
    39, 60, 62, 94, 145, 160, 162, 165,
    180, 185, 255, 285, 290, 291, 294,

295, 302, 310, 312
Swift, H.C. 179, 339, 343, 351
Swinnerton, A.J. 159

T

Taunton Commission 384
Taylor, F.R. 84, 97, 349
Teacher, K. 273, 274
Tebbutt, N. 6, 118, 119, 125, 175
tennis 123, 131, 133
Things to Come 27, 88
Thurleigh 98, 101, 226, 279, 323, 324, 327, 328
Time and Tide 10
The Times 10, 14, 54, 160
Tingay, L. 97, 187
Titmuss, R. 15, 274
Tomaschoff, W.T. 70, 89
    Contribution (WT) 30
Tricker, R. 187
Triggs, R. 347
Turner, R.L. 55, 186, 206, 354, 355
Turner, Rev. R.H. 5, 63, 65, 66, 67, 186, 357
Twinwoods 101, 330
Tyrell, R.A. 224

U

Ulph, R.A. 344, 351
U.S.A. 28, 30, 265
U.S.A.A.F. 98, 102, 226, 279, 322ff
U.S.S.R. (see Soviet Union)

V

V1 174, 280, 285, 290, 318, 319, 379
V2 174, 285, 290, 291, 292, 318, 379
Vaughan, W.A. 315, 317
VE Day 352, 353, 355, 360
V for Victory 202
Victory Hall 152
Vincent, E. 106

VJ Day 359, 360
von Rintelen 303
Vulliamy, B.L. 115, 186, 279, 280

W

Wade, D.D. 54, 128, 129, 260, 291
    Contributions (DDW) 3, 8, 33, 42, 46, 47, 48, 55, 128, 129, 233, 260, 264, 284, 286, 291
Waite, Terry 63
Waldman, R. 202, 203
Waldman, S. 123, 125, 338
Walker, I.
    Contributions (IW) 102, 145, 188, 222, 286, 313, 314
Walker, S.D. 348
War Weapons Week 278
Ware, F.E. 343, 351
Warships Week 279, 280
Wash, R.G. 349
Webb, G. 304
Webber, J. 52, 374
    Contributions (JW) 6, 32, 52, 117, 135, 374, 377,
Welch, C. 80, 85, 153
Weston, J. 289, 363
    Contributions (JWes) 41, 85, 188, 288, 289, 290, 291, 324, 326, 328, 363, 372
Weston, R. 146
Whitebread, W.J. 108, 118, 152, 157, 297
    Contributions (WJW) 6, 34, 106, 119, 152, 157, 298, 323
Whitebrook, J. 344, 346, 351
Wildman, R. 153
Williams, P.E. 334, 338
Williams, Sir R. Vaughan 192
Williamson, L.J. 229
Wilson, R.C. 344, 351
Wilton, Jean 246
Wings for Victory Week 254, 279
Winton, D. 159, 232

Wisher, J.H. 342, 343, 351
Women's Voluntary Service
    (WVS) 5, 281, 282, 294
Wood, Sir Henry 192
Woodruff, G. 196, 322, 358
    Contributions (GW) 73, 196, 323,
    358
Woolton, Lord 267, 274
Woolton Pie 267
Woolworths 48, 193, 255
Workers Playtime 202
Works Wonders 202
Worshipful Company of
    Brewers 135, 381, 382, 384
Wright, Eileen (née Card) 233
Wright, W. 291

Y

Yanks 322ff
Yardley, R.J.T. 345, 351
Young Communists League
    (YCL) 171
Young, D. 228
Young, M. 158

JOHN
BUNYANS
STATUE

RIGBYS
SHOP·MILL

RUSSELL
PARK
CAFÉ